STUDY GUIDE

to accompany

Krugman/Wells/Myatt
macroeconomics
CANADIAN EDITION

Rashid Khan
McMaster University

WORTH PUBLISHERS

Study Guide
by Rashid Khan
to accompany
Krugman/Wells/Myatt: Macroeconomics, Canadian Edition

Printed in the United States of America

Text design: Lee Ann Mahler/S. B. Alexander

ISBN 13: 978-0-7167-6158-7
ISBN 10: 0-7167-6158-0

First printing 2006

Worth Publishers
41 Madison Avenue
New York, NY 10010
www.worthpublishers.com

Contents

Preface

This Study Guide is designed for use with *Macroeconomics* by Paul Krugman, Robin Wells, and Anthony Myatt. It is intended to help evaluate your understanding of the material covered in the textbook and thereby reinforce the key concepts you need to learn. For each chapter of the textbook, the Study Guide provides an introduction, fill-in-the-blank chapter review, learning tips, and a set of multiple-choice questions as well as more comprehensive problems and exercises. Answers along with helpful explanations can be found at the end of each chapter.

Students often use an answer section to simply check if they have gotten the "right" answer. We caution you to use the answer section accompanying each chapter to really evaluate your comprehension of the material. In economics, the reasoning used in coming to the conclusions and correctly modeling the problems are as important as coming to an accurate answer. We have provided explanations for each problem in order for you to check that your understanding of the concepts has been appropriately applied. The understanding of economics can be accomplished through study of concepts, graphs, and equations.

Throughout this Study Guide, you will find activities that test your knowledge of the material through each of these methods. In some cases, the material may go beyond what has been covered in your class. We have used an * to denote questions that can be considered *optional.* These questions may contain more mathematical material than is required in your course.

The study of economics has the potential of altering the way you evaluate and understand the world. We feel that your use of this guide will help you in your study of basic macroeconomics principles and will provide a jumping-off point for further study in the economics field.

Acknowledgments

Thanks are due to a number of people for helping to create this Study Guide. Rashid Khan (McMaster University) was aided by the work of Rosemary Cunningham (Agnes Scott College), Elizabeth Sawyer Kelly (University of Wisconsin-Madison), and Martha Olney (University of California-Berkeley). Susan Kamp (University of Alberta) provided a further economic review of the material. Editorial and production guidance were provided by the supplements team at Worth Publishers: Marie McHale, Eve Conte, and Stacey Alexander.

STUDY GUIDE

chapter **1**

First Principles

The core of economic analysis involves four principles.

- *Scarcity of resources*

- *Opportunity costs*

- *Marginal analysis*

- *Gains from choices*

In reading this chapter, we will learn about why and how we make choices. We will see the gains from trade and the efficiency of a market system.

How Well Do You Understand the Chapter?

Use the following list of words to complete the blanks in the review of the chapter. The words may be used more than once or not at all. If you find yourself having difficulties, please refer back to the appropriate section in the text.

better off	free	margin	opportunity
choices	gains	marginal	natural
efficiency	governmental	market failure	scarce
efficiently	human	maximum	specialization
either-or	incentives	many	specializes
equilibrium	income	natural	standard
equity	interactions	produce	trade-off
exploit	inefficient	opportunities	unlimited
forego			

1. Since wants are _____ and resources are _____, individuals have to make _____ as to which wants are to be fulfilled by which resources. Because of scarcity of resources, a selection of one choice means that we _____ another choice. A resource is anything that can be used to _____ something else.

2. We distinguish between _____ resources, which include labour, skill, and intelligence, and _____ resources, which include resources from the physical environment, such as minerals and natural gas. When individuals

decide what they should buy, they are constrained by _____ and time, but this merely reflects an economy that is constrained in what it can produce by _____ resources.

3. When we choose between two choices, we make a(n) _____ choice based on the real cost of the choices. The real cost of any item is its _____ cost: what you must give up in order to get the item. Every choice we make has a(n) _____ cost: choosing an item or activity implies not choosing some other item or activity.

4. Some choices we make are not either–or issues but are matters of how much. These decisions are made at the _____ by comparing the costs and additional benefits of doing a little bit more of an activity versus doing a little bit less. The study of these kinds of trade-offs at the margin is called _____ analysis.

5. Individuals make decisions guided by the principle that they should _____ opportunities to make themselves better off. In fact, this principle of people taking advantage of all _____ to make themselves better off is the basis of all predictions by economists about economic behaviour. People respond to _____; a change in incentives will alter people's behaviour.

6. An economy is a system for coordinating the productive activities of many people. In a market economy, there are _____ participants. Each participant's opportunities, and hence choices, depend to a large extent on the _____ made by other people. For us to understand a market economy, we must understand the _____ of many individuals.

7. We enjoy a higher _____ of living when we interact with one another through trade. There are _____ from trade that arise from _____, when different individuals engage in different tasks. It is critical for us to understand that the economy as a whole can produce more when each person _____ and then trades with other people.

8. All markets move toward equilibrium. An economic situation is in equilibrium when no individual would be _____ doing something different. The fact that markets move in a predictable way toward _____ allows us to understand economic interactions.

9. We can apply the principle that resources should be used as _____ as possible to achieve society's goals as a standard for evaluating an economy's performance. An economy's resources are used efficiently when they are used in a way that fully exploits all _____ to make everyone better off. A(n) _____ outcome has occurred if it is now possible to make someone better off without making someone else worse off. An efficient economy produces the _____ gains from trade that are possible from the available resources.

10. Efficiency is not the only criterion for evaluating an economy. People also care about issues of fairness, or _____. Usually there is a(n) _____ between equity and efficiency; policies that promote _____ usually entail a cost of decreased efficiency, while policies that promote _____ usually entail a cost of decreased equity.

11. Perfectly competitive markets achieve _____. In a market economy, where individuals are _____ to choose what they want to consume and what they want to produce, people will choose to take advantage of all _____ to make themselves better off.

12. It is possible for the market outcome to be inefficient and for _____ to occur. When markets fail to achieve efficiency, _____ intervention can improve society's welfare. Government policies can provide incentives to change how society's resources are used to move society closer to a(n) _____ outcome.

Learning Tips

TIP #1: Resources are scarce.

"Scarcity" of "resources" means a limited supply of resources, which are used to satisfy competing needs and uses. Examples of resources are: land, labour, entrepreneur skills, and so forth.

Question: Which of the following statements is true?

A) Technological progress will solve the problem of scarcity of resources.
B) Money is classified as a resource.
C) Clean air and water are considered to be scarce resources.
D) Machinery and equipment are considered to be non-resource items.

Answer: C

TIP #2: Every activity has an opportunity cost; opportunity cost is what you give up in order to get something else (the next best alternative).

There is no such thing as a "free lunch." Because resources are limited, it is always necessary to give up something to get something else.

Question: Which of the following statements is **false?**

A) The opportunity cost of going to university is the foregone income that you could have earned elsewhere.
B) Standing in line for six hours at the Air Canada Center to buy U2 concert tickets is not an opportunity cost.
C) The opportunity cost can be zero if unemployed people can be put to work.
D) If resources were not scarce, opportunity costs can be zero.

Answer: B

4 CHAPTER 1 FIRST PRINCIPLES

TIP #3: Incremental or marginal costs and benefits are core topics in marginal analysis. Decisions like what to do with your next hour, or next dollar, are marginal decisions. Consider an activity and see its incremental (marginal) benefit and incremental (marginal) cost.

Question: Suppose you are considering renting a movie for $5 or going to a movie theater, which will cost you $10. Which of the following statements is **false?**

A) The marginal cost of an extra movie rental is $5.
B) The marginal cost of going to a movie theater is $10.
C) The marginal cost of a movie rental is cheaper than the marginal cost of going to a movie theater.
D) The marginal cost of renting a movie is higher than the marginal cost of going to a movie theater.

Answer: D

TIP #4: When we consider all available opportunities, our choices reflect maximum benefits.

People exploit opportunities to make themselves better off.

Question: Which of the following statements is **false**?

A) If you have two choices, and the first will improve your health while the second will harm your health, you will choose the first.
B) If the price of parking at your university increases, more students will use the public transit system to go to your university.
C) A higher price of gasoline will not affect consumers' choices regarding fuel-efficient cars.
D) If earnings of economics graduates increases relatively more than earnings of graduates in other areas, there will be a greater demand for enrollment in the economics department.

Answer: C

TIP #5: There are gains from trade.

When we compare autarky (no-trade) with trade, we see mutual gains from trade. A country can specialize in a good in which that country is relatively more efficient (due to lower opportunity costs). That country can thus receive gains from trade by exchanging its goods for more of another good from another country than what it will get within the domestic economy.

TIP #6: Markets move toward equilibrium.

An economic situation is in equilibrium when no individual would be better off doing something different.

Question: Consider a situation of shortages, where the quantity of goods supplied is less than the quantity of goods demanded. Which of the following correctly describes this scenario?

A) This is an equilibrium situation in the market.
B) For the given quantity of goods supplied, the price that the buyers are willing to pay is greater than the supply price.
C) For the given quantity of goods supplied, the price that the buyers are willing to pay is lower than the supply price.
D) The marginal net benefit in the given situation is negative.

Answer: B

TIP #7: In general, market equilibrium leads to efficiency.

The fact that markets move toward equilibrium is why we can predict market outcomes. The perfectly competitive market equilibrium is an efficient outcome, because it means that economy's resources are used efficiently and that all opportunities are exploited to make everyone better off.

TIP #8: There exists a conflict between efficiency and equity. When there is a market failure, government intervention can improve society's welfare.

People care about issues of fairness and equity. There is a trade-off between equity and efficiency. Policies that promote equity (for example, transfer payments to individuals) often come at a cost of decreased efficiency, and vice versa.

Multiple-Choice Questions

1. The real cost of going to a movie on Saturday night includes
   a. the cost of the movie ticket.
   b. the cost of the popcorn and soda you buy at the movie theater.
   c. the value to you of whatever activity you would have done had you chosen not to go to the movie.
   d. all of the above.

2. When Ross decides whether he should eat another dessert, economics says he
   a. only considers the price of the dessert.
   b. compares the benefits and costs of eating another dessert.
   c. considers how much additional exercise he will need to do to avoid gaining weight from eating the dessert.
   d. considers whether he can do so without anyone else noticing.

3. In making choices people find that
   a. resources are scarce and that they cannot do everything or have everything that they would like.
   b. the real cost of a choice is what you must give up in order to enjoy that choice.
   c. people make choices that will make them better off.
   d. all of the above are true.

4. Which of the following statements is true?
   a. If people were less wasteful we could eliminate problems due to scarcity of resources.
   b. People usually make choices without regard to the additional benefits and costs of those choices.
   c. People consider the opportunity costs of choices.
   d. The incentives, or the rewards for certain types of behaviour, rarely influence people's decisions at the margin.

5. Specialization in production and trade
   a. increases the amount of goods and services available to an economy.
   b. benefits only the economically stronger nation.
   c. reduces opportunity costs of production to zero.
   d. may eliminate any problems posed by scarce resources.

6. Which of the following statements is true?
a. Resources should be used as equitably as possible in order to achieve society's goals for efficiency.
b. There is a tendency for markets to move toward equilibrium.
c. Government intervention in markets never improves society's welfare.
d. Trade may make one nation worse off.

7. When a market is not in equilibrium
a. there will be a tendency for the market to continue to not be in equilibrium unless there is government intervention.
b. there are opportunities available to people to make themselves better off.
c. it must be because the government has intervened in the market, resulting in the market's failure to reach equilibrium.
d. no individual would be better off doing something different.

8. We know that resources are being used efficiently when
a. scarcity is no longer an issue.
b. an economy utilizes every opportunity to make people better off.
c. there are still gains from trade available.
d. we achieve equity.

9. The concept of equity focuses on
a. how to produce the maximum possible output from a given amount of resources.
b. how governments can intervene to make markets work better.
c. the issue of fairness.
d. the amount of physical plant and equipment an employer owns.

10. Government intervention in a market can improve society's welfare when
a. the market outcome is equitable.
b. the market fails to provide certain goods.
c. the market outcome is efficient.
d. we have exploited all opportunities to make people better off.

11. When people interact in markets we know that
a. we may move further from equilibrium.
b. some participants will be worse off.
c. this interaction must increase economic efficiency.
d. this interaction must achieve equity.

12. People respond to incentives because
a. markets move toward equilibrium.
b. incentives act as rewards that encourage people to behave in certain ways.
c. incentives exploit opportunities to make people better off.
d. incentives exploit opportunities to make people worse off.

13. When individuals decide how much of an activity they should do,
a. this is an example of marginal analysis.
b. this involves a comparison of the trade-off between the marginal costs and marginal benefits of doing more of the activity.
c. they are making a decision at the margin.
d. all of the above.

14. Which of the following is an example of an equity issue?
   a. The Mayor of Toronto has agreed to provide more shelters for homeless people.
   b. The resources will be inefficiently used if there are trade restrictions on imported goods.
   c. Freer trade will lead to more efficient uses of resources.
   d. Unemployment Insurance benefits promote economic efficiency.

15. Which of the following statements is true?
   a. Free market equilibria for all goods and services provide for efficient outcomes.
   b. There is no conflict between efficiency and equity.
   c. More equitable income distribution will promote more efficient uses of resources.
   d. The policies that promote equity often come at a cost of decreased efficiency.

Problems and Exercises

Read each question carefully and then write your answers in the space provided or on a separate sheet of paper.

1. Using the list of principles of individual choice below, explain which principle(s) each of the following situations illustrates.
   i.   Resources are scarce.
   ii. The real cost of something is what you must give up to get it.
   iii. "How much?" is a decision at the margin.
   iv. People usually exploit opportunities to make themselves better off.
   a. To attend your economics lecture at 9:00 in the morning, you miss breakfast.

   b. To decide whether you should work one more hour per week, you compare the benefits from that additional hour of work to the costs of giving up an hour of exercise each week.

   c. To decide whether you should get one more hour of sleep or attend your economics lecture this week, you compare the benefits of attending the lecture to the costs of not allocating that time to additional sleep.

   d. Your professor offers extra credit and reports that many students in your class have taken advantage of that opportunity.

   e. A bicycle shop in town offers a much lower price for a bike tune-up than its competitors. Appointments for tune-ups at the shop fill up quickly.

2. Using the list of principles below, explain which principle(s) of interaction each of the following situations illustrates.
   i.   There are gains from trade.
   ii. Markets move toward equilibrium.
   iii. Resources should be used as efficiently as possible to achieve society's goals for efficiency.
   iv. Perfectly competitive markets usually lead to efficiency.
   a. A bicycle shop owner and his landlord meet to negotiate their rent contract for the next year. After meeting, the shop owner agrees to extend his lease for two years instead of one year, while the landlord agrees to give him a 10% discount on his rental charge in exchange for the longer lease.

   b. The Ricardos are choosing between eating at home and going to a restaurant for dinner. If they go to a restaurant, it will cost $25 to feed their family of four. If they stay home, the cost of the groceries will be $13.50. They estimate that the time preparing the meal is worth $5.00. The family stays home.

   c. At the Shopper's Paradise, the checkout lines are rarely different in length.

   d. At the university library, a student can check out books with a human librarian or through an automated scanner. The automated scanner is faster than a librarian, but it is often unreliable and can't perform certain transactions. (For example, if an individual owes fines to the library, they will need to see the librarian to settle those fines.) No one uses the automated scanner until there are at least five individuals in line for the librarian.

3. For each of the following situations identify the nature of the market failure and provide examples of how government interaction can improve society's welfare when market failure occurs.
   a. While manufacturing its product, a firm generates a substantial amount of pollution. This pollution does not affect the firm, but it causes a community located downwind to experience higher levels of respiratory disease.

   b. Research and development at a firm has the potential to significantly improve human health but, because their research costs exceed the firm's direct benefits, they do not conduct the research.

    c. Land developers refuse to set aside land for parks and nature trails, so the new developments in a community do not offer these amenities.

4. Describe the opportunity costs when you decide to rent a DVD movie instead of going to a movie theater.

*5. Consider the following demand-supply equations.

$$Q^D = 200 - 2P \quad \text{(demand equation)}$$
$$Q^S = 2P \qquad \text{(supply equation)}$$

where Q^D is quantity demanded, Q^S is quantity supplied and P is price

a. Find the predicted price and quantity in a market-equilibrium situation.

b. Why will Q = 80 not be an efficient output?

Answers to How Well Do You Understand the Chapter

1. unlimited, scarce, choices, forego, produce

2. human, natural, income, scarce

3. either-or, opportunity, opportunity

4. margin, marginal

5. exploit, opportunities, incentives

6. many, choices, interactions

7. standard, gains, specialization, specializes

8. better off, equilibrium

9. efficiently, opportunities, inefficient, maximum

10. equity, trade-off, equity, efficiency

11. efficiency, free, opportunities

12. market failure, governmental, efficient

Answers to Multiple-Choice Questions

1. The real cost of going to a movie on Saturday night is what you must give up in order to go out. This opportunity cost includes the price of the movie ticket, the cost of the soda and popcorn that one gets to nibble on while watching the movie, and the forgone chance to do something else that evening. **Answer: D.**

2. In this case, the best answer is the one that captures the essence of the economic approach to making decisions. Answer B focuses on the comparison of benefits to costs. We can see that the other answers only consider some aspect of the benefit or cost. **Answer: B.**

3. All of the statements are true: since resources are scarce, people must choose among alternative uses of those resources; opportunity cost measures the real cost of choosing something; and people do opt to do those things that make them better off. **Answer: D.**

4. Resources are not scarce because of wastefulness but because they are limited in quantity. People do consider the additional benefits and additional costs when making choices, and these decisions at the margin are influenced by incentives. The only statement that is true is that people do consider opportunity costs when making choices. **Answer: C.**

5. Specialization in production and trade increases total production and allows for greater levels of consumption in all countries, not just the economically stronger nation. However, it does not eliminate opportunity costs or the scarcity of resources. **Answer: A.**

6. Markets tend toward equilibrium. Resources should be used as efficiently as possible, rather than as equitably as possible, to achieve society's goals for efficiency. Government can improve society's welfare, and trade never makes any nation worse off. **Answer: B.**

7. When markets are not in equilibrium, there are unexploited opportunities to make at least one person better off while making no one else worse off. Given that people always act to make themselves better off, the market will move toward equilibrium. **Answer: B.**

8. Resources are efficiently used when every opportunity to make people better off has been exploited. At that point, there are no longer any gains from trade. Resources are still scarce but are used efficiently. **Answer: B.**

9. Equity focuses on fairness. **Answer: C.**

10. When markets fail, government intervention can increase welfare. A good may not be produced by an individual firm because the marginal costs exceed the marginal benefits; yet, if side effects were considered, the good should be produced. When this happens, the government can provide the good. **Answer: B.**

11. The only statement that is true about interaction in markets is that it must increase efficiency. **Answer: C.**

12. Incentives are the rewards that people receive when they engage in certain activities. Answers C and D seem attractive as potential answers but are nonsensical: an incentive cannot exploit, or take advantage of, an opportunity. **Answer: B.**

13. All of the statements are true: individuals when deciding how much of an activity to do should compare the costs and benefits of doing just a little bit more of the activity. This comparison of "just a little bit more" is what is meant by making a decision at the margin; it is an example of marginal analysis. **Answer: D.**

14. All choices, except A, deal with efficiency issues. **Answer: A.**

15. When we see market imperfections or when we see public goods, pollution, etc., the market outcomes are not efficient outcomes. Therefore, the option A is wrong. The option B is wrong, because there are conflicts and tradeoffs between efficiency and equity. The equitable distribution of income will lead to less efficient use of resources. Therefore, the policies that promote equity often curtail efficiency. **Answer: D.**

Answers to Problems and Exercises

1. a. This statement illustrates principles (i) and (ii). Since resources—in this case, time—are scarce, it is impossible to do everything: you can either eat breakfast or attend class (i). The real cost of something is what you must give up to get it; in this case, the real cost of attending the lecture is the breakfast you could have eaten (ii).

   b. This statement illustrates principles (i), (ii), and (iii). Resources are scarce; therefore, choices must be made as to how to use those scarce resources (i). The real cost of working is measured by what is given up: in this case, exercise (ii). "How much?" is a decision at the margin: you decide how much work you should do each week by comparing the benefit of an additional hour of work to the cost (the lost exercise) of an additional hour of work (iii).

c. This statement illustrates principles (i), (ii), and (iii). Resources are scarce; you must choose between sleep and attending the lecture (i). The real cost of the lecture is measured by what you must give up in order to get the lecture; you give up sleep (ii). "How much?" is a decision at the margin: you decide whether you should sleep an extra hour or attend the lecture by comparing the benefit of an extra hour of sleep to the cost (the lecture you must give up) of attending the lecture (iii).

d. This statement illustrates principles (iii) and (iv). "How much?" is a decision at the margin: students electing to do the extra credit consider the marginal benefit of doing the work to the marginal cost and conclude that the marginal benefit is greater than the marginal cost (iii). People usually take advantage of opportunities to make themselves better off; many students perceive that doing the extra credit will help their grade and that failure to do the extra credit will hurt their grade (iv).

e. This statement illustrates principles (i) and (iv). Resources are scarce, and our choices reflect our valuation of how best to use those scarce resources; people choose to tune up their bikes since they view it as a good use of their scarce resources (i). People usually take advantage of opportunities to make themselves better off; since this is a bargain for those who can get appointments, people will try to take advantage of the offer (iv).

2. a. This statement illustrates principles (i), (ii), (iii), and (iv). Since both the shop owner and the landlord agree to this new rental agreement, it must be the case that the new lease is beneficial to both parties. The landlord gets the certainty of an occupied building for a longer period of time, while the shop owner gets the certainty of a business address and a reduced rent. This illustrates that there are gains from trade (i), that markets lead to efficiency (iv) and tend toward equilibrium (ii), and that resources should be used as efficiently as possible (iii).

b. This statement illustrates principles (iii) and (iv). The Ricardos recognize that the cost of eating out exceeds the cost of eating at home. Since these costs reflect the opportunity costs of eating, this family chooses to eat at home since this choice leaves them better off (they have $6.50 they can spend on other goods and services each time they forgo eating out). This illustrates that the real cost of something is what you must give up to get it and that resources should be used as efficiently as possible. The family can clearly compare the costs of eating at home to the costs of eating out due to the existence of markets; this enables them to decide on the most efficient use of their resources (iii) due to a market outcome that is efficient (iv).

c. This statement illustrates principles (ii), (iii), and (iv). Markets move toward equilibrium; since it is not an equilibrium for some checkout lines to have shorter waits than other checkout lines, we can anticipate that people will distribute themselves across the various checkout lines until the wait is approximately equal in all checkout lines (ii). In addition, checkout lines with equal waiting time imply an efficient use of resources since no reallocation of waiting shoppers will result in a reduction in waiting time for shoppers (iii). Lastly, this efficient use of resources occurs through the natural market mechanism: markets tend toward efficiency (iv).

d. This statement illustrates principles (ii), (iii), and (iv). The decision to use the automated scanner or the librarian takes into account the kind of transaction the individual must do (e.g., if an individual owes fines to the library, they will want to see the librarian to settle those fines since they cannot do that with the automated scanner), as well as the relative checkout speeds of the two choices. Individuals recognize that the automated scanner is quicker than waiting in line once there are at least five people in line. This illustrates the concept that markets move toward equilibrium (ii). It also illustrates the efficient use of resources, since people choose their line based on their perception of the optimal strategy for reducing their waiting time (iii and iv).

3. a. The firm fails to take into account the side effects of their production on the community. Government intervention in the form of establishing fines for pollution or enacting laws to curb certain undesirable behavior could help the market achieve a more efficient outcome.

  b. Market failure occurs because beneficial research is not undertaken, since the firm considers only *their* costs of this research and *their* benefits from the research and ignores the health benefits to others. The market does not take into account the side effects (the benefits received or costs incurred by those outside the firm) of their decisions. Government intervention to subsidize the research expenditures could alter the incentives firms face with regard to undertaking research.

  c. Developers will not provide parks and nature trails because they do not directly benefit from them. Since parks and nature trails benefit everyone, they need to be provided by the government. The government could establish laws or provisions to ensure that certain amounts of natural resources are considered off-limits for development.

4. The opportunity costs of going to a movie theater can be higher than those for a DVD rental. The opportunity costs of going to a movie theater include travel costs, parking costs, costs for waiting in line for tickets, over-priced refreshment costs, and so forth. The opportunity costs for DVD rental can be less.

5. a. Using market equilibrium condition, set $Q^D = Q^S$ and find $P = 50$ and $Q = 100$.
  b. When $Q = 100$, the total net benefit is 5,000. When $Q = 80$, the total net benefit is 4,800.

chapter 2

Economic Models: Trade-offs and Trade

Economic models are simplified representations of the real world. They deal with a set of variables, describe how these variables, given some assumptions, are related and provide some economic outcomes. After reading this chapter, we will understand the production possibility frontier (PPF) and the meaning of the opportunity cost. We will be able to comprehend the gains from trade after we analyze the theory of comparative advantage. The circular-flow diagram will allow us to see how the economy works through income-spending flows.

How Well Do You Understand the Chapter?

Fill in the blanks using the following terms to complete the following statements. Terms may be used more than once. If you find yourself having difficulties, please refer back to the appropriate section in the text.

absolute advantage	*flow*	*less*	*points*
change	*flows*	*lower*	*positive economics*
circular-flow	*forecasts*	*models*	*production*
comparative advantage	*gain*	*money*	*possibility frontier (PPF)*
constant	*gains from trade*	*normative economics*	*simplified*
economy	*goods and services*	*non feasible*	*specialization*
efficiency	*households*	*opportunities*	*specialized*
efficient	*income*	*opportunity cost(s)*	*straight*
expenditures	*increase*	*outward*	*trade-offs*
factor markets	*input-output*	*payment(s)*	*transactions*
feasible	*labour*	*physical*	*two*

1. A model is a(n) _____ description of the real world. In our economic models, we will focus on how, other things remaining constant, a change in just one factor affect an economic outcome.

2. The three _____ developed in this chapter are the production possibility frontier (PPF) model, a model that helps economists think about the _____ every economy faces; the comparative advantage model, which illustrates the _____; and the circular-flow diagram, which helps economists analyze the monetary _____ that occur in the economy as a whole.

3. The production possibility frontier (PPF) considers a simplified economy that produces only _____ goods. Points that lie inside the curve or on the curve represent _____ points of production for the economy. Points lying beyond the curve represent production choices that are not feasible for this economy given its level of resources and its technology. This model illustrates the economic concept of _____, since it is impossible to increase the production of one good without decreasing the production of the other good if an economy is producing at a point on its PPF.

4. The _____ is a good way to illustrate the general economic concept of efficiency. Points on the production possibility frontier are _____; there is no way to produce more of one good without producing _____ of the other good.

5. The _____ of producing one good is not just the amount of money it costs but also everything else that must be given up to get that good.

6. The shape of the PPF curve is usually bowed out from the origin; the _____ of producing more of one good increases as more of that good is produced.

7. The PPF also helps us to understand the meaning of economic growth. Economic growth is illustrated as a(n) _____ shift of the production possibility frontier, indicating that it is now possible to produce more of both goods. A(n) _____ shift of the production possibility frontier implies an expansion of the economy's ability to produce _____.

8. The _____ model uses the production possibility frontier concept to illustrate the gains from specialization and _____. Individuals or countries have a comparative advantage in producing a good when they can produce that good with a relatively lower opportunity cost. By specializing, according to their _____ and then engaging in trade, individuals and countries are better off. One of the most important insights for economies is that there are _____ even if one of the trading parties isn't especially good at anything.

9. We can use the _____ model to explore the gains from trade. To do this, we simplify by replacing the curved PPF line with a(n) _____ line PPF. This simplifies the model by making the opportunity cost of production _____ for any given production possibility frontier.

10. If one individual or nation can produce 1 more unit of a good with relatively lower opportunity costs, we say that they have a(n)_____ in the production of that good. However, trade can take place even when one individual or nation has a(n) _____ in producing all goods. Trade is based on _____ and not absolute advantage. The comparative advantage model clearly illustrates that _____ and trade result in a higher level of production.

11. The circular-flow diagram of an economy is a simplified model of the relationship between _____ and firms. It helps economists analyze the _____ that takes place in a market economy. The simplest of economic transactions is barter, in which an individual directly _____ a good or service he or she has for a good or service he or she wants.

12. The _____ diagram represents two kinds of flows around a circle: flows of _____, such as goods, labour, or raw materials in one direction; and flows of _____.

13. The _____ diagram consists of two kinds of markets: the markets for _____, in which households buy the goods and services they want from firms; and _____, the markets where firms hire factors of production from households. The factor market we know best is the _____ market, where workers are paid for their time. Households earn _____ in factor markets and then spend that _____ in the markets for goods and services. In the circular-flow diagram, income equals _____.

14. Economic analysis is useful in both positive and normative economics. _____ economics uses analysis to answer questions about the way the world works; this type of analysis has right and wrong answers. _____ economics employs analysis to answer questions about how the world should work. Positive economics analysis can be used to make predictions, or _____ about the future.

Learning Tips

TIP #1: The production possibility frontier provides a simple model to illustrate scarcity, opportunity cost, trade-offs, economic growth, and the distinction between efficient and inefficient points.

A production possibility frontier for a person or an economy illustrates the maximum amount of two goods that can be produced in a given amount of time given a fixed level of resources and technology. The production possibility frontier is a boundary between points that are feasible but inefficient (points inside the production possibility frontier) and points that are infeasible (points outside the production possibility frontier); thus, all points on the production possibility frontier are both feasible and efficient. Moving along the production possibility frontier, we can produce more of one good only by producing less of the other good. The opportunity cost of producing more of one good is measured as the number of units of the other good that must be forgone. Economic growth occurs when the production possibility frontier shifts out from the origin: an increase in resources or an improvement in technology will shift the production possibility frontier out, indicating an expansion in the productive capacity of the economy, as shown in Figure 2.1.

Figure 2.1

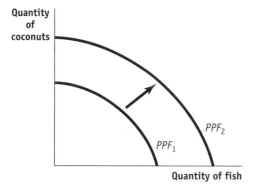

TIP #2: The model of comparative advantage illustrates why specialization and trade is advantageous to people and countries even if a person or a country does not have the absolute advantage in producing any good.

It is possible for individuals or countries to be better off if they specialize according to their comparative advantage and then trade with one another. A country has a comparative advantage in producing a good if it can produce the good at lower opportunity cost than can another country. For example, if country A's opportunity cost of producing one more unit of fish is two units of coconuts, while country B's opportunity cost of producing one more unit of fish is three units of coconuts, then country A should produce fish and trade with country B, which should produce coconuts. For example, even though the United States can absolutely produce more cars and textiles than a smaller country like Malaysia, there are still gains to be had from specialization according to one's comparative advantage and then trading. In this case, Malaysia has a comparative advantage in the production of textiles while the United States has a comparative advantage in the production of cars.

TIP #3: The circular-flow diagram of the economy illustrates the relationship between households and firms as they interact in both the product and the factor markets.

Households provide factors of production, while firms produce goods and services using those factors. Households use the income they earn from selling their factors of production to purchase the goods and services produced by the firms. In the circular-flow diagram (see p. 22), income equals expenditures. The circular-flow diagram depicts two flows: the flows of factors of production and goods and services, and the flows of income and expenditures.

TIP #4: The distinction between positive and normative economics is that the former is about how things are, while the latter is about how things should be.

Positive economics is concerned with descriptive, and hence objective, statements. Normative economics is concerned with prescriptive, and hence subjective, statements. Positive economics describes how the economy works, while normative economics focuses on how the economy should work. The statement "an increase in tax rates will result in a decrease in the amount of labor that will be provided in the market" is an example of a positive statement since it is a statement that can be proven true or false (it is an objective statement). While the statement "Canada should increase tax rates in order to generate higher levels of revenue for school funding" is a normative opinion that expresses what should be done from the speaker's point of view (it is a subjective statement). We can contrast the distinction between positive and normative statements by realizing that, once we agree on the facts, a positive statement will be either true or false; while, with a normative statement, the debate is not over the facts, but over the values and opinions held by different indivduals.

Multiple-Choice Questions

Use the following information to answer the next four questions.

Funland produces two goods, bicycles and yo-yos. In the following table, different feasible production combinations are given for Funland. Assume that Funland's production possibility frontier is linear between combinations A to B, B to C, C to D, etc.

Combination	Bicycles per year	Yo-Yos per year
A	1,000	0
B	800	8,000
C	600	12,000
D	400	15,000
E	200	17,000
F	0	18,000

1. If Funland is currently producing at combination B, the opportunity cost of producing 1,000 more yo-yos is
   a. 200 bicycles.
   b. 50 bicycles.
   c. 750 bicycles.
   d. 4,000 yo-yos.

2. If Funland is currently producing at point E, the opportunity cost of producing 10 more bicycles is
   a. 1 yo-yo.
   b. 10 yo-yos.
   c. 100 yo-yos.
   d. 1,000 yo-yos.

3. Funland's production possibility frontier exhibits
   a. constant opportunity cost.
   b. increasing opportunity cost.
   c. decreasing opportunity cost.
   d. both increasing and decreasing opportunity cost.

4. If Funland is currently producing 400 bicycles per year and 12,000 yo-yos per year, we know
   a. Funland is not at an efficient level of production.
   b. Funland is producing at a point inside its production possibility frontier.
   c. Funland could increase production of yo-yos without decreasing its production of bicycles.
   d. all of the above are true.

5. A straight-line production possibility frontier differs from a bowed-out production possibility frontier because the opportunity cost of producing one more unit of the good on the horizontal axis
   a. decreases as you move down the curve.
   b. increases as you move down the curve.
   c. is constant as you move down the curve.
   d. varies as you move down the curve.

6. Economic models
   a. should accurately represent the real world.
   b. are always complicated mathematical models.
   c. do not provide insight into economic outcomes since they do not accurately reflect the real world.
   d. are a simplified representation of reality.

7. The other things equal assumption means that
   a. all variables are equally important and that any change in one variable will result in the same outcome as an equivalently sized change in any other variable.
   b. all economic models share the same set of assumptions.
   c. the economic effect of a change in a single variable will be analyzed while holding all other variables constant.
   d. it does not matter what assumptions we make when building economic models.

8. Points that lie outside a country's production possibility frontier are
   a. efficient but not feasible.
   b. efficient and feasible.
   c. feasible.
   d. not feasible.

9. The shape of the production possibility frontier is bowed out from the origin due to
   a. scarcity of resources.
   b. specialization of resources.
   c. comparative advantage.
   d. absolute advantage.

10. If a country discovers new resources, this will, other things equal, result in the country's production possibility frontier
   a. shifting out from the origin.
   b. shifting in toward the origin.
   c. remaining the same as it was.
   d. either shifting in or out depending upon the type of resources.

Use the following information to answer the next two questions.

Two countries, Small Land and Big Land, have exactly the same amount of resources to use in the production of milk and bread. Their production possibility frontiers are given in the following graphs.

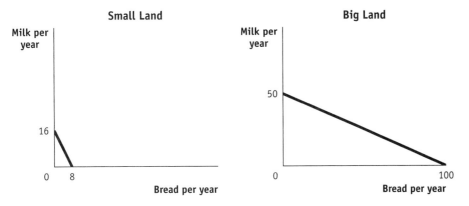

11. Which of the following statements is true?
   a. Small Land does not have a comparative advantage in the production of bread or milk.
   b. Big Land has a comparative advantage in the production of bread.
   c. Big Land has a comparative advantage in the production of milk.
   d. Small Land has a comparative advantage in the production of bread.

12. If Small Land and Big Land both specialize and then trade, then we know
   a. that both countries will benefit from this trade.
   b. that only Big Land will benefit from this trade.
   c. that only Small Land will benefit from this trade.
   d. it is impossible to know with certainty whether there are benefits from trade without further information.

13. Specialization and trade are beneficial to two countries
   a. provided their opportunity costs of production are not the same for all goods that they produce.
   b. when each country specializes in producing the good that it can produce at the lowest opportunity cost.
   c. even when one country can absolutely produce more than the other country.
   d. all of the above.

14. The circular-flow diagram of the economy illustrates
   a. the economic relationship between households and firms.
   b. the relationship between the markets for goods and services and the markets for factors of production.
   c. the equality between expenditure on goods and services and income received by factors of production.
   d. all of the above.

15. Suppose a business has two employees, Ellen and Ruth. The owner of the business wants Ellen and Ruth to take 12 orders and wrap 24 packages. Ellen and Ruth estimate their output as shown in the following table.

	Orders taken per hour	Packages wrapped per hour
Ellen	4	6
Ruth	1	5

Which of the following is true?
a. Since Ruth has an absolute disadvantage in the production of both types of goods, Ellen has a comparative advantage in the production of both types of goods.
b. If Ellen and Ruth do not cooperate and each takes half of the orders and wraps half of the packages, Ellen will work 3.5 hours, while Ruth will work approximately 14.5 hours.
c. Since Ellen has an absolute advantage in both types of goods, there are no gains from specialization.
d. If Ellen and Ruth both specialize according to their comparative advantage and produce only one type of good, Ellen will need to work only 3 hours.

16. Which of the following is a normative statement?
a. Due to advances in health care, people live longer and therefore Social Security expenses have increased.
b. Unemployment increased last year, even though the government sector followed an expansionary economic policy.
c. A 5% decrease in people's income will lead to a 3% decrease in people's consumption of mild cheese.
d. The main goal of the government should be to achieve an annual growth rate for the economy of 7%.

17. Which of the following statements is true about the circular-flow diagram shown here?

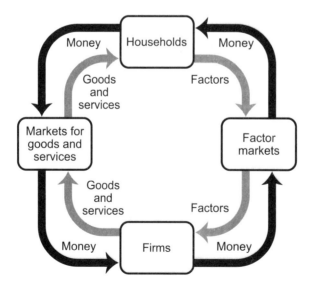

a. The circular-flow diagram allows businesses to make transactions between each other.

b. The circular-flow diagram models government interactions with firms and households.

c. The circular-flow diagram illustrates the economic relationship between households and firms.

d. The circular flow diagram helps us understand both saving and investment behavior in the economy.

18. When economists engage in forecasting, this is an example of

a. normative economics.

b. positive economics.

c. the absolute advantage economists have in this area of expertise.

d. providing a prescription for the economy.

Answer questions 19–22 on the basis of the following table of the production possibility frontier of a given economy, which produces only two goods with given resources and a given technology.

Quantity of coconuts	Quantity of fish
20	0
18	1
16	2
14	3
12	4
10	5
8	6
6	7
4	8
2	9
0	10

19. The opportunity costs of

a. 10 units of fish is zero quantity of coconuts.

b. 20 units of coconut is zero quantity of fish.

c. 1 unit of fish is 2 units of coconuts.

d. an extra unit of fish increases.

20. The opportunity cost of 1 extra unit of fish is

a. –2 units of coconut.

b. –0.5 unit of coconut.

c. +2 units of coconut.

d. +0.5 units of coconut.

21. Suppose, due to the current unemployment situation, the economy is producing 5 units of fish and 6 units of coconuts. The opportunity cost of adding 2 more units of fish is

a. 4 units of coconuts.

b. 2 units of coconuts.

c. 1 unit of coconut.

d. zero unit of coconut.

Answer questions 22–30 on the basis of the following table. Assume that there are two countries: country A and country B, with identical resources. The production functions are given in the accompanying table.
Quantities are litre bottles.

Country A		Country B	
Wine	Beer	Wine	Beer
100	0	50	0
80	10	40	10
60	20	30	20
40	30	20	30
20	40	10	40
0	50	0	50

22. Which of the following statements is true?
   a. Country A has a comparative advantage in both wine and beer.
   b. Country B has a comparative disadvantage in both wine and beer.
   c. Country A has an absolute advantage in wine.
   d. Country B has an absolute advantage in beer.

23. The opportunity cost of an additional unit of beer in Country A is
   a. 100 bottles of wine.
   b. 20 bottles of wine.
   c. 10 bottles of wine.
   d. 2 bottles of wine.

24. The opportunity cost of an additional unit of beer in country B is
   a. 1 bottle of wine.
   b. 10 bottles of wine.
   c. 20 bottles of wine.
   d. 50 bottles of wine.

25. The opportunity cost of an additional unit of beer is
   a. less in country A.
   b. less in country B.
   c. higher in country B.
   d. impossible to determine.

26. Which of the following statements is true?
   a. Country A has a comparative advantage in beer production.
   b. Country B has a comparative advantage in beer production.
   c. Country A has a comparative advantage in both beer and wine production.
   d. Country B has a comparative advantage in both beer and wine production.

27. The opportunity cost of an additional unit of wine in country A is
   a. 50 bottles of beer.
   b. 20 bottles of beer.
   c. 1 bottle of beer.
   d. 0.5 bottle of beer.

28. The opportunity cost of an additional unit of wine in country B is
   a. 1 bottle of beer.
   b. 10 bottles of beer.
   c. 20 bottles of beer.
   d. 50 bottles of beer.

29. Which of the following statements is true?
   a. Country A has a comparative advantage in wine production.
   b. Country B has a comparative advantage in wine production.
   c. Country A has a comparative advantage in wine production, because it has an absolute advantage in wine production.
   d. Country B has a comparative advantage in beer production, because it has an absolute advantage in beer production.

30. The table indicates that
   a. country A should specialize in wine production, export wine to country B, and import beer from country B.
   b. country B should specialize in wine production, export wine to country A, and import beer from country A.
   c. country A should not trade with country B, because it has nothing to gain.
   d. country B should produce wine only.

Problems and Exercises

1. Pacifica is an isolated country producing rice and coconuts. The following table shows different combinations of rice and coconuts that Pacifica can produce in a year. Due to limited resources and technology, as Pacifica increases production of one good it must decrease production of the other good.

Maximum annual output options	Rice (bushels)	Coconuts (pounds)
A	2,000	0
B	1,600	250
C	1,200	450
D	800	600
E	400	700
F	0	800

a. Graph combinations A–F on the following graph and then connect these combinations to create Pacifica's production possibility frontier.

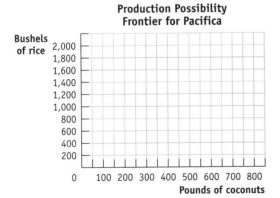

Production Possibility Frontier for Pacifica

b. Consider the following production combinations for Pacifica. For each combination determine which of the following classifications best describes the combination:
   I. The combination is feasible and efficient: the combination is on the production possibility frontier.

II. The combination is feasible but inefficient: the combination is inside the production possibility frontier.

III. The combination is not feasible: the combination is outside the production possibility frontier.

    i. 300 pounds of coconuts, 1,200 bushels of rice

    ii. 450 pounds of coconuts, 1,400 bushels of rice

    iii. 500 pounds of coconuts, 600 bushels of rice

    iv. 725 pounds of coconuts, 600 bushels of rice

    v. 250 pounds of coconuts, 1,600 bushels of rice

c. What is the opportunity cost of producing:
    i. 600 pounds of coconuts instead of zero pounds of coconuts?

    ii. 1,600 bushels of rice instead of 800 bushels of rice?

    iii. 700 pounds of coconuts instead of 250 pounds of coconuts?

2. Suppose an economy produces only two goods, oats and cotton, using only labor and land. This country's production possibility frontier for this year is given in the following graph.

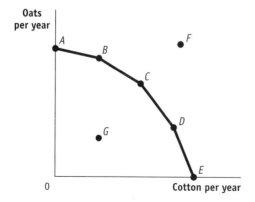

a. Which point on the graph will this economy produce at if it devotes all of its resources to oat production? Explain your answer.

b. Which point on the graph represents a feasible but inefficient point for this economy? Explain your answer.

c. Which point on the graph may become feasible if this economy experiences economic growth? Explain your answer.

d. Explain how you would measure the opportunity cost of moving from point C to point B.

3. Joe and Betty both produce butter and cheese. The following table provides information about some of the combinations of butter and cheese Joe and Betty can produce from their given resources and technology. Assume that both Joe and Betty have linear production possibility frontiers and that they each have the same amount of resources.

Joe's production		Betty's production	
Pounds of butter	Pounds of cheese	Pounds of butter	Pounds of cheese
100	0	120	0
80	30	90	40
60	60	60	80
40	90	30	120
20	120	0	160

a. Draw Joe's and Betty's production possibility frontiers on the following graphs.

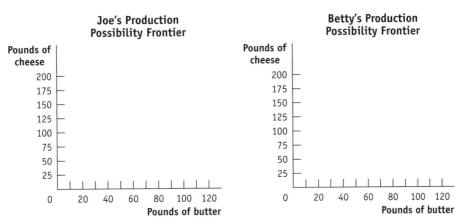

b. Which individual has the absolute advantage in the production of butter?

c. Which individual has the absolute advantage in the production of cheese?

d. What is the opportunity cost of producing one pound of butter for Joe?

e. What is the opportunity cost of producing one pound of butter for Betty?

f. What is the opportunity cost of producing one pound of cheese for Joe?

g. What is the opportunity cost of producing one pound of cheese for Betty?

h. Who has the comparative advantage in the production of butter?

i. Who has the comparative advantage in the production of cheese?

4. George and Kim own a cleaning and yard service business and are its only source of labor. George can rake 1 yard in 1 hour or clean 1 house in 4 hours. Kim can rake 1 yard in 2 hours or clean 1 house in 2 hours.
   a. Fill in the following table for George and Kim.

George		Kim	
Hours to rake a yard	Hours to clean a house	Hours to rake a yard	Hours to clean a house
_____	_____	_____	_____

   b. Fill in the following table showing production possibility combinations that are feasible and efficient for George and Kim if they each work 40 hours.

George's production possibilities		Kim's production possibilities	
Number of yards raked	Number of houses cleaned	Number of yards raked	Number of houses cleaned
0	_____	0	_____
_____	5	_____	10
_____	0	_____	0

On the following graphs, draw George's and Kim's production possibility frontiers if they each work 40 hours.

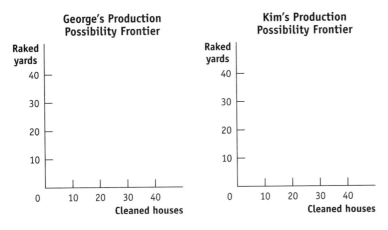

George's Production Possibility Frontier

Kim's Production Possibility Frontier

    c. If George and Kim specialize according to their comparative advantages, what will George do?

    d. If George and Kim work independently and each cleans and rakes at every house, what is the maximum number of houses they can clean and rake if they each work 40 hours?

    e. If George and Kim both agree to work 40 hours, what is the maximum number of houses that can receive both services if they specialize and work cooperatively?

5. Use the simple circular-flow diagram to answer this set of questions.
    a. Firms produce goods and services. What do firms receive when they produce these goods and services?

    b. Firms purchase factors of production from households. What do firms do with these factors of production?

    c. Households purchase goods and services from firms. Where do households acquire the funds to make these purchases?

    d. Households provide factors of production to firms. What motivates households to provide these factors of production?

    e. If firms hire larger amounts of factors of production, what do you anticipate will happen to the level of the production of goods and services?

6. The statements below are either positive or normative. Identify each statement. Explain your answer.

 a. The Canadian welfare system should provide greater monetary support to program participants.

 b. A tax on gasoline will reduce consumption of gasoline.

 c. A tax on gasoline is a more efficient way to finance highway construction than imposing user fees in the form of highway tolls.

7. Consider an economy that produces two goods, X and Y, with all resources fully employed. Use the accompanying table to answer the following questions.

Quantity of X	Quantity of Y
21	0
19	1
17	2
15	3
13	4
11	5
9	6
7	7
5	8
3	9
1	10
0	11

 a. What is the opportunity cost of 11 units of Y? The opportunity cost of one unit of Y? The opportunity cost of 21 units of X? The opportunity cost of one unit of X?

 b. Consider a combination of 5 units of X and 5 units of Y. Do you think that resources are under-utilized? What is the opportunity of adding 3 units of Y, with X staying at 5 units?

 c. What is the shape of the PPF line? Is opportunity cost constant or increasing?

8. Consider the story of two castaways. The accompanying table shows the PPF functions of Tom and Lloyd.

Tom's PPF		Lloyd's PPF	
Coconuts	Fish	Coconuts	Fish
100	0	50	0
80	10	40	10
60	20	30	20
40	30	20	30
20	40	10	40
0	50	0	50

 a. In what line of activity does Tom have the comparative advantage? Why?

 b. In what line of activity does Lloyd have the comparative advantage? Why?

c. If they specialize and agree to trade, what will be the total output of coconuts and fish?

d. Suppose they agree to trade one coconut for 2/3 fish (in other words, 1 fish for 3/2 coconuts). If Tom trades 48 coconuts, how many fish will he get in exchange? Assume that before trade took place, Tom consumed 52 coconuts and Lloyd consumed 18 fish. What will be the combination of consumption after trade and before trade for Tom? What will be the combination of consumption after trade and before trade for Lloyd? Is trade beneficial to both parties? Why?

Answers to How Well Do You Understand the Chapter

1. simplified

2. models, trade-offs, gains from trade, transactions

3. two, feasible, trade-offs

4. production possibility frontier (PPF), efficient, less

5. opportunity costs

6. opportunity costs

7. outward, outward, goods and services

8. comparative advantage, trade, comparative advantage, gains from trade

9. comparative advantage, straight, constant

10. comparative advantage, absolute advantage, comparative advantage, specialization

11. households, transactions, trades

12. circular-flow, input-output, payments

13. circular-flow, goods and services, factor markets, labour, income, income, expenditures

14. positive, normative, forecasts

Answers to Multiple-Choice Questions

1. Funland can increase its production of yo-yos only if it decreases its production of bicycles. Between combinations B and C, Funland can produce 20 yo-yos for every bicycle it does not produce; thus, if Funland produces 1,000 additional yo-yos, it must give up 1,000 divided by 20, or 50 bicycles. **Answer: B.**

2. The opportunity cost of producing an additional bicycle for Funland given its initial production at combination E is 10 yo-yos. If Funland increases its production of bicycles by 200, it must give up 2,000 yo-yos, therefore the opportunity cost of producing these 10 additional bicycles is 100 yo-yos. **Answer: C.**

3. Funland's production possibility frontier illustrates increasing opportunity cost, since as more and more bicycles are produced, increasingly larger amounts of yo-yos must be given up. For example, in order to produce 200 additional bicycles at combination E, Funland must reduce production of yo-yos by 2,000, while in order to produce 200 additional bicycles at combination D, Funland must reduce production of yo-yos by 3,000. Increasing opportunity cost is also true if Funland increases its production of yo-yos; increasing amounts of yo-yo production entail increasingly larger opportunity costs. **Answer: B.**

4. The data in the table tell us Funland can produce 400 bicycles per year while simultaneously producing 15,000 yo-yos per year. When Funland produces 400 bicycles per year and only 12,000 yo-yos, it uses resources inefficiently. Therefore, Funland is producing at a point inside the production possibility frontier. **Answer: D.**

5. Only one of these answers can be correct. The slope of a straight line is constant, and therefore the opportunity cost of producing one more unit of the good, measured by how much of the other good you must give up in order to produce one more unit of the first good, is constant. **Answer: C.**

6. Economic models are an attempt to simplify the real world while allowing economists to focus on the impact of changes in specific variables on economic outcomes. Economic models should be as simple as possible while still providing insight into the economic question they address. **Answer: D.**

7. The other things equal assumption is used in economic models to allow the model builder to focus on the impact of a change in a single variable on the model while all the other variables do not change. **Answer: C.**

8. Only points that lie on a country's production possibility frontier are efficient; points inside the production possibility frontier can be produced (they are feasible) but do not represent the maximum amount of production that is possible given the country's resources and technology; points outside the production possibility frontier cannot be produced with the country's available resources and technology (they are not feasible). **Answer: D.**

9. Production possibility frontiers illustrate scarcity of resources since the frontier acts as a boundary between those production combinations that are feasible and those that are not feasible. However, the bowed-out shape of the production possibility frontier is due to specialization of resources: when small amounts of one good are produced, we can increase the production of that good with a relatively small decrease in the production of the second good since we can use resources that are particularly well suited for the production of the first good. However, when large amounts of a good are produced, resources that are less well suited for that good's production are used, and thus relatively more of the other good's production must be sacrificed. **Answer: B.**

10. The discovery of new resources will make it possible for a country to produce more, causing its production possibility frontier to shift out away from the origin. **Answer: A.**

11. Small Land has a comparative advantage in the production of milk since its opportunity cost of milk production (1/2 unit of bread for every unit of milk it produces) is less than Big Land's opportunity cost of milk production (2 units of bread for every unit of milk it produces). In contrast, Big Land has the comparative advantage in the production of bread since its opportunity cost of bread production (1/2 unit of milk) is less than Small Land's opportunity cost of bread production (2 units of milk). **Answer: B.**

12. Specialization and trade based on comparative advantage is mutually beneficial to both trading partners. **Answer: A.**

13. The benefits from trade arise because of comparative advantage, the ability to produce a good with lower opportunity cost than a competitor can. Countries will mutually benefit from trade provided they have different opportunity costs of production and they each produce according to their comparative advantage. This beneficial trade does not depend upon absolute advantage. **Answer: D.**

14. The circular-flow diagram represents two flows between households and firms: (i) the flow of goods and services as well as the flow of factors of production; and (ii) the flow of money as payment for goods and services or as income received by factors of production. The model provides a simple representation of the equality between expenditure on goods and services and income received by factors of production. **Answer: D.**

15. The absolute advantage in the production of both goods belongs to Ellen. Ruth has the comparative advantage in wrapping presents, while Ellen has the comparative advantage in taking orders. If they each produce 6 orders and 12 wrapped packages, Ellen will work 3.5 hours (1.5 hours taking 6 orders and 2 hours wrapping packages), while Ruth will work 8 hours and 24 minutes (6 hours taking 6 orders and 2 hours and 24 minutes wrapping packages). If they both specialize and produce only one type of good, Ellen can produce 12 orders in 3 hours, while it will take Ruth 4 hours and 48 minutes to wrap 24 packages. **Answer: D.**

16. A positive statement is an objective or descriptive statement, while a normative statement is subjective or prescriptive. Statement D expresses an opinion or a subjective evaluation and is therefore a normative statement. **Answer: D.**

17. The circular flow diagram does not include government, saving, or investment; nor does it allow businesses to make transactions between each other. It provides a simple representation of the economic relationship between households and firms. **Answer: C.**

18. Although forecasting may serve as a guide to policy, it is still a prediction rather than a prescription: a forecast is an example of positive economics. **Answer: B.**

19. Opportunity costs are constant. The opportunity costs of 1 extra unit of fish are 2 coconuts. **Answer: C.**

20. We cannot consider negative costs. **Answer: C.**

21. Adding 2 more units of fish (by drawing unemployed people into gainful employment) will not reduce the output of coconuts. We started with 5 fish and 6 coconuts and now we have 7 fish and 6 coconuts. Therefore, the opportunity cost of 2 extra units of fish is zero. **Answer: D.**

22. Country A has an absolute advantage in wine, because country A can produce 100 bottles of wine, while country B can produce 50 bottles of wine. **Answer: C.**

23. Since the opportunity cost of 10 bottles of beer in country A is 20 bottles of wine, the opportunity cost of 1 bottle of beer is 2 bottles of wine. **Answer: D.**

24. Since the opportunity cost of 10 bottles of beer in country B is 10 bottles of wine, the opportunity cost of 1 bottle of beer is 1 bottle of wine. **Answer: A.**

25. Since 1 < 2, the opportunity cost of beer is less in country B. **Answer: B.**

26. Since opportunity costs are lower in country B, country B has the comparative advantage in beer production. **Answer: B.**

27. Since the opportunity cost of 20 bottles of wine in country A is 10 bottles of beer, the opportunity cost of 1 bottle of wine is 0.5 bottles of beer. **Answer: D.**

28. Since the opportunity cost of 10 bottles of wine in country B is 10 bottles of beer, the opportunity cost of 1 bottle of wine is 1 bottle of beer. **Answer: A.**

29. Since opportunity cost is lower in country A, country A has the comparative advantage in wine production. **Answer: A.**

30. Country A should specialize in wine and country B should specialize in beer. Trading will be beneficial to both countries. **Answer: A.**

Answers to Problems and Exercises

1. a. The production possibility frontier for Pacifica is shown in the following graph.

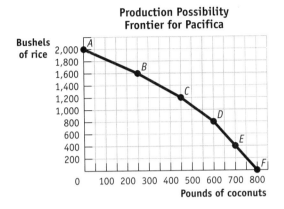

**Production Possibility
Frontier for Pacifica**

Bushels of rice (y-axis): 2,000, 1,800, 1,600, 1,400, 1,200, 1,000, 800, 600, 400, 200

Pounds of coconuts (x-axis): 0, 100, 200, 300, 400, 500, 600, 700, 800

Points: A, B, C, D, E, F

   b. In answering this question, you need to decide whether the given point lies on the production possibility frontier (answer I), lies inside the production possibility frontier (answer II), or lies outside the production possibility frontier (answer III).
   i. Since Pacifica can produce 450 pounds of coconuts and 1,200 bushels of rice, it follows that Pacifica can easily produce 300 pounds of coconuts and 1,200 bushels of rice. **Answer: II.**
   ii. Since the point corresponding to 450 pounds of coconuts and 1,200 bushels of rice lies on Pacifica's production possibility frontier, it follows that the point corresponding to 450 pounds of coconuts and 1,400 bushels of rice lies outside its production possibility frontier. **Answer: III.**
   iii. Since Pacifica can produce 800 bushels of rice and 600 pounds of coconuts, it must also be possible for Pacifica to produce 600 bushels of rice and 500 pounds of coconuts (a reduction in the production of both goods). **Answer: II.**
   iv. Since Pacifica can produce 700 pounds of coconuts and 400 bushels of rice on its production possibility frontier, it must follow that 725 pounds of coconuts and 600 bushels of rice (an increase in the production of both goods) represent a point that lies outside Pacifica's production possibility frontier. **Answer: III.**
   v. Since this point is given in the table, it represents a point that lies on Pacifica's production possibility frontier. **Answer: I.**
   c. The opportunity cost of moving from one point to another point on the production possibility frontier is measured by how many units of one good are given up in order to increase production of the other good.
   i. 1,200 bushels of rice
   ii. 350 pounds of coconuts
   iii. 1,200 bushels of rice

2. a. Point *A* represents the maximum amount of oats that can be produced by this economy. Any other point on the production possibility frontier relative to point *A* results in some production of cotton and a reduction in oat production.
   b. Point *G* is feasible since it is a production combination that lies inside the production possibility frontier. However, it is not efficient since it would be possible to increase oat or cotton production without decreasing production of the other good.

   c. Point *F* currently is not a feasible point for production for this economy since it lies beyond the production possibility frontier. However, if there is economic growth the production possibility frontier will shift out, resulting in an ability to produce more of both goods.

   d. The opportunity cost of moving from point *C* to point *B* is measured by the units of cotton per year that must be given up in order to increase oat production.

3. a.

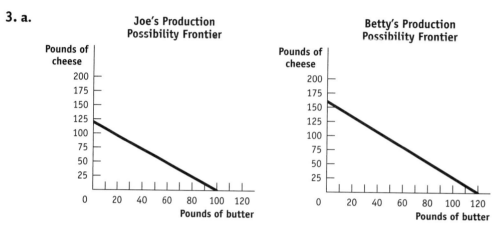

   b. Betty has the absolute advantage in the production of butter since she can produce more butter than Joe (120 pounds versus 100 pounds) from the same amount of resources.

   c. Betty has the absolute advantage in the production of cheese since she can produce more cheese than Joe (160 pounds versus 120 pounds) from the same amount of resources.

   d. The opportunity cost of producing one pound of butter for Joe is 1.2 pounds of cheese.

   e. The opportunity cost of producing one pound of butter for Betty is 4/3 pounds of cheese.

   f. The opportunity cost of producing one pound of cheese for Joe is 0.833 pound of butter.

   g. The opportunity cost of producing one pound of cheese for Betty is 3/4 pound of butter.

   h. Joe has the comparative advantage in the production of butter since his opportunity cost, 1.2 pounds of cheese, is less than Betty's opportunity cost of 4/3 pounds of cheese.

   i. Betty has the comparative advantage in the production of cheese since her opportunity cost of cheese production is lower than Joe's (3/4 pound of butter versus 0.8 pound of butter).

4. a.

George		Kim	
Hours to rake a yard	Hours to clean a house	Hours to rake a yard	Hours to clean a house
1 hour	4 hours	2 hours	2 hours

b.

George's production possibilities		Kim's production possibilities	
Number of yards raked	Number of houses cleaned	Number of yards raked	Number of houses cleaned
0	10	0	20
20	5	10	10
40	0	20	0

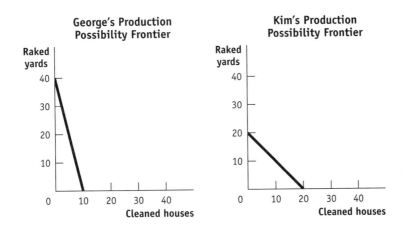

George's Production Possibility Frontier

Kim's Production Possibility Frontier

c. George will rake yards since his opportunity cost of raking yards (1/4 clean house) is smaller than Kim's opportunity cost of raking yards (1 clean house).

d. Working 40 hours, George can clean and rake at 8 houses (he will use 32 hours to clean the 8 houses and another 8 hours to rake their yards). Working 40 hours, Kim can clean and rake at 10 houses (she will use 20 hours to clean the 10 houses and 20 hours to rake their yards). The number of houses independently and completely served by George and Kim is 8 + 10 = 18 houses.

e. Kim will specialize and clean 20 houses using her 40 hours. George will rake the yards of these 20 houses, and that will use 20 of his 40 hours. With his remaining 20 hours George can clean and rake 4 homes. Together George and Kim can provide both services to 24 houses if they specialize and cooperate with one another.

5. a. Firms earn money from selling goods and services to households.

b. Firms use factors of production to produce the goods and services they sell to households.

c. Households purchase goods and services using the income they receive from selling factors of production to firms.

d. Households provide factors of production to firms in order to receive income that they then spend on goods and services.

e. Production of goods and services will increase since firms will have more factors of production available to them to produce goods and services.

6. a. This statement is an example of normative economics since it expresses how one person thinks the world should work rather than expressing a factual, objective statement.

b. This statement is an example of positive economics since it is a statement that can be analyzed and determined to be either true or false independent of the analyst's values.

c. This statement is an example of positive economics since the two methods of financing highway construction can be compared as to which method achieves the goal most efficiently.

7. a. 21 units of X; 21/11 units of X; 11 units of Y; 11/21 units of Y
   b. no; zero
   c. straight line; constant opportunity cost

8. a. Coconuts. Tom's opportunity cost for 1 coconut is 1/2 fish, while Lloyd's opportunity cost for 1 coconut is 1 fish. Tom's opportunity cost is relatively lower than Lloyd's opportunity cost.
   b. Fish. Lloyd's opportunity cost for 1 fish is 1 coconut, while Tom's opportunity cost for 1 fish is 2 coconuts. Lloyd's opportunity cost is relatively lower than Tom's opportunity cost.
   c. 100 units of coconuts and 50 units of fish.
   d. 32 units of fish. For Tom, the consumption after the trade, coconuts = 52 and fish = 32. Before trade, coconuts = 52 and fish = 24.
   For Lloyd, the consumption combination after trade, fish = 18, coconuts = 48. Before trade, fish = 18, coconuts = 32.
   Trade is beneficial to both. The consumption basket is higher after trade.

chapter **2** Appendix

Graphs in Economics

This appendix reviews how to look at graphs and simple equations. Some basic math principles and relations between variables help us to understand economic theories and concepts. The authors discuss how graphs describe relationships between variables and how to look at slopes and maximum values.

How Well Do You Understand the Chapter?

Fill in the blanks using the following terms to complete the following statements. Terms may be used more than once. If you find yourself having difficulties, please refer back to the appropriate section in the text.

absolute value	interpretation	pie	two
arc	left	point(s)	unrelated
average	length	positive	value
causality	linear	price	variable(s)
constant	maximum	relationship	vertical
decreases	minimum	right	x-variable
dependent	negative	run	x-axis
graph(s)	non-linear	slope	y-variable
horizontal	numerical	straight	zero
increases	observation	tangent	
independent	omitted	time	
infinity	percentage	truncated	

1. When studying economics, _____ are the visual images used to illustrate ideas and enhance understanding. _____ _____ in economics typically depict the relationship between economic variables. A(n) _____ is a quantity that can take on more than one _____, for example; a person's age, a household's income, and the price of a bicycle are all variables. Most economic models describe the _____ between two economic variables while holding all other _____ constant.

2. In a two-axis _____, one variable is called the *x*-variable and the other variable is called the _____. The *x*-variable is measured along the horizontal axis, while the *y*-variable is measured along the _____ axis. The horizontal axis and the vertical axis intersect at the origin, where both the *x*-variable and the *y*-variable have a value of

_____. As you move to the right along the _x_-axis, the value of the _x_-variable _____. As you move up from the origin along the _y_-axis, the value of the _y_-variable _____. Graphs often represent a causal relationship: the value of the independent valuable affects the value of the _____ variable.

3. A straight line on a graph depicts a(n) _____ relationship between the two variables. A curved, or _____ line depicts a non-linear relationship. Two variables have a(n) _____ relationship when an increase in one variable leads to an increase in the other variable. Two variables have a negative relationship when an increase in one variable leads to _____ in the other variable. A curve depicting a positive relationship slopes upward to the _____, while a curve depicting a(n) _____ relationship slopes downward to the right. The point at which a curve crosses the _____ axis is called the horizontal intercept. The horizontal intercept shows the value of the _____ when the _y_-variable equals _____. The point at which a curve crosses the vertical axis is called the _____ intercept; the vertical intercept shows the value of the _____ when the _x_-variable equals _____.

4. A _____ measures the steepness of the curve and tells you how responsive the _y_-variable is to changes in the _x_-variable. On a linear curve, the slope is calculated by dividing the "rise" between two points by the "_____" between these same two points. The rise measures the change in the _y_-variable, while the _____ measures the change in the _x_-variable. If two variables have a(n) _____ relationship, the slope of the curve representing this relationship will have a positive value; if two variables have a negative relationship, the slope of the curve representing this relationship will have a(n) _____ value. The slope of a horizontal line is always _____, while the slope of a vertical line is always equal to _____.

5. As you move along the curve, a linear curve has _____ slope. If the curve slopes upward to the right and gets increasingly steeper, it has _____ increasing slope; if the curve slopes upward to the right and gets increasingly flatter, it has _____ decreasing slope.

6. There are _____ methods for calculating the slope of a non-linear relationship. The _____ method of slope measurement calculates a(n) _____ slope of the curve between two points by drawing a straight line between the two points on the curve and calculating the slope of that straight line. The _____ method of slope measurement calculates the slope of the curve at a particular point by finding the slope of the straight line which is _____ to the curve at that point. A tangent line is a straight line that just touches a(n) _____ curve at a particular point.

7. When the slope of a curve changes from positive to negative, it creates a(n) _____ point on the curve; when the slope of a curve changes from negative to positive, it creates a(n) _____ point on the curve.

8. Numerical graphs display numerical information. Time-series graphs, scatter diagrams, pie charts, and bar graphs are examples of _____ graphs. In a time-series graph, _____ is graphed on the horizontal axis, while values of a variable that occurred at those times are graphed on the vertical axis. A scatter diagram consists of a set of _____, where each point corresponds to an actual _____ of the x-variable and y-variable. A(n) _____ chart depicts the share of a total amount that is accounted for by various components, where the share is typically expressed as a(n) _____. A bar graph employs bars of various height or _____ to indicate a variable's values.

9. Graphs can be constructed, intentionally or unintentionally, in ways that are misleading and may lead to inaccurate conclusions. The scale used in constructing a graph can influence your _____ of the data being presented. Sometimes the scale on a graph is _____, where part of the range of values on an axis is omitted; truncation of a scale can influence interpretation of the graph's data. A scatter diagram can lead the viewer to believe that two variables are related, but this may be a misinterpretation of the data if the observed relationship is due to an unobserved effect of a third _____ on each of the other two variables. This _____ variable creates the erroneous appearance of a direct causal relationship between the two represented variables. It is important to understand how graphs may mislead or be interpreted incorrectly since policy decisions, business decisions, and political arguments are often based on the _____ of numerical graphs. The mistake of reverse causality occurs when the dependent variable is erroneously taken as a(n) _____ variable, while the independent variable is erroneously taken as a(n) _____ variable.

Learning Tips

TIP #1: The construction and interpretation of graphs is crucial in economics.

Graphs give the economist a handy way to show relationships between variables. Graphs often present a concept in a clear visual image that can take many words to explain.

TIP #2: There are two methods for calculating the slope of a curved line: the arc method and the point method.

Both methods are used in the book. The arc method calculates an average slope of a curve by drawing a straight line between two points on the curve and calculating the slope of that straight line. The point method calculates the slope of the curve at a particular point by finding the slope of the straight line tangent to the curve at that point.

TIP #3: There are a variety of ways to present data in graphical form.

Economists use two-variable graphs, pie charts, bar graphs, and scatter diagrams. Each of these forms provides insights on the relationship between variables.

TIP #4: Numerical graphs can present data in a misleading manner.

Sometimes graphs can distort relationships, and sometimes this distortion is intentional. Common problems include altering the scale used in the construction of a graph, using a truncated scale, or misrepresenting the direction of causality between variables.

Multiple-Choice Questions

1. A variable
   a. is a numerical value.
   b. is a quantity that can take on more than one value.
   c. has a constant value in economic models.
   d. depicts the relationship between two economic measures.

2. Economic models often use two-variable graphs to portray the relationship between two different variables while allowing other variables that might influence the relationship
   a. to vary.
   b. to increase.
   c. to decrease.
   d. to stay constant.

3. Which of the following statements is true?
   a. In general, the x-axis measures the independent variable and the y-axis measures the dependent variable.
   b. Price, although an independent variable, is by convention always measured on the y-axis.
   c. At the origin, the value of both variables is zero.
   d. All of the above are true.

4. A straight line in a graph
   a. has constant slope.
   b. indicates that the two variables have a linear relationship.
   c. may have a slope that is positive, negative, equal to zero, or equal to infinity.
   d. is all of the above.

5. A curved line in a graph
   a. has constant slope.
   b. must have either positive or negative slope.
   c. has a slope measure that varies as you move along the curve.
   d. has a slope of infinity.

6. Which of the following statements is true?
   a. If the x- and y-variables have a positive relationship, then as the x-variable increases in value the y-variable decreases in value.
   b. The x- and y-variables have no causal relationship to each other when a graph of the two variables is either a vertical or a horizontal line.
   c. If the x- and y-variables have a negative relationship, then as the y-variable decreases in value the x-variable also decreases in value.
   d. The vertical intercept corresponds to that point on the vertical axis where the value of the y-variable equals zero.

7. As you move rightward along the horizontal axis, a curve with positive increasing slope
   a. slopes downward.
   b. slopes upward and gets flatter.
   c. slopes upward and gets steeper.
   d. slopes downward and gets steeper.

8. The arc method of calculating the slope of a curve
   a. involves drawing a straight line between two points on the curve and then calculating the slope of that straight line.
   b. calculates a measure of the average slope of the curve between two points on the curve.
   c. does not require the drawing of a line tangent to the curve at a particular point on the curve.
   d. is all of the above.

9. A maximum point occurs when
   a. the x-variable is maximized.
   b. the x-variable equals zero.
   c. the slope of the curve changes from positive to negative.
   d. the slope of the curve changes from negative to positive.

10. Which of the following types of graphs would be best to use if you wanted to depict the relationship between time and another variable?
   a. time-series graph
   b. scatter diagram
   c. pie chart
   d. bar graph

11. The information in a pie chart represents
   a. different points, where each point corresponds to an actual observation of the x- and y-variables.
   b. the share of a total amount that is accounted for by various components, usually given as percentages.

    c. different values of the variables by height or length.
    d. different values of the variables as they vary over time.

12. Graphs may be misleading to the viewer because of the
    a. choice of scale that is used in creating the graph.
    b. truncation of the x- and/or y-axis.
    c. lack of clarity about what information is being presented.
    d. all of the above.

13. Suppose there is a relationship between two variables. When the researcher wrongly believes that the first variable causes the changes in the second variable, when in fact it is the second variable causing changes in the first variable, we call this a problem of
    a. an omitted variable.
    b. a truncated graph.
    c. reverse causality.
    d. misleading scale.

14. Given the equation of $x = 10 - 2y$, where the x-variable is in the horizontal axis,
    a. the slope of the graph is −2.
    b. the slope of the graph is not constant.
    c. the vertical intercept is 10.
    d. the vertical intercept is 5.

15. Consider the equation of $x = 20 + 4y$, where the x-variable is in the horizontal axis. Which of the following statements is **false?**
    a. The slope of the graph is 1/4.
    b. The intercept in the horizontal axis is 20.
    c. The intercept in the vertical axis is 5.
    d. The slope is positive and constant.

Problems and Exercises

1. Consider the five sets of data below.

Set A		Set B		Set C		Set D		Set E	
X	Y	X	Y	X	Y	X	Y	X	Y
10	1	0	5	5	8	0	10	0	15
10	2	1	4	6	8	1	12	1	10
10	3	2	3	7	8	2	14	2	7
10	4	3	2	8	8	3	16	3	5

Suppose you were to graph each of the data sets in a two-variable graph with the x-variable on the horizontal axis and the y-variable on the vertical axis.
    a. Which data set(s) represent(s) a horizontal line?

    b. Which data set(s) has/have a slope of infinity?

c. Which data set(s) depict(s) a positive relationship?

d. Which data set(s) depict(s) a negative relationship?

e. Which data set(s) depict(s) a linear relationship?

f. Which data set(s) has/have a slope greater than zero?

g. What is the absolute value of the slope of data set B?

h. What is the absolute value of the slope of data set D?

2. Use the following graph to answer this question. Note that this graph is not drawn to scale.

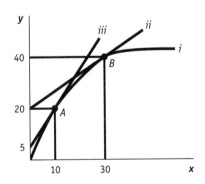

a. What is the y-intercept of line *iii*?

b. Which line is drawn tangent to the curve *i* at point B?

c. Using the arc method, calculate the slope between points A and B.

d. Using the point method, what is the slope at point A?

e. Using the point method, what is the slope at point *B?*

f. What is the relationship between the slope found in question 2c with the slopes found in questions 2d and 2e?

3. For each of the following pairs of variables, identify the independent variable and explain why you think it is the independent variable.
   a. Price of hamburgers and quantity of hamburgers consumed.

   b. Interest rates and the quantity of loans a bank makes.

4. Study the following four graphs. For each of the following statements, indicate which graph matches the statement. In addition, identify which variable would appear on the horizontal axis and which variable would appear on the vertical axis.

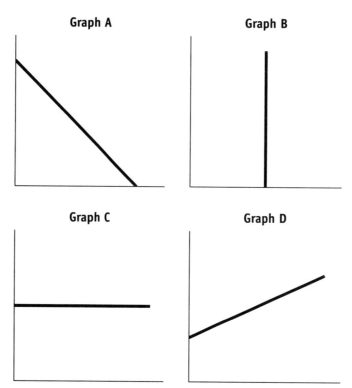

Graph A   Graph B

Graph C   Graph D

   a. If the price of football tickets decreases, more people attend the game.

   b. Older adults have more health problems than younger adults.

   c. No matter the price there are a fixed number of original Vincent van Gogh paintings.

d. Regardless of the quantity of corn a farmer produces, he or she will still sell it for the prevailing market price.

5. Consider the following data.

Year	Number of applications for admission to EastBay University
1980	4,000
1990	6,000
2000	9,000
2005	21,000

a. Graph the preceding data on both of the following graphs, using linear segments to connect the four observations with one another.

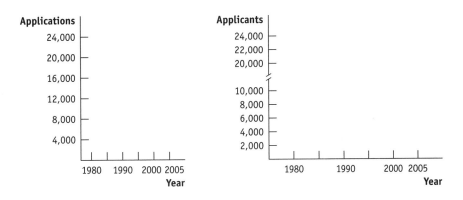

b. Compare and contrast the two graphs you have drawn in part a.

6. Consider the equation of $x = 20 - 0.5y$ and draw the x-variable as the horizontal axis.
  a. What is the intercept of the horizontal axis?

  b. What is the intercept of the vertical axis?

  c. What is the slope of the graph? Is the slope constant, increasing, or decreasing as values of y change?

  d. What is the value of x when $y = 12$ and when $y = 8$?

  e. Consider the second equation of $x = 10 + 0.5y$. Given both equations, solve for y and for x.

Answers to How Well Do You Understand the Chapter

1. graphs, graphs, variable, values, relationship, variables

2. graph, *y*-variable, vertical, zero, increases, increases, dependent

3. linear, non-linear, positive, decreases, right, negative, horizontal, *x*-variable, zero, vertical, *y*-variable, zero

4. slope, run, run, positive, negative, zero, infinity

5. constant, positive, negative

6. two, arc, average, point, tangent, non-linear

7. maximum, minimum

8. numerical, time, points, observation, pie, percentage, length

9. interpretation, truncated, variable, omitted, interpretation, independent, dependent

Answers to Multiple-Choice Questions

1. A variable is a measure of something, such as price or quantity, that can vary numerically; thus, a variable is a quantity that can take on more than one value. **Answer: B.**

2. Economic models use two-variable graphs in order to present a visual image of the relationship between these two variables. Other variables that might affect the relationship between the two variables are held constant to simplify the analysis. **Answer: D.**

3. Each of these statements is correct. Although the independent variable is typically placed on the horizontal axis, price, by convention, is always placed on the vertical axis. At the origin, where the x-axis intersects the y-axis, both variables have a value of zero. **Answer: D.**

4. By definition a straight line in a graph is linear; it therefore depicts a linear relationship. In addition, a straight line has constant slope since the ratio of the change in the y-variable to the change in the x-variable is constant along the entire line. Straight lines can slope up to the right (positive slope), slope down to the right (negative slope), be horizontal (slope of zero), or be vertical (slope of infinity). **Answer: D.**

5. A curved line's slope varies as you move along the curve since the ratio of the change in the y-variable to the change in the x-variable is not constant. The slope of a curved line is positive if the line curves upward as you move to the right along the x-axis, and negative if the line curves downward as you move to the right along the x-axis. A curved line can contain both positively and negatively sloped segments. **Answer: C.**

6. The x- and y-variables have a positive relationship when both variables move together: if x increases in value, then y increases in value, or if x decreases in value, then y decreases in value. The x- and y-variables have a negative relationship when the variables move in opposite directions: if x increases in value, then y decreases in value, and vice versa. The vertical intercept is the value of y when the x-variable (not the y-variable) equals zero. A vertical or horizontal line indicates that there is no relationship between the two variables: if the line is vertical, the y-variable changes values without affecting the x-variable, and if the line is horizontal, the x-variable changes values without affecting the y-variable. **Answer: B.**

7. A curve with a positive slope slopes upward. If the slope is positive and increasing, this means that the change in the *y*-variable increases faster than the change in the *x*-variable. This is true only if the line is upward sloping and gets increasingly steep. **Answer: C.**

8. Drawing a straight line between two points on the curve and then calculating the slope of that straight line is the arc method. The arc method is an approximation of the slope of the curve between the two chosen endpoints: it is an average slope. The tangent line is necessary when calculating slope using the point method, not the arc method. **Answer: D.**

9. A maximum point refers to the point where the *y*-variable reaches its maximum value; this will occur at that point where the slope changes from positive to negative. **Answer: C.**

10. A time-series graph depicts the value of a variable graphed at different points in time. **Answer: A.**

11. Different points, where each point corresponds to an actual observation of the *x*- and *y*-variables, describes a scatter diagram. A bar graph depicts different values of the variables by height or length, while a time-series graph shows different values of the variables as they vary over time. A pie chart is the share of a total amount that is accounted for by various components, usually given as percentages. **Answer: B.**

12. It is important to realize that graphs may be misleading to a viewer because of the scale that is used in constructing the graph, the values omitted from the *x*-axis or the *y*-axis (the case of the truncated axis), or because it is not clear what numerical information the graph is providing. **Answer: D.**

13. When two variables are related, researchers need to investigate whether the first variable determines the value of the second variable or vice versa. Getting the direction of causality wrong is termed reverse causality. **Answer: C.**

14. Slope is rise over run and it is constant at –0.5. When *x* is zero, *y* is 5. **Answer: D.**

15. Slope is 1/4 and it is constant. When *x* is zero, *y* is –5. **Answer: C.**

Answers to Problems and Exercises

1. a. Set C, since the *y*-variable is constant at 8 while the *x*-variables change.
 b. Set A has a slope of infinity. Slope is defined as the ratio of the change in the *y*-variable to the change in the *x*-variable, and in this case the change in the *x*-variable is equal to zero.
 c. Set D, since as the *x*-variable increases in value the *y*-variable also increases in value.
 d. Set B and set E, since the *x*-variable and *y*-variable move in opposite directions: as one variable increases in value the other variable decreases in value.
 e. Sets A, B, C, and D all depict linear relationships, since each of these sets has constant slope.
 f. Set A and set D, since set A has a slope of infinity and set D has a slope of 2.
 g. Set B's slope is –1, so the absolute value of the slope of this set would be 1.
 h. The absolute value of the slope of data set D is 2.

2. a. The *y*-intercept of line *iii* is the value of *y* when the *x*-variable equals zero. In this case the value of the *y*-intercept is 5.
 b. Line *ii* is drawn tangent to curve *i* at point *B* since it just touches the curve at point *B*.
 c. To calculate the slope between points *A* and *B* using the arc method, we need to find the change in the *y*-variable and divide this by the change in the

x-variable. The change in the *y*-variable equals 20 (40 – 20) and the change in the *x*-variable equals 20 (30 – 10). The ratio of these changes, or the slope, using the arc method is 20/20, or 1.

d. The slope at point *A* using the point method is equal to the slope of the line drawn tangent to the curve at point *A*. The slope of line *iii* is 15/10 = 1.5.

e. The slope at point *B* using the point method is equal to the slope of the line drawn tangent to the curve at point *B*. The slope of line *ii* is 20/30 = 0.67.

f. The slope measure found using the arc method is an average slope. When we compare this average slope to the measures of slope we calculated using the point method, we find that the average slope measure's value lies between the more precisely calculated slope measures we found using the point method.

3. a. Price of hamburgers is the independent variable since the price influences the quantity of the good consumed.

b. An interest rate is the price of borrowing funds (money). As a price it is the independent variable that affects the quantity of loans made by an individual or a bank.

4. a. Graph A depicts this situation, with the quantity of people attending the game on the horizontal axis and the price of football tickets on the vertical axis.

b. Graph D depicts this situation, with the age of adults on the horizontal axis and health problems on the vertical axis.

c. Graph B depicts this situation, with the quantity of paintings on the horizontal axis and the price on the vertical axis. (Price, although the independent variable, is placed on the vertical axis by convention.)

d. Graph C depicts this situation, since the farmer can sell as much corn as she or he would like without affecting the market price. Quantity of corn would be on the horizontal axis and price of corn would be on the vertical axis.

5. a.

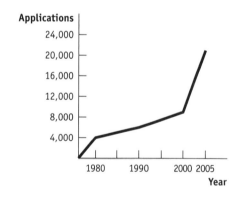 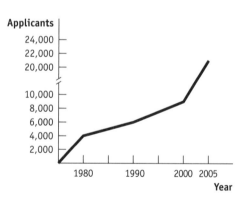

b. The two graphs visually have a different impact on the viewer: the left graph uses a smaller scale on both axes, and this leads the increase from year 2000 to year 2005 to appear quite steep (which it is, since it represents more than a 100% increase in the number of applicants between the year 2000 and the year 2005). The right graph spreads out the scale of the *x*-axis and also truncates part of the *y*-axis, and this distorts the data shown in the graph. This example is meant to reinforce the importance of choice of scale in making graphs as well as the potential impact on interpretation when a scale is truncated.

6. a. 20
   b. 40
   c. –2; constant
   d. 14; 16
   e. *y* = 10 and *x* = 15

chapter 3

Supply and Demand

This chapter introduces the economic analysis of demand and supply. After reviewing market demand and market supply, we will be able to see how a competitive market works. The main determinants of demand are the following:

- *price of the product in question*

- *prices of related goods*

- *income of the buyers*

- *tastes of the buyers*

- *expectations*

The main determinants of supply are the following:

- *price of the product itself*

- *prices of inputs*

- *technology*

- *expectations*

After studying this chapter and working out the following problems, you will know how the equilibrium price and quantity are solved. You will also know how new equilibrium is established when either demand or supply change or both change.

How Well Do You Understand the Chapter?

Use the following list of words to complete the blanks in the review of the chapter. Words may be used more than once or not at all. If you find yourself having difficulties, please refer back to the appropriate section in the text.

along	equal	larger	positive
change	fall	left	right
complements	higher	less	smaller
constant	increase	lower	smaller
decrease	indeterminate	more	substitutes
demand	inferior	negative	supply
down	larger	normal	up

1. According to the law of demand, as price increases, the quantities demanded
_____, and as price decreases, the quantities demanded
_____. Other things being equal, a higher price for a good leads
people to demand a(n) _____ quantity of goods. When price falls,
we move _____ a given demand curve. A demand curve shows a(n)
_____ relationship between price and quantity demanded.

2. The demand curve of a given good will shift to the _____ if the
price of a complement good increases. Two goods are _____ if a fall
in the price of one good leads consumers to buy less of the other goods. Other
things being equal, as the prices of substitute goods increase, people demand a(n)
_____ quantity of the other good. Apples and oranges are
_____. Oatmeal cookies and tea are _____. If there is
an increase in the price of butter, there will be a(n) _____ in the
demand for margarine.

3. Assume that peanut butter and bread are complements. If there is an increase in
the price of peanut butter, the quantity demanded of peanut butter will
_____. As a result, the demand curve of bread will shift to the
_____.

4. Assume that the good X is normal. If the income of the consumers increases, the
demand curve of good X will shift to the _____. With economic
downturns, we observed that the demand curve of a Kraft dinner shifted to the
right; therefore, a Kraft dinner is a(n) _____ good.

5. As your student income depletes at the end of the winter term in your university,
you buy more macaroni and cheese dinners. Therefore, as far as you are concerned,
macaroni and cheese dinners are _____ goods. Inferior goods are
not bad goods. Inferior goods are those goods that show a(n) _____
relationship between income and demand.

6. There is a well-founded expectation that Ontario will raise the tax on cigarettes in
tomorrow's budget announcement. As a result, demand for cigarettes in Ontario
will _____ today.

7. Other things being equal, as price increases, suppliers are willing to supply a(n)
_____ quantity of a given good. As price decreases, sellers are willing
to supply a(n) _____ quantity of a given good.

8. With technological improvements, the supply curve of digital cameras has shifted
to the _____.

9. With increased energy prices, the production costs of goods will
_____, and as a result, the supply curve of goods in Canadian mar-
kets will shift to the _____.

10. When the equilibrium in a competitive market is established, the quantity demanded of a good is _____ to the quantity supplied. Changes in the equilibrium prices will occur if there is a change (shift) in either _____ or _____.

11. If a severe frost problem damages the production of oranges, the supply curve of oranges will shift to the _____ and the price of oranges will _____. As a result, the price of apples may increase, because of a(n) _____ in the demand for apples.

12. Consider an initial equilibrium situation. If both demand and supply double, the equilibrium price will remain _____. If the demand curve shifts to the right and the supply curve shifts to the left, the equilibrium price will _____, but the effect on equilibrium quantity will be _____.

13. Consider an initial equilibrium situation of a digital camera. Assume that supply of a digital camera doubled due to great technological improvements, while demand increased by 50%. As a result, the new equilibrium price of a digital camera should be _____ than the old equilibrium price, and the new equilibrium quantity of a digital camera should be _____ than the old equilibrium quantity.

14. If the demand curve shifts to the left while the supply curve shifts to the right, the new equilibrium quantity is _____.

Learning Tips

TIP #1: The demand curve shows the relationships between price and quantity demanded.

Other things being equal, as price increases, the quantity demanded of goods decreases. Higher price is associated with lower quantities demanded. The law of demand shows that consumers are willing to buy more at lower prices. The movement along a given demand curves shows the effects of price and price only on the quantities demanded. See Figure 3.1.

Figure 3.1

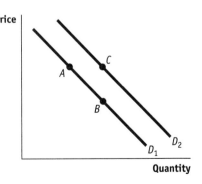

Question: Consider the movement from point A to point B (in Figure 3.1), which can be explained by

A) higher-consumer income.
B) the higher price of related goods.
C) the higher price of the good itself.
D) the lower price of the good itself.

Answer: D

TIP #2: The shift of demand curve is related to other variables, beside that of price itself. The other variables are: the price of related goods, income, tastes, and expectations.

If the price of **substitutes** increases, the demand curve for the good under consideration will shift to the right. If the price of **complements** increases, the demand curve under consideration will shift to the left. As income increases, the demand curve for **normal goods** will shift to the right.

As income increases, the demand curve for **inferior goods** will shift to the left. Normal goods are those goods that are positively related to income. Inferior goods are those goods that are negatively related to income. Any favorable effects of changes in consumers' tastes shift the demand curve to the right. Expectations regarding future shortages, future taxes, and future price hikes will shift the demand curve to the right at the present time. **Make sure that you know the distinction between moving along a curve and a shift of the curve.**

Question: See Figure 3.1. All of the following will cause a movement from A to C **except**

A) higher-consumer income.
B) higher price of substitutes.
C) expectation about future shortages.
D) lower price of the good itself.

Answer: D

TIP #3: The supply curve shows the relationships between price and quantity supplied.

The law of supply shows that sellers are willing to supply more when price increases. As price increases, the quantity supplied increases. **Make sure that you know the distinction between moving across a given supply curve and a shift of the supply curve.** The movement up along a given supply curve shows the effects of price and price alone. Across a given supply curve, we see a positive relation between price and quantity supplied. A shift of the supply curve is caused by variables, other than the price itself. Reduced input prices and technological improvements shift the supply curve to the right. See Figure 3.2.

Figure 3.2

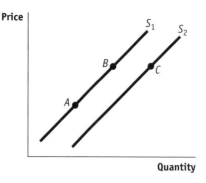

Question: Consider the movement from point A to point B (in Figure 3.2), which can be explained by

A) higher prices.
B) lower prices.
C) lower wages.
D) improved cost-saving technology.

Answer: A

Question: Movement from point A to point C (in Figure 3.2) can be explained by all of the following, **except**

A) the higher price of the good itself.
B) lower wages.
C) improved cost-saving technology.
D) entry of new firms.

Answer: A

TIP #4: A competitive equilibrium is found when quantity demanded is equal to quantity supplied.

At the market-clearing price, the price that consumers are willing to pay is equal to the price that sellers are asking for selling their goods, at the same quantity.

TIP #5: Changes in demand (shift factors), or changes in supply (shift factors), or changes in both demand and supply will bring about new equilibrium outcomes.

If both demand and supply increase, the equilibrium quantity will increase, but the effect on equilibrium price will be indeterminate. We must know the magnitudes of changes in both demand and supply to determine if price increases, decreases, or stays the same. If the increase in demand is greater than the increase in supply, price will increase. If the increase in demand is matched by the increase in supply, then price will not change. If the increase in demand is less than the increase in supply, then price will go down.

If demand increases and supply decreases, the equilibrium price will increase, but the effect on equilibrium quantity will be indeterminate, because we don't know the extent of the shifts.

Figure 3.3

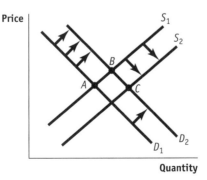

Points to remember:
A) If the demand curve shifts to the right (from D_1 to D_2) and supply curve does not change (the given supply curve is S_1), then both equilibrium price and equilibrium quantity will increase. See the movement from point A to point B in Figure 3.3.
B) If the supply curve shifts to the right (from S_1 to S_2) and demand curve shifts does not change (the given demand curve is D_2), then the equilibrium price will fall and equilibrium quantity will increase. See the movement from point B to point C in Figure 3.3.
C) The movement across a given supply curve is caused by the shift of the demand curve.
D) The movement across a given demand curve is caused by the shift of the supply curve.

TIP #6: A table may help you to identify the change to equilibrium as a result of simultaneous changes to demand and supply.

You can fill in the rows for the change in demand and the change in supply, then just add up the columns. For example, Table 3.1 shows that when there is an increase in both demand and supply in a market, equilibrium quantity definitely increases, but we cannot determine what will happen to equilibrium price.

Table 3.1

	Equilibrium price	Equilibrium quantity
Increase in demand	Increase	Increase
Increase in supply	Decrease	Increase
Net effect	???	Increase

Other possible combinations of changes in demand and supply are shown in Tables 3.2, 3.3, and 3.4.

Table 3.2

	Equilibrium price	Equilibrium quantity
Decrease in demand	Decrease	Decrease
Decrease in supply	Increase	Decrease
Net effect	???	Decrease

Table 3.3

	Equilibrium price	Equilibrium quantity
Increase in demand	Increase	Increase
Decrease in supply	Increase	Decrease
Net effect	Increase	???

Table 3.4

	Equilibrium price	Equilibrium quantity
Decrease in demand	Decrease	Decrease
Increase in supply	Decrease	Increase
Net effect	Decrease	???

Multiple-Choice Questions

The demand and supply schedules in the accompanying table reflect the weekly demand and supply of movie tickets in a small town. Answer the next four questions based on this schedule.

Price	Quantity demanded	Quantity supplied
$4.00	1,200	0
5.00	1,000	200
6.00	800	400
7.00	600	600
8.00	400	800
9.00	200	1,000

1. As the price of movie ticket falls from $8 to $7,
  a. the quantity demanded of movie tickets increases from 400 to 600.
  b. the quantity supplied of movie tickets rises from 600 to 800.
  c. the demand for movie tickets increases from 400 to 600.
  d. the supply of movie tickets decreases from 800 to 600.

2. The market for movie tickets will be in equilibrium when the
  a. equilibrium price is $6.00 and the equilibrium quantity is 400.
  b. equilibrium price is $6.00 and the equilibrium quantity is 800.
  c. equilibrium price is $7.00 and the equilibrium quantity is 600.
  d. equilibrium price is $5.00 and equilibrium quantity is 1,000.

3. If there is an increase in the demand for movie tickets, then at a price of $7
  a. quantity demanded will equal 600.
  b. quantity demanded will be less than 600.
  c. quantity demanded will be more than 600.
  d. it is impossible to tell the level of quantity demanded.

4. At a price of $9, there is a
  a. surplus of 1,000 movie tickets.
  b. shortage of 800 movie tickets.
  c. surplus of 800 movie tickets.
  d. surplus of 200 movie tickets.

5. During the fall of 2002, many vacationers on cruise liners became ill while on board their ships. Consequently, there was a
  a. decrease in the quantity demanded of cruise vacations but no change in demand for cruise vacations.
  b. decrease in the demand for cruise vacations.
  c. increase in the quantity supplied of cruise vacations but no change in supply of cruise vacations.
  d. increase in the supply of cruise vacations.

6. If the market for pencils clears, then we know
  a. that everyone who wanted to buy a pencil can.
  b. that everyone who wanted to sell a pencil can.
  c. that everyone who wanted to buy or sell a pencil at the equilibrium price can.
  d. that the market is not in equilibrium.

7. If there is an increase in the price of chocolate, we know that in response the
   a. demand for chocolate will decrease.
   b. quantity demanded for chocolate will decrease.
   c. supply of chocolate will decrease.
   d. quantity supplied of chocolate will decrease.

8. Which of the following would lower the equilibrium price of tea?
   a. a decrease in the price of coffee
   b. an increase in income and tea is a normal good
   c. an increase in the price of inputs in the production of tea
   d. an increase in a fungus that has destroyed a large proportion of the tea crop

9. As a result of the increased wage package negotiated by the hospital and the hospital workers' union,
   a. quantity supplied of hospital services will increase, with no change in supply.
   b. supply of hospital services will increase.
   c. quantity supplied of hospital services will decrease, with no change in supply.
   d. supply of hospital services will decrease.

10. The Smith family eats both meat and potatoes on a regular basis and we need to know how the family views these goods. If the price of meat rises and the family eats more potatoes, then the two goods must be
   a. substitutes.
   b. complements.
   c. inferior.
   d. normal.

11. Folklore tells us that pregnant women like to eat ice cream with pickles. If they were the only consumers of both goods, an increase in the price of pickles would
   a. decrease the demand for pickles.
   b. increase the demand for ice cream.
   c. increase the demand for pickles.
   d. decrease the demand for ice cream.

12. Toward the end of the month when money gets tight, Sara eats a lot of peanut butter sandwiches. Sara doesn't eat them because she likes them but because they're cheap. If Sara experiences an increase in income, we expect her
   a. demand for peanut butter sandwiches will increase.
   b. demand for peanut butter sandwiches will decrease.
   c. supply of peanut butter sandwiches will increase.
   d. supply of peanut butter sandwiches will decrease.

13. In the market for videotape rentals, the equilibrium price has fallen and the equilibrium output has risen. Which of the following may explain these changes?
   a. Prices of movie tickets have increased.
   b. Royalties paid to actors based on videotape rentals have fallen.
   c. DVD players have fallen in price.
   d. The government has begun to offer free concerts in parks and museums.

14. Equilibrium in the fish market is disturbed by two different events: (i) a report by the Canadian Medical Association announces that increased consumption of fish is associated with lower heart disease, and (ii) fishermen are banned from fishing in environmentally sensitive areas that previously were important sources for their catch. In the market for fish,
a. equilibrium price will increase and equilibrium output will decrease.
b. both equilibrium price and output will increase.
c. equilibrium price will increase but there will be no change in equilibrium output.
d. equilibrium price will increase but we don't have enough information to determine the change in equilibrium quantity.

15. How will the market for bicycles be affected by an increase in the price of gasoline and an increase in the desire for exercise?
a. The equilibrium price and quantity of bicycles will increase.
b. The equilibrium price of bicycles will fall and the equilibrium quantity will increase.
c. The equilibrium price of bicycles will rise but we don't have enough information to determine the change in equilibrium quantity.
d. The equilibrium output of bicycles will rise but we don't have enough information to determine the change in equilibrium price.

16. A new fertilizer doubles the grape harvest in the California wine country, while at the same time the government decreases the minimum age to purchase alcoholic beverages to 18. In the market for wine,
a. both the equilibrium price and quantity of wine will increase.
b. the equilibrium price will remain the same while the equilibrium quantity will increase.
c. the equilibrium price of wine will rise but we don't have enough information to determine the change in equilibrium quantity.
d. the equilibrium quantity will increase but we don't have enough information to determine the change in equilibrium price.

17. People become more conscious about the fat content in fast-food burgers at the same time as fast-food workers' wages decrease. In the market for fast-food burgers,
a. there is an increase in equilibrium price and a decrease in equilibrium quantity.
b. there is a decrease in equilibrium price and an increase in equilibrium quantity.
c. the equilibrium price will fall but we don't have enough information to determine the change in equilibrium quantity.
d. the equilibrium output will rise but we don't have enough information to determine the change in equilibrium price.

18. Car buyers are increasingly concerned about the low gas mileage associated with sports utility vehicles (SUVs), and the Canadian Auto Workers Union (the union that covers many of the workers producing automobiles in Canada) receives large pay increases for its members. In the market for SUVs,
a. there is an increase in equilibrium price and a decrease in equilibrium quantity.
b. there is a decrease in equilibrium price and an increase in equilibrium quantity.
c. the equilibrium price will rise but we don't have enough information to determine the change in equilibrium quantity.
d. the equilibrium output will fall but we don't have enough information to determine the change in equilibrium price.

19. If in the market for a particular type of tennis ball the equilibrium price has risen but equilibrium quantity has stayed the same, then
   a. the demand and supply of these tennis balls must have risen.
   b. the demand for these tennis balls must have risen but the supply must have fallen.
   c. the demand and supply of these tennis balls must have fallen.
   d. the supply of these tennis balls must have risen but the demand must have fallen.

20. If in the market for oranges the equilibrium quantity has risen but equilibrium price has stayed the same, then
   a. the demand and supply of oranges must have risen.
   b. the demand for oranges must have risen but the supply must have fallen.
   c. the demand and supply of oranges must have fallen.
   d. the supply of oranges must have risen but the demand must have fallen.

21. Consider the demand and supply graphs of pizza and identify one of the following statements as a "movement along a given demand curve."
   a. lower price of pizza sauce
   b. sudden increase in the number of buyers
   c. increase in consumer income
   d. increase in the prices of the substitutes of pizza

22. According to the law of demand for a given good (as reflected in a given demand curve)
   a. as income increases, consumers buy more of the normal goods.
   b. as price increases, consumers buy less of the given good.
   c. as prices of substitutes increase, consumers buy more of the given good.
   d. as tastes improve, consumers buy more of the given good.

23. An increase in the quantity supplied of pizza can be caused by
   a. a rightward shift of the supply curve.
   b. an increase in income with the assumption that pizza is a normal good.
   c. technological progress in the pizza production.
   d. lower wages of the pizza workers.

24. Which of the following statements is **false?**
   a. At the market-clearing price, the quantity demanded is equal to quantity supplied.
   b. As the price of oranges increases, the demand for oranges decreases.
   c. As income increases, the demand for normal goods increases.
   d. As the number of producers increases, the supply in the market increases.

25. Which of the following statements is true?
   a. If two goods are complements, a decrease in the price of one good will cause the demand for the other good to decrease.
   b. If two goods are substitutes, an increase in the price of one good causes the demand for the other good to increase.
   c. The movement along a demand curve is caused by income changes.
   d. The movement along a supply curve is caused by changes in wages.

26. The likely reason for the scalper's price being higher than the official ticket price for the Calgary Flames playoff game against the Tampa Bay Lightning in the Stanley Cup Final is
a. an increase in the demand for the playoff game tickets.
b. an increase in the supply of the playoff game tickets.
c. an increase in governmental subsidies to sports and entertainment.
d. an increase in the popularity of Don Cherry, an outspoken CBC commentator in the CBC *Hockey Night*.

27. You expect that you will have less income during the end of the school term (because you have over-spent your beer budget during the term). As a result, the inferior good in your consumption basket is
a. beer, because you are buying less beer now.
b. movie tickets, because you are buying less movie tickets now.
c. a Kraft dinner, because you are buying more Kraft dinners now.
d. beer, because you hate beer now.

28. During the past year, consumers' income has increased by 5%. Other things being constant, demand for lobster increased by 20%, the demand for steak increased by 18%, demand for tuna increased by 1% and demand for some other products decreased by 15%. Therefore
a. tuna is an inferior good, because it showed the least increment.
b. only lobster and steak are normal goods.
c. only lobster, steak, and tuna are the normal goods.
d. lobster, steak, tuna, and other goods are normal goods.

29. We have observed that lobster prices in the Atlantic Canada fall during the peak summer-harvest season, even though Atlantic Canada receives the highest number of tourists during the peak harvest season. We can conclude that
a. the percentage increase in supply of lobster is less than the percentage increase in demand for lobster.
b. the percentage increase in supply of lobster is greater than the percentage increase in demand for lobster.
c. the demand curve of lobster has shifted to the left.
d. the supply curve of lobster has shifted to the right, while the demand curve of lobster has shifted to the left.

30. Your professor used to recommend few textbooks for reading, but students were not required to buy any of them. But this year, your professor has made the textbook by Krugman, Wells, and Myatt the mandatory textbook and students are required to buy it. This year was also a significant year for the company that published this textbook, because the company implemented strategic cost-saving measures. Therefore
a. the price of the textbook should increase.
b. the price of the textbook should decrease.
c. the price of the textbook may increase or decrease.
d. the demand for the competing textbooks must increase.

31. Increased supply of the textbook by Krugman, Wells, and Myatt is caused by
a. an increase in the demand for the textbook.
b. an increase in the price of the textbook.
c. an increase in the popularity of the textbook.
d. a decrease in the printing costs of the textbook.

32. The price of movie rentals has gone down recently because
   a. the price of VCRs has gone down significantly.
   b. the price of a movie theatre ticket has gone up.
   c. there is an increase in the number of movie rental stores.
   d. there is an increase in the popularity of the DVDs.

Consider the following market for pita bread and answer Questions 33–34 on the basis of the accompanying table, where the demand schedules of three individuals are given. The market demand is composed of three individuals' demand functions. The market supply at respective prices is given too.

Price per pita bread	Quantity demanded by Sarah	Quantity demanded by Rinku	Quantity demanded by Sholok	Market supply
$0.30	10	15	20	12
0.40	9	13	16	16
0.50	8	11	12	20
0.60	7	9	8	24
0.70	6	7	4	28

33. At a price of $0.30 per pita bread, the market will have a _____ pita breads; as a result, the price of pita bread will go _____.
   a. surplus of 20; down
   b. surplus of 33; down
   c. shortage of 33; up
   d. shortage of 20; up

34. The market-clearing price is
   a. $0.30.
   b. $0.40.
   c. $0.50.
   d. $0.60.
   e. $0.70.

35. Many consumers use carrot muffins and coffee as _____. If the price of coffee increases, then the demand curve of carrot muffins with respect to price of carrot muffin will _____.
   a. substitutes; shift to the right
   b. complements; shift to the right
   c. complements; shift to the left
   d. substitutes; shift to the left

36. Which of the following statements is **false?**
   a. As more buyers enter the market, the market demand curve shifts to the right.
   b. As income falls, the demand for an inferior good increases.
   c. One explanation for a movement up along a given supply curve is that more producers enter the market as price increases.
   d. Higher price of gasoline may reduce the demand for automobiles.

37. Consider the market for recycled products. What will be the outcome if consumer preferences change favorably toward recycled products and if, at the same time, production technology of recycled products has improved?
a. The price of recycled products may increase or decrease.
b. The quantity of recycled products may increase or decrease.
c. The price of recycled products must increase.
d. The quantity of recycled products must increase.

38. For an inferior good, a fall in consumers' income combined with increases in production costs, will lead to a
a. higher price of the inferior good.
b. lower price of the inferior good.
c. higher quantity (bought and sold) of the inferior good.
d. lower quantity (bought and sold) of the inferior goods.

39. The other day you noticed that the price as well as the quantity bought and sold of organic vegetables in the farmers market had recently increased. One possible explanation could be
a. increased production costs of organic vegetables along with an unchanged demand schedule.
b. a shift in consumers preference toward organic vegetables.
c. a fall in income with the assumption that organic vegetables are normal goods.
d. lower production costs of organic vegetables.

40. The price of a ticket to the last hockey game played by Wayne Gretzky in Ottawa Senator's hockey arena increased because
a. scalpers kept the price too high.
b. the ticket supply was reduced drastically.
c. there was an increase in demand.
d. there was an increase in supply.

41. Students are parking in no-parking zones in the street, because of a massive shortage of parking spots on campus. One can conclude that the price for parking on campus is
a. above the equilibrium price.
b. below the equilibrium price.
c. too high.
d. at the equilibrium price.

Answer question 42–43 on the basis of the following graph.

U2 is giving a concert in the Air Canada Centre in September 2005. The seating capacity (20,000 seats) is given by the vertical supply curve. The demand function is given by D_1 line.

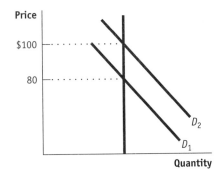

42. The equilibrium price of a ticket to the U2 concert is
   a. $80.
   b. $100.
   c. $120.
   d. $160.

43. If the concert is a sold-out event and if the market demand curve shifts to D_2 on the day of the concert, the scalper's price for a ticket will be
   a. $80.
   b. $100.
   c. $120.
   d. $160.

Optional questions: Answer questions 44–45 on the basis of the following competitive model

$$Q = 400 - 15P + 2Y \quad \text{(Demand function)}$$
$$Q = -100 + 10P \quad \text{(Supply function)}$$

Where P is price, Q is quantity, and Y is income.

*44. If $Y = 1,000$, the equilibrium P and Q are
   a. 100 and 900, respectively.
   b. 100 and 1,700, respectively.
   c. 180 and 900, respectively.
   d. 180 and 1,700, respectively.

*45. If income doubles, the new equilibrium P and Q will be
   a. 100 and 900, respectively.
   b. 100 and 1,700, respectively.
   c. 180 and 900, respectively.
   d. 180 and 1,700, respectively.

Problems and Exercises

Read each question carefully and then write your answers in the space provided or on a separate sheet of paper.

1. Answer the following questions based on the weekly market demand schedule for cups of coffee at the College Coffee Shop, as well as the demand schedules for three students, Ann, Brad, and Ceci, shown in the accompanying table.

Price	Ann's demand	Brad's demand	Ceci's demand	Everyone else's demand	Market demand
$0.25	10	5	20	—	8,000
0.50	9	4	19	—	7,000
0.75	8	3	18	—	6,000
1.00	7	2	17	—	5,000
1.25	6	1	16	—	4,000
1.50	5	0	15	—	3,000
1.75	4	0	14	—	2,000
2.00	3	0	13	—	1,000

a. In the table on the previous page, fill in Everyone else's weekly demand for coffee (i.e., the market less Ann, Brad, and Ceci).

b. Draw Ann's, Brad's, and Ceci's weekly demands for coffee. Do the individuals' demand curves and schedules show the "law of demand"?

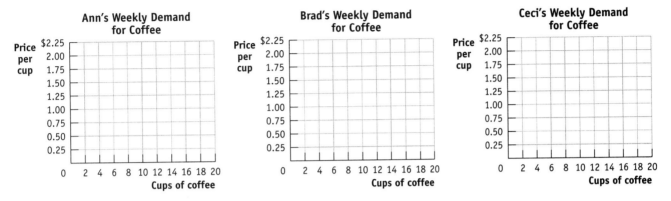

c. Draw the demand curve for the weekly market demand for coffee in the following figure. Do the preceding market demand schedule and the demand curve in the following figure show the law of demand?

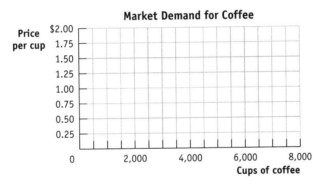

d. If the price of coffee rises from $1.00 to $1.50, will the market demand for coffee or the quantity demanded of coffee change? How will it change?

e. If there is an increase in the price of tea, will the market demand for coffee or the quantity demanded of coffee change? How will it change?

f. If there is an increase in the price of tea but Ceci's demand for coffee does not change, does Ceci see coffee and tea as substitutes?

g. If there is an increase in income and Brad reduces his consumption of coffee (perhaps in favor of espresso), is coffee a normal or inferior good for Brad? How will Brad's demand curve for coffee change?

h. What will happen to Ceci's demand for her new favorite coffee, "April Rain," which is only available during the month of April, as April comes to an end?

2. The Campus Coffee Shop's weekly supply schedule of cups of coffee is shown in the following table. Graph the market supply curve in the following figure and answer the questions below.

Price	Market supply
$0.25	3,500
0.50	4,000
0.75	4,500
1.00	5,000
1.25	5,500
1.50	6,000
1.75	6,500
2.00	7,000

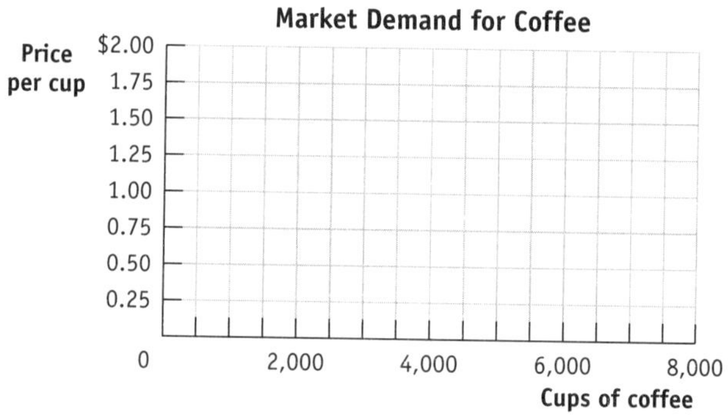

Market Demand for Coffee

a. When the price of a cup of coffee rises, does the quantity supplied of coffee increase or decrease? Describe how an increase in the price of coffee might change the supply curve in the preceding graph.

b. If there is an increase in the wages paid to students who work in the coffee shop, will the supply curve shift to the left or right?

c. If several developing countries begin exporting coffee, will the supply curve shift to the left or right?

3. The following table shows the market demand and supply schedules for cups of coffee at the Campus Coffee Shop. Graph the demand and supply curves in the following figure.

Price	Demand	Supply
$0.25	8,000	3,500
0.50	7,000	4,000
0.75	6,000	4,500
1.00	5,000	5,000
1.25	4,000	5,500
1.50	3,000	6,000
1.75	2,000	6,500
2.00	1,000	7,000

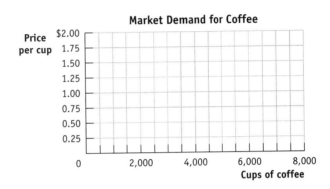

Market Demand for Coffee

a. What is the equilibrium price and equilibrium level of output?

b. What quantity is demanded and what quantity is supplied at a price of $0.75 per cup of coffee? Is there a shortage or surplus at that price? By how much do they differ? Would you expect the price of a cup of coffee to change?

c. What quantity is demanded and what quantity is supplied at a price of $1.75 per cup of coffee? Is there a shortage or surplus at that price? By how much do they differ? Would you expect the price of a cup of coffee to change?

d. If we assume coffee is a normal good, how will an increase in income affect demand? If there is an increase in income and demand increases by 1,500 cups per week at every price, what will be the new equilibrium price and output of coffee?

e. Returning to the original supply and demand curves, what will happen to demand and/or supply of coffee if there is a decrease in the price of tea? If the price of tea falls and the demand for coffee decreases by 1,500 cups per week at every price, what will be the new equilibrium price and output of coffee?

f. Returning to the original supply and demand curves, how will an increase in the price of coffee beans affect the demand and/or supply of coffee? If the increase in the price of coffee beans increases such that the supply of coffee falls by 1,500 cups per week at every price, what will be the new equilibrium price and output of coffee?

4. In each of the following markets, explain what will happen, if anything, to supply and demand, and how the new equilibrium price and quantity compare to the initial equilibrium price and output.

a. Chocolate: Compare the market for chocolate for a week during January and during the week leading up to Valentine's Day. How do the equilibrium price and equilibrium quantity of chocolate compare during the two times of year?

b. Milk: A ban on the use of certain hormones for cows radically lowers the amount of milk each cow produces.

c. Tofu: The American Medical Association releases a report extolling the virtues of tofu at the same time as a frost destroys the soybean (main ingredient in tofu) crop.

d. Economists: More colleges require students to take an economics class, while universities graduate more economists with Ph.D. degrees.

e. Film: The prices of digital cameras fall and film manufacturers develop a new technology that lowers the cost of producing film.

f. Child Car Seats: The number of babies being born falls, while at the same time additional government regulations raise the cost of producing car seats.

5. The following table pertains to hypothetical demand and supply schedules of lobster in Canada. Prices are expressed as dollars per kg of lobster. The quantities are expressed in thousand kg.

Price per kg	Quantity demanded	Quantity supplied
$ 6	140	60
8	120	80
9	110	90
10	100	100
11	90	110
12	80	120
13	70	130
14	60	140
15	50	150
16	40	160
20	0	200

a. Is $6 the market-clearing price? If so, explain why. If not, why not?

b. When price is $8, what is the magnitude of excess demand or shortage? What happens to price when there is an excess demand in the market?

c. When you plot a demand curve, what is the slope ($\Delta P/\Delta Q$) of this demand curve?

d. When price is $14, what is the amount of surplus? What happens to price when there is a surplus in the market?

e. What is the market-clearing price? What is the equilibrium quantity?

6. Consider demand and supply schedules of good X in Canada and in the Rest of the World (ROW).

Price	Demand in Canada	Supply in Canada	Demand in ROW	Supply in ROW
30	70	30	997	762
40	60	40	996	1,016
50	50	50	995	1,270
60	40	60	994	1,524

a. Fill in the columns of world demand and supply schedules.

Price	Demand in the world	Supply in the world
$30	1,067	792
40	_____	_____
50	_____	_____
60	_____	_____

b. Find the equilibrium world price. Is Canada an exporter or importer at the world price? Why?

c. If there is a total ban on foreign imports, what will be the price in Canada? Will the price in ROW be higher or lower than the price in Canada? Why?

7. In 2004, the NHL playoff between the Ottawa Senators and the Toronto Maple Leafs was dubbed as the Battle of Ontario. The 7th and deciding playoff game in Toronto was a sold-out game. Explain why the scalpers' price was significantly higher than the official price.

8. Explain with the help of a graph why the following statement is true or false.

"A recent study showed that eating spinach helps reduce heart attacks, causing an increase in the demand for spinach. This increase in demand caused a higher price for spinach in the market. This higher price will in turn reduce the demand for spinach."

*9. *Optional question:* Consider the following demand equation of spinach.

$Q = 200 - 0.5P + 0.2P^O + 0.3Y$, where Q is the quantity of spinach, P is the price of spinach, P^O is the price of substitutes, and Y is the income.

a. Re-write the above equation assuming that $P^O = 20$ and $Y = 1,000$.

b. In part a, is the equation that is described a demand equation or a supply equation? Why?

c. Is spinach a normal good or an inferior good? Why?

d. Consider the original equation and justify that the other good is not a complement.

*10. *Optional question:* Consider the following competitive model where Q is the quantity and P is the price.

$Q = 100 - P$ (Demand function in Canada)
$Q = P$ (Supply function in Canada)
$Q = 1,000 - 0.1P$ (Demand function in the ROW)
$Q = 25.4P$ (Supply function in the ROW)

a. If Canada is a closed economy (Canada does not engage in trade in the world market), then what will be the equilibrium price in Canada? What will be the equilibrium price in the ROW?

b. Derive the world demand function and the world supply function.

c. Find the equilibrium price and quantity. Is Canada an exporter or importer (circle the correct choice) at the world market price? What is the advantage to consumers in Canada if Canada participates in world trade instead of remaining in isolation?

11. Consider the following demand and supply schedules of PEI potatoes.

Price (P)	Quantity demanded (Q_D)	Quantity supplied (Q_S)
$10	0	15,000
8	2,000	12,000
6	4,000	9,000
4	6,000	6,000
2	8,000	3,000
0	10,000	0

a. What is the equilibrium price and equilibrium quantity?

b. Derive the demand equation.

c. Derive the supply equation.

d. Use the demand and supply equations that you derived and solve for P and for Q.

e. Draw graphs to show the results for all the equations you just derived.

12. Consider the market for apples (normal good) and assume an initial competitive equilibrium of apples. Trace the effects of the following in the accompanying table.

Cause	Demand curve	Demand curve	Price change	Quantity change
	Specify the shift (*leftward* or *rightward*) of the demand curve, or state that there is *no shift*.	Specify the shift (*leftward* or *rightward*) of the demand curve, or state that there is *no shift*.	Specify *zero* if price does not change, or insert *plus* sign if price increases, or insert *minus* sign if price decreases, or put a *question mark* if price remains the same, or increases or decreases.	Specify *zero* if quantity does not change, or insert *plus* sign if quantity increases, or insert *minus* sign if quantity decreases, or put a *question mark* if quantity remains the same, or increases or decreases.
Early frost damaging the crop.	No shift	Leftward	+	−
New health reports indicate that eating apples helps fight cancer.				
Increase in consumers' income and increase in wages for the workers in apple orchards.				
Increase in the demand for apple ciders and more government subsidies for the apple growers.				

13. The consumer report on the beer industry shows that, during the last year, beer consumption in Ontario has increased by 40%, while average price of beer has gone down by 10%. Explain these statistical results.

14. Explain why each of the following statements is true or false.
   a. As price of apples fall, demand for apples increases.

   b. As income falls, demand for apples may increase or decrease.

   c. (Assume that spinach is a normal good). The demand for spinach increased due to a report linking eating spinach to better health and at the same time, consumers' income falling because of a severe recession. As a result, the demand for spinach must increase.

   d. Consider a given demand curve. The reason for a down-sloping demand curve is that as price goes down, more buyers enter the market.

   e. When more sellers enter the market, the supply curve shifts to the right.

15. Draw demand-supply graphs for chicken and fish. Consider a drop in the supply of chicken and trace its effect on price and quantity in both markets.

Answers to How Well Do You Understand the Chapter

1. decrease, increase, smaller, along, negative

2. left, substitutes, larger, substitutes, complements, increase

3. fall (decrease), left

4. right, inferior

5. inferior, negative

6. increase

7. larger, smaller

8. right

9. increase, left

10. equal, demand, supply

11. left, increase, increase

12. constant, increase, indeterminate

13. lower, higher

14. indeterminate

Answers to Multiple-Choice Questions

1. As the price of movie tickets falls, only quantity demanded and quantity supplied of tickets per week changes—a change in price will not change the supply or demand of movie tickets. As the price falls from $8 to $7, from the demand schedule we see that quantity demanded rises from 400 to 600 tickets per week, while quantity supplied falls from 800 to 600 tickets per week. **Answer: A.**

2. The market is in equilibrium when quantity demanded equals quantity supplied. This happens in the market for movie tickets at a price of $7.00. At any price higher than $7, quantity supplied is greater than quantity demanded; at any price below $7, quantity demanded is greater than quantity supplied. **Answer: C.**

3. An increase in demand will shift the demand curve to the right. At every price, more will be demanded. Therefore, after an increase in demand, more than 600 tickets will be demanded at a price of $7. **Answer: C.**

4. We know that at a price higher than $7 (the equilibrium price), there will be an excess supply. At $9, quantity supplied is 1,000 tickets and quantity demanded is 200 tickets. Therefore, there is an excess supply, or surplus, of 800 movie tickets. **Answer: C.**

5. As cruise line vacationers became ill, there was a decrease in the demand for cruises (a shift to the left in the demand curve). This created an excess supply of cruises at the initial equilibrium price and the price for cruises fell. As the price fell, there was an increase in quantity demanded of cruises (a movement down the new demand curve) and a decrease in quantity supplied (a movement down the supply curve). **Answer: B.**

6. When the market for pencils clears, the market is in equilibrium. This means that at the market price the quantity demanded of pencils equals the quantity supplied of pencils. Some people may want to buy or sell a pencil but cannot or do not want to at that price. **Answer: C.**

7. If the price of chocolate rises, there will be an increase in the quantity supplied of chocolate and a decrease in the quantity demanded of chocolate. There is no change to either demand or supply of chocolate because of a change in its price. **Answer: B.**

8. The price of tea will fall if there is either a decrease in demand or an increase in supply. If there is a decrease in the price of coffee, quantity demanded of coffee will increase, and since coffee and tea are substitutes, the demand for tea will decrease. On the other hand, an increase in income will increase the demand for tea (tea is a normal good) and the price of tea would rise. Both the increase in the price of inputs and a destruction of the tea crop would decrease the supply of tea and its price would rise. **Answer: A.**

9. Increased wages for hospital workers raises the cost of providing hospital services. The supply of hospital services will decrease. **Answer: D.**

10. As the price of meat rises, the family's quantity demanded of meat will fall. If at the same time it eats more potatoes, the family must be substituting potatoes for meat. The family views the two goods as substitutes. **Answer: A.**

11. Ice cream and pickles are complements for pregnant women. As the price of pickles rises, there will be a decrease in the quantity demanded of pickles and a decrease in the demand for ice cream. **Answer: D.**

12. Since Sara eats peanut butter sandwiches because they're cheap and not because she likes them, a peanut butter sandwich is an inferior good for her. When her income rises, we expect that her demand for peanut butter sandwiches will decrease. **Answer: B.**

13. If the equilibrium price of videotape rentals has fallen and the equilibrium quantity has risen, there must have been an increase in the supply of videotape rentals. This will happen if royalties paid to actors based on videotape rentals fall (a decrease in the price of an input). If the prices of movie tickets rise, there would be an increase in demand of videotape rentals, resulting in an increase in both the equilibrium price and quantity of videotape rentals. If the price of DVD players falls, there would be an increase in quantity demanded of DVD rentals, and since DVD rentals and videotape rentals are substitutes, there would be a decrease in demand for videotape rentals. The decrease in demand would decrease both the equilibrium price and quantity of videotape rentals. There would also be a decrease in demand of videotapes if the government began to offer free concerts—concerts and video-tape rentals are substitute goods. **Answer: B.**

14. The report from the American Medical Association will increase the demand for fish because of fish's beneficial health effects, and the ban from fishing in environ-mentally sensitive areas will decrease the supply of fish. Using the following table, we see that this will definitely increase the equilibrium price of fish, but we cannot determine the effect on the equilibrium quantity. **Answer: D.**

	Equilibrium price	Equilibrium quantity
Increase in demand	Increase	Increase
Decrease in supply	Increase	Decrease
Net effect	Increase	???

15. An increase in the price of gasoline and an increase in the desire for exercise will both increase the demand for bicycles. Consequently, there will be increases in the equilibrium price and quantity of bicycles. **Answer: A.**

16. The doubling of the grape harvest in California will increase the supply of wine, while the reduction in the minimum drinking age will increase the demand for wine. Using the accompanying table, we see that these two changes will increase the equilibrium quantity of wine, but we are not certain if the equilibrium price will rise or fall. **Answer: D.**

	Equilibrium price	Equilibrium quantity
Increase in demand	Increase	Increase
Increase in supply	Decrease	Increase
Net effect	???	Increase

17. As consumers become more fat conscious, there will be a decrease in the demand for fast-food burgers. The decrease in the minimum wage earned by many fast-food workers will increase the supply of fast-food burgers. Using the accompanying table, we see that the decrease in demand and increase in supply will definitely lower the equilibrium price, but the equilibrium quantity may rise, fall, or stay the same. **Answer: C.**

	Equilibrium price	Equilibrium quantity
Decrease in demand	Decrease	Decrease
Increase in supply	Decrease	Increase
Net effect	Decrease	???

18. Concern about low gas mileage with SUVs will decrease the demand for those cars, while the increase in pay for the United Auto Workers will decrease the supply of SUVs. Using the following table, we see that the equilibrium output of SUVs will fall but we can't say what will happen to the equilibrium price. **Answer: D.**

	Equilibrium price	Equilibrium quantity
Decrease in demand	Decrease	Decrease
Decrease in supply	Increase	Decrease
Net effect	???	Decrease

19. If the equilibrium price of a particular type of tennis ball has risen, it must mean that the demand has risen (putting upward pressure on price) but the supply has decreased (also putting upward pressure on price). Since the equilibrium quantity did not change, the pressure for quantity to rise with the increase in demand is offset by the pressure for quantity to fall with the decrease in supply. **Answer: B.**

20. If the equilibrium quantity of oranges has risen, it must mean that the demand and supply have both increased—both put upward pressure on quantity. Since the equilibrium price did not change, the pressure for price to rise with the increase in demand is offset by the pressure for price to fall due to the increase in supply. **Answer: A.**

21. The production costs of pizza will go down due to the lower price of pizza sauce. As a result, the supply curve of pizza will shift to the right and price will go down across a given demand curve. **Answer: A.**

22. According to the law of demand, as price increases, quantity demanded decreases. All other choices, except choice **b**, show shifts of the demand curve. **Answer: B.**

23. This question deals with "movement across a supply curve." An increase in income shifts the demand curve to the right; price increases, and as a result, more quantity is supplied. **Answer: B.**

24. As price increases, "quantity demanded" decreases; price-fall does not lead to the change (shift) of the demand curve. **Answer: B.**

25. For substitutes, an increase in price of one good leads to a rightward shift in the demand curve of the other good. **Answer: B.**

26. An increase (rightward shift) in the demand for playoff game tickets will lead to higher scalper's price. **Answer: A.**

27. An inferior good is exemplified by the fact that a fall in income leads to more demand. A Kraft dinner is an inferior good here. **Answer: C.**

28. A normal good shows that higher income is positively related to greater demand. Lobster, steak, and tuna are normal goods, because they exhibited positive increase in demand along with positive increase in income. **Answer: C.**

29. Increase in supply is greater than the increase in demand, causing a lower price of lobster. **Answer: B.**

30. The question shows that both demand and supply increased. Since we don't know the extent of those increases, we cannot conclude whether price should increase, fall, or remain constant. **Answer: C.**

31. All factors in this question will cause shifts of the demand curve. Increase in supply of the textbooks is caused by fall in the printing costs. **Answer: D.**

32. Lower price of VCRs means more quantity of VCRs demanded, which will cause a rightward shift in the demand for movie rentals and a higher price for them. Higher price of movie theatre ticket means less demand for movie tickets and more demand for movie rentals; as a result, the price for movie rentals should increase. Similarly, increase in the popularity of DVD movies means a higher price of movie rentals. More supply of movie rentals due to more stores will cause a rightward shift of the supply curve and a lower price of movie rentals. **Answer: C.**

33. The market demand at a price of $0.30 is 45 units, while the market supply is 12. Therefore, there is a shortage of 33 and price will go up. **Answer: C.**

34. Quantity demanded is equal to quantity supplied when price is $0.60. **Answer: D.**

35. Coffee and carrot muffins are complements. Higher price of coffee means less coffee demanded, and less demand for coffee means less demand for carrot muffins. **Answer: C.**

36. Across a given supply curve, the number of producers is constant. As more producers enter the market, the supply curve shifts to the right. **Answer: C.**

37. Since both demand and supply curves have shifted to the right, more quantities will be bought and sold. But the effect on price is unknown without knowledge of the extent of the shifts. **Answer: D.**

38. For inferior goods, a fall in income will lead to an increase in demand. Higher production costs mean lower output at given prices (i.e., a leftward shift of the supply curve). Therefore, price will definitely increase, but the effect on quantity is unknown, because we don't know the extent of the shifts. **Answer: A.**

39. The first choice in this question should lead to lower quantity bought and sold with higher price. Fall in income should cause the demand curve to shift to the left and result in a lower price. The fourth choice in this question should cause a lower price. Rightward shift of the demand curve means a higher price and more quantity traded. **Answer: B.**

40. Increase in demand. **Answer: C.**

41. Shortages occur when the price is below the equilibrium price. **Answer: B.**

42. See where the demand curve D_1 intersects the vertical supply curve. **Answer: A.**

43. New equilibrium price is $100. **Answer: B.**

44. When $Y = 1,000$, the demand function is $Q = 2,400 - 15P$

$$-100 + 10P = 2,400 - 15P$$
$$25P = 2,500$$
$$P = 100 \text{ and } Q = 900$$

Answer: A.

45. $-100 + 10P = 4,400 - 15P$

$$25P = 500$$
$$P = 180 \text{ and } Q = 1,700$$

Answer: D.

Answers to Problems and Exercises

1. a. To find Everyone Else's demand, take the total market demand and subtract the demands of Ann, Brad, and Ceci.

Price	Ann's demand	Brad's demand	Ceci's demand	Everyone else's demand	Market demand
$0.25	10	5	20	7,965	8,000
0.50	9	4	19	6,968	7,000
0.75	8	3	18	5,971	6,000
1.00	7	2	17	4,974	5,000
1.25	6	1	16	3,977	4,000
1.50	5	0	15	2,980	3,000
1.75	4	0	14	1,982	2,000
2.00	3	0	13	984	1,000

b. The preceding demand schedules and the demand curves in the following figures show the "law of demand." As the price of the good increases, quantity demanded decreases.

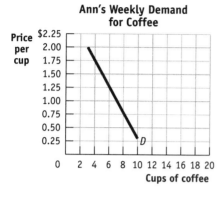

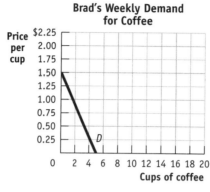

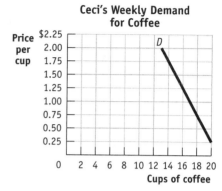

c. The weekly market demand curve for coffee in the following figure shows the law of demand: when price falls, quantity demanded rises.

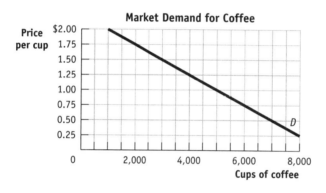

d. As the price of coffee rises from $1.00 to $1.50, there is only a change in quantity demanded. It will fall from 5,000 cups to 3,000 cups.

e. Coffee and tea are substitutes. As the price of tea increases, there will be an increase in the demand for coffee. At all prices, consumers will want to purchase more coffee.

f. If the price of tea does not affect Ceci's demand for coffee, she does not see tea as a substitute for coffee.

g. If Brad reduces his consumption of coffee when there is an increase in income, coffee is an inferior good for Brad. His demand curve for coffee will shift to the left.

h. As the month comes to an end, Ceci's demand for coffee will rise since she expects not to be able to have any more "April Rain" once May arrives.

2. The market supply curve for coffee is shown in the following figure.

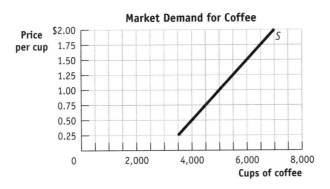

Market Demand for Coffee

a. There is a positive relationship between the price of a cup of coffee and quantity supplied. An increase in the price of coffee will result in a movement up the supply curve but not a shift in the supply curve.

b. An increase in the wages paid to students who work in the coffee shop will decrease supply (less will be supplied at every price) and shift the supply curve to the left.

c. An increase in the number of developing countries exporting coffee will increase supply (more will be supplied at every price), shifting the supply curve to the right.

3. The market supply and demand curves for coffee are shown in the following figure.

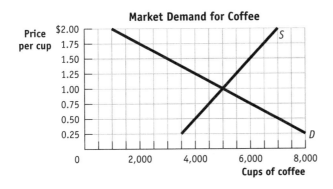

Market Demand for Coffee

a. In equilibrium, the market clears—the amount consumers wish to buy is equal to the amount firms wish to sell. In this case, the equilibrium price is $1.00 per cup and the equilibrium level of output is 5,000 cups of coffee.

b. At a price of $0.75, quantity demanded is 6,000 cups of coffee per week and quantity supplied is 4,500 cups of coffee per week. There is an excess demand of coffee (a shortage) equal to 1,500 cups per week. As a result, the price of a cup of coffee will increase.

c. At a price of $1.75, quantity demanded is 2,000 cups of coffee per week and quantity supplied is 6,500 cups of coffee per week. There is an excess supply of coffee (a surplus) equal to 4,500 cups per week. As a result, the price of a cup of coffee will decrease.

d. If coffee is a normal good, an increase in income will increase the demand for coffee. If the demand for coffee increases by 1,500 cups per week at every price, the new equilibrium price will be $1.25 per cup and the new equilibrium quantity will be 5,500 cups, as shown in the following figure.

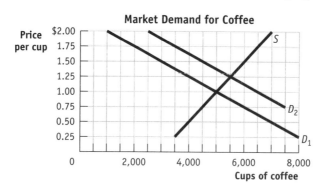

e. Assuming coffee and tea are substitutes, a decrease in the price of tea will lower the demand for coffee but will not affect the supply of coffee. If the demand for coffee falls by 1,500 cups per week at every price, the new equilibrium price will be $0.75 per cup and the new equilibrium quantity will be 4,500 cups, as shown in the following figure.

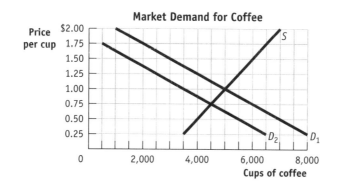

f. Since coffee beans are an input in the production of coffee, an increase in their price will reduce the supply of coffee. If the supply of coffee falls by 1,500 cups per week at every price, the new equilibrium price will be $1.25 per cup and the new equilibrium quantity will be 4,000 cups, as shown in the following figure.

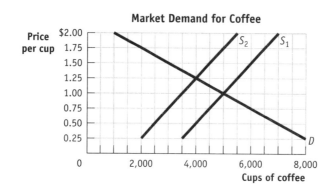

4. a. Chocolate: During the week leading up to Valentine's Day the demand for chocolate increases, and there are increases in the equilibrium price and the equilibrium quantity of chocolate.

b. Milk: If a ban on the use of certain hormones lowers the amount of milk each cow produces, there will be a decrease in the supply of milk. As a result, the equilibrium price of milk will increase and equilibrium quantity will decrease.

c. Tofu: The report extolling the virtues of tofu will increase demand, while the frost that destroys the soybean crop will decrease supply. To see how these two factors affect equilibrium price and equilibrium output, we can look at each effect individually and then find the net effect.

	Equilibrium price	Equilibrium quantity
Increase in demand	Increase	Increase
Decrease in supply	Increase	Decrease
Net effect	Increase	???

Equilibrium price will definitely rise, but we cannot determine what will happen to the equilibrium quantity.

d. Economists: When more colleges require students to take an economics course, the demand for economists to teach those courses will increase. The bumper crop of new economics Ph.D.'s will increase the supply of economists. Again, we need to look at how these two factors affect equilibrium price and equilibrium output. We can look at each effect individually and then find the net effect.

	Equilibrium price	Equilibrium quantity
Increase in demand	Increase	Increase
Increase in supply	Decrease	Increase
Net effect	???	Increase

The equilibrium quantity will definitely increase, but we cannot determine how the equilibrium price will change.

e. Film: Since digital cameras are a substitute for film cameras, as the price of digital cameras fall there will be a decrease in the demand for film. Supply will increase as film manufacturers develop a new technology that lowers the cost of producing film. Here is how each factor affects equilibrium price and equilibrium output:

	Equilibrium price	Equilibrium quantity
Decrease in demand	Decrease	Decrease
Increase in supply	Decrease	Increase
Net effect	Decrease	???

These changes to the film market will definitely decrease equilibrium price, but we cannot determine what will happen to equilibrium quantity.

f. Child car seats: Demand will fall due to the lower birth rate, and supply will decrease as the government regulations increase the cost of producing car seats. Here is how each factor affects equilibrium price and equilibrium output:

	Equilibrium price	Equilibrium quantity
Decrease in demand	Decrease	Decrease
Decrease in supply	Increase	Decrease
Net effect	???	Decrease

These changes to the child car seat market will definitely decrease equilibrium quantity, but we cannot determine what will happen to equilibrium price.

5. a. $6 is not a market-clearing price, because quantity demanded exceeds quantity supplied.
   b. Excess demand is 40 kg. Price will increase.
   c. –1/10.
   d. Surplus is 80 kg. Price will decrease.
   e. $P = 10 and $Q - 100$ kg.

6. a. Demand: 1,056, 1,045, and 1,034; Supply: 1,056, 1,320, and 1,584.
   b. Price is $40. Canada imports 20, because the Canadian demand exceeds the Canadian supply.
   c. Price in Canada is $50. The price in ROW should be lower, because the ROW has a larger supply available for the ROW markets (due to zero import by Canada).

7. The 7th playoff game was a sell-out game. There was a huge increase in demand for this deciding game in Toronto. Because of manifold increases in demand, the scalpers had a bonanza; they sold the tickets at about four times higher than the official ticket price.

8. The statement is false. Increase in demand shifts the demand curve to the right. As a result, price increases. Increase in price causes an increase in quantity supplied. See the accompanying graph, where the initial equilibrium point is point A and the new equilibrium point is B.

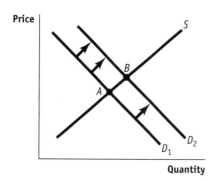

9. a. $Q = 502 - 0.5P$
   b. It is a demand equation, because quantity (Q) is negatively related to price (P) when we consider a demand function.
   c. It is a normal good, because quantity (Q) is positively related to income (Y).
   d. For complements, quantity (Q) is negatively related to price of other goods. In this question, P_O is positively related to Q; that means, we are dealing with substitutes.

10. a. Set Q demanded equal to Q supplied and solve price (P).
   $100 - P = P$. Therefore, in Canada, $P = 50$ and $Q = 50$.
   Use the condition that
   $1000 - 0.1P = 25.4P$
   In ROW, $P = 39.22$ and $Q = 996.19$
   b. $Q = 1100 - 1.1P$ (world demand function)
   $Q = 26.4P$ (world supply function)
   c. World price = 40 and equilibrium $Q = 1,056$.
   Canada imports 20 units.
   Consumers benefit due to lower price.

11. a. $P = \$4$ and $Q = 6,000$.
   b. $Q_D = 10,000 - 1000P$.
   c. $Q_s = 1,500P$.
   d. From $1,500P = 10,000 - 1,000P$, we solve P as $\$4$ and Q as $6,000$.

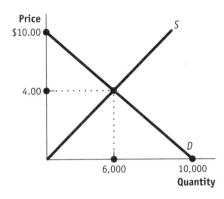

12.

Demand curve	Supply curve	Price change	Quantity change
Rightward	No shift	+	+
Rightward	Leftward	+	?
Rightward	Rightward	?	+

13. The beer industry witnessed an increase in demand. At the same time, supply curve of beer shifted to the right. The increase in supply was greater than the increase in demand and as a result, the price of beer has gone down.

14. a. False. As price of apples fall, the *quantity demanded* for apples increases. This is a movement on a given demand curve. When we say "demand for apples increases," we mean a rightward shift of the demand curve, caused by anything but the price of apples.
   b. True. If apples are considered as normal goods, then demand will fall; but if apples are considered as inferior goods, then demand will increase.
   c. False. The favorable health report will shift the demand curve to the right, but the income effect will shift the demand curve to the left. Since we don't know the extent of these shifts, we cannot conclude that the demand for spinach will increase.
   d. False. On a given demand curve, the number of buyers is fixed.
   e. True.

15.

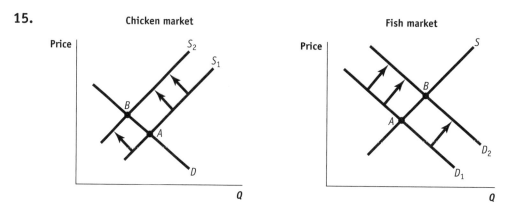

The supply curve in the chicken market will shift to the left, causing a higher price of chicken.

If chicken and fish are substitutes, then an increase in chicken price will cause a rightward shift of the demand curve of fish. As a result, the price of fish will increase.

chapter 4

The Market Strikes Back

Apply the demand-supply framework that you learned in the last chapter and see how price controls, quotas, and taxes work in our economy in Canada. Generally, the government imposes price controls, quotas, and taxes to protect consumers, to protect producers, or to raise tax-revenues; these measures lead to debates and criticisms. You will see that whenever government does intervene in markets, it causes some inefficiencies, which will be explained in this chapter.

How Well Do You Understand the Chapter?

Fill in the blanks using the following terms, or circle the correct answer to complete the following statements. Terms may be used more than once. If you find yourself having difficulties, please refer back to the appropriate section in the text.

black	greater	license	rent
both	high	less	rise
burden	ignore	minimum	resources
consumers	increase(s)	price ceiling	sales
decrease(s)	illegal	price control(s)	shortage
down	inefficiencies	price floor	surplus
excise	low	producers	up
fall	lower	quota	wedge

1. The government may try to affect markets by imposing _____ that specify either a minimum or maximum price in a market. A(n) _____ is the maximum price that can be charged in a market; price floor is a(n) _____ price. Whenever the government intervenes in markets, inefficiencies such as _____, or black market, prices may develop.

2. The government would impose a ceiling if it believed that the equilibrium price of a(n) good in an uncontrolled (free) market is too _____ for consumers to pay. When the government imposes a ceiling that is lower than the market equilibrium price, quantity demanded will be quantity supplied, resulting in a _____ of the good. Rent control is an example of a(n) _____.

3. The government would impose a(n) _____ if it believed the equilibrium price of a good in an uncontrolled (free) market is too low for producers to earn respectable incomes. This is a way to protect the _____ of a good. When the government imposes a price floor that is higher than the market equilibrium price, quantity demanded will be _____ than quantity supplied, resulting in a(n) _____ of the good. Minimum wage is an example of a(n) _____.

4. In creating either a surplus or shortage of the good, the government creates _____ in the market. With a price ceiling and the resulting _____, consumers waste _____ searching for the good, while producers offer goods of inefficiently _____ quality. With a(n) _____ and the resulting surplus, there will be an inefficient allocation of _____ among sellers, with producers offering goods of inefficiently _____ quality.

5. With price controls, a(n) _____ market, or illegal market, may develop. When either demanders or suppliers are not able to purchase or sell what they wish to at the government-imposed price-ceiling, the illegal price will be _____ than the mandated (official or legal) ceiling price.

6. The government may also affect the market equilibrium price and output by imposing a quantity control. Whenever the government imposes a(n) _____, a limit to the amount that can be sold, or requires a(n) _____, which limits the number of suppliers in a market, it will not only affect the amount of the good that is exchanged but also the price at which it is exchanged.

7. When the government imposes a quantity control it drives a(n) _____ between the demand price, the price that consumers are willing to pay for the amount available under the quantity control, and the supply price, the price at which producers are willing to offer the amount available under the quantity control. The demand price is _____ than the supply price, and this difference is known as the price _____ or quota _____.

8. Quantity controls also may have some _____ associated with them. As long as the demand price of a given quantity is _____ than the supply price, there is a missed opportunity.

9. When government assesses a(n) _____ tax, a per-unit tax on a particular good, it also affects the market equilibrium price, output, and results in _____.

10. If the per-unit tax is collected from the producers, the supply curve will shift _____ by the amount of the tax. Consequently, the price that consumers will pay will _____; but after producers remit the tax revenue to the government, producers will receive a(n) _____ price than before the tax. The _____, or cost, of the tax is borne by _____ the producers, and the consumers when we have normal-looking demand supply graphs.

11. If the tax is collected from the _____, the demand curve will shift _____ by the amount of the tax. Consequently, the price that consumers will pay to the producers will be _____ but they will also have to pay the tax, leading to a total price, the price to producers plus tax, that is _____ than the price before the tax. Again, _____ producers and consumers share the burden of the tax.

12. Since the imposition of the tax _____ the amount of the good exchanged, there is an opportunity cost. Since the tax has discouraged some mutually beneficial transactions, we say that there is an excess _____, or deadweight loss, from a tax.

Learning Tips

TIP #1: When the government imposes a price ceiling, be sure the price ceiling is below the equilibrium price; if it isn't, the price ceiling won't affect the market. Similarly, when the government imposes a price floor, be sure the price floor is above the equilibrium price to affect the market.

If the government sets a price ceiling above the equilibrium price, the price control will not affect the market equilibrium price. See Figure 4.1. At the price ceiling, quantity supplied will be greater than quantity demanded and the price in the market will fall until it returns to its original equilibrium price. The price ceiling only restricts the price from rising.

Figure 4.1

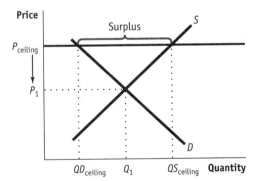

If the government sets a price floor below the equilibrium price, the price control will not affect the market equilibrium price. At the price floor, quantity demanded will be greater than quantity supplied and the price in the market will rise until it returns to its original equilibrium price. The price floor only restricts the price from falling. See Figure 4.2.

Figure 4.2

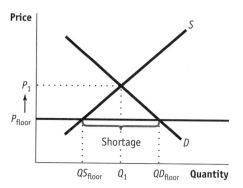

Question: Consider Figure 4.2. Which of the following statements is **incorrect?**

A) Effective ceiling price is set a point below the uncontrolled (free) market equilibrium price.
B) There will a shortage with a ceiling price.
C) Effective floor price is set a point above the uncontrolled (free) market equilibrium price.
D) When the ceiling price is imposed, the black market price is always lower than the uncontrolled (free) market price.

Answer: D

TIP #2: Remember that the government can use either an excise tax or license sales to change the equilibrium price and output in a market. Either way, the government can raise the same amount of revenue.

By imposing an excise tax or a quantity control, the government drives a wedge between the demand price and the supply price. When the government imposes a tax, the price wedge is equal to the amount of the tax. See Figure 4.3a. When the government grants licenses as a means of quantity control, the price wedge is the quota rent. See Figure 4.3b. If the government sells licenses to produce output and sets the price of each license equal to the price wedge, it can generate the same revenue as the excise tax; you can see this by comparing Figure 4.3a with Figure 4.3b.

Figure 4.3a   **Figure 4.3b**

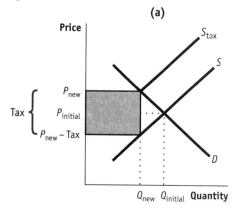   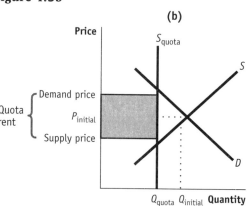

Question: Consider Figure 4.3a. Which of the following statements is **incorrect?**

A) With the per-unit tax, after-tax price exceeds the initial no-tax equilibrium price by the amount of the per-unit tax.

B) Tax reduces the quantity sold.
C) Tax reduces the sellers' income.
D) There is a deadweight loss with tax.

Answer: A

TIP #3: The question of "who pays the tax?" is more than just a question of who remits the tax money to the government. It doesn't matter whether the buyers or the sellers are required to send the tax to the government because the tax burden is usually shared by the buyers and the sellers.

Figure 4.4a illustrates an example of the government imposing a per-unit tax to be paid by the consumers, while Figure 4.4b shows an example of a per-unit tax to be paid by the producers.

Figure 4.4a   **Figure 4.4b**

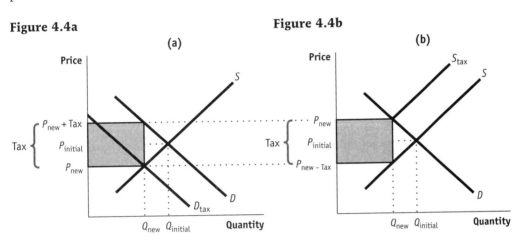

Question: Consider Figure 4.4a. Which of the following statements is **incorrect?**

A) After the per-unit tax is imposed, the seller's price net of tax is higher than the initial no-tax equilibrium price.
B) After the per-unit tax is imposed, the buyer's final price (which includes per-unit tax) is higher than the initial no-tax equilibrium price.
C) Both consumers and producers are worse off as a result of the per-unit tax.
D) Tax reduces quantity sold.

Answer: A

Although the new price falls to P_{new} in Figure 4.4a, where the consumer is required to "pay the tax," that price represents the price that producers receive after the imposition of the tax. Since the consumer must pay that price plus the tax, the cost to the consumer of the good is P_{new} + Tax after the imposition of the tax. The portion of the tax paid by the consumer and the portion paid by the producer does not depend upon who is nominally required to pay the tax. While the producer is nominally responsible for the tax in Figure 4.4b, the market price rises to P_{new} and the consumer pays that price; the producer only receives P_{new} − Tax after the tax is paid to the government. Figure 4.4b shows that the price the consumer pays and the price the producer receives are identical to the prices shown in Figure 4.4a, even though in that figure we assumed that the consumer was nominally responsible for the tax. The price the consumer pays and the price the producer receives is the same whether the consumer or the producer is required to "pay the tax."

TIP #4: You can determine how much of the tax is paid by the consumer and by the producer by comparing the old equilibrium price with the new equilibrium price and the tax.

Since it does not matter who actually "pays the tax," we can look at the burden of the tax assuming the producer pays the tax. Figure 4.5 shows the government's revenue from the tax and the consumer's and producer's share of the tax.

Figure 4.5

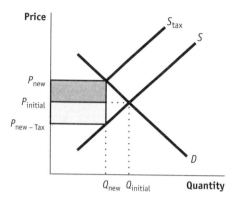

The government's revenue is the amount of the tax (the difference between the supply curves, or $P_{new} - [P_{new} - Tax]$) times the quantity exchanged after the imposition of the tax (Q_{new}). It is the sum of the shaded rectangles. The consumer pays a higher price with the tax (P_{new} versus $P_{initial}$) on the quantity exchanged after the imposition of the tax (Q_{new}), so the consumer's burden is ($P_{new} - P_{initial}$) times Q_{new}. The producer receives a lower price ($P_{new} - Tax$ versus $P_{initial}$) with the tax on the quantity exchanged after the imposition of the tax (Q_{new}), so the producer's burden is ($P_{initial} - [P_{new} - Tax]$) times Q_{new}.

Multiple-Choice Questions

1. The government might impose a price ceiling in a market for a good if it believed that the price in the market was
   a. too high for the consumers of the good.
   b. too low for the consumers of the good.
   c. too high for the producers of the good.
   d. too low for the producers of the good.

2. When the government imposes a price floor in a market, which of the following inefficiencies may occur?
   a. The good may be offered for sale with inefficiently low quality.
   b. The good may be offered for sale with inefficiently high quality.
   c. A shortage of the good may occur.
   d. A black market may develop, where the good or service is exchanged at a price higher than the price floor.

3. Rent controls are inefficient because they result in
   a. cheaper housing for some renters than in the absence of the controls.
   b. lower-quality housing for some renters than in the absence of controls.
   c. shorter waits for rent-controlled housing.
   d. a surplus of rent-controlled apartments.

The following five questions are based on the demand and supply schedules in the accompanying table reflecting the weekly demand and supply of movie tickets in a small town.

Price	Quantity demanded	Quantity supplied
$4.00	1,200	0
5.00	1,000	200
6.00	800	400
7.00	600	600
8.00	400	800
9.00	200	1,000

4. To provide affordable entertainment for teens—and get them off the streets at night—the local government imposes a price ceiling of $5.00 on movie tickets. Consequently,
   a. there are 1,000 happy patrons who are now able to see movies for only $5.00 per ticket.
   b. there are 800 frustrated patrons who would like to buy a ticket at $5.00 but cannot get one.
   c. there are 200 frustrated moviegoers who would like to buy a ticket at $5.00 but cannot get one.
   d. nothing happens to the equilibrium price or quantity of movie tickets; the price ceiling is ineffective.

5. To provide affordable entertainment for teens—and get them off the streets at night—the local government imposes a price ceiling of $8.00. Consequently,
   a. there are 800 happy patrons who are now able to see movies for only $8.00 per ticket.
   b. there are 400 frustrated patrons who would like to buy a ticket at $8.00 but cannot get one.
   c. there are 200 frustrated moviegoers who would like to buy a ticket at $8.00 but cannot get one.
   d. nothing happens to the equilibrium price or quantity of movie tickets; the price ceiling is ineffective.

6. If the government limits the number of movie tickets sold to 400 tickets each week by requiring a license to sell tickets, the quota rent for the holders of the licenses would be
   a. $7 per ticket.
   b. $6 per ticket.
   c. $4 per ticket.
   d. $2 per ticket.

7. To raise revenue to improve the parks in the town, the government imposes a tax of $2 on movie tickets, collected from the theater owners. As a result, the price of movie tickets rises to
   a. $9 and the equilibrium level of tickets bought and sold is 200 each week.
   b. $9 and the equilibrium level of tickets bought and sold is 1,000 each week.
   c. $8 and the equilibrium level of tickets bought and sold is 400 each week.
   d. $7 and the equilibrium level of tickets bought and sold is 600 each week.

8. If the government imposed a tax of $2 on movie tickets, it would raise revenue equal to
   a. $400.
   b. $800.
   c. $1,200.
   d. $2,000.

The accompanying figure describes the market for unskilled labor in a particular town. Use this graph to answer the next two questions.

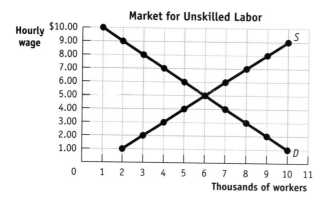

Market for Unskilled Labor

9. If the government imposes a minimum wage of $6.00, then
   a. employment will fall to 5,000 workers and unemployment will be equal to 1,000 workers.
   b. employment will fall to 6,000 workers and unemployment will be equal to 2,000 workers.
   c. employment will fall to 5,000 workers and unemployment will be equal to 2,000 workers.
   d. employment will fall to 6,000 workers and unemployment will be equal to 1,000 workers.

10. At a minimum wage of $6.00, unemployment will result because
    a. 1,000 workers will lose jobs, and 1,000 workers will enter the labor force but not find jobs as the wage rises from $5.00 to $6.00.
    b. 2,000 workers will lose jobs as the wage rate rises from $5.00 to $6.00.
    c. 2,000 workers will enter the labor force but not find jobs as the wage rate rises from $5.00 to $6.00.
    d. 5,000 workers will lose jobs as the wage rate rises from $5.00 to $6.00.

11. Many economists believe that the minimum wage in Canada does not create unemployment (or a surplus of workers) because
    a. the minimum wage is below the equilibrium wage and therefore is ineffective.
    b. the minimum wage is above the equilibrium wage and therefore is ineffective.
    c. most minimum wage workers are teenagers.
    d. the minimum wage is a voluntary program.

12. As long as the demand price of a given quantity exceeds the supply price,
    a. there is a missed opportunity.
    b. there is a shortage of the good.
    c. producers have no incentive to sell the product.
    d. consumers have no incentive to buy the product.

13. When the government imposes a tax in a market and collects the tax from the producers,
    a. the price of the good rises by the full amount of the tax.
    b. the supply curve shifts down by the full amount of the tax.
    c. the supply curve shifts up by the full amount of the tax.
    d. both the demand and supply curves shift up by the full amount of the tax.

14. When the government imposes a tax in a market and collects the tax from the consumers,
   a. the price of the good rises by the full amount of the tax.
   b. the demand curve shifts down by the full amount of the tax.
   c. the supply curve shifts up by the full amount of the tax.
   d. both the demand and supply curves shift up by the full amount of the tax.

15. The excess burden, or deadweight loss, of a tax comes about because
   a. the consumers pay a higher price than they would without the tax.
   b. both producers and consumers are hurt by the tax.
   c. the tax lowers the quantity exchanged and some mutually beneficial transactions do not take place.
   d. of all of the above.

16. The following figure shows a simplified market for taxi rides during the average evening rush hour in Montreal. Given the number of taxi medallions, the maximum number of rides available during an average rush hour is 20,000. The evening rush-hour quota rent is

   a. $4.
   b. $6.
   c. $8.
   d. $12.

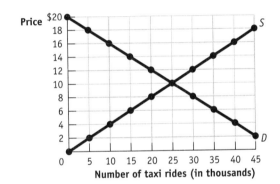

17. The following figure shows a market in which the government has imposed a quota of 1,000 units. The government could also reduce the amount exchanged in the market to 1,000 by imposing a tax equal to

   a. $1.
   b. $2.
   c. $3.
   d. $4.

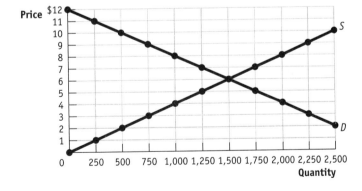

18. The minimum wage has
   a. some positive employment effects.
   b. some negative employment effects.
   c. made all unskilled workers worse off.
   d. made all unskilled workers better off.

19. Which of the following statements is true?
    a. Minimum wages in Canada are, on an average, higher (in terms of purchasing power) than at any time in the last 30 years.
    b. Job-training programs can simultaneously increase the equilibrium wage and employment in Canada.
    c. Job-training programs can increase the equilibrium wage but will not affect employment situation in Canada.
    d. Job-training programs cannot increase the equilibrium wage of unskilled workers.

20. The following figure shows a market in which the government has imposed a tax. Which of the following statements about the graph is correct?

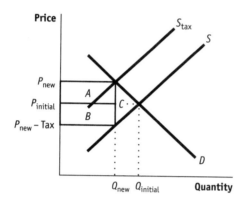

    a. Rectangle A represents the portion of the tax paid by the producers.
    b. Rectangle B represents the portion of the tax paid by the consumers.
    c. The sum of rectangles A and B represents the government's revenue from the tax.
    d. Triangle C represents the government's tax revenue from the tax.

21. Consider the labour market for unskilled workers. With more job-training schemes in Canada, the demand for labour will shift to the _____ and the wage rate as well as employment will _____.
    a. right; increase
    b. left; decrease
    c. right, decrease
    d. left, increase

Answer questions 22–25 on the basis of the following demand and supply schedules of blueberries. Quantities are expressed in thousand kg.

Price per kg	Quantity demanded	Quantity supplied
$1.00	100	20
1.50	90	30
2.00	80	40
2.50	70	50
3.00	60	60
3.50	50	70
4.00	40	80
4.50	30	90
5.00	20	100

22. With a price ceiling of $1.50 per kg, the shortages will be
   a. 30 thousand kg.
   b. 40 thousand kg.
   c. 50 thousand kg.
   d. 60 thousand kg.

23. With a price ceiling of $1.50 per kg, the black market price can be as high as
   a. $5.
   b. $6.
   c. $3.
   d. none of the above.

24. Instead of a ceiling price, the Nova Scotia government imposes a per-unit tax of $1.00 per kg. As a result, the post-tax market price will be
   a. $4.00.
   b. $3.50.
   c. $3.00.
   d. none of the above.

25. As a result of a per-unit tax of $1.00 per kg, total tax revenues will be
   a. $50 thousand.
   b. $60 thousand.
   c. $70 thousand.
   d. none of the above.

Problems and Exercises

Read each question carefully and then write your answers in the space provided or on a separate sheet of paper.

1. The following table shows the market demand and supply curves for 18-hole golf games per week at the golf courses in Midvale City. (For simplicity we're assuming that all golf courses and tee times are equally desirable.) Graph the demand and supply curves in the following figure.

Price per 18-hole golf game	Demand for 18-hole golf games (in thousands)	Supply for 18-hole golf games (in thousands)
$10	10	0
20	9	1
30	8	2
40	7	3
50	6	4
60	5	5
70	4	6
80	3	7
90	2	8
100	1	9
110	0	10

Market for Golf Games

Price of golf game, $110 to 10; Quantity of golf games (in thousands) 0 to 10.

a. The market-clearing price is _____ and the market-clearing level of output is _____ games.

b. One of the candidates for mayor of Midvale City is running on a platform that proposes to keep the price of an 18-hole golf game affordable to everyone by imposing a price ceiling of $20 for an 18-hole game. If he is elected, what will happen to the price and the number of golf games played? What types of inefficiencies might result?

c. Another candidate for mayor of Midvale City proposes to reward some of her biggest contributors, the owners of the golf courses, by imposing a price floor of $80 per game of golf. If she is elected, what will happen to the price and number of golf games played? What types of inefficiencies might result?

d. A third candidate for mayor is running on a "Family First" platform and is concerned about how golf separates families. He is proposing to limit the number of golf games to 3,000 per week. If he is elected, what will happen to the price and number of golf games played? What types of inefficiencies might result?

2. Canada has a long history of Marketing Boards to protect farm income and farm price.

The province of Prince Edward Island is famous for island spuds. The following table shows the hypothetical demand and supply schedules of PEI potatoes.

Price per kg	Demand (in thousand kg)	Supply (in thousand kg)
$1.00	100	20
1.10	90	30
1.20	80	40
1.30	70	50
1.40	60	60
1.50	50	70
1.60	40	80
1.70	30	90

a. If the Potato Marketing Board in PEI did not intervene, what will be the equilibrium unregulated free market price and quantity?

b. If the Marketing Board imposes a price floor of $1.60 per kg, what will be the surplus in the market? If the government buys this surplus, what will be the cost of buying? What will be the total farm income?

c. Suppose instead of buying surplus potatoes, the government decides to provide farmers with subsidy of $0.40 per kg, what will be the total subsidy payments to the farmers?

3. The Pelmar County supervisor has proposed a tax on beer as a way to both curb excessive drinking and to raise the needed revenue to cover its budget deficit. The monthly supply and demand curves for beer (we're assuming all beer is the same) are shown in the accompanying figure. Answer the following questions assuming the government imposes a tax of $1 per six-pack and collects the tax from the producers.

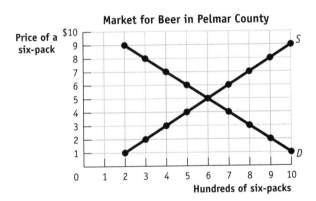

Market for Beer in Pelmar County

a. After the imposition of a tax of $1 per six-pack, what is the new equilibrium price and output of beer?

b. What is the government's revenue from the tax?

c. How much of the $1 tax is paid by the consumers and how much by the producers?

4. Suppose the Canadian government is considering some price support policies to provide income assistance to Canadian wheat farmers in the prairies. The quantities of demand and supply in bushels are shown in the following table.

Price per bushel	Quantity demanded	Quantity supplied
$10	800	1,200
8	900	1,100
6	1,000	1,000
4	1,100	900
2	1,200	800

a. If the government sets a price-floor of $10.00, how many bushels will be produced? What will be the surplus? If the government buys surplus wheat (to be donated to the Third World countries), how much will it cost the government?

b. Suppose the government sets a target price of $10.00 and output quota at 1,200 bushels. Find the market price at which 1,200 bushels of wheat will be purchased by consumers. If the government gives (as subsidy) to farmers an amount equal to the difference between market price and target price for each bushel of wheat, how much will it cost the government?

c. Which option is cheaper to the government? Which option will be chosen by the farmers?

5. Explain why the following statement is true or false: If the demand curve is vertical, the burden of excise tax is shared by both consumers and producers.

6. The hypothetical demand and supply functions of Atlantic lobsters are the following:

$$Q^D = 220 - 10P$$
$$Q^S = -80 + 20P$$

In the above equations, Q^D is the quantity of lobsters demanded, Q^S is the quantity of lobster supplied, and P is the price of lobsters per kg.
a. Find the equilibrium price and quantity.

b. If output is restricted to 80 kg, what will be the price at which consumers are willing to buy 80 kg, and what will be the price at which lobster fisherman are willing to sell 80 kg?

c. Given your answer in **b,** what will be the quota rent?

d. Instead of using a quota system, find the appropriate per-unit excise tax to ensure that lobster fisheries are limited to 80 kg. What will be the tax revenues? What will be the deadweight loss?

7. Explain with a diagram why the following statement is true or false: "Other things remaining constant, the steeper the demand curve of labour, the less the negative employment effects due to the minimum wage regulations."

Answers to How Well Do You Understand the Chapter

1. price controls, price ceiling, minimum, illegal

2. high, shortage, price ceiling

3. price floor, producers, less, surplus, price floor

4. inefficiencies, shortage, resources, low, price floor, sales, high

5. black, greater

6. quota, license

7. wedge, greater, wedge, rent

8. inefficiencies, greater

9. excise, inefficiencies

10. up, increase, lower, burden, both

11. consumers, down, less, greater, both

12. decreases, burden

Answers to Multiple-Choice Questions

1. When the government imposes a price ceiling (a maximum price), it does so because it believes that the equilibrium price is too high. The producers want a high price but consumers want a low price. By setting a maximum price below the equilibrium price, the government is trying to help the consumers. **Answer: A.**

2. When the government imposes a price floor (a minimum price) in a market, a surplus results. Since producers will be competing with one another for customers but not on the basis of price, they may offer some perks with the good. **Answer: B.**

3. Rent controls are a price ceiling and create shortages of apartments. Owners have little incentive to keep up these apartments, and consequently they are often of lower quality. **Answer: B.**

4. At a price of $5.00 per ticket, 1,000 tickets will be demanded but only 200 will be supplied. Therefore, 200 people will be able to buy tickets and 800 will not. **Answer: B.**

5. When the government imposes a price ceiling of $8 tickets will be demanded, 800 will be supplied, and a surplus will result. The surplus would cause prices to fall—and they can fall because the price ceiling is only a maximum price. The price of a movie ticket will fall back to the equilibrium price of $7. **Answer: D.**

6. If the government limits the number of movie tickets sold to 400, the demand price of those 400 tickets would be $8.00, while the supply price of the tickets would be $6.00. The quota rent is the difference between the demand price and the supply price, or $2 per ticket. **Answer: D.**

7. A tax of $2 on movie tickets will shift the supply curve for movie tickets up by $2, as shown in the following figure. The new equilibrium price will be $8 per ticket and 400 tickets will be bought and sold. **Answer: C.**

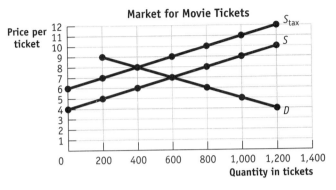

Market for Movie Tickets

8. From the preceding figure we can see that 400 tickets would be exchanged with the tax and the government would earn $800 from the tax (= $2 × 400). **Answer: B.**

9. At a $6 minimum wage, 7,000 workers will be looking for jobs, but firms will only want to hire 5,000 of them. There will be 2,000 unemployed workers. **Answer: C.**

10. As the wage rises from the equilibrium wage of $5 to the $6 minimum wage, 1,000 workers will lose their jobs (firms would hire 6,000 workers at a wage of $5, but at $6 only 5,000 will be hired). Also, 1,000 workers who were not willing to work at $5 enter the labor force at a wage of $6 but are not able to find jobs. **Answer: A.**

11. If the minimum wage is set below the equilibrium wage, it will have no effect on the market and therefore the minimum wage will not create unemployment. This is the situation that many economists believe exists for the minimum wage in the United States. **Answer: A.**

12. When the demand price exceeds the supply price for a given quantity, there is a shortage of the good and the market would be better off with more exchanged. There is a missed opportunity. **Answer: A.**

13. When the government imposes a tax in a market and the tax is collected from the producers, the supply curve will shift up by the full amount of the tax. Producers want the same price for supplying a particular quantity plus the tax. **Answer: C.**

14. When the government imposes a tax in a market and the tax is collected from the consumers, the demand curve will shift down by the amount of the tax. The demand curve reflects that price paid to the producer. Consumers are only willing to pay the same price for a particular quantity, but now part of the payment is to the government and the rest is to the producer. **Answer: B.**

15. Since a tax lowers the amount of the good exchanged, some mutually beneficial transactions that would have taken place do not. This is the excess burden, or deadweight loss, of a tax. **Answer: D.**

16. The quota rent is the difference between the demand price and the supply price for the quota. At the quota of 20,000 rides, the quota rent is $4 (= $12 – $8). **Answer: A.**

17. If the tax were $4 per unit, the supply curve would shift up by $4 and intersect the demand curve at a price of $8 and quantity of 1,000 units. **Answer: D.**

18. Use given demand-supply curves with wage rate at the vertical axis and quantity of labour at the horizontal axis and set the minimum wage above the free-market wage rate (where demand and supply curves intersect). The gap between demand and supply at the minimum wage is the amount of unemployment. **Answer: B.**

19. A job-training program shifts the demand for labour curve to the right. As a result, both wage and employment increase. **Answer: B.**

20. Rectangle *A* is the portion of the tax paid by the consumers, rectangle *B* is the portion paid by the producers. Together rectangles *A* and *B* represent the government's tax revenue. **Answer: C.**

21. A job-training program shifts the demand for labour curve to the right. **Answer: A.**

22. See the gap between quantity demanded and quantity supplied when the ceiling price is $1.50. **Answer: D.**

23. If the quantity supplied is 30 thousand kg at the ceiling price of $1.50, there are consumers who will be willing to buy 30 thousand kg at a price of $4.50. Therefore, $4.50 is the highest black market price. **Answer: D.**

24. When consumers buy 50 thousand kg at a final (gross) price of $3.50, it is equal to the supply price of $2.50 (net of tax), at which sellers are willing to supply 50 thousand kg of blueberries. **Answer: B.**

25. With *Q* = 50 thousand kg and tax = $1.00, tax revenues = $50 thousand. **Answer: A.**

Answers to Problems and Exercises

1.

Market for Golf Games

a. The market-clearing price is $60 and the market-clearing level of output is 5,000 games.

b. A price ceiling of $20 for an 18-hole game will insure that the price of an 18-hole game is $20, but only 1,000 games will be offered for sale at that price. There will be an excess demand of 8,000 games—a lot of people who would like to play for $20 a game will be disappointed. We might expect to see golf courses requiring golf carts that would rent for very high rates (wasted resources); certain players might make side payments to employees to ensure that they get to play (wasted resources); and the owners of the golf courses might not keep the greens and fairways in their best condition (inefficiently low quality).

c. A price floor of $80 will insure that the price of a golf game will be $80, but only 3,000 games will be played at that price. Since the owners of the golf courses would like to supply 7,000 games at that price, there will be a surplus in the market. The owners might try to attract more players by offering cheap or free golf cart rentals (wasted resources and inefficiently high quality), lessons by pros (wasted resources and inefficiently high quality), and drinks at the 19th hole (wasted resources).

d. If the mayor imposes a quota of 3,000 games, the price of a golf game will rise to $80 and there will be a price wedge, or quota rent, of $40 (= $80 – $40). Some inefficiencies would include missed opportunities; golfers would be willing to pay $70 per game for 1,000 additional golf games and the golf courses would offer those 1,000 games for $50 per game. Also, there's an incentive on the part of both golfers and golf courses to ignore the law.

2. Use the data in the table.
   a. Price = $1.40, quantity demanded and supplied = 60 thousand kg.
   b. At the floor price, quantity demanded = 40 thousand kg and quantity supplied = 80 thousand kg. Therefore, surplus = 40 thousand kg. Cost of buying this surplus = $1.60 times 40 thousand kg = $64 thousand.
   c. With a subsidy of $0.40 per kg, quantity demanded and supplied will be 80 thousand kg. The total subsidy costs to the government = $32 thousand.

3. a. If the government imposes a tax of $1 per six-pack, the supply curve with the tax will shift up by the amount of the tax. Before the tax, producers were willing to supply 600 six-packs for $5 each; after the tax they require $6 to supply 600 six-packs. The new equilibrium price with the tax is $5.50 per six-pack, and the equilibrium quantity is 550 six-packs per month.

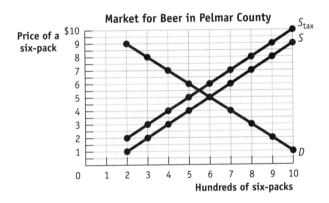

Market for Beer in Pelmar County

b. The government's revenue is the tax, $1, times the new equilibrium quantity, 550 six-packs, or $550 per month.
   c. The consumers were paying $0.50 more per six-pack after the tax on 550 six-packs, or $275. The producers are receiving $0.50 less per six-pack after the tax on 550 six-packs, or $275. The consumers and producers are paying equal amounts of the tax.

4. a. Quantity produced = 1,200 bushels. Since quantity demanded is 800 bushels, surplus equals 400 bushels. The cost of buying this surplus is $4,000.
   b. The difference between target price and market price (when consumers buy 1,200 bushels) is $8. If $8 is subsidized for each bushel, it will cost the government $9,600.
   c. Buying surplus is cheaper for the government. The farmers are indifferent between two options, because they will earn $12,000 in total in both options.

5. False. With a vertical demand curve, an excise tax (which shifts the supply curve), the price increases by the amount of the tax. The total burden of tax falls on consumers.

6. a. $P = $10; Q = 120$
   b. Consumers are willing to pay = $14; producers are willing to sell at = $8.
   c. Quota rent = (80) ($14 – $8) = $480.

d. Appropriate excise tax = $6
Tax revenue = $6(80) = $480
Deadweight loss = (1/2)(40)($4) + (1/2)(40)($2) = $120

7. True. See the following graph.
With the demand curve of D_1, the unemployment is $L_1 - L_3$.
With the steeper demand curve of D_2, the unemployment is $L_2 - L_3$ and it is less than the previous unemployment.

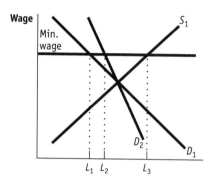

chapter 5

Consumer and Producer Surplus

This chapter provides a detailed analysis of consumer surplus and producer surplus. To understand consumer surplus, we need to see that an individual's demand curve reflects his or her willingness to pay for a given amount of a good. We assume that an individual will be willing to pay less and less for an additional quantity of a given good. Consumer surplus is the difference between what a buyer is willing to pay and what he or she actually pays. To understand producer surplus, we need to see that an up-sloping supply curve represents the producers' supply price, which in turn represents their costs. Producer surplus is the difference between what producers receive for quantities sold and what it costs at various quantities of output. Generally, an unregulated free market brings an equilibrium outcome where quantity demanded is equal to quantity supplied at the market clearing price. This equilibrium is considered an efficient outcome because it maximizes the combined consumer and producer surplus. This chapter explains why there is a loss of surplus if we are not at the efficient point and why gains in trade exist. We also measure the deadweight loss of an excise tax as the loss of surplus.

How Well Do You Understand the Chapter?

Fill in the blanks using the terms below to complete the following statements. Terms may be used more than once. If you find yourself having difficulties, please refer back to the appropriate section in the text.

above	deadweight loss	larger	sum
below	decrease(s)	lowest	surplus
beneficial	efficient	market(s)	total
best	enough	market failure	total surplus
better	excise tax	minimum	triangle
cannot	externality	price	under
consumer(s)	gains	price elasticities	willingness to pay
consumer surplus	government	producer	worse off
costs	increase(s)	producer surplus(es)	

1. We can view a demand curve as the _____ curve of each potential consumer. Each consumer will benefit if the _____ is less than his or her willingness to pay. We measure that benefit (the individual consumer surplus) by the difference between the consumer's _____ and the market price. Total consumer surplus is just the _____ of the individual consumer surpluses, and we measure it graphically as the area _____ the demand curve and _____ the market price. The term _____ refers to both individual and to total consumer surplus.

2. A(n) _____ in price increases consumer surplus via two channels: a gain to consumers who would have bought at the original price and a gain to consumers who are persuaded to buy by the lower price. A(n) _____ _____ in the price of a good reduces consumer surplus in a similar fashion.

3. There is a similar distinction between a firm's individual producer surplus and total producer surplus. An individual firm benefits from selling a good in a(n) _____ as long as it can cover their _____. The cost of each potential producer is the _____ price at which he or she is willing to supply a unit of that good. The difference between the price received and the seller's costs is its _____. Total producer surplus is just the sum of all individual _____. We can measure total producer surplus as the area _____ the supply curve and below the market _____.

4. When the price of a good _____, producer surplus increases through two channels: the gains of those who would have supplied the good in the original, lower price and the gains of those who are induced to supply the good by the higher price. A(n) _____ in the price of a good similarly leads to a fall in producer surplus. The term _____ is often used to refer to both the individual and to the total producer surplus.

5. Markets make everyone _____ off, and we can measure this by the total _____ in a market (the total net gain to society from the production and consumption of a good). The _____ surplus represents the _____ from trade. Some markets are efficient and maximize _____. Any possible rearrangement of consumption or sales, or a change in the quantity bought and sold, _____ total surplus. Another way to look at the efficiency of markets is to say that we _____ make anyone better off without making someone else _____.

6. If we try to reallocate equilibrium output in a market among consumers, consumer surplus will _____. The market allocates the good to those consumers who have the highest _____. If we try reallocating equilibrium output in a market among sellers, _____ will fall. The market allocates the right to sell the good to the producers with the _____ cost.

7. In perfectly competitive markets, the market equilibrium is the _____ outcome for every individual consumer and producer. It maximizes _____ and _____ surplus. However, sometimes _____ occurs when markets fail to be efficient. Markets may fail to be efficient in a sense that there may not be _____ buyers and/or sellers in a market, and therefore either one or more buyers or sellers can influence the market _____. Also, it is possible that the actions of buyers and/or sellers affect others (this is called a(n) _____), and the market equilibrium may not maximize consumer and producer surplus. Finally, it may be that some goods, by their very nature, are unsuited for efficient management by

_____ .

8. Both producers and consumers bear the burden of a(n) _____ and the relative burden depends on the _____ of the supply and demand curves. There is an excess burden or _____ of a tax because some mutually _____ transactions did not take place. The deadweight loss can be measured as a loss of both consumer surplus and _____ _____ surplus. Some of the loss of the total surplus becomes revenue to the _____. The difference between the loss of _____ and the tax revenue is the excess burden or _____ of the tax. We measure it graphically as the _____ representing the potential surplus of the mutually beneficial transactions that did not take place. The larger the elasticity of demand or elasticity of supply, the _____ is the deadweight loss of the tax.

Learning Tips

TIP #1: You can only measure consumer surplus as the triangle under the demand curve and above the market price if there are a large number of buyers. You can only measure producer surplus as the triangle above the supply curve and under the market price if there are a large number of sellers.

If you only have a few buyers or a few sellers, as in Figure 5.1 (Figures 5-2 and 5-7 in the text), you must calculate each individual's surplus and then add them together to get the market consumer or producer surplus. Each individual's consumer surplus is measured as the difference between that individual's willingness to pay and the market price. Each individual's producer surplus is measured as the difference between the market price and the individual's cost.

Figure 5.1

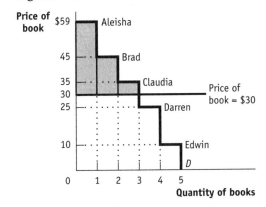
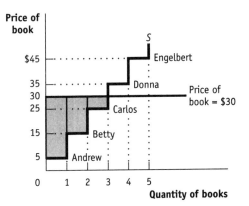

Question: Consider Figure 5.1. Assume that the price of each book is $30, the total consumer surplus is

A) $59.
B) $49.
C) $45.
D) $30.

TIP #2: Producer and consumer surplus changes when the price of a good changes.

As the price of a good rises, quantity demanded will fall. Since consumers buy fewer goods at higher prices, and on those goods there is a smaller difference between willingness to pay and the market price, consumer surplus must decline. The reverse is true for a decrease in price.

As the price of a good rises, quantity supplied will rise. Since producers supply more goods at higher prices, and on those goods and the others that had been supplied there is a larger difference between market price and cost, producer surplus must increase. The reverse is true for a decrease in price.

TIP #3: The combined loss in consumer and producer surplus exceeds the revenue to the government when the government imposes a tax in the market.

Since fewer units of the good are exchanged, the consumer and producer surplus earned on those units no longer sold is lost to everyone. In Figures 5.2 and 5.3, consumer surplus is shown as triangle A, producer surplus as triangle B; rectangle C represents the government's revenue and triangle F is the total loss (deadweight loss) in producer and consumer surplus because of the tax.

Figure 5.2

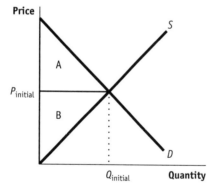

Figure 5.3

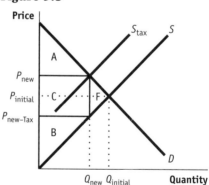

TIP #4: The excess burden or deadweight loss of a tax will be greater the larger the price elasticities of demand and supply.

The excess burden or deadweight loss of the tax comes about because of the loss of total surplus that results when transactions that are mutually beneficial to consumers and producers do not take place. A tax will discourage a larger number of transactions when the demand and supply curves are relatively price elastic. Compare Figures 5.4 and 5.5. In Figure 5.4, the demand and supply curves are relatively price inelastic when compared with Figure 5.5. If the government imposes the same per-unit tax in both markets, the loss of consumer and producer surplus will be much larger in Figure 5.5 than in Figure 5.4. This is because when the supply and demand curves are relatively price elastic, the tax will discourage more transactions than when the curves are relatively price inelastic. (The more elastic curves indicate that the consumers and producers are more responsive to changes in prices.)

Figure 5.4

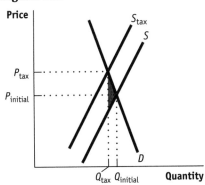

Figure 5.5

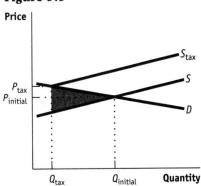

Multiple-Choice Questions

1. The demand curve shows
   a. the maximum amount consumers are willing to pay for particular units of a good.
   b. the minimum amount consumers are willing to pay for particular units of a good.
   c. the average amount consumers are willing to pay for particular units of a good.
   d. that consumers want to pay the lowest price possible.

Answer the next three questions based on the following demand schedule and curve for six buyers of tickets to a dress rehearsal of a new play at the local college.

Potential buyer	Willingness to pay
A	$10
B	9
C	7
D	6
E	5
F	2

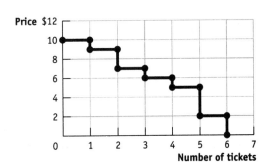

2. If the price of a ticket to the dress rehearsal is $6, how many tickets will be sold?
   a. 1
   b. 3
   c. 4
   d. 5

3. At a price of $5 per ticket, total consumer surplus would equal
   a. $2.
   b. $4.
   c. $12.
   d. $24.

4. If the college imposed a price ceiling of $2 for the dress rehearsal, the number of tickets sold would be _____ and consumer surplus would equal _____.
  a. 4; $5
  b. 5; $15
  c. 5; $6
  d. 6; $27

5. When the quantities we are dealing with are relatively large, we can identify total consumer surplus on a graph as the
  a. area above the demand curve and below the price.
  b. area above the demand curve and above the price.
  c. area below the demand curve and below the price.
  d. area below the demand curve and above the price.

6. As the price of a good increases, consumer surplus
  a. increases.
  b. decreases.
  c. stays the same.
  d. may increase, decrease, or stay the same.

7. As the price in a market falls,
  a. consumer surplus decreases because some consumers leave the market, reducing consumer surplus.
  b. consumer surplus decreases because the consumers who remain in the market receive a lower consumer surplus.
  c. consumer surplus increases because consumers who would have bought the good at the higher price earn more consumer surplus, and new consumers enter the market who also earn consumer surplus.
  d. consumer surplus may increase, decrease, or stay the same.

8. If the demand curve is perfectly price elastic,
  a. consumer surplus will equal zero.
  b. consumer surplus will equal producer surplus.
  c. consumer surplus will equal total surplus.
  d. consumer surplus will be greater than producer surplus.

9. After waiting in line for three hours to buy two $50 tickets for a concert, someone offered Agnes $160 for her two tickets. Agnes refused even though she knew that comparable seats were still available for $50 per ticket if she waited in line again for three hours. We know that the opportunity cost of Agnes's time is
  a. greater than or equal to $60 per hour.
  b. less than or equal to $60 per hour.
  c. greater than or equal to $20 per hour.
  d. less than or equal to $20 per hour.

10. We measure total producer surplus as the
  a. area above the supply curve and below the price.
  b. area above the supply curve and above the price.
  c. area below the supply curve and below the price.
  d. area below the supply curve and above the price.

11. As the price of oranges rises, the producer surplus in the orange market
   a. increases.
   b. decreases.
   c. does not change.
   d. may increase, decrease, or stay the same.

12. Economists say markets are efficient when
   a. opportunity costs are minimized.
   b. total revenue is maximized.
   c. total surplus is maximized.
   d. it is possible to make someone better off while making another worse off.

13. If the free-market equilibrium price of an orange is $0.50, Lucy is willing to buy an orange but Liam is not. If we let Lucy buy the orange but then take it away from her and give it to Liam,
   a. consumer surplus will rise.
   b. consumer surplus will fall.
   c. producer surplus will rise.
   d. producer surplus will fall.

14. Markets may not be efficient if
   a. opportunity costs are present.
   b. only monetary costs are present.
   c. no monetary costs are present.
   d. externalities are present.

15. When the government imposes a price floor above the equilibrium price in a market, consumer surplus _____ and total surplus _____.
   a. may fall; may rise
   b. will fall; will fall
   c. will rise; will rise
   d. may rise; may fall

16. When the government imposes a price floor above the equilibrium price in a market, producer surplus
   a. will rise.
   b. will fall.
   c. will not change.
   d. may rise, fall, or stay the same.

17. If the demand curve for a good is perfectly price inelastic and the government imposes a tax in the market,
   a. there will be no deadweight loss.
   b. the government's tax revenue will equal the loss in producer surplus.
   c. the government's tax revenue will be more than the loss in producer surplus.
   d. the government's tax revenue will be less than the loss in producer surplus.

Use the accompanying figure to answer the next three questions.

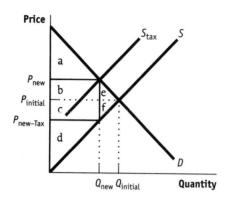

18. Before the government introduces a tax in the market, consumer surplus is represented by
a. areas a, b, and c.
b. areas a, b, and e.
c. areas e and f.
d. areas c, f, and d.

19. After the government introduces a tax in the market, the government's revenue is represented by
a. areas a, b, and c.
b. areas a, b, c, and d.
c. areas e and f.
d. areas b and c.

20. The deadweight loss from the tax is equal to
a. areas a, b, and c.
b. areas a, b, and e.
c. areas e and f.
d. areas b, c, e, and f.

21. Assume that the market demand curve is perfectly price inelastic and the supply curve is up-sloping. When an excise tax is imposed, the deadweight loss will be
a. the maximum positive value.
b. zero.
c. more than zero.
d. less than zero.

Answer questions 22–23 on the basis of the following:

There are 4 consumers willing to pay the following prices for 1-hour of Internet games in an Internet café. Andrew is willing to pay $10, Sarah is willing to pay $8, Rinque is willing to pay $6, and Sholok is willing to pay $4.

22. If the price of the Internet game is $5, the total consumer surplus will be
a. $24.
b. $20.
c. $18.
d. $9.

23. If the price of the Internet game decreases to $3, the total consumer surplus will increase by
 a. $16.
 b. $9
 c. $7.
 d. $2.

*24. When the demand function is $Q^D = 100 - P$ and the supply function is $Q^S = 4P$, the maximum total surplus is gained when the amount bought and sold is
 a. 20.
 b. 40.
 c. 80.
 d. 100.

*25. When the demand function is $Q^D = 100 - P$ and the supply function is $Q^S = 4P$ and the market equilibrium is an efficient outcome, the total surplus will be
 a. $8,000.
 b. $6,400.
 c. $5,200.
 d. $4,000.

Problems and Exercises

Read each question carefully and then write your answers in the space provided or on a separate sheet of paper.

1. There are five signed lithographs of Picasso's *Peace Dove* in excellent condition. Abner, Buddy, Carlos, Dylan, and Edgar currently own them but would be willing to sell if the price were right (higher than their opportunity cost). Lydia, Mira, Nicole, Olivia, and Pia would all like to buy one of those lithographs but each has a different willingness to pay. The accompanying table shows the willingness to pay (maximum price) of the buyers and the opportunity costs (minimum price) of the sellers.

Seller	Minimum price	Buyer	Maximum price
Abner	$1,200	Lydia	$1,000
Buddy	4,500	Mira	5,000
Carlos	3,000	Nicole	2,500
Dylan	2,500	Olivia	1,500
Edgar	2,800	Pia	2,000

 a. Draw figures similar to Figures 5-1 and 5-6 in your text showing the willingness to pay for the Picasso lithograph of the buyers and the cost for the lithograph of the sellers.

b. All lithographs sell for the same price. How many lithographs will be bought and sold? What will be the price of the lithographs? Who will sell and who will buy the lithographs?

c. What is the total amount of consumer surplus? producer surplus? total surplus?

d. Show consumer and producer surplus graphically.

e. If there were more interested buyers for lithographs of Picasso's *Peace Dove* and the market price of the lithograph rose to $3,000, calculate the new values of consumer and producer surplus for the above individuals. Why have they changed?

f. If there were more lithographs of Picasso's *Peace Dove* in excellent condition available and the market price of the lithograph fell to $2,000, calculate the new values of consumer and producer surplus for the above individuals. Why have they changed?

2. The following table shows the market demand and supply schedules for cups of coffee at the Campus Coffee Shop. Graph the demand and supply curves and find the equilibrium price and equilibrium output.

Quantity	Supply price	Demand price
0	$0.00	$3.00
1,000	0.50	2.00
2,000	1.00	1.00
3,000	1.50	0.00
4,000	2.00	
5,000	2.50	

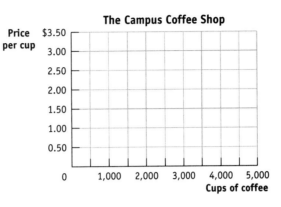

a. At the equilibrium price, graphically show consumer surplus, producer surplus, and total surplus.

b. If the government imposed a quota on the Campus Coffee Shop such that they could not sell more than 1,000 cups of coffee, what will be the new price and output at the shop? How will the quota affect consumer, producer, and total surplus?

c. If the government imposed a $0.50 price ceiling in the market for coffee, what will be the new price and output at the Campus Coffee Shop? How will the price ceiling affect consumer, producer, and total surplus?

3. The government is considering imposing the same tax in the markets shown in the following figures. Which of the markets will have the largest deadweight loss? Which will have the smallest deadweight loss? Since governments would like to minimize the deadweight loss associated with a tax, can you advise the government as to what types of price elasticities of demand will minimize the deadweight loss?

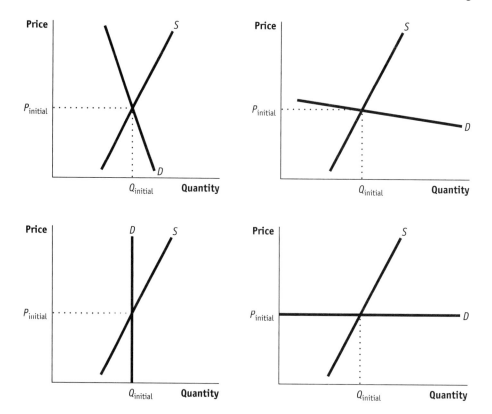

4. In each of the following markets explain what will happen, if you can, to consumer, producer, and total surplus. Show your answers graphically.
   a. Bottled Water: A newspaper reports an unhealthy level of bacteria in tap water.

   b. Milk: A ban on the use of certain hormones for cows radically lowers the amount of milk each cow produces.

c. Gasoline: The government lowers the excise tax on gasoline products.

5. Consider the following table.

Units of goods	Willingness to pay by Sarah	Willingness to pay by Prima
1	$50	$40
2	$40	$35
3	$30	$30
4	$20	$25
5	$10	$20
6	$ 0	$15
7	$ 0	$10
6	$ 0	$ 5

a. If the price is $14 per unit, how many units of goods will be bought by Sarah and by Prima? What will be the total consumer surplus?

b. If the price goes down to $6, how many units of goods will be bought by Sarah and by Prima? What will be the total consumer surplus?

6. Consider the following schedule of demand and supply of pizza in Hamilton, Ontario.

Price of pizza	Quantity of pizza demanded	Quantity of pizza supplied
$8	1	7
7	2	6
6	3	5
5	4	4
4	5	3
3	6	2
2	7	1

a. Find the equilibrium price, equilibrium quantity, consumer surplus, producer surplus, and total surplus.

b. Hamilton City decided to impose an excise tax of $2 per pizza. Find the equilibrium price, equilibrium quantity, consumer surplus, producer surplus, and total surplus.

*7. Consider the following equations.

$P = 10 - Q$ [Price (P) that consumers are willing to pay for a given quantity (Q)]
$P = Q$ [Price (P) that producers are asking for a given quantity (Q)]

We assume that, in an equilibrium situation, the price that consumers are willing to pay is equal to the asking price of producers.
a. Find the equilibrium P and Q. Find the total surplus.

b. If the excise tax is $4 per unit of output, what will be the total surplus, total tax collections, and deadweight loss?

Answers to How Well Do You Understand the Chapter

1. willingness to pay, price, willingness to pay, sum, under, above, consumer surplus

2. decrease, increase

3. market, costs, minimum, producer surplus, producer surpluses, above, price

4. increases, decrease, producer surplus

5. better, surplus, total, gains, total surplus, decreases, cannot, worse off

6. decrease, willingness to pay, producer surplus, lowest

7. efficient, consumer, producer, market failure, enough, price, externality, markets

8. excise tax, price elasticities, deadweight loss, beneficial, producer, government, total surplus, deadweight loss, triangle, larger

Answers to Multiple-Choice Questions

1. The demand curve reflects the highest amount that consumers are willing to pay for particular units of a good. **Answer: A.**

2. At a price of $6, consumers are only willing to purchase 4 tickets. **Answer: C.**

3. At a price of $5, consumers are willing to purchase 5 tickets. The consumer surplus will equal the sum of $5 (the surplus earned on the first ticket), $4 (the surplus earned on the second ticket), $2 (the surplus earned on the third ticket), and $1 (the surplus earned on the fourth ticket) for a total of $12. There is no consumer surplus earned on the fifth ticket. **Answer: C.**

4. At a price ceiling of $2, the college will sell 6 tickets and the ticket buyers will earn a surplus of $27. Compared with the answer for a price of $5, consumer surplus increases by $3 on each of the original 4 tickets sold and $3 on the fifth ticket sold. **Answer: D.**

5. Consumer surplus is the difference between what consumers are willing to pay for particular units and what they actually pay. We measure this as the area under the demand curve (willingness to pay) and above the market price. **Answer: D.**

6. As the price of a good increases, some consumers leave the market and those who remain earn a lower consumer surplus on each unit that they continue to buy—both lead to a decrease in consumer surplus. **Answer: B.**

7. As the price of a good falls, more consumers enter the market, and those who were already in the market earn a higher consumer surplus on each unit that they continue to buy—both lead to an increase in consumer surplus. **Answer: C.**

8. If the demand curve is perfectly price elastic, consumers are only willing to buy units of the good at one particular price. That price must be the market price. Since there is no difference between the price consumers are willing to pay and the market price, there is no area below the demand curve and above the market price and consumer surplus is zero. The figure below shows the answer graphically. **Answer: A.**

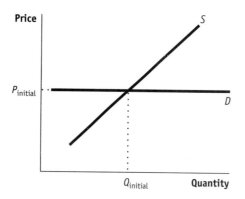

9. Agnes would earn $60 for the three-hour wait to get additional tickets, or $20 per hour. Since she chooses not to sell her tickets, $160 must be equal to or lower than the price of the tickets plus the opportunity cost of her time. Agnes values her time at a rate equal to or greater than $20 per hour. **Answer: C.**

10. Producer surplus measures the difference between the market price of a good and the price at which producers are willing to sell particular units. We measure producer surplus as the area under the market price and above the supply curve. **Answer: A.**

11. As the price of oranges rises, more sellers enter the market and those who were already in the market earn a higher producer surplus—both lead to an increase in producer surplus. **Answer: A.**

12. Markets are efficient when they allocate goods in such a way that no one can be made better off without someone else being made worse off. This is true in equilibrium because the total surplus is maximized. **Answer: C.**

13. Since Lucy is willing to buy an orange at a price of $0.50, that price must reflect at least the value that Lucy attributes to oranges. Since Liam does not buy an orange at a price of $0.50, he values the orange at something less than $0.50. When we take an orange away from Lucy and give it to Liam, consumer surplus must fall. **Answer: B.**

14. Markets may not be efficient if an individual buyer or seller does not take the market price as given (for example, a monopolist) and/or if there are welfare effects influencing individuals other than the market participants (an externality). **Answer: D.**

15. The government imposes a price floor above the market price. As the accompanying figures show, as the price rises, both consumer surplus (triangle A) and total surplus (triangle A plus area with diagonal lines) will fall. **Answer: B.**

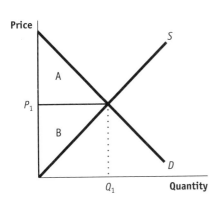 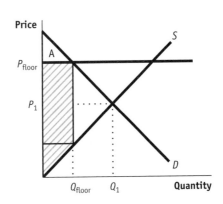

16. The government imposes a price floor above the market price. As the price rises, the number of units sold declines. Producers will earn a larger producer surplus on each unit it sells but they will sell fewer units. Producer surplus may rise, fall, or stay the same. **Answer: D.**

17. The figure below shows that as the government imposes a tax in a market where the demand curve is perfectly price inelastic, there will be no deadweight loss. Triangle B is the producer surplus both before and after the tax and rectangle C is the government's revenue from the tax. **Answer: A.**

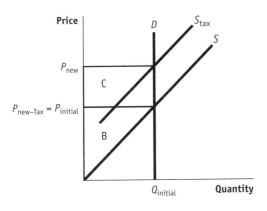

18. Consumer surplus is the area under the demand curve and above the market price. This includes areas a, b, and e. **Answer: B.**

19. The government's revenue is the per-unit tax ($= P_{new} - [P_{new} - Tax]$) times the new quantity exchanged (Q_{new}). This area is represented by areas b and c. **Answer: D.**

20. The deadweight loss is the combined loss of consumer and producer surplus when the government imposes the tax. This is areas e and f. **Answer: C.**

21. With the vertical demand curve, the price increases by the amount of the excise tax. The total loss of surplus is equal to the total tax revenues. Therefore, there is zero deadweight loss. **Answer: B.**

22. $P = \$5$, the consumer surplus for Andrew is $5, for Sarah, $3 and for Rinque, $1. The total consumer surplus is $9. **Answer: D.**

23. When $P = \$3$, the consumer surplus for Andrew is $7, for Sarah, $5, for Rinque, $3, and for Sholok, $1. The total consumer surplus is $16. The increase in consumer surplus is $16 − $9 = $7. **Answer: C.**

24. When $Q^D = Q^S$, the equilibrium P is $20 and the equilibrium Q is 80 units. **Answer: C.**

25. At the equilibrium outcome, the total consumer surplus is $3,200 and the total producer surplus is $800. Therefore, the total surplus is $4,000. **Answer: D.**

Answers to Problems and Exercises

1. a.

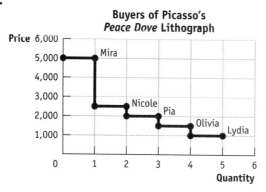

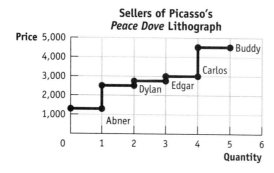

b. Abner and Dylan sell their lithographs to Mira and Nicole for $2,500. See the following figure.

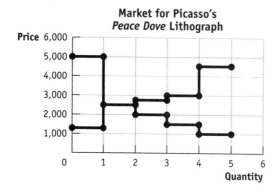

c. Consumer surplus is $2,500: Mira earns $2,500 in consumer surplus (she was willing to pay $5,000 but only pays the market price of $2,500), but Nicole does not earn anything (she was only willing to pay the market price of $2,500). Producer surplus is $1,300: Abner earns $1,300 in producer surplus (his costs were only $1,200 but he received $2,500), but Dylan does not earn any (his costs equaled the market price of $2,500). Total surplus is $3,800.

d.

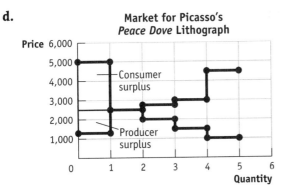

Market for Picasso's
Peace Dove Lithograph

e. At a price of $3,000, only Mira (out of our five buyers) would buy the lithograph and she would earn consumer surplus of $2,000. Abner, Dylan, and Carlos would sell their lithographs and they would earn producer surplus of $2,300 ($1,800 for Abner, $500 for Dylan, and nothing for Carlos). As the price rose, consumer surplus fell because Nicole dropped out of the market and Mira earned a smaller consumer surplus, while producer surplus rose because both Abner and Dylan earned a larger producer surplus and Carlos came into the market.

f. At a price of $2,000, Mira, Nicole, and Pia would buy the lithograph and they would earn consumer surplus of $3,500 ($3,000 for Mira, $500 for Nicole, and nothing for Pia). Only Abner would sell the lithograph and he would earn producer surplus of $800. As the price fell, producer surplus fell because Dylan no longer sells his lithograph and Abner receives a smaller producer surplus, while consumer surplus rose because Pia came into the market and both Mira and Nicole earned a larger consumer surplus.

2.

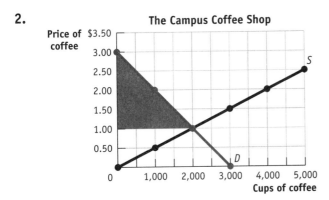

The Campus Coffee Shop

a. The equilibrium price is $1.00 per cup of coffee and the equilibrium output is 2,000 cups of coffee per week. Consumer surplus is the area below the demand curve and above the price—the upper triangle. Producer surplus is the area above the supply curve and under the price—the bottom triangle. Total surplus is the sum of consumer and producer surplus, or the two triangles combined.

b. At a quota of 1,000 cups of coffee, the Campus Coffee Shop will sell the 1,000 cups at $2.00 per cup. Consumer surplus will fall under the quota to the triangle above $2.00 and below the demand curve—the shaded triangle. Consumer surplus will always fall when a quota is imposed.

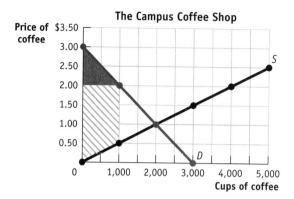

In this situation, producer surplus will increase under the quota to the area under $2 and above the supply curve up to a quantity of 1,000 cups—the area with diagonal lines. However, in general producer surplus may be higher or lower under a quota depending on how the gain in producer surplus on the quantity sold with the quota compares to the loss of producer surplus on the units that were sold initially but not under the quota.

Total surplus in the coffee market is definitely lower compared with the original equilibrium in the market. Total surplus will always decrease when a quota is imposed.

c. With a $0.50 price ceiling, the Campus Coffee Shop will sell 1,000 cups of coffee at $0.50 per cup.

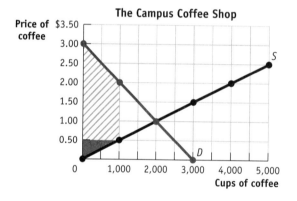

Comparing the market equilibrium with no government intervention with the $0.50 price ceiling, producer surplus will definitely be lower; it is represented by the shaded triangle. If a price ceiling is effective, producer surplus will definitely decrease. Consumer surplus (represented by the area with diagonal lines) appears to be the same with the price ceiling. In this case, it appears that the gain in consumer surplus on the first 1,000 cups equals the loss of consumer surplus on the 1,000 cups not consumed. However, in general, under an effective price ceiling, consumer surplus may increase, decrease, or stay the same. Total surplus is definitely lower compared with the original equilibrium in the coffee market. Total surplus always decreases with a price ceiling.

3. In the graphs below, the supply curve is the same but the demand curve shows differing price elasticities of demand. When the government imposes the same tax in the market, the supply curve shifts up by the same amount in each graph to S_{tax}. In the top two graphs, we see that when the price elasticity of demand is larger (the graph on the right), the deadweight loss due to the tax is larger than it is when the price elasticity of demand is smaller (the graph on the left). In the two bottom graphs, the one on the left shows a perfectly price inelastic demand curve (price elasticity of demand equals 0), while the one on the right shows a perfectly price elastic demand curve (price elasticity of demand is infinite). When the price elasticity of demand is zero, there is no deadweight loss for the tax. As the demand curve has greater elasticity, the deadweight loss gets larger and it is at its largest when the price elasticity of demand is infinite.

We could show a similar relationship between the price elasticity of supply and the deadweight loss if we held the demand curve constant and allowed the price elasticity of supply to vary. When the price elasticity of supply is zero (supply curve is vertical), there will be no deadweight loss, and the deadweight loss will get larger as the price elasticity of supply gets larger (as the supply curve becomes more horizontal).

If the government wants to minimize the deadweight loss from a tax, it should impose a tax in a market where the relative price elasticities of demand and supply are small.

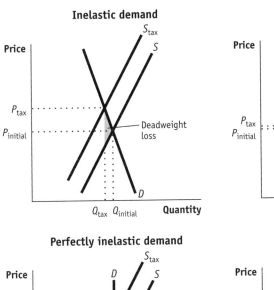

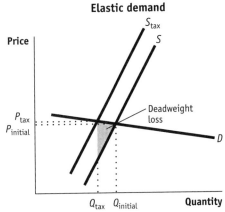

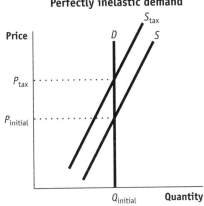

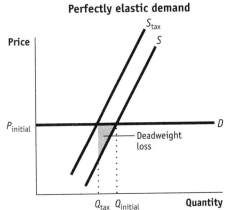

4. a. The demand for bottled water rises, increasing price and quantity. As price and quantity rise, producer surplus definitely rises but we can't say what will happen to consumer surplus. Consumer surplus may rise or fall—price has risen but so has the consumer's willingness to pay. From the graph below, we see that total surplus must rise.

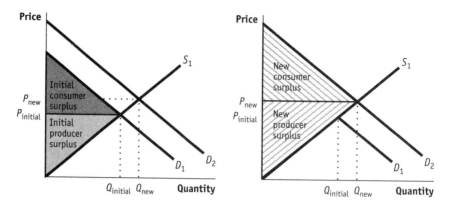

b. The ban on hormones will decrease the supply of milk, increasing price and lowering output. As shown in the graphs below, as price rises, consumer surplus definitely falls (fewer units are purchased and there is a lower surplus on those units consumers still buy). We can't tell what will happen to producer surplus—price has risen but so have costs. Total surplus definitely falls.

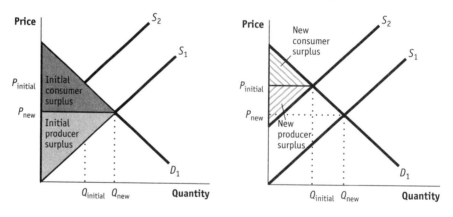

c. As the government lowers the excise tax, the supply of gasoline will increase, lowering price and raising output. As illustrated in the graphs below, consumer surplus will definitely increase—more consumers will enter the market and consumer surplus on the initial units sold will increase. Producer surplus may rise, fall, or stay the same—prices fall but so do costs. Total surplus increases.

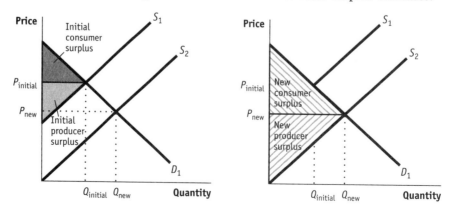

5. a. Sarah buys 4 units. Her total consumer surplus = $36 + $26 + $16 + $6 = $84

Prima buys 6 units. Her total consumer surplus = $26 + $21 + $16 + $11 + $6 + $1 = $81

Total surplus = $84 + $81 = $165

b. Sarah buys 5 units. Her total consumer surplus = $44 + $34 + $24 + $14 + $4 = $120

Prima buys 7 units. Her total consumer surplus = $34 + $29 + $24 + $19 + $14 + $9 + $4 = $133

Total surplus = $253

6. a. $P = \$5$, $Q = 4$, consumer surplus = $6, producer surplus = $6, and total surplus = $12

b. $P = \$6$, $Q = 3$, consumer surplus = $3, producer surplus = $3, and total surplus = $6

7. a. $Q = 5$, $P = \$5$, and total surplus = ($12.50 + $12.50) = $25. At the market equilibrium, the supply-price is equal to the demand-price; using this condition, we can solve equilibrium output, where quantity demanded is equal to quantity supplied. From $Q = 10 - Q$, we can solve $Q = 5$ and $P = \$5$.

b. $Q = 3$, $P = \$7$, total surplus = ($4.50 + $4.50) = $9, total tax collections = $12, and deadweight loss = $4. With tax, the after-tax supply-price is $4 + Q$. Set the new supply-price equal to the demand price and solve new Q. $Q + 4 = 10 - Q$. Therefore, $Q = 3$ and the after-tax $P = \$7$. The total tax revenue = $(3(\$4)) = \$12$. To find the deadweight loss, we need to find out pre-tax total surplus and after-tax total surplus. At the initial equilibrium, the consumer surplus = $[(\$5(5))/2]$ = $12.5 and producer surplus = $[(\$5(5))/2] = \$12.5$. Therefore, the total surplus is $25. After the tax, the consumer surplus = $[(\$3(3))/2] = \$4.5$ and producer surplus = $[(\$3(3))/2] = \$4.5$.

Therefore, the total surplus is $9.

The loss of total surplus = $25 − $9 = $16.

The deadweight loss = Loss of total surplus − tax revenue = $16 − $12 = $4.

chapter 6

Macroeconomics: The Big Picture

This chapter provides an overview of macroeconomics and discusses how macroeconomics, the study of the economy as a whole, differs from microeconomics. The chapter introduces the concepts of business cycles, long-run growth, inflation, deflation, and the distinction between open economies, where countries trade with one another, and closed economies, where there is no international trade.

How Well Do You Understand the Chapter?

Fill in the blanks using the terms below or circle the correct answer to complete the following statements. Terms may be used more than once. If you find yourself having difficulties, please refer back to the appropriate section in the text.

aggregate(s)	fiscal policy	monetary policy	short-run
capital flows	fluctuations	mutually	spending
closed	GDP	nominal	stability
consumer price	GDP deflator	open	stabilization policy
cycle	growth	output	standard of living
decreases	import(s)	paradox of thrift	trade
discouraged workers	increase(s)	percentage	underemployment
exchange rate	inflation rate	rationale	unemployment
expansion	interest rate	real	zero
export(s)	labour force	recession	
financial	microeconomics	scarce	

1. Macroeconomics is the study of the _____ economy or the economy as a whole. Central topics in macroeconomics include the determination of the overall level of output, prices, and employment in economy. Macroeconomics also considers exports, _____, and _____ in an open economy. Microeconomics, on the other hand, focuses on the production and consumption of specific goods and the allocation of _____ resources among competing uses. _____ analyzes how individuals and firms make decisions.

2. Macroeconomics uses various economic aggregates to study the economy. Economic _____ are measures of economic variables that summarize data collected from different markets for goods, services, workers, and assets.

Examples of economic aggregates include _____, aggregate output, investment, and savings. In the short run, when the economy is in a(n) _____ phase, jobs are plentiful; when the economy is in a(n) _____ phase, jobs are difficult to find. A business _____ consists of a period of short-run ups and downs of output.

3. Macroeconomics also studies long-run economic growth and its causes. Long-run economic _____ is measured as percentage change of the economy's overall output per person. Long-run growth in an economy raises the level of aggregate income and results in a higher _____ for people.

4. In the short run, the combined effect of individual decisions may have a very different impact on the economy than what any one individual intended. For example, when individual households fear and expect a(n) _____, they reduce their expenditure and save more in order to prepare for this expected recession, which, in turn, brings less aggregate income and less saving. This is known as the _____. Yet the effect of many households acting in a thrifty manner is to plunge the economy into a deeper _____.

5. Macroeconomics provides a(n) _____ for government intervention to reduce short-term _____ in the economy. Fiscal policy refers to government _____ and taxation policy, while monetary policy refers to the control of _____ and quantity of money in circulation. Both fiscal policy and monetary policy are useful tools for offsetting the _____ fluctuations in the macroeconomy.

6. Employment measures the total number of people working in the economy, while _____ is the total number of people who are actively looking for work but currently not working. The sum of employment plus unemployment equals a country's _____. The labour force does not include _____ workers (those workers who are not currently working and who have given up seeking jobs, because they do not believe they will find a job). The labour statistics do not measure _____ (the number of people who are working but whose wages are low, because these workers do not work as many hours as they would like, and/or because they are working at lower-paying jobs). Both the number of employed and the number of unemployed can be expressed in terms of a(n) _____; we then refer to the employment rate and the unemployment rate. The unemployment rate is never equal to _____ since there are always people who are seeking employment or are between jobs. In a(n) _____, the unemployment rate increases. In an expansion, the unemployment rate _____. The economy's output level and unemployment rate move in opposite directions; when the economy's output increases, the economy's unemployment rate _____. The economy's total output is the total production of final goods and services and is referred to as real gross domestic product, or real _____.

7. The _____ refers to policy efforts directed at reducing the severity of business cycle fluctuations. Stabilization may take the form of _____, in which the government alters its spending and/or taxing policies in order to help smooth short-run economic fluctuations; or it may take the form of _____ in which the economy is stabilized through changes in the quantity of money in circulation and through _____.

8. Secular long-run growth, or long-run growth, occurs when aggregate _____ per person increases. This growth in the economy occurs over several decades and does not refer to the short-run increase in aggregate output that occurs during a(n) _____. In the long run, economic growth is essential in order for wages and the standard of living in an economy to

_____.

9. The distinction between nominal and real values is important to macroeconomics. _____ values are measures that have not been adjusted for changes in prices over time, while _____ values are measures that have been adjusted for changes in prices. The overall level of prices in an economy is the aggregate price level. Inflation is a(n) _____ in the aggregate price level, while deflation is a(n) _____ in the aggregate price level. Two measures of the aggregate price level are the _____ and the _____ index. Economics view price _____ as a desirable goal for an economy. The _____ measures the annual percentage change in the aggregate price level.

10. We call an economy that does not engage in international trade a(n) _____ economy. An economy that participates in international trade is a(n) _____ economy. Countries engage in international trade because this trade is _____ beneficial to them. When studying open economies the movement of the _____, or the values of different national currencies to one another, is important. Changes in the exchange rate can affect a country's aggregate price level and its _____ balance. The trade balance measures the difference between the value of _____ (the value of the goods and services a country sells to other countries) and its _____ (the value of the goods and services a country buys from other countries). Countries trade _____ assets, as well as goods and services; international movements of financial assets are referred to as

_____.

Learning Tips

TIP #1: Studying economics requires learning both new vocabulary and a new way of thinking.

This chapter provides an overview of macroeconomics, the topics covered in the study of macroeconomics, and general definitions of macroeconomic variables. You will need to familiarize yourself with this information and vocabulary.

TIP #2: Macroeconomics focuses on the economic behavior of the overall economy, while microeconomics focuses on the economic behavior of individuals, firms, and specific markets.

Macroeconomics studies topics like the determination of the aggregate level of output, the aggregate price level, the level of employment, short-run economic fluctuations, and long-run economic growth. Microeconomics considers topics like supply and demand in particular markets, profit maximization by firms, and utility maximization by individuals.

TIP #3: Aggregation of data is at the heart of macroeconomics.

This chapter briefly describes the meaning of aggregation and gives examples of aggregated measures like employment, real GDP, and the overall price level. The concept of aggregation is important to understand as you begin your study of macroeconomics.

TIP #4: In macroeconomics, the aggregate effect is often greater than the sum of the individual effects.

In macroeconomics we find that the sum of many individual actions accumulates to produce outcomes that are larger than the simple sum of these individual actions. The combined effect of individual decisions can be much different from the intentions that any one individual had. The text provides an example of this with the paradox of thrift.

TIP #5: The phases of business cycle are: expansion, peak, recession, and trough.

In expansion, output ↑ and unemployment rate ↑. In recession, output ↓ and unemployment rate ↑.

TIP #6: Short-run stabilization policies are used to smooth short-run economic fluctuations.

Fiscal policy and monetary policy are considered as stabilization policies. Growth policy is a long-run policy instituted to increase productivity and improve the standard of living.

Multiple-Choice Questions

1. Macroeconomics, unlike microeconomics,
    a. considers the behavior of individual firms and markets.
    b. focuses on the production and consumption of particular goods.
    c. tries to explain increases in living standards over time.
    d. finds that the behavior of individuals is more important in determining economic activity than is the aggregate summation of this behavior.

2. Which of the following statements is true?
  a. In macroeconomics, there is no role for government intervention in the economy.
  b. In microeconomics, the prices determined in economic models are aggregate price levels for the economy.
  c. Microeconomics studies business cycle fluctuations in the economy.
  d. Fiscal and monetary policy may be helpful in reducing short-term economic fluctuations in the economy due to adverse economic events.

3. Which of the following is NOT an aggregate macroeconomic variable?
  a. Savings: the sum of household, government, and business savings during a given year
  b. Investment: the addition to the economy's supply of productive physical capital
  c. Bicycle production: the total number of bicycles manufactured in an economy during a given year
  d. Capital account: the total net amount of assets sold to foreigners

4. In a recession,
  a. unemployment increases, aggregate output decreases and people enjoy higher living standards.
  b. unemployment increases while aggregate output and aggregate income decrease.
  c. aggregate output and aggregate income decrease, eventually leading, in all cases, to an economic depression.
  d. aggregate output must fall for at least three consecutive quarters.

5. Government intervention in the economy
  a. is called fiscal policy if it involves a policy change that alters the interest rate or the level of money in circulation in the economy.
  b. is called fiscal policy if it involves changing government spending or taxing in order to offset the economic effects of short-run fluctuations in the macroeconomy.
  c. is particularly useful in helping economies in the long run.
  d. is only helpful during economic recessions.

6. Economic growth
  a. refers to increases in real GDP over the long run.
  b. refers to short-term fluctuations in real GDP.
  c. is best measured using the employment rate.
  d. is of little importance to economists.

7. A country's labour force
  a. is the sum of the country's unemployed and employed workers.
  b. includes discouraged workers.
  c. excludes underemployed workers.
  d. is all of the above.

8. Which of the following statements is true?
  a. An economy that is not in a recession will have an unemployment rate equal to zero.
  b. In an economic expansion, the unemployment rate decreases while aggregate output increases.
  c. An economy's output level and employment rate move in opposite directions.
  d. Both b and c are correct.

9. Stabilization policy refers to
   a. maintaining the same policy no matter whether the economy is in a recession or an expansion.
   b. adopting a policy to reduce policy fluctuations in order to follow a predictable policy pattern.
   c. maintaining a fixed level of money in circulation in the economy.
   d. none of the above.

10. Which of the following statements is true?
   a. Nominal measures do not adjust for price changes over time.
   b. Real measures do adjust for price changes over time.
   c. Nominal and real measures of the same variable may increase simultaneously but not necessarily at the same rate of change.
   d. All of the above are true.

11. Inflation occurs when
   a. the aggregate level of output increases.
   b. the unemployment rate decreases.
   c. the aggregate price level rises over time.
   d. consumers' purchasing power increases over time.

12. A country that trades goods and services with another country is known as
   a. an open economy.
   b. a real economy.
   c. a nominal economy.
   d. a closed economy.

13. A change in a country's exchange rate
   a. increases the country's trade balance.
   b. affects the country's aggregate price level.
   c. alters the country's trade balance.
   d. Both b and c are correct.
   e. Both a and b are correct.

14. Capital flows measure
   a. the international trade of goods and services.
   b. the international trade of financial assets.
   c. the amount of investment businesses make during a year.
   d. the performance of the stock market.

15. Which of the following statements is true?
   a. Microeconomics deals with exports and imports of all goods and services in Canada.
   a. Macroeconomics deals with exports and imports of all goods and services in Canada.
   b. Microeconomics deals short-run stabilization policies in Canada.
   c. Macroeconomics deals with lobster price in Canada.

16. Which of the following statements is true?
   a. Macroeconomics studies both stabilization policy and long-run growth policy.
   b. Macroeconomics studies only the short-run stabilization policy.
   c. Macroeconomics studies only the long-run growth policy.
   d. Microeconomics studies both stabilization policy and long-run growth policy.

17. The paradox of thrift is an example of
  a. fallacy of composition.
  b. stabilization policy.
  c. growth policy.
  d. secular long-run growth.

18. The actual unemployment rate in a recession can be higher if we count
  a. discouraged workers as unemployed.
  b. part-time workers as employed.
  c. discouraged workers as unemployed and part-time workers as employed.
  d. discouraged workers as employed and part-time workers as employed.

19. Sir John Maynard Keynes strongly supported
  a. long-run growth policies.
  b. monetary policy.
  c. fiscal policy.
  d. non-interventionist policy.

20. Consider an economy with 900 employed workers and 100 unemployed workers. Suppose 50 unemployed workers become discouraged workers. Which of the following statements is false?
  a. The unemployment rate should not change.
  b. The labour force would decrease to 950.
  c. The original unemployment rate was 10%.
  d. The unemployment rate has dropped to approximately 5.3%.

21. All of the following are examples of economic aggregates except
  a. current account balance
  b. aggregate output and price level
  c. deflation rate
  d. the price of an IBM share

22. Recession phase is characterized by all of the following except
  a. increasing unemployment rate
  b. increasing price.
  c. falling output.
  d. falling employment rate.

23. GDP deflator indicates
  a. inflation or deflation rate of domestically produced goods and services.
  a. inflation or deflation rate of imported goods and services.
  b. inflation or deflation rate of both domestically produced goods and services as well as imported goods and services.
  c. nominal value of GDP.

24. Economic growth is the result of all of the following except
  a. stabilization policy.
  b. growth of labour force.
  c. growth of capital.
  d. technological progress.

25. Capital flows can be seen
  a. as current account item in the balance of payment.
  b. as current account as well as a capital account item in the balance of payment.
  c. international capital flows due to the differential interest rates in the world.
  d. international output flows due to the differential interest rates in the world.

Problems and Exercises

1. For each of the following questions identify whether the question is more appropriate for the study of microeconomics or macroeconomics, and why.

   a. What will happen to nominal wages in our community if Corporation X, an employer of 1,000 people, decides to relocate its plant to a different state?

   b. What will happen to real GDP if the federal government continues to run record levels of government deficit?

   c. If the Fed increases the money supply, what will happen to the interest rate in our economy?

   d. Does our unemployment rate understate the level of unemployment because of its treatment of discouraged workers?

   e. What will the effect of recent tropical storms be on the price of bananas?

2. Suppose that people anticipate an economic recession and decide to increase their rate of saving so they are better prepared financially for the recession. Explain why this response might actually make the recession worse.

3. This chapter distinguishes between an economic expansion as part of the business cycle and long-run economic growth. Concisely explain the difference between these two terms.

4. In the beginning of 2003, suppose the population in Neverland was 2 million people and the level of real GDP, or aggregate output, was $40 million. During 2003 population increased by 2%, while real GDP increased by 5%. During this same period, the aggregate price level was constant. Furthermore, suppose these growth rates continued into 2004 and 2005.
Fill in the following table using the previous information. (Make all calculations to two places past the decimal.)

	Beginning of 2003	Beginning of 2004	Beginning of 2005	Beginning of 2006
Real GDP				
Population				
Real GDP/person				

5. In the beginning of 2003, suppose the population in Funland was 2 million people and the level of real GDP, or aggregate output, was $40 million. During 2003 population increased by 3%, while real GDP increased by 3%. During 2004 population increased by 4%, while real GDP increased by 3%. During 2005 population increased by 5%, while real GDP increased by 3%.
  a. Fill in the following table using the previous information. (Make all calculations to two places past the decimal.)

	Beginning of 2003	Beginning of 2004	Beginning of 2005	Beginning of 2006
Real GDP				
Population				
Real GDP/person				

  b. What do you know about this country's standard of living between the beginning of 2003 and the end of 2005? Explain your answer.

  c. In comparing your answers in problem (4) to your answers in problem (5), what major concept do these problems illustrate?

6. Suppose there are 12,000 people living in Macroland. Of these 12,000 people, 1,000 are either too old to work or too young to work. Of the remaining individuals, 5,000 are employed with full-time jobs; 3,000 are employed part time, but wish to work full time; and 1,000 are underemployed, but working full-time jobs; 1,000 are currently not working but are looking for work; and the remainder are discouraged workers.

a. What is the size of the labour force in Macroland?

b. What is the employment rate in Macroland?

c. What is the unemployment rate in Macroland?

d. What percentage of the total population are discouraged workers?

e. Suppose you are told that 100 people find jobs for every $10,000 increase in the level of output. If you wanted the unemployment rate to equal 8%, what would the change in output need to be? Assume no changes in the number of young and old in the population or in the number of discouraged workers.

f. Suppose the government department in Macroland is responsible for compiling unemployment statistics and redefines the employed as including only those with full-time jobs. How does this change the unemployment rate, given the initial information?

7. Consider the following items. Then fill in the blanks; write "1", if the item is a microeconomic variable and write "2" if it is a macroeconomic variable.

   a. Money supply in Canada. _____
   b. Exchange rate of Canadian dollar. _____
   c. Inflation and deflation rate. _____
   d. Unemployment rate in New Brunswick. _____
   e. Student enrolment in Canada. _____
   f. Student loan in Canada. _____
   g. Price of gasoline in Canada. _____
   h. Price of gold in Canada. _____
   i. Price of Tim Horton share in Canada. _____
   j. Price of Tim Horton Coffee in Canada. _____
   k. Average salary of university professors at McMaster University. _____

8. Suppose the labour force in the smallest province in Canada, PEI, is 60,000; 20% of this labour force is currently unemployed. Imagine the following scenarios occur simultaneously.
   i. 4,000 workers become discouraged and stop searching for jobs.
   ii. 2,000 workers retire.
   iii. 4,000 workers who had retired now filled 4,000 part-time positions.

Calculate the current unemployment rate and the total labour force after the previous events occur.

Answers to How Well Do You Understand the Chapter

1. aggregate, imports, capital flows, scarce, Microeconomics.

2. aggregates, unemployment, expansion, recession, cycle.

3. growth, standard of living

4. recession, paradox of thrift, recession

5. rationale, fluctuations, spending, interest rate, short-run

6. unemployment, labour force, discouraged workers, underemployment, percentage, zero, recession, decreases, decreases, GDP

7. stabilization policy, fiscal policy, monetary policy, interest rate

8. output, expansion, increase

9. Nominal, real, increase, decrease, GDP deflator, consumer price, stability, inflation rate

10. closed, open, mutually, exchange rate, trade, exports, imports, financial, capital flows

Answer to Multiple-Choice Questions

1. Macroeconomics studies the aggregate economy, not individual action; in studying the aggregate economy, macroeconomics seeks to explain the factors that determine a country's standard of living. In macroeconomics we are reminded that the aggregation of individual behavior often has a larger impact than just the sum of these individual behaviors. **Answer: C.**

2. In the aggregate economy, output and employment fluctuate in the short run. Macroeconomic theory analyzes the effect of fiscal and monetary policy on short-run economic fluctuations and provides a rationale for government intervention to lessen the economic impact of business cycles. **Answer: D.**

3. Although each of these variables is aggregated to some extent, the bicycle production for the year only aggregates in a market for a single product rather than aggregating over multiple markets. **Answer: C.**

4. A recession, by definition, occurs when aggregate output decreases and income decreases. As the economy produces a smaller level of output, employment of labour decreases since less labour is needed to produce the smaller level of output. Not all recessions turn into depressions, and there is no uniform agreement about the length of time aggregate output must decrease for the downturn in economic activity to be viewed as a recession. **Answer: B.**

5. Government intervention in the economy is called fiscal policy, if it involves a change in government spending and/or taxation implemented to reduce short-run business cycle fluctuation in the economy. Government intervention in the economy is called monetary policy, if it involves a change in the interest rate or a change in the amount of money in circulation in the economy implemented in order to reduce short-run business cycle fluctuation in the economy. **Answer: B.**

6. Economic growth is measured as an increase in the level of real GDP in the economy. This increase refers to an increase over the long run, rather than a short-run economic expansion. **Answer: A.**

7. The labour force is defined as the sum of the employed and unemployed workers in an economy where the unemployed workers excludes those not working and not actively seeking employment (discouraged workers) and where the number of employed workers is not adjusted to reflect the number of underemployed workers. **Answer: A.**

8. This question centers on the relationship between aggregate output and employment: as aggregate output increases, employment also increases and hence, unemployment decreases. An economy can reduce its level of unemployment but can not eliminate unemployment, since there will always be people newly entering the labour force and searching for their first jobs. **Answer: B.**

9. Stabilization policy refers to the use of government policy, fiscal or monetary, to reduce short-run economic fluctuations in the economy. **Answer: D.**

10. All of these statements are true, since nominal measures do not adjust for price level changes over time while real measures do adjust for price level changes. It is also possible for both nominal and real measures to increase at the same time, but for the rate of increase to vary. **Answer: D.**

11. Inflation is defined as the increase in the aggregate price level over time. **Answer: C.**

12. A country that engages in international trade is referred to as an open economy, while a country that does not trade is a closed economy. **Answer: A.**

13. Change in a country's exchange rate alters the prices of goods and services and hence, the aggregate price level; and such a change alters the relative attractiveness of the country's goods and services to other economies. Its trade balance may increase as it exports more goods and services, or decrease as it imports more goods and services. **Answer: D.**

14. Capital flows measure the buying and selling of financial assets to international trading partners. **Answer: B.**

15. Macroeconomics deals with economic aggregates of output, exports, imports, etc. Stabilization policy is a macroeconomic issue. Lobster price is a microeconomic variable. **Answer: B.**

16. The short-run stabilization and long-run growth are covered in macroeconomics. **Answer: A.**

17. According to the fallacy of composition, what is true for some is true for all. Paradox of thrift is an example of the fallacy of composition. **Answer: A.**

18. The unemployment rate goes up when unemployed people become discouraged and drop out of the job market. **Answer: A.**

19. Keynes emphasized fiscal policy intervention during the Great Depression of 30s. **Answer: C.**

20. The unemployment rate has decreased from 10% to 5.3%. **Answer: A.**

21. The price of IBM share is a microeconomic variable. **Answer: D.**

22. Recession is characterized by falling price. **Answer: B.**

23. The GDP deflator is an index of the prices of domestically produced goods. It does not take into account consumer prices of imported goods. **Answer: A.**

24. The stabilization policies are aimed at short-run economic fluctuations, not at long-run growth. **Answer: A.**

25. Capital flows is a capital account item in the balance of payment. It is affected by interest differentials. **Answer: C.**

Answers to Problems and Exercises

1. a. Microeconomics: this question is directed at understanding the local effect of this corporation's move instead of its total effect across the aggregate economy.
  b. Macroeconomics: this question focuses on the aggregate performance of the economy.
  c. Macroeconomics: this question considers the impact of monetary policy on the aggregate economy.
  d. Macroeconomics: this question addresses the accuracy of the economy-wide measure of the level of unemployment.
  e. Microeconomics: this question considers the price of a specific good rather than the overall price level in the economy.

2. Even though the individual's decision is a rational path to follow, the effect of many individuals making this decision is to reduce spending dramatically in the aggregate economy. As spending decreases, producers respond by decreasing their production and reducing their use of labour. This paradox of thrift has the effect of worsening the recessionary tendencies in the economy.

3. An economic expansion is a short-run increase in the level of aggregate output that may not be sustained indefinitely, while long-run economic growth reflects a sustainable increase in an economy's ability to produce more goods and services.

4.

	Beginning of 2003	Beginning of 2004	Beginning of 2005	Beginning of 2006
Real GDP	$40 million	$42 million	$44.1 million	$46.31 million
Population	2 million	2.04 million	2.08 million	2.12 million
Real GDP/person	$20	$20.59	$21.20	$21.84

5. a.

	Beginning of 2003	Beginning of 2004	Beginning of 2005	Beginning of 2006
Real GDP	$40 million	$40.12 million	$41.32 million	$42.56 million
Population	2 million	2.06 million	2.14 million	2.24 million
Real GDP/person	$20	$19.48	$19.31	$19

  b. The standard of living in Funland between the beginning of 2003 and the end of 2005 is decreasing, since the rate of population growth exceeds the rate of real GDP growth.
  c. Problems (4) and (5) illustrate the importance of the growth rates of population and real GDP in determining the standard of living. In problem (4), the standard of living increases since real GDP grows as a faster rate than the rate of population increase, while in problem (5), the standard of living decreases since the population growth rate is greater than the rate of real GDP growth.

6. a. The labour force is defined as the number of employed workers plus the number of unemployed workers. The number of employed workers equals the sum of full-time workers, part-time workers, and underemployed workers, or, in this example, 9,000 workers. The number of unemployed workers is equal to the 1,000 workers who are currently not working, but who are actively looking for work. Thus, the labor force equals 10,000 workers.

b. Employment Rate = [Employed/(Labour Force)] × 100 = (9,000/10,000) × 100 = 90%
c. Unemployment Rate = [Unemployed/(Labour Force)] × 100 = (1,000/10,000) × 100 = 10%
d. Percentage of Discouraged Workers in Population = [(Discouraged Workers)/Population] × 100 = (1,000/12,000) × 100 = 8.33%
e. The current unemployment rate is 10%. To reduce the unemployment rate to 8% requires that 200 of the currently unemployed workers find jobs. If output increases by $10,000 for every 100 people who find jobs, then output must increase by $20,000 for 200 people to find employment.
f. Using the new definition of employment, the number of employed now equals 6,000, and the unemployed would increase by 3,000 for a total of 4,000 unemployed. This change in definition results in a much higher unemployment rate (30%) and a much lower employment rate (60%). The definitions underlying calculations do matter.

7. a. Money supply in Canada: 2
 b. Exchange rate of Canadian dollar: 2
 c. Inflation and deflation rate in Canada: 2
 d. Unemployment rate in New Brunswick: 2
 e. Student enrolment in Canada: 2
 f. Student loan in Canada: 2
 g. Price of gasoline in Canada: 1
 h. Price of gold in Canada: 1
 i. Price of Tim Horton share in Canada: 1
 j. Price of Tim Horton Coffee in Canada:1
 k. Average salary of university professors at McMaster University: 1

8. Labour force = 60,000 – 4,000 – 2,000 + 4,000 = 58,000

Unemployment rate = 8,000/58,000 or 13.79%.

chapter 7

Tracking the Macroeconomy

This chapter focuses on the idea of economic aggregation and what aggregation means when measuring the level of aggregate production, the level of aggregate employment, and the level of aggregate prices. In this chapter, a more complicated circular-flow diagram of the economy is presented. This diagram provides an illustration of different ways to calculate aggregate production or gross domestic product (GDP). The chapter also discusses the distinction between nominal and real GDP; how to calculate the unemployment rate; the relationship between economic growth and the unemployment rate; and the calculation of price indexes as measures of the aggregate price level.

How Well Do You Understand the Chapter?

Fill in the blanks using the terms below or circle the correct answer to complete the following statements. Terms may be used more than once. If you find yourself having difficulties, please refer back to the appropriate section in the text.

circular-flow diagram	factors of production	government spending	market price money	sum total factor income
consumer price index	factors of production	growth imports	national accounts	total market value
consumption	final	imports	negative	transfer payments
data	financial	income	nominal GDP	underestimate
deflator	financial	index	overestimate	unemployment
disposable income	financial markets	inflation rate	price	unemployment rate
domestic economy	firms	intermediate	price level	value added
double counting	GDP per capita	investment	producer price index	variables
expenditure	goods and services	labour	quantities	
exports	government	labour market conditions	Real GDP	
factor income		living		

1. Good macroeconomic policy depends on good measurement of key economic
_____ that provide information about how the aggregate economy is
performing. These key macroeconomic variables include the level of aggregate
income and aggregate output, the level of employment and unemployment, and the
level and rate of change of _____ in the economy.

The national income and expenditure accounts, or _____, provide a
set of statistical _____ that indicate the country's state of economic
performance.

2. A(n) _____, focusing on money flows, illustrates the key concepts underlying the national accounts. Note that the flow of _____ into each market or sector must be equal to the flow of money out of each market or sector. The circular-flow diagram includes the output market, the factor market, and the _____ market. The sectors represented in the more complicated circular-flow diagram in this chapter include households, _____, the government, and the rest of the world. The circular-flow diagram provides a simplified illustration of national income and national expenditure. Here's a brief summary of each sector's activity.

3. Households receive _____ from selling their factors of production to firms. Households receive income from selling their _____. They also receive dividends and interest income from their indirect ownership of physical capital used by firms; and rental income from selling the use of their land. Households gain income they earn from selling _____ and then use this income to purchase _____, to pay their taxes, and to provide private savings to the _____. Household income net of taxes and government transfers is called _____.

4. The government collects tax revenue and then returns part of this money as _____. The sum of tax revenue net of transfer payments plus funds the government borrows from the financial markets is then used by the government to purchase and services.

5. Firms hire _____ to produce goods and services, but they also expend funds to buy goods and services. This investment spending on productive physical capital is included in the national accounts as part of total spending on goods and services. Investment spending also includes expenditure on inventories, since these inventories will contribute to greater future sales of a firm. Construction of new homes is also included in _____, since a new home produces a future stream of housing services for the people who live in the house.

6. The rest of the world participates in the _____ by purchasing goods and services produced in that economy (the domestic economy's _____), by selling goods and services to the domestic economy (the domestic economy's _____), and by making transactions in the domestic economy's financial markets.

7. The _____ markets receive funds from households, as well as from the rest of the world. These funds provide the basis for loans to the government, firms, and the rest of the world.

8. The GDP (from the expenditure side) is the sum of consumer spending on goods and services, investment spending, _____ spending, and the difference between spending on exports and imports. GDP is the _____ of all _____ goods and services produced in an economy during a given period of business cycle. The _____ goods and services are those items that are used as inputs for the production of final goods and services. In calculating GDP, care must be taken to avoid _____.

9. There are four different ways to calculate GDP. One method is to add up the total value of final goods and services produced in an economy during a given period. An alternative method is to add up total _____ on domestically produced final goods and services in the economy. A third method of computing GDP is to sum the total value of _____ paid by firms in the economy to households. A fourth method is to add up the _____ by firms at each stage of production. All four methods will yield identical values of GDP for an economy during a given time period.

10. We can write an equation for an economy's GDP: GDP = $C + I + G + X - IM$, where C is _____ spending, I is _____ spending, G is _____ spending, X is spending on domestically produced goods and services by foreigners (the domestic economy's exports), and IM is spending on _____, or spending on goods and services produced by foreign economies. We refer net export as $X - IM$.

11. Gross National Product, or GNP, is the _____ earned by citizens of a country irrespective of where they reside. GDP, in contrast, is the total factor of income earned in a country without regard to the citizenship of the owners of those _____.

12. GDP can change over time because the economy is producing more or because the _____ of the goods and services it produces have increased. _____ calculates the value of aggregate production during a given time period, using prices from some given base year. In effect, it uses constant prices. In contrast, _____ is the calculation of GDP using current prices. Real GDP measures allow one to compare the _____ in aggregate output in an economy over time.

13. In comparing GDP across countries, we can eliminate differences in population size by dividing each country's GDP by its population to get _____, which is the average GDP per person. Real GDP per capita is one of many important determinants of human welfare: it measures what a country can do, but it does not address how that country uses that output to affect the standard of _____.

14. The labour force is the sum of the number of employed workers and the number of unemployed workers. The unemployed category includes those currently not working, but actively seeking employment. The unemployed category excludes discouraged workers. The _____ is the percent of the labour force that is unemployed. It is an indicator of _____ and not a literal measure of the number of people unable to find jobs. The actual unemployment rate may _____ true unemployment, because it does not correct for the fact that it takes time for someone looking for work to find a job. The actual unemployment rate may _____ true unemployment, because it excludes discouraged workers.

15. In general, there is a(n) _____ relationship between growth in the economy and the rate of unemployment. That is, falling real GDP is associated with a rising _____ rate.

16. Economists measure changes in the aggregate _____ by tracking changes in the cost of buying a given market basket. A price _____ measures the cost of purchasing a given market basket in a given year, where that cost is normalized so it is equal to 100 in the base year. To calculate the cost of the market basket, multiply the _____ of each good in the market basket times its price and then _____ these products. Then use this information to calculate a price _____ by dividing the cost of the market basket in the base year and then multiplying this ration by 100. An example of price index is the _____. The _____ is the percentage change per year in a price index. The _____, also known as the wholesale price index, measures the cost of a basket of goods typically purchased by producers. The GDP _____ is calculated as the ratio of normal GDP for that year to real GDP for that year (let's call it year *n*) times 100.

Learning Tips

TIP #1: It is important that you understand thoroughly the concepts underlying the more complicated circular-flow diagram presented in this chapter.

The circular-flow diagram tracks the flows of money in and out of different markets and sectors in the economy. The flows into a market or sector must equal the flows out of that market or sector. You will want to review this material and practice working some numerical examples.

TIP #2: A primary focus of this chapter is the topic of economic aggregation.

In order to discuss macroeconomic issues, we need to develop measures that will allow us to describe the macroeconomy. Economic aggregation addresses this issue. In this chapter, you need to fully understand the process of economic aggregation and how it relates to the measurement of economic production, employment, and the overall price level.

TIP #3: The national income accounts provide measures about the aggregate or overall economy; understanding the concept of economic aggregation is essential in the study of macroeconomics.

The national income accounts are data collected and provided by the government about aggregate economic performance. The national income accounts break down the components of total spending so we can study the behavior of households, firms, the government, and the foreign sector. The national income accounts also break down national income into wages, interest, rent, and other factor payments so we can analyze factor income.

TIP #4: There are multiple methods for calculating GDP, but each method yields the same measure of GDP for a given time period.

GDP calculation for an economy can be done using four methods: 1) multiply the price of final goods and services produced in an economy during a given time period by the quantities produced in that time period and then sum together these products; 2) add up the total expenditures in the domestic economy on final goods and services during a given time period by the sectors of the economy, or in other words, by households, government, firms, and the rest of the world; 3) add up the value added of production by firms in the domestic economy over the given time period; or 4) sum the value of factor payments in the domestic economy over the given time period. Each method yields the same value of GDP for the given time period. It is important for you to thoroughly understand the concepts underlying each of these approaches.

TIP #5: The distinction between real and nominal variables is important in macroeconomics.

We use prices to measure the relative value of goods and services, but because prices do not stay constant over time in an economy it is important to measure economic variables over time using methods that correct for these price changes. Real economic variables are variables calculated using prices from a designated base year. In contrast, nominal economic variables are calculated with current prices and therefore are measures that do not correct for price level fluctuations. It is important to realize that if there is inflation the national income and product accounts may indicate nominal GDP is increasing, even though real GDP may be decreasing, increasing, or staying constant.

TIP #6: To compare GDP across countries, we need real GDP per capita data.

For example, Canada's real GDP per capita for a given year is calculated by dividing Canada's real GDP by Canada's population.

TIP #7: There is a negative relationship between unemployment and real GDP.

We calculate the unemployment rate by dividing number of workers unemployed by the labour force (which is composed of the number of people employed plus the number of people unemployed). The actual unemployment rate may suffer from over-estimation or under-estimation.

Multiple-Choice Questions

1. Which of the following statements is true?
    a. In the circular-flow diagram of the economy, the flow of money into each market or sector is not necessarily equal to the flow of money coming out of each market or sector.
    b. GDP in Canada includes income earned by Canadian citizens living in foreign countries during a given time period.
    c. GNP in Canada measures the value of final goods and services produced within Canadian borders during a given time period.
    d. None of the above statements is true.

2. Households receive income from
    a. wages they earn from selling their labour.
    b. their indirect ownership of the physical capital used by firms.
    c. interest earned from bonds, dividends earned from stock ownership, and rent earned when they sell the use of their land to firms.
    d. All of the above are ways households earn income.

3. After the payment of taxes to the government, household income is referred to as
    a. transfer income.
    b. gross income.
    c. net income.
    d. disposable income.

4. Households, in the circular-flow diagram of the economy, can use their income to
    a. pay taxes, purchase goods and services, and engage in private saving.
    b. pay taxes and purchase goods and services only.
    c. purchase factors of production, pay taxes, or purchase goods and services.
    d. purchase factors of production, pay taxes, or engage in private saving.

5. Government raises funds through
    a. taxation and by borrowing in financial markets.
    b. taxation, purchases of goods and services, and by borrowing in financial markets.
    c. taxation, purchases of goods and services, and revenues received for intermediate goods produced by the government.
    d. taxation and transfer payments.

6. Suppose Country A sells $100 million worth of goods and services to Country B. Country B sells $50 million worth of goods and services to Country A. These are the only two countries in Macro World. Then,

a. net exports in Country B equal – $50 million.

b. net exports in Country A equal $150 million.

c. net exports in Country A equal $150 million.

d. net exports in Country B equal $50 million.

$X - IM$

$X = 50$

7. Investment spending includes

a. expenditures on new residential housing.

b. expenditures on new inventories by businesses.

c. expenditures by businesses on productive physical capital.

d. All of the above are included in investment spending.

Use the information and the following table to answer the next three questions. The table represents data about an economy's performance during a year. Suppose in the economy represented in the table there are only three firms: Canadian Racquet Co., which produces tennis racquets; Canadian Metal Co., which produces the various metals that go into racquet production; and Canadian Ore Co., which mines the ores needed for the manufacture of the metal. This economy produces 100 racquets that sell for $50 each.

	Canadian Racquet Co.	Canadian Metal Co.	Canadian Ore Co.	Total factor income
Value of sales	$5,000	$3,000	$500	
Intermediate goods	A	B		
Wages	3,000	1,000	100	C
Interest payments	100	50	20	D
Rent	500	100	50	E
Profit	200	750	130	F
Total expenditures by firm	5,000	3,000	500	
Value added per firm	G	H	I	

8. GDP for this hypothetical economy is equal to

a. $5,000 or the value of sales for Canadian Racquet Co.

b. $8,500 or the sum of the value added for the three firms.

c. $3,500 or the value of the intermediate goods used by the Canadian Racquet Co.

d. $980 or the sum of the profits for the three firms.

9. GDP can be measured using different methods. If you were using the factor payments' approach, which entries would you combine to get a measure of GDP?

a. G, H and I

b. A and B

c. A, B, C, and D

d. C, D, E, and F

10. GDP can be measured using the value added method. Using this method, which of the following values are correct for the missing entries in the table?

a. A = $3,000, B = $3,000, G = $2,000, H = $0, I = $500

b. A = $3,000, B = $500, G = $2,000, H = $2,500, I = $500

c. A = $3,000, B = $3,000, G = $0, H = $4,500, I = $500

d. A = $3,000, B = $500, G = $0, H = $4,500, I = $500

11. Double counting is
   a. the inclusion of the value of intermediate goods and services more than once when calculating GDP.
   b. the failure to include the value of intermediate goods in the final calculation of an economy's GDP.
   c. a process that artificially lowers the value of GDP.
   d. avoided if we do not use the value added method in calculating GDP.

Use the information in the following table to answer the next three questions.

	Price in 2005	Price in 2006
Oranges	$.50	$.40
Apples	.25	.40
Bananas	.40	.50

Suppose 2005 is the base year and the market basket for purposes of constructing a price index consists of 200 oranges, 100 apples, and 100 bananas.

12. What is the value of the price index in 2005?
   a. 1.15
   b. 100
   c. 165
   d. 190

13. What is the value of the price index in 2006, using 2005 as the base year?
   a. .97
   b. 1
   c. 100
   d. 103

14. What is the rate of inflation between 2005 and 2006 in this economy?
   a. 0%
   b. 3%
   c. 103%
   d. 67%, since two of the three prices increased between 2005 and 2006

15. In Macroland the GDP deflator for 2006 is 105, with 2005 the base year. Real GDP in 2006 equals $210 billion; therefore, nominal GDP in 2006 equals _____ while nominal GDP in 2005 equals _____.
   a. $220.5 billion; $200 billion
   b. $220.5 billion; $210 billion
   c. $200 billion; $210 billion
   d. $200 billion; $220.5 billion

Use the following information to answer the next two questions.

Suppose the adult population of Macronesia is 100,000 people. Of these 100,000 people, 20,000 are not in the labour force. Of the remaining 80,000 people, 16,000 have given up searching for a job and are not actively seeking work; 4,000 are unemployed and actively seeking work; 14,000 work part time; and the remainder are fully employed.

16. What is the unemployment rate in Macronesia?
   a. 5%
   b. 6.25%
   c. 8.5%
   d. 10%

17. What would happen to Macronesia's unemployment rate, relative to your answer in the last question, if discouraged workers were counted as unemployed workers?
   a. The unemployment rate would be unchanged.
   b. The unemployment rate would decrease.
   c. The unemployment rate would increase.
   d. The unemployment rate could increase, decrease, or remain the same.

18. Which of the following statements is true?
   a. In the circular-flow diagram, the households are considered as investors, because they use their savings to buy shares from the stock markets.
   b. In the circular-flow diagram, the households are considered as investors and the firms are considered as savers.
   c. In the circular-flow diagram, the households are considered as savers and the firms are considered as investors.
   d. In the circular-flow diagram, the governments are considered as investors and the households are considered as savers.

19. Which of the following statements is false?
   a. Canada's GNP is greater than Canada's GDP, if the total factor income earned by Canadians living abroad is greater than the total factor income earned by foreigners while residing in Canada.
   b. Canada's GNP is greater than Canada's GDP, if the total factor income earned by Canadians living abroad is less than the total factor income earned by foreigners while residing in Canada.
   c. Canada's GNP is equal to Canada's GDP, if the total factor income earned by Canadians living abroad is equal to the total factor income earned by foreigners while residing in Canada.
   d. If Canadians earned an income in Brazil, it should be a part of Brazil's GDP.

20. In a given year, the nominal GDP of country A has doubled, while the nominal GDP of country B has tripled. Both countries experienced 1% growth in population. We can definitely conclude:
   a. The growth rate of per capita real GDP of country A is higher than that of country B.
   b. The growth rate of per capita real GDP of country A is lower than that of country B.
   c. Assume that the inflation rates in both countries are identical. The growth rate of per capita real GDP of country A is higher than that of country B.
   d. Assume that the inflation rate of country A is 10% and inflation rate of country B is 20%. The growth rate of per capita real GDP of country A is lower than that of country B.

Answer Questions 21–22 on the basis of the following table:

All dollar figures are in billion dollars.

Year	Nominal GDP	Real GDP	
2001	$400	$400	=100
2002	$420	$400	=105
2003	$450	$409	=110
2004	$500	$476	=105

$$\frac{nominal\ GDP}{real\ GDP} \times 100 =$$

21. Compute the value of the GDP deflator for each year listed then select from the following statements the one that is false.
    a. The base year is 2001.
    b. The GDP deflator in the year 2002 is 105.
    c. The GDP deflator in the year 2003 is 110.
    d. The GDP deflator in the year 2004 is 95.

22. Compute the value of the GDP deflator for each year listed then select from the following statements the one that is false.
    a. The real GDP increased between 2001 and 2002.
    b. The real GDP decreased between 2002 and 2003.
    c. The overall price level of domestic goods decreased between 2003 and 2004.
    d. The increase in nominal GDP always implies inflationary trends.

23. If GDP is $400 billion, consumption is $250 billion, government expenditure $100 billion, and gross business investment is $125 billion, the net export is
    a. impossible to solve.
    b. – $75 billion. $400 = 250 + 100 + 125$
    c. + $75 billion.
    d. zero.

Use the table pertaining to National Income accounts of a given economy and answer Questions 24–27. All figures in billion dollars.

Disposable Income:	$320
Personal saving:	65
Government expenditures:	120
Gross business investment:	85
Depreciation:	30
Inventory investment:	0
Export:	60
Import:	70
Net income from foreign sources:	15
Indirect taxes minus subsidies:	18

24. Personal consumption is $G = 120$
    a. $320 billion. $I = 85$
    b. $255 billion. $C = ?$
    c. $237 billion. $X = 60$
    d. impossible to calculate from the accompanying table. $Im = 70$

25. Personal Income tax is
    a. $18 billion.
    b. $38 billion.
    c. $255 billion.
    d. impossible to calculate from the accompanying table.

26. If income tax is $60 billion, personal consumption is $255 billion, and personal saving is $65 billion, then the personal income should be
    a. $380 billion.
    b. $350 billion.
    c. $320 billion.
    d. impossible to calculate from the accompanying table.

27. Which of the following statements is false?
    a. The GDP is $450 billion.
    b. The GNP is $465 billion and the national income is $417 billion.
    c. The GNP is $440 billion and the national income is $392 billion.
    d. The net investment is $55 billion dollars.

28. Which of the following statements is true?

   a. Personal transfers from Federal Government are included in the GDP of Canada.

   ✗b. Intermediate goods are taken into account in the GDP calculation in Canada.

   c. Services provided by nannies are included in the GDP calculations, but parental care of children are excluded in the GDP calculations.

   d. Canada's GDP figures can be used as good indexes of income-distribution in Canada.

29. If the economy's GDP = $500 billion, C = $350 billion, I = $70 billion, G = $120 billion, and exports equal $50 billion, then the economy's imports should

   a. be $90 billion dollars. $500 = 350 + 70 + 120 + (50 - Im)$

   b. be $50 billion dollars.

   c. lead to trade surplus.

   d. lead to a trade deficit of $20 billion.

30. Which of the following statements is true?

   a. The consumer price index takes into account price-changes of both domestic and foreign goods consumed by a typical consumer.

   b. The consumer price index takes into account price-changes of only domestic goods consumed by a typical consumer.

   c. The consumer price index takes into account price-changes of only foreign goods consumed by a typical consumer.

   d. The GDP deflator takes into account price-changes of both domestic and foreign goods consumed by a typical consumer.

Problems and Exercises

1. You are given the following information about Macronesia. During 2005, the government of Macronesia spent $200 million on goods and services as well as $20 million on transfer payments, while collecting $150 million in taxes. During 2005 households paid $150 million in taxes, purchased goods and services worth $400 million, and received $800 million in the form of wages, dividends, interest, and rent. Firms in 2005 had $100 million of investment spending, and they borrowed or had stock issues of $170 million from the financial markets. In 2005 exports to this economy equaled $150 million while imports to this economy equaled $50 million. In the financial markets, there was foreign borrowing of $50 million and foreign lending of $20 million.

   a. Sketch a circular-flow diagram of Macronesia's economy showing the quantitative flows.

   b. What is GDP in 2005 in Macronesia?

   c. What is the value of disposable income in Macronesia in 2005?

d. What is the value of household saving in Macronesia in 2005?

e. Is the government running a balanced budget during 2005? Explain your answer.

f. Compute the flows of money into the financial markets and the flows of money out of the financial markets. Are they equal?

g. Compute the flows of money into the market for goods and services and the flows of money out of the market for goods and services. Are they equal?

h. Compute the flows of money into the factor markets and the flows of money out of the factor markets. Are they equal?

2. For the following list decide how the item affects the calculation of GDP for Macro States in 2005.
   a. A new house is constructed in Macro States during 2005.

   b. Bruce sells his house in Macro States without the help of a realtor in January 2005.

   c. The government purchases new textbooks for the schools of Macro States during 2005.

   d. Macro States sells 100,000 pounds of beef to Neverlandia during 2005.

e. Judy tutors Ellen's children in exchange for Ellen driving the children's carpool three days a week throughout 2005.

f. A candlemaker produces 500 candles during 2005 but only sells 200 candles during 2005; the other 300 candles are added to the candlemaker's inventories.

3. Suppose you are told that Finlandia produces three goods: tennis shoes, basketballs, and lawn mowers. The following table provides information about the prices and output for these three goods for the years 2004, 2005, and 2006.

Year	Price of tennis shoes	Quantities of tennis shoes	Price of basketballs	Quantities of basketballs	Price of lawn mowers	Quantities of lawn mowers
2004	$50	100	$10	200	$100	10
2005	52	108	10	205	100	12
2006	54	115	10	212	110	12

a. Using the previous information, fill in the following table.

Year	Nominal GDP
2004	
2005	
2006	

b. What was the percentage change in nominal GDP from 2004 to 2005?

c. What was the percentage change in nominal GDP from 2005 to 2006?

d. Using 2004 as the base year, fill in the following table.

Year	Real GDP
2004	
2005	
2006	

e. What was the percentage change in real GDP from 2004 to 2005?

f. What was the percentage change in real GDP from 2005 to 2006?

g. Using 2004 as the base year, fill in the following table.

Year	GDP deflator
2004	
2005	
2006	

4. In Macro Space, the price index is based upon a market basket consisting of 10 apples, 2 pizzas, and 5 ice cream cones. You are given prices for these three items for 2004, 2005, and 2006 in the following table.

Year	Price of apples	Price of pizzas	Price of ice cream cones
2004	$.50	$4.00	$1.00
2005	.52	3.85	1.10
2006	.49	3.90	1.30

a. Fill in the following table using year 2004 as your base year.

Year	Cost of market basket	Price index value
2004		
2005		
2006		

b. Using the information you computed in part (a), what was the rate of inflation between 2004 and 2005?

c. Using the information you computed in part (a), what was the rate of inflation between 2005 and 2006?

d. Fill in the following table using year 2005 as your base year.

Year	Cost of market basket	Price index value
2004		
2005		
2006		

e. Using the information you computed in part (d), what was the rate of inflation between 2004 and 2005?

f. Using the information you computed in part (d), what was the rate of inflation between 2005 and 2006?

g. Compare your answers in parts (b) and (c) to your answers in parts (e) and (f).

5. Suppose that there are 10,000 adults in Finlandia and that 5,000 of these adults are employed, 2,000 are unemployed, 500 are discouraged workers, and the rest are not currently working or seeking employment.
  a. What is the labor force equal to in Finlandia?

  b. What is the unemployment rate in Finlandia?

  c. What would the unemployment rate equal in Finlandia if discouraged workers were counted as unemployed workers?

  d. Currently Statistics Canada does not count discouraged workers as unemployed workers. How does this decision affect the calculated value of the unemployment rate?

  e. Suppose that for every $10,000 increase in GDP in Finlandia, unemployment decreases by 100 people. If GDP increases by $20,000, what will Finlandia's unemployment rate equal? Assume there is no change in the number of discouraged workers and that discouraged workers are not counted as unemployed workers.

  f. What is the relationship between GDP and unemployment?

6. State whether each of the following statements is true or false and explain why it is true or false.

  a. The GDP reflects the economic wellbeing of a nation.

  b. The actual unemployment rate may suffer from a downward bias as well as an upward bias.

7. Use the following table pertaining to National Income accounts of a given economy and answer the following questions. All figures in billion dollars.

Disposable Income:	$400
Personal saving:	90
Personal income tax:	75
Government expenditures:	150
Government transfers to individuals:	45
Gross business investment:	95
Depreciation:	30
Inventory investment:	0
Export:	60
Import:	40
Net income from foreign sources:	−15
Indirect taxes minus subsidies:	18

  a. Find net investment.

  b. Find consumption and personal income.

  c. Find GDP.

  d. Find GNP and national income.

8. Answer the following questions on the basis of the following table:

All dollar figures are in billion dollars.

Year	Nominal GDP	Price Index	Real GDP
2001	$400	100	
2002	$420		$400
2003	$450	120	
2004	$500	125	
2005		140	$420

a. Fill in the blanks in the accompanying table.

b. Which year experienced the highest percentage increase in nominal GDP?

c. Which year experienced the highest percentage increase in real GDP?

d. Which year experienced the highest percentage increase in price index?

Answers to How Well Do You Understand the Chapter

1. variables, price, national accounts, data

2. circular-flow diagram, money, financial, firms

3. income, labour, factors of production, goods and services, financial markets, disposable income

4. transfer payments

5. factors of production, investment

6. domestic economy, exports, imports

7. financial

8. government spending, total market value, final, intermediate, double counting

9. expenditure, factor income, value added

10. consumption, investment, government, imports

11. total factor income, factors of production

12. market price, Real GDP, nominal GDP, growth

13. GDP per capita, living

14. unemployment rate, labour market conditions, overestimate, underestimate

15. negative, unemployment

16. price level, index, quantities, sum, index, consumer price index, inflation rate, producer price index, deflator

Answers to Multiple-Choice Questions

1. An underlying principle of the circular-flow diagram is that the flow of money into a market or sector must equal the flow of money out of that market or sector. GDP measures the value of final production in an economy during a given time period, while GNP measures the value of final production in a country by its citizens no matter where they are located. **Answer: D.**

2. All three answers describe different ways households can earn income through their selling of factors of production—land, labour, and capital—to businesses. **Answer: D.**

3. By definition, household income less taxes is referred to as disposable income since this is the income that households are left to "dispose of" once they have paid their tax obligations. Households use this disposable income to make purchases of goods and services and for private saving. **Answer: D.**

4. Households use their income to pay taxes, to purchase goods and services, and to accumulate private saving. **Answer: A.**

5. The sources of funding for the government are tax revenue and the funds the government borrows in the financial markets. Transfer payments are not a source of revenue for the government, since they represent a redistribution of purchasing power from one individual to another individual in the economy. The government purchases goods and services but does not actually manufacture intermediate or final goods. **Answer: A.**

6. Net exports are defined as exports minus imports. Country A's net exports equal ($100 million – $50 million) or $50 million. Country B's net exports equal ($50 million – $100 million) or –$50 million. **Answer: A.**

7. Investment spending, by definition, is the sum of expenditure on productive physical capital, inventories, and new residential housing. **Answer: D.**

8. Since GDP is equal to the value of all final goods and services produced in an economy during a given time period, GDP for this economy can be found by multiplying the number of racquets produced during the given time period times their price. This yields $5,000. Alternatively, one could add up the total payments to factors of production: wages, interest payments, rent, and profit sum to $5,000. **Answer: A.**

9. To get the value of GDP using the factor payments approach, you would need to add up the sum of factor payments: this would be the sum of wages, interest payments, rent, and profit, or cells *C, D, E,* and *F.* **Answer D.**

10. The cost of intermediate goods in entry *A* is equal to the value of metal sales from Canadian Metal Co., or $3,000. The cost of intermediate goods in entry *B* is equal to the value of ore sales from Canadian Ore Co., or $500. The value added by Canadian Racquet Co., or entry *G,* is equal to the value of sales by this company minus the value of intermediate goods used by this company ($5,000 – $3,000 or $2,000). The value added by Canadian Metal Co., or entry *H,* is equal to the value of sales by this company minus the value of intermediate goods used by this company ($3,000 – $500 or $2,500); the value added by Canadian Ore Co., or entry *I,* is equal to the value of sales by this company minus the value of intermediate goods used by this company ($500 – $0 or $500). **Answer B.**

11. Double counting is when you count the production of an item more than once when calculating the value of GDP. This can arise because the good is used as an intermediate good in the production of a final good. For this reason, intermediate goods are not counted as part of GDP because this would result in an overstatement of the level of production that has occurred in an economy. **Answer: A.**

12. The value of a price index in the base year is always equal to 100. To calculate a price index in general, you need to calculate the ratio of the cost of the market basket in the current year to the cost of the market basket in the base year and then multiply this ratio by 100. In this question, the ratio is equal to 1 since the cost of the two market baskets is the same and thus, the price index equals 100. **Answer: B.**

13. Calculate the value of the market basket in the base year: (200 oranges) ($.5/orange) + (100 apples)($.25/apple) + (100 bananas)($.4/banana) = 165. Calculate the value of the market basket in 2006: (200 oranges)($.4/orange) + (100 apples)($.25/apple) + (100 bananas)($.5/banana) = 170. Then put these two values into the following formula:

Price Index = [(Cost of Market Basket in Current Year)/(Cost of Market Basket in Base Year)] × 100

Price Index = [(170)/(165)] × 100 = 103

Note that the market basket stays fixed when calculating a price index. **Answer: D.**

14. To calculate the inflation rate between two time periods, you need the price index for each time period. Then, use the following formula:

Inflation Rate = [(Price Index in Period 2 – Price Index in Period 1)/(Price Index in Period 1)] × 100

In this case,

Inflation Rate = [(103 – 100)/100] × 100 = 3%

Answer: B.

15. To answer this question, it is helpful to first organize the information you are given in a table.

Year	Price Index	Nominal GDP	Real GDP
2005	100		
2006	105		$210 billion

We know that in the base year nominal GDP equals real GDP, but we still need to calculate this value. We can calculate this value using the formula:

Price Index in 2006 = [(Real GDP in 2006)/(Real GDP in base Year)] × 100

Or, in this case

105 = [($210 billion)/(Real GDP in base year)] × 100

or

Real GDP in base year = $200 billion

To calculate Nominal GDP in 2006, we use the formula for the GDP deflator:

Price Index in 2006 = [(Nominal GDP in 2006)/(Real GDP in 2006)] × 100

Rearranging the formula we have

Real GDP in 2006 = [(Nominal GDP in 2006)/(Price Index in 2006)] × 100

or

$210 billion = [(Nominal GDP in 2006)/105] × 100

or

Nominal GDP in 2006 = $220.5 billion

Our completed table is

Year	Price Index	Nominal GDP	Real GDP
2005	100	$200 billion	$200 billion
2006	105	$220.5 billion	$210 billion

Answer: A.

16. Calculate the unemployment rate using this formula:

Unemployment rate = [(Number of Unemployed)/(Labour Force)] × 100

where the labour force is equal to the number of employed workers plus the number of unemployed workers. In this case, the unemployment rate = [(4,000)/(64,000)] × 100 or 6.25%. Note the labour force does not include discouraged workers (16,000) or the 20,000 people who are not currently in the labour force.
Answer: B.

17. The unemployment rate now equals $[(20,000)/(80,000)] \times 100$ or 25%. The unemployment rate increases when discouraged workers are counted as unemployed workers. **Answer: C.**

18. Households are savers and business firms are investors. **Answer: C.**

19. Canada's GNP should be less than Canada's GDP, if the total factor income earned by Canadians living abroad is less than the total factor income earned by foreigners while residing in Canada. **Answer: B.**

20. To compare real GDP per capita, we need inflation-adjusted per capita real GDP data. Since nominal GDP tripled in country B, while inflation rate is 20%, real GDP increased more in country B than that of country A, which experienced 10% inflation rate along with doubling of her nominal GDP. **Answer: D.**

21. GDP deflator = (Nominal GDP) $\times$ 100/Real GDP.

GDP deflator for 2002 = ($420/$400)100 = 105.

GDP deflator for 2003 = ($450/$409)100 = 110.02.

GDP deflator for 2004 = ($500/$476)100 = 105.04

Answer: D.

22. Between 2001 and 2002, real GDP remained constant. Between 2002 and 2003, real GDP increased. Since the GDP deflator of 2004 is 105.04, which is less than the GDP deflator of 2003, we can conclude that over-all price level of domestic goods is lower than that in 2003. Therefore, the option c is true. The option d is false, because the increase in nominal GDP can be caused by increases in output along with zero or negative inflation. **Answer: C.**

23. Since GDP = C + I + G + net export and since GDP = $250 billion and

(C + I + G) = $475, net export must be –$75 billion. **Answer: B.**

24. Disposable income equals personal consumption + personal saving and since disposable income is $320 billion and personal savings is $65 billion, the personal consumption can be calculated as $255 billion. **Answer: B.**

25. We know that disposable income equals personal income minus personal income tax. The table does provide data on disposable income, but it does not provide any data on personal income; therefore, we cannot calculate personal income tax. **Answer: D.**

26. Since personal income = personal consumption + personal saving + personal tax, we can calculate personal income as $380 billion = $255 billion + $65 billion + $60 billion. **Answer: A.**

27. GDP = $255 billion + $85 billion + $120 billion + $60 billion − $70 billion = $450. GNP = $450 billion + $15 billion = $465 billion. National income = $465 billion minus depreciation ($30 billion) minus indirect taxes less subsidies ($18 billion) = $417 billion. Net investment = $85 billion minus depreciation ($30 billion) = $55 billion. **Answer: C.**

28. The options a, b and d are false. The option d is true. **Answer: C.**

29. GDP = $500 billion = $350 billion + $70 billion + $120 billion + $50 billion minus import, we can calculate import as $90 billion and calculate deficit as $40 billion. **Answer: A.**

30. The options b, c and d are false. **Answer: A.**

Answers to Problems and Exercises

1. a.

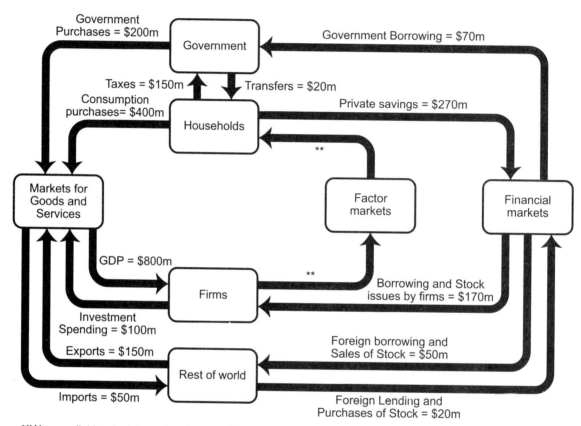

**Wages, dividends, interest, and rent = $800m

b. The value of GDP in 2005 in Macronesia is $800 million: this is equivalent to the sum of factor payments to households in the form of wages, dividends, interest, and rent. It is also equivalent to the sum of consumption spending, government spending, investment spending, and net exports.

c. Disposable income is income received by households less taxes plus transfers. In this problem, disposable income equals $670 million.

d. Household saving equals household income minus taxes plus transfers minus consumption spending, or $270 million. Household saving is the amount households have left of their income once they pay their taxes and make their consumer purchases.

e. No. The government spends $200 million, and its net tax collections equal $130 million. To finance this level of spending without a change in taxes, the government will need to borrow $70 million from the financial markets.

f. The flow of money into the financial markets must equal the flow of money out of the financial markets in order for these markets to be in equilibrium. Borrowing in the financial markets equals the sum of government borrowing

($70 million), plus firm borrowing ($170 million) plus foreign borrowing ($50 million); lending in the financial market is equal to the sum of household saving ($270 million) plus foreign lending ($20 million).

g. The flow of money into the market for goods and services must equal the flow of money out of the market for goods and services. In this case, these flows equal $800 million. The flow of money into the market for goods and services includes government spending of $200 million, household purchases of $400 million, investment spending by firms of $100 million, and net exports of $100 million for a total of $800 million. The flow of money out of the market for goods and services equals GDP or the sum of wages, dividends, interest, and rent ($800 million).

h. The flow of money into the factor markets must equal the flow of money out of the factor markets. In this problem, these flows equal $800 million. The flow of money into the factor markets is equal to GDP ($800 million), while the flow of money out of the factor markets must equal the sum of wages, dividends, interest, and rent ($800 million).

2. a. New home construction is included in GDP as investment spending.
   b. This is not included in GDP since the value of the house was counted in GDP the year the house was built.
   c. Textbook purchases by the government are included in GDP as government spending.
   d. Macro States exports beef and the value of these exports are included in the GDP of Macro States.
   e. Although there is production occurring, Ellen and Judy do not exchange money, and therefore this transaction does not get included in GDP.
   f. This increase in inventory is included in GDP as part of investment, since it represents new production in the economy of Macro States.

3. a.

Year	Nominal GDP
2004	$8,000
2005	8,866
2006	9,650

To calculate nominal GDP, multiply the price of each good times the quantity produced of that good and then sum together these products. For example, nominal GDP in 2004 = (Price of Tennis Shoes) (Quantity of Tennis Shoes) + (Price of Basketballs)(Quantity of Basketballs) + (Price of Lawn Mowers)(Quantity of Lawn Mowers) = $8,000.

b. The percentage change in nominal GDP from 2004 to 2005 was 10.83%: $[(8,866 - 8,000)/8,000] \times 10 \times 0 = 10.83\%$.

c. The percentage change in nominal GDP from 2005 to 2006 was 8.84%: $[(9,650 - 8,866)/8,866]100 = 8.84\%$.

d.

Year	Real GDP
2004	$8,000
2005	8,650
2006	9,070

To calculate real GDP, multiply the price of each good in the base year (2004) times the quantity produced of that good in a given year and then sum together these products. The value of real GDP will equal nominal GDP in the base year. In 2005, real GDP can be calculated as the following sum: ($50 per pair of tennis shoes)(108 pairs) + ($10 per basketball)(205 basketballs) + ($100 per lawn mower)(12 lawn mowers).

    e. The percentage change in real GDP from 2004 to 2005 was 8.13%: [(8,650 − 8,000)/8,000] × 100.

    f. The percentage change in real GDP from 2005 to 2006 was 4.86%: [(9,070 − 8,650)/8,650] × 100.

    g.

Year	GDP deflator
2004	(8,000/8,000) × 100 = 100
2005	(8,866/8,650) × 100 = 102.50
2006	(9,650/9070) × 100 = 106.39

4. a.

Year	Cost of Market Basket	Price index value
2004	(10)(.5) + (2)(4) + (5)(1) = $18	(18/18) × 100 = 100
2005	(10)(.52) + (2)(3.85) + (5)(1.1) = $18.4	(18.4/18) × 100 = 102.22
2006	(10)(.40) + (2)(3.9) + (5)(1.3) = $19.2	(19.2/18) × 100 = 106.67

    b. The rate of inflation between 2004 and 2005 was 2.22%: [(102.22 − 100)/100] × 100 = 2.22%.

    c. The rate of inflation between 2005 and 2006 was 4.35%: [(106.67 − 102.22)/102.22] × 100 = 4.35%.

    d.

Year	Cost of Market Basket	Price index value
2004	(10)(.5) + (2)(4) + (5)(1) = $18	(18/18.4) × 100 = 97.83
2005	(10)(.52) + (2)(3.85) + (5)(1.1) = 18.4	(18.4/18.4) × 100 = 100
2006	(10)(.40) + (2)(3.9) + (5)(1.3) = $19.2	(19.2/18.4) × 100 = 104.35

    e. The rate of inflation between 2004 and 2005 was 2.22%: [(100 − 97.83)/97.83] × 100 = 2.22%.

    f. The rate of inflation between 2005 and 2006 was 4.35%: [(104.35 − 100)/100] × 100 = 4.35%.

    g. Answers (b) and (c) are the same as answers (e) and (f). This is not surprising since the choice of a base year will generate different values for the price index, but the rate of change in prices between years should be equivalent no matter what year is chosen as the base year.

5. a. The labour force is equal to the sum of employed plus unemployed workers. In this case, the labour force is equal to 5,000 + 2,000, or 7,000.

    b. To find the unemployment rate use the formula

Unemployment Rate = (Unemployed/Labour Force) × 100

In this case, the unemployment rate equals (2,000/7,000) × 100 or 28.57%.

    c. If discouraged workers were counted as unemployed workers, the formula for calculating the unemployment rate would change to

Unemployment Rate* = (Unemployed + Discouraged Workers)/Labour Force) × 100

The unemployment rate would equal (2,500/7,000) × 100 or 33%.

    d. The decision by Statistics Canada to exclude discouraged workers from the calculation of the unemployment rate results in an understatement of the unemployment rate in the economy.

   e. Since GDP increases by $20,000, we know that unemployment decreases by 200 people (2,000 − 200 = 1,800). Thus, the unemployment rate is now equal to (1,800/7,000) × 100, or 25.72%.

   f. As GDP increases, unemployment decreases.

6. a. The statement is false. The GDP is not a good index of economic wellbeing, because

- It does not take into account income distribution.

- It does not take into account pollution, urban congestion, resource-depletion, etc.

- It does not take into account leisure and non-market activities.

- It does not take into account home-makers' contribution.

- It does not take into account spending on education as investment in human capital.

   b. The statement is true. The actual unemployment figure is an underestimation, when it does not take into account discouraged workers effect or underemployment. The actual unemployment figure is an overestimation, when it does not take into account of the people who are officially unemployed, but get paid for works under the table.

7. a. Net investment = $95 billion − $30 billion = $65 billion

   b. Consumption = $400 billion − $90 billion = $310 billion.

   Personal Income = $400 billion + $75 billion = $475 billion.

   c. GDP = $310 billion + $95 billion + $150 billion + $60 billion − $40 billion = $575 billion.

   d. GNP = $575 billion − $15 billion = $460 billion.

   National Income = $460 billion − $30 billion − $18 billion = $412 billion.

8. a. All dollar figures are in billion dollars.

Year	Nominal GDP	Price Index	Real GDP
2001	$400	100	**$400**
2002	$420	**105**	$400
2003	$450	120	**$375**
2004	$500	125	**$400**
2005	**$588**	140	$420

b.

Year	% Growth rate of nominal GDP
2002	5%
2003	7.14%
2004	11.11%
2005	17.6% **[The year of highest percentage increase]**

c.

Year	% Growth rate of real GDP
2002	0
2003	− 6.25%
2004	6.67% **[The year of highest percentage increase]**
2005	5%

d.

Year	% increase in the price index
2002	5%
2003	14.29% **[The year of highest percentage increase]**
2004	4.17%
2005	12%

chapter **8**

Long-Run Economic Growth

This chapter focuses on long-run economic growth and its sources. Long-run economic growth can be measured as the change in real GDP per capita over time. Comparison of real GDP per capita for different countries reveals different economic growth experiences: some countries have experienced rapid economic growth over time, while other countries have been much less fortunate. Long-run economic growth depends on productivity, which depends on physical capital, human capital, and technological progress. This chapter also discusses the convergence hypothesis: the theory states that relatively poor countries should have higher rates of growth of real GDP per capita than relatively rich countries.

How Well Do You Understand the Chapter?

Fill in the blanks using the terms below or circle the correct answer to complete the following statements. Terms may be used more than once. If you find yourself having difficulties, please refer back to the appropriate section in the text.

aggregate production function	domestic	growth rates	slows
	double	high	spending
annual	education	human capital	tax revenue
borrowing	GDP per capita	inflation investment	technological improvements
convergence	government	labour productivity	technology
convergence hypothesis	government intervention	real GDP	
diminishing returns	greater	saving	

1. A key economic statistic to measure economic growth is the growth of
_____ over time. When computing how long it takes real GDP per
capita to _____, the rule of 70 is useful. This rule states that the
number of years it takes a variable to double is approximately equal to 70 divided
by the _____ growth rate of the variable.

2. Long-run economic growth depends almost exclusively on increases in output per
worker, or _____. For the aggregate economy, we can measure
labour productivity as the _____ divided by the number of people
working. Increases in productivity are due to increases in physical capital, human
capital, or changes in _____. Physical capital refers to manmade
resources such as buildings and machines. _____ refers to the
improvements in labour productivity through education and knowledge.

3. The _____ is a mathematical equation describing the relationship between the level of output per worker (productivity) and the amount of human capital per worker, physical capital per worker, and the state of technology. The aggregate production function exhibits _____ to physical capital: holding the level of human capital per worker and the state of technology constant, increases in physical capital per worker increase output per worker by smaller and smaller amounts.

4. Total factor productivity is the percentage of _____ from a given set of factor inputs. It signifies the contribution to output due to changes in

_____.

5. _____ differ across countries and across periods of time. Countries with rapid growth tend to be countries with _____ growth rates in their physical capital, human capital, and/or technology. Countries that pursue policies and support institutions enhancing these three factors experience _____ economic growth. An economy increases its physical capital through _____ spending. This can be funded by _____ savings or by _____ funds from foreigners.

6. A well-functioning financial market is very important for economic growth because this allows directing savings into productive business _____. The _____ can increase the level of savings in an economy by collecting more in _____ than it spends. A government that spends in excess of its tax revenue (i.e., pursues fiscal deficit policy) may "crowd out" private _____. The government can also adversely affect saving and investment by pursuing inflationary monetary policy. _____ erodes the value of financial assets and this reduces individuals' incentives to

_____.

7. A country's human capital is primarily enhanced through government spending on _____. It has a significant impact on a country's economic growth rate. A country's infrastructure is also a critical factor of economic growth. Inadequate infrastructure _____ growth rates in an economy.

8. _____ are a key force behind economic growth. This depends on scientific advance. _____ on research and development (R & D) enhances the development of new technologies.

9. Political stability, well-defined property rights, and the appropriate level of _____ also play a role in long-run economic growth.

10. The _____ says that economic differences between countries, measured as real GDP per capita, tend to narrow over time. This suggests that differences in living standards between countries should narrow over time. Countries with relatively low _____ per capita will tend to have higher growth rates than countries with relatively high real GDP per capita. When there are differences in education, infrastructure, and political stability between countries, then there is no clear tendency toward _____ in the world economy as a whole.

Learning Tips

TIP #1: Real GDP per capita is a key statistic for measuring economic growth.

We use real GDP and not nominal GDP in measuring economic growth because we are interested in the increase in the quantity of goods and services being produced and not in the effects of an increase in the price level. We use real GDP per capita because we want to have a measure of average standard of living.

TIP #2: Familiarize yourself with the rule of 70 and how to apply it.

The rule of 70 provides a simple mathematical formula for estimating the amount of time it takes a variable that grows gradually over time to double. The rule of 70 states that the number of years it takes for a variable to approximately double is equal to 70 divided by the annual growth rate of the variable.

TIP #3: It is important to understand and know the sources of long-run economic growth.

Economic growth arises because of increases in productivity, or output per worker. This increase in productivity is due to increases in human capital per worker, physical capital per worker, and/or technological advance. Economic growth is enhanced by high levels of saving and investment spending, a strong educational system, adequate infrastructure, well-supported research and development, political stability, and appropriate levels of government intervention in the economy.

TIP #4: Productivity increases when physical capital per worker, human capital per worker, or technology increases.

Increases in productivity are the primary source of economic growth over time. It is important to understand what productivity is and how an economy's productivity can be improved. You should make sure you understand what an aggregate production function is and how it illustrates the relationship between productivity and the variables that determine productivity.

TIP #5: The concept of diminishing returns to physical capital is important.

Holding everything else constant, an increase in physical capital per worker will lead to smaller increases in productivity. Adding additional physical capital to a fixed level of labor and technology initially increases output at an increasing rate, but eventually each successive addition to physical capital per worker produces a smaller increase in output per worker.

TIP #6: **Investment spending determines the level of physical capital available to workers.**

Investment spending plays a vital role in determining an economy's rate of economic growth. Investment spending can be funded through domestic saving or through the borrowing of foreign saving.

TIP #7: **According to convergence hypothesis, differences in living standards should narrow over time, because countries with relatively low per capita real GDP will have higher growth rates than the counties with relatively high per capita real GDP.**

In reality, we don't see a clear tendency towards convergence because there are differences in education, infrastructure, and political stability between countries.

Multiple-Choice Questions

1. Real GDP per capita is
  a. the value of real GDP divided by the number of units of capital in an economy in a given time period.
  b. always increasing over time for any given economy.
  c. the value of real GDP divided by population for a given country.
  d. both b and c.

2. Suppose real GDP for Macronesia is $200 million in 2005. Furthermore, suppose population in Macronesia is 100,000 in 2005. If population increases to 105,000 in 2006 while GDP increases by 5%, then it must be true that real GDP per capita in Macronesia in 2006
  a. increased.
  b. decreased.
  c. stayed constant.
  d. may have increased, decreased, or remained constant.

3. Which of the following statements is true?
  a. Over the past century, Canada's real GDP per capita rose by nearly 794%.
  b. In 2003, India was still poorer than Canada was in 1900, as measured by real GDP per capita.
  c. Today nearly 50% of the world's population lives in countries that are poorer than Canada was in 1900, as measured by real GDP per capita.
  d. All of the above statements are true.

4. Suppose that real GDP per capita grows at 2% per year. How many years will it take for real GDP per capita to approximately double? It will take
  a. 70 years because of the rule of 70.
  b. 140 years, because the rule of 70 states that a variable will double in 70 years if the variable has an annual growth rate of 1%; therefore, a variable growing at 2% will take twice as long to double.
  c. 35 years, because the rule of 70 states that the number of years it takes for a variable to double is equal to 70 divided by the annual growth rate of the variable.
  d. 50 years, since at 2% per year it takes 50 years to reach 100% more than the initial real GDP per capita.

5. Which of the following has been most important in driving long-run economic growth?
   a. rising labour productivity or output per worker
   b. putting more people to work
   c. being a relatively rich country initially
   d. the availability of abundant natural resources

6. Productivity increases can be attributed to
   a. increases in physical capital or the amount of machinery and office space available to workers.
   b. increases in human capital or the level of workers' education.
   c. technological advances.
   d. all of the above.

7. Which of the following statements is true?
   a. An aggregate production function indicates how output per worker depends on the level of physical capital per worker, human capital per worker, and the state of technology.
   b. Holding everything else constant, an increase in human capital per worker reduces the level of output per worker.
   c. Holding everything else constant, a decrease in physical capital per worker increases the level of output per worker.
   d. All of the above are true.

8. Suppose the amount of human capital per worker and the state of technology are held constant. As physical capital per worker increases, each additional increase in physical capital per worker leads to
   a. greater increases in output per worker.
   b. greater decreases in output per worker.
   c. smaller increases in output per worker.
   d. smaller decreases in output per worker.

9. Economists often use the "other things equal" expression. This expression indicates
   a. that a group of variables is held constant while we examine how changing one variable affects our economic model.
   b. an individual views two possible outcomes as being equivalent in their impact.
   c. that the distribution of income is equal among all members of an economy.
   d. that equal amounts of all factors of production are used in the economy under study.

Use the following information to answer the next two questions.

An economy initially has 100 units of physical capital per worker. Each year it increases the amount of physical capital by 5%. According to the aggregate production function for this economy, each 1% increase in physical capital per worker, holding human capital and technology constant, increases output per worker by 1/5th of 1%, or .20%.

10. In two years time, what is the level of physical capital per worker in this economy?
   a. 110 units of physical capital per worker
   b. 105 units of physical capital per worker
   c. 110.25 units of physical capital per worker
   d. 210 units of physical capital per worker

11. Suppose output per worker is initially $1,000. After one year, what does estimated output per worker equal? Assume there is no inflation in this economy: real GDP equals nominal GDP.
    a. $1,000
    b. $1,001
    c. $1,010
    d. $1,100

12. An economy increases its level of physical capital per worker by increasing the level of investment spending. This can be achieved by
    a. having domestic residents spend more of their income on consumption spending.
    b. having domestic residents spend less of their income on consumption spending while increasing their domestic saving.
    c. borrowing foreign savings from residents of other countries.
    d. both a and c.
    e. both b and c.

13. "Crowding out" refers to a situation where
    a. government spending, financed through borrowing, reduces the level of consumption spending.
    b. government spending, financed through borrowing, encourages high levels of investment spending.
    c. government spending, financed through borrowing, stimulates saving by domestic residents.
    d. government spending, financed through borrowing, reduces private investment spending.

14. Monetary policy that leads to high levels of inflation may
    a. decrease the level of saving in an economy.
    b. decrease the level of investment spending in an economy.
    c. erode the value of financial assets in an economy.
    d. All of the above statements are true.

15. Which of the following statements is true?
    a. Countries with low levels of infrastructure typically experience low rates of economic growth.
    b. Infrastructure is primarily provided by private companies.
    c. Basic public health measures, like clean water, are not considered part of an economy's infrastructure.
    d. All of the above statements are true.

16. Long-run economic growth requires
    a. the imposition of bureaucratic restrictions on business and household activity.
    b. political stability and respect for property rights.
    c. extensive government intervention in markets in the form of import restrictions, government subsidies, and protection of firms from competitive economic pressures.
    d. all of the above.

17. Economic growth can be especially fast
    a. for countries playing "catch up" to countries that already have high real GDP per capita.
    b. for relatively poorer countries, if the convergence hypothesis holds true.
    c. if the country is able to benefit from adopting the technological advances already utilized in advanced countries.
    d. All of the above statements are true.

18. Long-run economic growth depends on
   a. physical capital and equipment.
   b. human capital.
   c. technology.
   d. all of the above.

19. Diminishing marginal productivity of capital per labour implies which of the following?
   a. Other things remaining the same, if labour doubles, capital also doubles.
   b. Other things remaining the same, the capital-labour ratio declines as output increases.
   c. Other things remaining the same, the capital-output ratio increases as output increases.
   d. Other things remaining the same, increases in physical capital per worker increases the output per worker by smaller and smaller amounts.

20. Imagine a graph with real GDP per worker on the vertical axis and physical capital per worker on the horizontal axis. If we assume diminishing marginal productivity of capital per worker, we will draw real GDP per worker line as a
   a. vertical line.
   b. horizontal line.
   c. linear line.
   d. non-linear (curved line).

21. Imagine a graph with real GDP per worker on the vertical axis and physical capital per worker on the horizontal axis. Technological improvement implies
   a. increasing marginal productivity of capital per worker.
   b. an upward shift of the real GDP per worker line at given levels of capital per worker.
   c. a downward shift of the real GDP per worker line at given levels of capital per worker.
   d. no shifts of the real GDP per worker line at given levels of capital per worker.

22. According to convergence hypothesis
   a. all countries should have identical growth rates.
   b. all developing countries will experience slower growth rates than those of the developed countries.
   c. differences in per capita real GDP between countries will tend to narrow over time.
   d. world poverty will decline over time.

23. Crowding out of private investment will occur
   a. when private sector conducts too many business ventures.
   b. when government sector borrows funds from the financial market to carry out budget deficits.
   c. when private sector borrows funds from the financial market to carry out investment projects.
   d. when government runs budget surplus and private sector borrows funds from the financial market to carry out budget deficits.

Answer questions 24-25 on the basis of the following:

Consider an economy with the following aggregate production function, when holding human capital per worker and technology constant.

 Define k as K/L and y as Y/L, where K stands for units of capital and L stands for units of labour. Assume fixed L.

The economy's production function is:
$y = 10(k)^{1/2}$

24. When $k = 100$, the output per worker is
a. 1,000.
b. 100.
c. 10.
d. 1/2.

25. When k increases to 400 from 100 (that is, k increases 4 times), then the output per worker should increase
a. 4 times.
b. 3 times.
c. 2 times.
d. 1.5 times.

Problems and Exercises

 1. You are given the following information about the country of Macronesia.

Year	Nominal GDP	CPI	Real GDP	Population
2003	$10 billion	100	10	1.0 million
2004	10.5 billion	105		1.05 million
2005	11.0 billion	108		1.08 million

a. What is the base year for the economy represented in the previous table? How did you identify the base year?

b. Calculate the missing values in the table. Calculate the missing value and then round to the nearest thousand million: e.g., 14,829,000,000 would be rounded to 14.8 billion.

c. Use the complete table to calculate the missing values in the following table. You will find it helpful to define real GDP in millions (for example, 14.8 billion is 14,800 million), since population is expressed in millions.

Year	Real GDP per capita
2003	
2004	
2005	

d. Let's compare the percentage changes in some of the variables we are working with in this problem. Use the following table to organize your calculations.

Year	Percentage change in nominal GDP	Percentage change in real GDP	Percentage change in population	Percentage change in real GDP per capita
2003				
2004				
2005				

e. In order for real GDP per capita to increase over time, what must be true about the relationship between the percentage change in real GDP and the percentage change in population?

f. Why do we focus on computing real GDP per capita instead of nominal GDP per capita?

2. Suppose real GDP per capita in Fun Land is $10,000 in 2005. Economists in Fun Land predict steady increases in real GDP in Fun Land of 7% a year for the foreseeable future.

a. According to the rule of 70, how many years will it take for Fun Land's real GDP per capita to double?

10

b. To verify your answer in (a), compute the values for real GDP per capita in the following table.

Year	Real GDP per capita
2005	$10,000
2006	10,700
2007	11,449
2008	12250.43
2009	
2010	
2011	
2012	
2013	
2014	
2015	

c. Is your value for real GDP per capita for 2015 equal to $20,000? If it differs, does this surprise you? Explain your answer.

3. The economy of Macro States estimates its aggregate production function as

$$Y/L = 50(K/L)^{1/2}$$

when technology and human capital per worker are held constant. In the equation Y is real GDP, L is the number of workers, and K is the quantity of physical capital. Macro States has 500 workers.

a. Calculate real GDP per worker (Y/L) and physical capital per worker (K/L) for the given levels of physical capital in the following table. Round (K/L) to the nearest hundredth and (Y/L) to the nearest whole number.

K	K/L	Y/L
$ 0	0	0
20	0.04	10
40	0.08	14
60	0.12	17
80	0.16	20
100	0.2	22
200	0.4	32
400	0.8	45

b. Plot Macro States' aggregate production function on the following graph, where physical capital per worker is measured on the x-axis and real GDP per worker is measured on the y-axis.

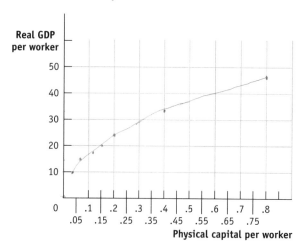

c. As physical capital per worker increases, what happens to real GDP per worker?

4. Suppose that Macro States increases its level of technology and human capital per worker relative to its economic condition in problem (3). Now, Macro States' economists estimate that the aggregate production function for Macro States is given by the equation

$$Y/L = 60(K/L)^{1/2}$$

a. Relative to the aggregate production function you plotted in (3b), what do you anticipate will happen to Macro States' aggregate production function because of this increase in human capital per worker and technology?

b. Compare productivity in Macro States in the initial situation to its new situation, assuming that Macro States has $100 worth of physical capital.

c. Why are increases in productivity important?

5. Suppose there are two countries, Macroland and Pacifica, that currently have real GDP per capita of $10,000 and $15,000, respectively. Furthermore, suppose Macroland's economy has an average annual growth rate of 2%, while Pacifica has an average annual growth rate of 1.4%.

   a. Compute real GDP per capita for both Macroland and Pacifica 50 years from now.

$$10000 + (1 + 0.02)^{50}$$

   b. Compute real GDP per capita for both Macroland and Pacifica 100 years from now.

   c. Initially, Macroland's real GDP per capita is 67% of Pacifica's real GDP per capita. After 50 years, what is the relationship of Macroland's real GDP per capita to Pacifica's real GDP per capita in percentage terms? What is this relationship after 100 years?

6. Briefly describe the factors that contribute to economic growth.

7. What is the convergence hypothesis? Describe the reasons for leading to the convergence outcome as predicted by the hypothesis?

8. Consider an economy with the following aggregate production function, when holding human capital per worker and technology constant.

Define $y = Y/L$ and define $k = K/L$.
Y is total output, K is capital and L is worker.
Assume fixed L.

Use the output per worker (y) function as
$y = 10k^{1/2}$

Use the marginal return of capital per worker (k) function as
$5/(k^{1/2})$

a. Fill in the following table:

k	y	Marginal return of capital per worker
9	30	$\frac{5}{3}$
16	40	$\frac{5}{4}$
25	50	$\frac{5}{5} = 1$
64	80	$\frac{5}{8}$
100	100	$\frac{5}{10}$

b. Circle the correct choice. As k increases, output increases/decreases at an increasing/constant/decreasing rate.

c. Assume that technological improvement has led to the following production function: $y = 20k^{1/2}$

Use the marginal return of capital per worker (K/L) function as: $10/(k^{1/2})$

Fill in the following table:

k	y	Marginal return of capital per worker
9	60	$\frac{10}{3}$
16	80	$\frac{10}{4}$
25	100	$\frac{10}{5}$
64		
100		

d. Circle the correct choice. As k increases, marginal return of capital per worker increases/decreases/or stays constant.

Answers to How Well Do You Understand the Chapter

1. GDP per capita, double, annual

2. labour productivity, real GDP, technology, Human capital

3. aggregate production function, diminishing returns

4. real GDP, technology

5. Growth rates, high, greater, investment, domestic, borrowing

6. investment, government, tax revenue, investment, Inflation, saving

7. education, slows

8. Technological improvements, Spending

9. government intervention

10. convergence hypothesis, real GDP, convergence

Answers to Multiple-Choice Questions

1. Real GDP per capita is defined as the value of real GDP in a country divided by that country's population. Real GDP per capita may increase, decrease, or remain steady over time. **Answer: C.**

2. In 2006, population in Macronesia increased by 5% as did real GDP. Since both population and real GDP increased by the same percentage amount, real GDP per capita is unaffected. **Answer: C.**

3. Answers (a), (b), and (c) are all drawn directly from the text and provide different perspectives on economic growth over time and in different regions. **Answer: D.**

4. This is a straightforward use of the definition of the rule of 70: this rule states that an estimation of the number of years it takes for a variable to double is equal to 70 divided by the annual growth rate of the variable. **Answer: C.**

5. Sustained economic growth occurs only when an economy steadily increases the amount of output each worker produces: in other words, long-run economic growth depends upon rising labour productivity. Putting more people to work can increase output in the short run, but it does not result in sustained economic growth. Long-run economic growth is possible in relatively poor countries (for example, South Korea before 1970) and countries endowed with low levels of resources (for example, Japan). **Answer: A.**

6. Each of these reasons—physical capital, human capital, and technological advances—contributes to increases in productivity, or the ability to produce more output per worker. **Answer: D.**

7. Answer (a) provides a definition of the aggregate production function. In answers (b) and (c), we know there is a relationship between output per worker and the amount of human capital per worker or physical capital per worker: in both cases, an increase in either human or physical capital, holding everything else constant, will lead to an increase in output per worker. **Answer: A.**

8. This question focuses on the concept of diminishing returns to physical capital: given an aggregate production function with a constant level of human capital per worker and state of technology, an increase in the quantity of physical capital per worker will lead the rate of productivity to fall while remaining positive. Thus, output per worker will increase but by smaller and smaller amounts. **Answer: C.**

9. The "other things equal" expression is used when economists want to single out the effect of a change in one variable on their economic model. To see this effect, all other variables that might affect the model are held constant, or equal to their initial value, while the single variable is allowed to change. **Answer: A.**

10. Physical capital per worker in the first year increases by 5%, or $(100)(1.05) = 105$ units. In the second year, physical capital per worker increases another 5%, or $(105)(1.05) = 110.25$ units. **Answer: C.**

11. Using growth accounting, we can estimate output per worker as being equal to the percentage change in physical capital per worker times the impact on output per worker. In this case, a 5% increase in physical capital per worker will lead to a 1% increase in output per worker. Since output is initially $1,000, a 1% increase in output will equal $1,010. **Answer: C.**

12. Investment spending depends upon the availability of savings. An increase in investment spending is possible either by increasing the level of domestic savings or by borrowing foreign savings. **Answer: E.**

13. "Crowding out" refers to the idea that government borrowing absorbs resources that could otherwise be used to promote economic growth. This government borrowing crowds out, or reduces, investment spending. **Answer: D.**

14. Inflation reduces the purchasing power of the dollar as well as the value of other financial assets. Monetary policy which leads to inflation will cause people to save less, since these saved dollars have less purchasing power over time. Lower levels of saving will lead to lower levels of investment. **Answer: D.**

15. Infrastructure includes roads, power lines, ports, information networks, and basic public health measures. Countries lacking this infrastructure find it hard to maintain high rates of economic growth. Infrastructure is primarily provided by government, not private enterprise. **Answer: A.**

16. Long-run economic growth requires political stability and well-defined property rights. Long-run economic growth is hindered by bureaucratic restrictions and excessive government intervention in markets. **Answer: B.**

17. The convergence hypothesis says that differences in real GDP per capita among countries tends to narrow over time because countries that start with lower GDP per capita tend to grow at faster rates than countries that start with higher GDP per capita. Answers (a) and (b) express comparable ideas. Relatively poor countries may experience fast economic growth if they implement existing technological advances. **Answer: D.**

18. Economic growth depends on all of the following: physical capital, human capital and technology. **Answer: D.**

19. Given technology and given human capital, increases in physical capital per worker will lead to smaller and smaller increases in the output per worker. **Answer: D.**

20. Because of the assumption of diminishing marginal productivity, the curve depicting real GDP per worker is a curved line with diminishing slope as we increase the quantity of capital per worker. **Answer: D.**

21. Technological improvement will shift the real GDP per worker curve upward. **Answer: B.**

22. According to convergence hypothesis, differences in per capita real GDP between countries will tend to narrow down over time. **Answer: C.**

23. With budget deficits, government borrows funds from the financial markets, which tends to raise the domestic interest rate, which in turns reduces (crowds out) private investment. **Answer: B.**

24. $y = 100$. **Answer: B.**

25. When $k = 100$, $y = 100$. When $k = 400$, $y = 200$.

Therefore, k increases by 2 times. **Answer: C.**

Answers to Problems and Exercises

1. a. 2003. The base year is that year with the CPI value of 100.
 b.

Year	Nominal GDP	CPI	Real GDP	Population
2003	$10 billion	100	$10 billion	1.0 million
2004	10.8 billion	105	10.3 billion	1.01 million
2005	11.5 billion	108	10.7 billion	1.02 million

 c.

Year	Real GDP per capita
2003	$10,000
2004	10,188
2005	10,441

 d.

Year	Percentage change in nominal GDP	Percentage change in real GDP	Percentage change in population	Percentage change in real GDP per capita
2003	—	—	—	—
2004	8%	2.9%	1%	1.9%
2005	6.5%	3.5%	1%	2.5%

 e. The percentage change in real GDP must be greater than the percentage change in population for real GDP per capita to increase over time.
 f. Real GDP per capita allows us to track the increase in the quantity of goods and services available in our economy rather than just the effects of a rising price level.

2. a. Ten years, since the rule of 70 says the number of years it takes for a variable to double is approximately equal to 70 divided by the annual growth rate of the variable.

b.

Year	Real GDP per capita
2005	$10,000
2006	10,700
2007	11,449
2008	12,250
2009	13,108
2010	14,026
2011	15,007
2012	16,058
2013	17,182
2014	18,385
2015	19,672

c. The value of real GDP per capita for 2015 is $19,672, which is less than the estimated $20,000. This is not surprising since the rule of 70 is an estimation of the number of years it takes a variable to double rather than a numerically precise calculation.

3.

a.

K	K/L	Y/L
$ 0	$ 0	$ 0
20	.04	10
40	.08	14
60	.12	17
80	.16	20
100	.2	22
200	.4	32
400	.8	45

b.

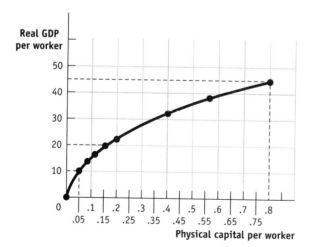

c. Real GDP per worker increases as physical capital per worker increases, but it increases at a diminishing rate. For example, if we hold the number of workers and all other variables constant, real GDP per worker increases by $4 when physical capital increases from $20 to $40, but real GDP per worker increases by $3.50 when physical capital increases from $40 to $60.

4. a. Macro States aggregate production function will shift up relative to its initial position for every level of physical capital per worker. We can see this by recalculating output per worker given the new aggregate production function.

K	K/L	Y/L
$ 0	$ 0	$ 0
20	.20	12.00
40	.28	16.80
60	.35	21.00
80	.40	24.00
100	.45	27.00

b. Productivity is defined as output per worker. When physical capital equals $100, output per worker is initially $22.50; while, after the increase in human capital per worker and technology, output per worker increases to $27.00.

c. Increases in productivity are important because they indicate that each worker on average is now producing a greater level of output. This, in turn, makes it possible for people on average to experience higher standards of living.

5. a. Real GDP per capita in Macroland in 50 years will equal $(\$10{,}000)(1 + .02)^{50}$ or $26,916. Real GDP per capita in Pacifica in 50 years will equal $(\$15{,}000)(1 + .014)^{50}$, or $30,060.

b. Real GDP per capita in Macroland in 100 years will equal $(\$10{,}000)(1 + .02)^{100}$, or $72,446. Real GDP per capita in Pacifica in 100 years will equal $(\$15{,}000)(1 + .014)^{100}$, or $60,240.

c. In 50 years, Macroland's real GDP per capita to Pacifica's real GDP per capita in percentage terms is 89.5%, while in 100 years, it is 120.3%.

6. Factors that contribute to economic growth are
   a. physical capital and equipment.
   b. human capital and a skilled labour force.
   c. technology.
   d. infrastructure.

7. The convergence hypothesis says that the differentials in per capita real GDP between countries will reduce over time, because the countries with low per capita real GDP will tend to have higher growth rates than countries with high per capita real GDP. In reality, the convergence does not take place, because there are differences between countries with respect to political and economic stability, infrastructure, health and education, and social and institutional factors.

8. a.

k	y	Marginal return of capital per worker
9	30	5/3
16	40	5/4
25	50	5/5
64	80	5/8
100	100	5/10

b. As k increases, output increases at a decreasing rate.

c.

k	y	Marginal return of capital per worker
9	60	10/3
16	80	10/4
25	100	10/5
64	160	10/8
100	200	10/10

d. As k increases, marginal return of capital per worker decreases.

chapter 9

Savings, Investment Spending, and the Financial System

This chapter examines the relationship between saving and investment and how financial markets facilitate economic growth. The chapter also discusses four principal types of assets: stocks, bonds, loans, and bank deposits. It examines the role of financial intermediation in the economy and how financial intermediation enables investors to diversify while simultaneously reducing their exposure to risk and the costs of their transactions, while increasing their access to liquidity. The chapter discusses the determination of stock prices and the effect of stock market fluctuations on the macroeconomy.

How Well Do You Understand the Chapter?

Fill in the blanks using the terms below or circle the correct answer to complete the following statements. Terms may be used more than once. If you find yourself having difficulties, please refer to the appropriate section in the text.

asset(s)	economic growth	imports	loanable fund market	portfolio
bank deposits		income		positive
banks	efficient markets hypothesis	inflows	losing	private savings
borrow	expectations	interest	macroeconomic	profit
borrowed	exports	interest rate	mutual fund	rate of return
borrowers	financial assets	investment spending	negative	risk(s)
budget balance	financial intermediaries	irrationally	negative effect	riskier
capital inflow(s)		lender	net revenue	savers
closed	financial risk	lent	nominal interest rate	savings
deficit	fluctuations	liability		sources
demand	government spending	life insurance companies	open	stock market indexes
demanded	government transfers	liquid	outflows	supply
deposit	greater than	liquidity	pension funds	surplus
ease		loan	physical	transaction costs
			physical capital	
			physical inflows	

1. Long-run _____ depends on a well-functioning financial system that can link _____ with excess funds to _____ who need funds to finance productive investment activities. Domestic savings and foreign savings are the two _____ of savings in an economy. The financial system provides the mechanism for increasing _____, a critical source of productivity growth. _____ refers to spending on physical capital, while financial investment refers to the purchase of financial _____ like stocks, bonds, or existing real estate. Human capital is primarily provided by the government through its support of education, while physical capital, excluding infrastructure, is provided through private _____.

2. The saving-investment spending identity states that savings is always equal to investment whether the economy is a(n) _____ economy or a(n) _____ economy with trade. In a(n) _____ economy, investment spending, I, can be written as $I = GDP - C - G$. Private savings, $S_{Private}$, in a closed economy can be expressed as total income plus _____ minus taxes and consumption or $S_{Private} = GDP + TR - T - C$. When the government spends more than it collects in tax revenue, it runs a budget _____, and when the government spends less than it collects in tax revenue, it runs a budget _____. A budget surplus is equivalent to _____ by the government. The _____, $S_{Government}$, is equal to taxes minus government transfers and government spending, or $S_{Government} = T - TR - G$. A positive budget balance indicates the government has a saving (surplus), while a _____ budget balance indicates the government has negative saving (deficit). National Savings, NS, is the sum of _____ plus government savings, or $NS = GDP - C - G$.

3. In an open economy, savings need not be spent on _____ of capital in the same country where the savings occurred. Countries can receive _____ of savings from other countries, and countries can generate _____ of savings to other countries. We call the net effect of international inflows and outflows of funds on the total savings available for investment spending in a country its net _____, or KI. Capital inflow can be positive or negative: when capital inflow is _____, the inflow of funds into a country exceeds the outflow of funds; and when capital inflow is _____, the inflow of funds into a country is less than the outflow of funds.

4. A positive capital inflow represents funds _____ from foreigners, while a negative capital inflow represents funds _____ to foreigners. Capital inflow is related to a country's _____ and imports (IM). If a country spends more on _____ than it earns from its exports (X), it is suffering a trade deficit and it must _____ the difference from foreigners. That borrowing is equal to the county's capital inflow. This implies that a country's _____ is equal to the difference between imports and exports, or $KI = IM - X$. In an open economy, investment spending equals national savings (or the sum of private savings and government savings) plus _____, or $I = S_{Private} + S_{Government} + KI = NS + KI$.

5. The _____ is a hypothetical market where savers who _____ funds, interact with borrowers who _____ funds. The loanable funds market maximizes the gains from trade between lenders and borrowers. The equilibrium price, or interest rate, equates the quantity of funds _____ with the quantity of funds supplied. This _____ is the return a lender receives for allowing borrowers the use of a dollar for one year. The real interest rate is the interest rate adjusted for changes in prices over the length of the loan, while the _____ is the interest rate unadjusted for changes in prices.

6. A business (firm) will borrow funds to finance a project provided that the _____ on the project exceeds the cost of borrowing for the project; that is, a project will be undertaken by a business only if the rate of return is equal to or _____ the interest rate levied on the loan. The rate of return, measured as a percent, is equal to the _____ from the project divided by the cost of the project times 100, or written in equation form: *Rate of Return = [(Increase in Revenue–Cost of Project)/(Cost of Project)] x 100.*

7. "Crowding out" refers to the _____ on private investment spending caused by government budget deficits. If the government's budget _____ results in crowding out of private investment, less _____ capital is accumulated each year in the economy. This can, holding everything else constant, result in lower long-run _____.

8. Some _____ is essential for long-run economic growth. For example, government expenditure on infrastructure is critical. The _____ impact of crowding out is based on the assumption of "other things being equal", whereby all government spending necessary for the economy's infrastructure has occurred and any additional government expenditure resulting in a budget _____ will reduce the level of private _____.

9. Households invest their savings and wealth, or accumulated savings, by purchasing _____ in financial markets. These are paper claims that provide the buyer of the claim future income from the seller of the claim. They represent a(n) _____ to the purchaser of the claim and a(n) _____ to the seller of the claim. For example, if you borrow funds from a bank, the loan represents an asset to the bank, because the bank will receive a(n) _____ in the future from the loan. And it represents a liability to you, since you must repay the funds you have borrowed at some point in the future.

10. The financial system provides borrowers and lenders a cost-effective way to reduce costs and risk while enhancing their liquidity. _____ are the expenses suppliers and demanders incur when they negotiate and execute a transaction. _____ refers to the uncertainty about future outcomes that involve financial losses and gains. A risk-averse person views potential losses and gains in an asymmetrical way; the total decrease in the person's welfare from losing a given amount of money is _____ the total increase in the person's welfare from gaining an equivalent amount of money. The risk-averse person is willing to expend a greater amount of resources to avoid _____ a dollar than he or she is willing to expend to gain a dollar.

11. Asset diversification (or the holding of different types of financial and physical assets) reduces the level of _____ an individual faces. Liquidity refers to the _____ with which an asset can be converted into cash. A liquid asset is easily converted into cash, while an illiquid asset cannot be easily converted into cash.

12. The four primary types of financial assets are loans, bonds, stocks, and _____. A loan is an agreement between a particular _____ and a particular borrower. Loans are typically tailored to the needs of the borrower. A bond is a promise to repay the owner of the bond a specific amount at some point in the future plus yearly _____ for the life of the bond. Information about the bond-issuer is freely available from bond-rating agencies that assess the credit-worthiness of the bond-issuer. Bonds are easy to resell, which enhances their _____. A stock is a share in the ownership of a company. Owning a share of stock in a given company is _____ than owning a bond from this same company; stock ownership generally results in a higher return for an investor than a bond, but it also carries higher _____.

13. _____ are institutions that transform funds gathered from many individuals into financial assets. Four important financial intermediaries are mutual funds, pension funds, _____, and banks.

- A(n) _____ creates a diversified stock portfolio and then re-sells shares of the stock portfolio to individual investors. This enables investors with a small amount of money to indirectly invest in a diversified _____, which yields a better return for any given level of _____ than would otherwise be available to the investor.

- _____ are non-profit institutions that collect savings from their members and then invest these funds in a wide variety of assets to provide retirement income for their members.

- _____ collect funds from policyholders to guarantee payments to the policyholders' beneficiaries when the policyholders die. Life insurance companies increase individual welfare by reducing risk.

- _____ are institutions that gather funds from depositors and then use these funds to make loans. Banks enhance financial liquidity while serving the financing needs of those borrowers who do not want to use the stock or bond market.

14. A bank _____ is an asset for the individuals depositing their funds at the bank and a liability for the bank. A bank _____ is an asset for the bank and a liability for the individuals who borrow the funds. Bank deposits provide _____ assets to the owners of these deposits while simultaneously providing a source of funds to finance the illiquid investments of borrowers.

15. _____ are numbers intended as a summary of average prices in the stock market. Three examples are The Dow Jones Industrial Average, the S&P 500, and the NASDAQ.

16. _____ in the financial system can be a source of macroeconomic instability. The value of a(n) _____ comes from its ability to generate higher future consumption of goods and services. This future income can be earned as interest or dividends, or it can be earned from selling the asset in the future at a(n) _____. Therefore, the value of an asset today depends upon investors' beliefs about the future value of the asset. For example, stock prices will change in response to changes in investors' _____ about future stock prices.

17. There are two principal competing viewpoints about how stock-price _____ are determined. The _____ says that asset prices always include all publicly available information: this implies that stock prices are fairly valued and stockprices are neither over-priced nor under-priced. A contrasting view holds that markets often behave _____, leading to the possibility that some stocks are under-priced and represent potential profit-making opportunities for the investor. There is no reason to assume stock prices will be stable. Stock-price fluctuations can have major _____ effects requiring policy-maker intervention.

Learning Tips

TIP #1: It is important to understand that savings and investment spending are always equal whether the economy is open or closed.

This is an accounting fact and is referred to as the savings-investment spending identity.

TIP #2: It is important to know and understand the formulas and definitions of investment spending, private savings, the budget balance, national savings, and capital inflow.

This chapter includes a number of equations which provide a mathematical expression of important relationships between variables. Make sure you familiarize yourself thoroughly with these formulas:

$I = GDP - C - G$ in a closed economy

$S_{Private} = GDP + TR - T - C$

$S_{Government} = T - TR - G$

$NS = S_{Private} + S_{Government} = GDP - C - G$ in a closed economy

$KI = IM - X$ in an open economy

$I = S_{Private} + S_{Government} + (IM - X)$ in an open economy

$I = NS + KI$

TIP #3: It is important to understand that some government spending is essential for a well-functioning economy.

An economy cannot function without a basic infrastructure that includes a well-functioning system of law and order including a court system, a public health system to prevent the spread of disease, and systems of transportation, communication, and education. When economists discuss the crowding out of private investment spending because of government budget deficits, they are assuming that this additional government spending is spending that is in excess of this basic infrastructure.

TIP #4: A business project will be undertaken if the rate of return of that project is equal to or greater than the market interest rate.

As the interest rate increases, fewer business projects will be undertaken and less investment will occur. Other things remaining the same, additional G will lead to a budget deficit, which will reduce investment; this is called the crowding out effect.

TIP #5: The financial system provides borrowers and lenders cost-effective ways to reduce risks, while enhancing liquidity.

Asset diversification (holding different kinds of assets) reduces the risk an individual faces. *Liquidity* refers to the ease at which an asset can be converted into cash.

TIP #6: Financial intermediaries are institutions that transfers funds gathered from many individuals into financial assets.

Four financial intermediaries are: mutual funds, pension funds, life insurance companies, and banks.

TIP #7: The demand and supply of loanable funds determine the market interest rate.

The demand for funds is negatively related to the interest rate, and the supply of funds is positively related to the interest rate. Changes in demand, changes in supply, or changes (shift of the curves) in both demand and supply will lead to a new equilibrium quantity of funds and a new equilibrium interest rate.

TIP #8: Instability in the financial market can be a source of macroeconomic instability.

Stock-price fluctuations can have major macroeconomic effects requiring intervention from policy-makers.

Multiple-Choice Questions

1. Financial markets are beneficial
   a. to savers, since they provide interest payments for the use of savers' funds.
   b. to borrowers, since they provide a source of funds for productive investments.
   c. to the government, since they provide both a use for surplus government funds and a source of funds should the government run a deficit.
   d. All of the above statements are true statements.

2. Investment spending includes all of the following EXCEPT
   a. the construction of a new residence during the current year.
   b. the purchase of a new piece of equipment at a factory during the current year.
   c. the purchase of a home, built twenty years ago, during the current year.
   d. the acquisition of new computers for a business during the current year.

3. Sources of funds for investment spending include
   a. domestic savings.
   b. foreign savings.
   c. the Bank of Canada.
   d. All of the above are correct.
   e. Both a and b are correct.

4. Which of the following statements is true?
   a. In an open economy, the only source of funds for investment spending is domestic savings.
   b. In a closed economy, the only use of savings is to provide funds to finance government deficits.
   c. In a closed economy, the only source of funds for investment spending is domestic savings.
   d. Both a and b are true.
   e. Both b and c are true.

5. Which of the following statements is true?
   a. $I = GDP - C - G$ in a closed economy.
   b. $GDP = C + I + G + X - IM$ in an open economy.
   c. $GDP = S_{Private} + T + C - TR$
   d. $S_{Government} = T - TR - G$
   e. All of the above statements are true.

6. When government spending is greater than net taxes,
   a. government savings is positive.
   b. there is a budget surplus.
   c. there is a positive surplus.
   d. there is a budget deficit.

7. The term budget balance can be abbreviated as $S_{Government}$. The value of $S_{Government}$ is
   a. positive when the government is running a budget surplus.
   b. positive when the government is running a budget deficit.
   c. negative when the government is running a budget deficit.
   d. zero when the government's expenditure equals its net taxes.
   e. a, c, and d.

8. Which of the following statements is true about national savings in a closed economy?
   a. National savings is the sum of domestic savings plus the budget balance.
   b. National savings is GDP minus consumption spending minus government spending.
   c. National savings is always equal to investment spending.
   d. All of the above statements are true.

9. Capital inflow is
   a. the net inflow of foreign funds plus domestic savings into an economy.
   b. the net inflow of funds into a country, or the total inflow of foreign funds into a country minus the total outflow of domestic funds to other countries.
   c. the total outflow of domestic funds to other countries minus the net inflow of foreign funds into a country.
   d. the total outflow of domestic funds to other countries plus the net inflow of foreign funds into a country.

10. Economists differentiate between these types of capital: physical capital, human capital, and financial capital. Which of the following statements is false?
   a. Human capital includes changes in the level of education or training workers possess.
   b. Physical capital includes changes in inventories.
   c. Financial capital refers to the funds available in an economy for investment spending.
   d. Financial capital refers to expenditures on manufacturing equipment.

11. Suppose a country exports $50 million worth of goods and services, while it imports $60 million worth of goods and services. This country
   a. has a positive capital inflow.
   b. lends funds to foreigners.
   c. has a negative capital inflow.
   d. Both a and b are correct.
   e. Both b and c are correct.

12. In an open economy, investment spending equals
   a. domestic savings.
   b. private savings plus the budget balance.
   c. the sum of private savings, the budget balance, and the difference between imports and exports.
   d. private savings plus capital inflows.

13. The loanable funds market
   a. provides a market where savers and borrowers can make mutually beneficial transactions.
   b. uses supply and demand to determine an equilibrium price or interest rate.
   c. interest rate is the return a lender receives for allowing borrowers the use of a dollar for one year.
   d. All of the above statements are true.

Use the following information to answer the next two questions.

Suppose Joe lends Maxine $100 for the year. At the end of the year, Maxine repays Joe the $100 plus an additional payment of $15 for the use of Joe's money during the year.

14. Assuming there is no inflation during the year, what is the interest rate Maxine pays Joe?
  a. .15%
  b. 1.5%
  c. 15%
  d. 115%

15. Maxine, when borrowing the funds from Joe, anticipates the inflation rate for the year will be 10%, while Joe expects it to be 7%. Inflation is actually 8% for the year. Which of the following statements is true?
  a. Joe benefits unexpectedly from this higher than expected inflation rate.
  b. Maxine benefits unexpectedly from this lower than expected inflation rate.
  c. The nominal interest rate for this loan is 7%.
  d. The real interest rate for this loan is 7%.

16. A business has two possible investment projects available to it for the coming year. The following table summarizes the information the business has about these projects.

Project	Projected increase in revenues from project	Cost of project
Project A	$10,000	$9,000
Project B	15,000	13,500

Suppose the interest rate is 10%. Which of the following statements is true?
  a. Both projects are equally attractive to the firm in terms of their rate of return.
  b. Both projects represent a situation where the rate of return is less than the interest rate.
  c. Neither project will be undertaken by the business during the coming year.
  d. Both b and c are correct.

17. When the government runs a deficit, this shifts the
  a. supply of loanable funds curve to the right.
  b. supply of loanable funds curve to the left.
  c. demand for loanable funds curve to the right.
  d. demand for loanable funds curve to the left.

18. Which of the following is an asset from a bank's perspective?
  a. Joe's checking account deposit of $500 at the bank.
  b. Mike's car loan of $2,000 that he borrowed from the bank.
  c. Mary's savings account balance of $325 at the bank.
  d. From the bank's perspective, a, b, and c are all assets.

19. Financial markets provide a means for
  a. reducing risk for borrowers and lenders.
  b. reducing transaction costs for borrowers and lenders.
  c. enhancing liquidity for borrowers and lenders.
  d. All of the above statements are true.

20. A person who is willing to spend more resources to avoid losing a fixed sum of money than is willing to expend on gaining the same sum of money is
  a. a risk lover.
  b. risk averse.
  c. displaying diminishing returns to risk.
  d. irrational.

21. Which of the following assets is most liquid?
  a. a home with a market value of $200,000
  b. a checking account balance of $1,000
  c. a three-carat diamond engagement ring
  d. a rare edition of an out-of-print book

22. Financial intermediaries
  a. transform funds gathered from many individuals into financial assets.
  b. provide a means of increasing risk for investors as well as business owners.
  c. only invest in bonds.
  d. only invest in stocks.

23. Banks
  a. provide liquidity to lenders.
  b. serve the financing needs of borrowers who do not use or cannot be served by the stock and bond markets.
  c. accept deposits from individuals who have excess funds.
  d. All of the above statements are true.

24. Stock market prices are neither overvalued or undervalued according to
  a. irrational exuberance.
  b. the theory of stock market "bubbles."
  c. the efficient markets hypothesis.
  d. All of the above statements are true.

25. Suppose the current market price of a one-year bond is $1,200. You are planning to buy a New Brunswick Utility bond. The bond promises to pay $1,260 after one year. You expect zero inflation. Which of the following statements is correct?
  a. You should buy the bond because the rate of return is 5%.
  b You should not buy the bond because the rate of return is higher than 5%.
  c. You should buy the bond if the market interest rate is less than 5%.
  d. You should buy the bond if the market interest rate is more than 5%.

26. Consider a closed model, where investment equals national savings. Which of the following equations is incorrect?
  a. Investment (I) = national savings (NS) = GDP − G − C.
  b. Private savings (S_P) = GDP + transfers (TR) − taxes (T) − consumption (C).
  c. Government savings (S_G) = $T − TR − G$.
  d. I = GDP + $TR − G − C$.

27. Consider a closed economy. If GDP = $600, consumption (C) = $260, government expenditure (G) = $100, transfers (TR) = $20, and taxes (T) = $60, then investment equals
  a. $200.
  b. $240.
  c. $340.
  d. $460.

28. Consider a closed economy. At present, the GDP = $600, consumption (C) = $260, government expenditure (G) = $100, transfers (TR) = $20, and taxes (T) = $60. If G increases by 100, while the other figures remain constant, then investment
   a. should not change.
   b. should decrease by $100.
   c. may increase or decrease.
   d. should decrease by more than $100.

29. In an open model, the GDP = $600, consumption (C) = $260, government expenditure (G) = $100, transfers (TR) = $20, taxes (T) = $60, and domestic business investment (I) is $190. Therefore, the net capital inflow (KI) is
   a. plus $50.
   b. minus $50. $600 = 260 + 100 + 190$
   c. zero.
   d. none of the above.

30. In an open model, GDP = $600, consumption (C) = $260, government expenditure (G) = $100, transfers (TR) = $20, taxes (T) = $60, and domestic business investment (I) is $190. If G increases from $100 to $200, while other data just given remain constant, then net capital inflow (KI) is
   a. plus $50.
   b. minus $50.
   c. zero.
   d. none of the above.

31. Consider a closed model with an initial equilibrium situation in the market for loanable funds along with balanced budgets. If the government now runs a budget deficit and borrows funds from the market, then
   a. the demand curve of loanable funds will shift to the left, and the new equilibrium interest rate will be lower than the initial equilibrium interest rate.
   b. the supply curve of loanable funds will shift to the left, and the new equilibrium interest rate will be higher than the initial equilibrium interest rate.
   c. the demand curve of loanable funds will shift to the right, and the new equilibrium interest rate will be higher than the initial equilibrium interest rate.
   d. the supply curve of loanable funds will shift to the right, and the new equilibrium interest rate will be lower than the initial equilibrium interest rate.

32. Consider a closed model with an initial equilibrium situation in the market for loanable funds. Assume that the government has adopted tax reforms that led to an increase in the private savings. As a result,
   a. the demand curve of loanable funds will shift to the left.
   b. the supply curve of loanable funds will shift to the left.
   c. the demand curve of loanable funds will shift to the right, and the new equilibrium interest rate will be higher than the initial equilibrium interest rate.
   d. the supply curve of loanable funds will shift to the right, and the new equilibrium interest rate will be lower than the initial equilibrium interest rate.

Answer Questions 33-35 on the basis of the following table. All figures in billion dollars.

Assume zero budget-deficit and closed economy.

Interest rate	Quantity of funds demanded	Quantity of funds supplied
16%	$200	$800
14%	$300	$700
12%	$400	$600
10%	$500	$500
8%	$600	$400
6%	$700	$300

33. The equilibrium interest rate is _____ and the equilibrium quantity of funds is _____.
    a. 10%; $500 billion
    b. 12%; $700 billion
    c. 12%; $600 billion
    d. 14%; $700 billion

34. (Assume that the supply schedule remains unchanged. If the government decides to run a budget deficit and borrows $200 billion from the market, the equilibrium interest rate will be _____ and the equilibrium quantity of funds will be _____.
    a. 10%; $500 billion
    b. 12%; $700 billion
    c. 12%; $600 billion
    d. 14%; $700 billion

35. Given the scenario described in Question 34, the crowding out of private investment will be
    a. $200 billion.
    b. $100 billion.
    c. $50 billion.
    d. zero.

Problems and Exercises

1. You are given the following information about the open economy of Macroland for 2005.

GDP	$100 billion
C	70 billion
T	15 billion
TR	8 billion
G	20 billion
X	10 billion
IM	12 billion

   a. What is the level of investment spending in Macroland in 2005?
   b. What is the level of capital inflow for Macroland in 2005? Is Macroland borrowing from foreigners or lending to foreigners? Explain your answer.
   c. What is private savings equal to in Macroland in 2005?
   d. What is the budget balance equal to in Macroland in 2005?

e. Does national savings plus capital inflow equal investment spending for this economy in 2005?

f. Is the government of Macroland saving or borrowing funds in 2005? Explain your answer.

2. Use the following information about the three economies, Funland, Upland, and Downland, to answer the following questions.

	Funland	Upland	Downland
GDP	$1,000	$5,000	$4,000
C	800	3,500	$3,000
I	80	800	800
G	100	800	300
X	50	400	400
IM	30	500	500
T	50	600	600
TR	20	200	200

a. Fill in the missing information in this table.

b. From the information you are given and your calculations in part (a), fill in the following table.

	Funland	Upland	Downland
$S_{Private}$	170	1100	600
$S_{Government}$	-70	-400	100
KI	-20	100	-100

c. Now, calculate capital inflow, private saving, and investment spending as a percentage of GDP for each economy. Report your calculations in an organized table.

d. What is the budget balance as a percentage of GDP for Funland, Upland, and Downland?   -7%, -8%, 2.5%

e. Are Funland, Upland, and Downland running a budget deficit or a budget surplus? How does your answer relate to the capital inflow each economy experiences?

3. Suppose in a closed economy, the demand for loanable funds can be expressed as $r = .1 - .00005Q$ and the supply of loanable funds can be expressed as $r = .00005Q$, where r is the real interest rate expressed as a decimal (for example, 8% is expressed as .08 in the equation) and Q is the quantity of loanable funds. Assume the government initially has a budget balance of zero.

a. What is the equilibrium real interest rate and the equilibrium quantity in the loanable funds market?

b. Suppose the government's budget balance decreases to −$100 at every real interest rate. What will happen to the demand and supply of loanable funds with this change? What do you predict will happen to the equilibrium interest rate and the equilibrium quantity in the loanable funds market?

c. Does crowding out occur in this economy when the budget balance is −$100? Explain your answer.

4. For each of the following decide whether they represent investment in physical assets, investment in financial assets, or investment in human capital. For each example also decide whether it represents investment spending.
   a. The government increases expenditures on education for children and training for post-high school graduates.
   b. Michael purchases a $100 bond issued by a local company that provides technical support for computer users.
   c. Susan purchases $1,000 worth of filing cabinets and office desks for her business office.
   d. A neighboring country purchases $10 million in Federal government bonds.
   e. Mary purchases a newly constructed factory that manufactures auto parts.

5. A business is analyzing a potential project. The two employees analyzing the project agree that the cost of the project is $100,000, but they disagree about the projected rate of return. One employee argues that the rate of return will be 8%, while the other argues that the rate of return will be 12%. Since the interest rate the business faces is 10%, the project's viability is in dispute. What could lead to the different rates of return these employees have calculated?

6. Briefly identify critical areas of government spending that are necessary if an economy is to experience economic growth.

7. Briefly describe three important problems that lenders and borrowers face and how the financial system addresses these three problems.

8. Consider the following demand and supply schedules of loanable funds. All figures are in billion dollars. Assume zero budget deficits and a closed economy.

Interest rate	Quantity of funds demanded	Quantity of funds demanded
16%	$200	$800
14%	$300	$700
12%	$400	$600
10%	$500	$500
8%	$600	$400
6%	$700	$300

   a. Consider the equilibrium outcomes:
   The interest rate is _____.

   The private savings is _____.

   The government savings is _____.

   The private business investment is _____.

b. The government has decided to run a budget deficit and increases government spending (G) by $400. Assume that the supply schedule remains unchanged. Consider the new equilibrium outcome:

The interest rate is _____.

The private savings is _____.

The government savings is _____.

The private business investment is _____.

The crowding out effect is _____.

9. Consider a closed economy with the following information:

GDP = $800 billion

C = $500 billion

T = 100 billion

G = $130 billion

Transfers = 0

Find the following:

$I =$

Private savings =

Government savings =

National savings =

10. Consider an open economy. All figures are in million dollars. Answer the following questions

a. X = $120

IM = $80

T = $125

G = $200

I = $100

Find private savings.

b. Private savings = $205

$T = \$125$

$G = \$200$

$I = \$100$

Find capital inflow.

c. GDP = $900

$T = \$125$

$G = \$200$

$I = \$100$

$C = \$560$

If G increases by $100, while GDP and consumption stay constant, what will be the change in the capital inflow?

11. a. Consider a closed economy.
GDP $= C + I + G$.

$C = GDP + TR - T - S_P$

$S_G = T - G$

National savings (NS) $= S_P + S_G$

Prove that $NS = I$.

b. Consider an open economy.

GDP $= C + I + G + X - IM$

$C = GDP + TR - T - S_P$

$S_G = T - G$

National savings (NS) $= S_P + S_G$

Prove that $NS - I = X - IM$.

Answers to How Well Do You Understand the Chapter

1. economic growth, savers, borrowers, sources, physical capital, Investment spending, assets, investment spending

2. closed, open, closed, government transfers, deficit, surplus, savings, budget balance, negative, private savings

3. physical, inflows, outflows, capital inflows, positive, negative

4. borrowed, lent, exports, imports, borrow, capital inflow, capital inflow

5. loanable fund market, supply, demand, demanded, interest rate, nominal interest rate

6. rate of return, greater than, net revenue

7. negative effect, deficit, physical, economic growth

8. government spending, negative, deficit, investment spending

9. financial assets, asset, liability, income

10. Transaction costs, Financial risk, greater than, losing

11. risks, ease

12. bank deposits, lender, interest, liquidity, riskier, risk

13. Financial intermediaries, life insurance companies, mutual fund, portfolio, risk, Pension funds, Life insurance companies, Banks

14. deposit, loan, liquid

15. Stock market indexes

16. Fluctuations, asset, profit, expectations

17. expectations, efficient markets hypothesis, irrationally, macroeconomic

Answers to Multiple-Choice Questions

1. Financial markets provide funds for those who need to borrow funds, as well as a means of earning interest for those with surplus funds. **Answer: D.**

2. Investment spending refers to spending on the economy's stock of physical capital. It includes spending on physical equipment, inventories and new construction. It does not include the selling of a pre-existing structure since this represents a change of ownership rather than new productive capacity. **Answer: C.**

3. The Bank of Canada is not a source of funds for investment spending, while domestic and foreign savings do provide funds for investment spending. **Answer: E.**

4. A closed economy does not have any economic interaction with the rest of the world while an open economy does. A closed economy finances its investment spending solely through domestic savings, while an open economy funds its investment spending through both domestic and foreign savings. **Answer: C.**

5. We know that GDP is equal to total spending on goods and services in an open economy (answer b); in a closed economy there are no imports or exports so GDP is equal to total domestic spending on goods and services (answer a). Private savings plus consumption plus net transfers equals GDP (answer c), and government savings is equal to net taxes minus the level of government spending (answer d). **Answer: E.**

6. If the government spends more than its net revenue, it runs a budget deficit or a negative surplus. This implies that government saving is negative. **Answer: D.**

7. By definition $S_{Government}$ is equal to government net taxes (taxes minus transfers) minus government spending. When $S_{Government}$ is greater than zero this indicates that net taxes exceed government spending: this is a budget surplus. When $S_{Government}$ is less than zero this indicates that government spending exceeds net taxes: this is a budget deficit. **Answer: E.**

8. All of these statements are true by definition. **Answer: D.**

9. Capital inflow measures the total level of funds available in a country to finance investment spending. It consists of the inflow of foreign funds into the economy minus the outflow of domestic funds to other economies, or the net inflow of funds into an economy. **Answer: B.**

10. Expenditures on manufacturing equipment are considered physical capital and not financial capital. **Answer: D.**

11. Capital inflow is defined as imports minus exports: in this case, capital inflow is positive. When capital inflow is positive the country spends more on imports than it earns from exports and must therefore borrow the difference from foreigners. **Answer: A.**

12. In any economy, investment spending equals savings. In an open economy, savings is equal to the sum of private saving, the budget balance, and capital inflows. Capital inflow is defined as the difference between imports and exports. **Answer: C.**

13. The loanable funds market is a hypothetical market where savers can lend money or supply funds to borrowers, the demanders of funds. The price for borrowing funds is the interest rate, or the return the lender of funds receives for loaning out a dollar for a year. **Answer: D.**

14. To calculate the interest rate Maxine pays, use the following formula:

Interest Rate = [(Total Payment at end of year − Amount of Loan)/(Amount of Loan)] × 100

which yields the following:

Interest Rate = [115 − 100)/(100)] × 100 = 15%

Answer: C.

15. When making the loan, Joe, with his expected inflation rate of 7%, anticipates a real interest rate of 8%; when the actual inflation rate is 8% rather than 7%, Joe's real interest rate on the loan falls to 7% and he is worse off than he anticipated. When making the loan, Maxine, with her expected inflation rate of 10%, anticipates a real interest rate of 5%; when the actual inflation rate is 8% rather than 5%, Maxine's real interest rate on the loan rises to 7% and she is worse off than she anticipated. The nominal interest rate is 15%, while the real interest rate is the nominal interest rate minus the inflation rate or 7%. **Answer: D.**

16. The rate of return for both projects is 11%, which is greater than the interest rate. Since both projects have the same rate of return, they are equally attractive to the business from the perspective of their rate of return. **Answer: A.**

17. When the government runs a deficit, it becomes a borrower in the loanable funds market and this implies that the demand curve for loanable funds shifts to the right at any given interest rate. **Answer: C.**

18. Joe's checking account balance is an asset from Joe's perspective and a liability from the bank's perspective. Mary's saving account balance is similarly an asset from her perspective and a liability from the bank's perspective. Mike's car loan represents an asset for the bank since Mike is legally obligated to repay the funds he has borrowed; the car loan represents a liability from Mike's perspective. **Answer: B.**

19. Answers (a), (b), and (c) focus on three problems that financial markets address for borrowers and lenders. **Answer: D.**

20. This statement is the definition of a risk-averse person. **Answer: B.**

21. The checking account balance is the most liquid asset in this list, since it can be effectively used as cash at most business locations. The other three assets must be sold to a buyer in order to convert them into cash: this transaction takes time and reduces the liquidity of these assets. **Answer: B.**

22. Financial intermediaries provide a means for reducing risk for investors and business owners when they gather funds from many individuals and then invest these funds in a diversified portfolio of financial assets that can include stocks as well as bonds. **Answer: A.**

23. Banks do provide liquidity for lenders in the form of deposits that can be accessed easily, while at the same time banks provide funds to finance the illiquid investments of borrowers. **Answer: D.**

24. The efficient markets hypothesis says that all publicly available information about a stock is already included in the stock's price. Thus, all stocks are fair-valued: they are neither underpriced nor overpriced. **Answer: C.**

25. We know that $(1 + r) = \$1,260/\$1,200$, where r is rate of return. We can solve r as 5%. If r is greater or equal to market interest, one should buy the bond. **Answer: C.**

26. The first three options are correct. We know that investment (I) = national savings (NS) = GDP − G − C. **Answer: D.**

27. Since investment (I) = national savings (NS) = GDP − G − C, we can see that investment equals $ 240 after we take into account the following: GDP = $600, G = $100 and C = $260. **Answer: B.**

28. Since GDP, private savings, and consumption did not change, increase of G by $100 will bring investment down by $100. **Answer: B.**

29. We know that GDP = C + I + G + X − IM and X − IM − minus capital inflow. Therefore, X − IM = $600 − $260 − $190 − $100 = $50. Therefore, capital inflow is minus $50. **Answer: B.**

30. We know that GDP = C + I + G + X − IM and X − IM = minus capital inflow. Therefore, X − IM = $600 − $260 − $190 − $200 = −$50. Therefore, capital inflow is plus $50. **Answer: A.**

31. When the government increases its borrowings from the market, the demand curve for funds shifts to the right and the interest rate increases. **Answer: C.**

32. When private savings increase due to tax reforms, the supply curve for funds shifts to the right and the interest rate decreases. **Answer: D.**

33. Interest rate = 10% and equilibrium quantity is $500 billion. **Answer: A.**

34. The quantity of demand for funds increases by $200 billion at each and every interest rate, while the supply schedule remains unchanged. The new equilibrium interest rate = 12% and equilibrium quantity is $600 billion. **Answer: C.**

35. At the old equilibrium interest rate of 10%, investments were $500 billion. At the new interest rate of 12%, private investments are $400 billion. Therefore, private investments had gone down (crowding out effect) by $100 billion. **Answer: B.**

Answers to Problems and Exercises

1. a. The level of investment spending can be calculated using the formula GDP = C + I + G + (X − IM). Using the information in the table and solving for I we find investment spending is equal to $12 billion.
   b. Capital inflow equals imports minus exports or $2 billion. Since capital inflow for Macroland in 2005 is a positive number we know capital is flowing into Macroland from other countries and therefore Macroland is borrowing funds from foreigners.
   c. We can calculate private savings, $S_{Private}$, using this formula:

$$S_{Private} = GDP + TR - T - C$$

   Using the information from the table, $S_{Private}$ equals $23 billion.
   d. We can calculate the budget balance, $S_{Government}$, using the following formula:

$$S_{Government} = T - TR - G$$

   Using the information from the table, $S_{Government}$ equals −$13 billion.
   e. Yes, national savings plus capital inflow is equivalent to private savings plus the budget balance plus capital inflow. For Macroland in 2005 this sums to $12 billion which is equivalent to the level of investment spending.
   f. The government of Macroland has a negative budget balance in 2005. This indicates that the government is running a budget deficit and is therefore borrowing funds.

2. a. To find investment spending for any of the economies use the formula GDP = C + I + G + X − IM. For Funland investment spending equals $80, in Upland investment spending equals $800, and in Downland investment spending equals $800.
   b. To find $S_{Private}$, use the formula $S_{Private} = GDP + TR - T - C$. To find $S_{Government}$, use the formula $S_{Government} = T - TR - G$. To find KI use the formula $KI = IM - X$. using the formulas and the given information you can complete the table as follows:

	Funland	Upland	Downland
$S_{Private}$	170	1,100	600
$S_{Government}$	−70	−400	100
KI	−20	100	100

c. Capital inflows as a percentage of GDP can be calculated as $[KI/GDP] \times 100$. This formula can be modified for all the other percentage calculations by replacing KI in the numerator with the relevant variable. Here are the calculations organized in a table.

	Funland	Upland	Downland
Capital inflow as a percentage of GDP	−2%	2%	2.5%
Private savings as a percentage of GDP	17%	22%	15%
Investment spending as a percentage of GDP	8%	16%	20%

d. We can answer this question using the information we calculated in part (b) or we can use the formula $I = S_{Private} + S_{Government} + KI$ and solve for $S_{Government}$ while measuring all terms as a percent of GDP. The first method calculates the budget balance as a percentage of GDP for Funland as $[−70/1,000] \times 100$ or −7%; for Upland as $[−400/5,000] \times 100$ or −8%; and for Downland as $[100/4,000] \times 100$ or 2.5%. Using the equation we get $S_{Government}$ for Funland as −7% (since $S_{Government}$ = 8% − 17% − (−2%); $S_{Government}$ for Upland as −8% (since $S_{Government}$ = 16% − 22% − 2%); and $S_{Government}$ for Downland as 2.5% (since $S_{Government}$ = 20% − 15% − 2.5%).

e. Funland is running a government deficit of $70, since Funland collects $50 in taxes and expends $20 on transfers and $100 on government spending. This implies Funland's government is borrowing funds: since private savings in Funland equals $170 and the capital inflow equals −$20, this indicates that Funland is lending funds to foreigners because their level of private savings is sufficient to cover the government's budget deficit as well as its level of investment spending.

Upland is running a government deficit of $400, since Upland collects $600 in taxes and expends $200 on transfers and $800 on government spending. When we look at the relationship between I, $S_{Private}$, $S_{Government}$, and KI, we find that Upland's capital inflow is a positive $100 so Upland is borrowing from foreigners. Private savings is equal to $1,100, government savings is −$400, and capital inflow is $100, resulting in investment spending in Upland of $800.

Downland is running a government surplus of $100, since Downland collects $600 in taxes and expends $200 on transfers and $300 on government spending. When we look at the relationship between I, $S_{Private}$, $S_{Government}$, and KI, we find that Downland's capital inflow is a positive $100; so Downland is borrowing from foreigners. Private savings is equal to $600, government savings is $100, and capital inflows is $100, resulting in investment spending in Downland of $800.

3. a. To find the equilibrium quantity in the loanable funds market set demand equal to supply or $.1 − .00005Q = .00005Q$. Solving for Q, we get Q equals $1,000. The equilibrium interest rate equals $.00005Q$, using the supply equation, or $.1 − .00005Q$, using the demand equation. Substituting 1,000 for Q, we get the equilibrium real interest rate, r, equals 5%.

b. The government is now running a deficit and must demand funds in the loanable funds market. At every real interest rate, demand for loanable funds has now increased by $100. Thus, the demand curve shifts to the right. There is no shift in the supply of loanable funds with this change. When the demand curve shifts, there is a movement along the supply curve: we anticipate the equilibrium real interest rate and quantity of loanable funds will increase when the government runs a negative budget balance.

c. In this economy, there is partial crowding out when the budget balance is −$100. Investment spending decreases when the government's budget balance is −$100.

4. a. Increases in expenditures on education and training represent investment in human capital.
   b. Michael's purchase of the bond represents an investment in a financial asset, since Michael will receive a payment in the future as compensation for the use of his money today.
   c. Susan's purchases represent investment spending, since they are investment in physical capital.
   d. The purchase of government bonds by a country or by an individual represents an investment in a financial asset.
   e. Mary's purchase represents investment spending, since it is an investment in physical capital.

5. a. Since we know that the rate of return equals [(Increase in Revenue − Cost of the Project)/Cost of the Project] × 100, it must be that the two employees do not agree about the size of the increase in revenue. If the rate of return is 8% and the cost of the project is $100,000, then we can solve the equation for the increase in revenue. In this case, the increase in revenue equals $108,000. If the rate of return is 12%, then the increase in revenue equals $112,000.

6. Answers to this question will vary but will include expenditures on public health, on systems of law and order including the court system, education systems, communication systems, and transportation systems. Economies that lack basic health, fail to educate their population, support corrupt legal systems, or do not provide basic infrastructure will lack the core supports necessary for economic growth.

7. Lenders and borrowers face three broad categories of problems: the problem of transaction costs, the problem of risk, and the problem of achieving the desired level of liquidity.

Transactions costs refer to the costs of making transactions: both borrowers and lenders face transaction costs when they commit to borrowing or lending funds. The financial system reduces transaction costs by making the arrangements between lenders and borrowers more efficient. For example, a business can borrow funds from a bank much more efficiently than it can borrow the same amount of funds from 1,000 potential lenders.

Financial risk, or risk, refers to the uncertainty people face with regard to future outcomes that involve financial gains and losses. The financial system helps borrowers and lenders share the risk they are exposed to through diversification, since this diversification, or investing in assets with unrelated risks, reduces the total risk of loss the individual faces.

The financial system also addresses the need for liquidity for investors. Stocks and bonds as well as banks provide a mechanism for individuals to have liquid assets while also enabling the financing of illiquid investments.

8. a. The interest rate is 10%.
   The private savings is $500 billion.
   The government savings is zero.
   The private business investment is $500 billion.
   b. The interest rate is 14%.
   The private savings is $700 billion.
   The government savings is minus $400 billion.
   The private business investment is $300 billion.
   The crowding out effect is $200 billion.

9. From data provided, we can solve the following:

I = \$800 billion – \$500 billion – \$130 billion = \$170 billion

Private savings = GDP – T – C = \$800 billion – \$100 billion – \$500 billion = \$200 billion

Government savings = \$100 billion – \$130 billion = \$30 billion

National savings = \$200 billion – \$30 billion = \$170 billion

10. a. Private savings + Government savings–Investment = X – IM

Private savings + [\$125 – \$200] – \$100 = \$120 – \$80

Private savings = \$215

b. Private savings + Government savings – Investment = X – IM

X – IM = – Capital inflow

\$205 – \$75 – \$100 = \$30.

c. When G = \$200, net export was \$40; capital inflow was minus \$40.

When G is \$300, net export = – \$60; capital inflow is \$600.

Therefore, capital inflow has increased by \$60.

11. a. Since national savings (NS) = S_P + S_G = S_P + T – G – TR,

We can show that SI = I

b. Since national savings (NS) = S_P + S_G = S_P + T – G – TR, we can prove that

NS – I = X – IM

chapter 10

Aggregate Supply and Aggregate Demand

This chapter develops the basic model of aggregate supply (*AS*) and aggregate demand (*AD*) that describes the relationship between the level of aggregate output and the aggregate price level. A distinction is made between the short-run *AS* curve, where the aggregate price level is positively related to the aggregate output level, and the long-run *AS* curve, a vertical curve where aggregate output is at the economy's potential output and independent of the aggregate price level. This model enables us to find both the short-run and the long-run macroeconomic equilibrium. The chapter further explores the economic changes that result in the *AD* or *AS* curves shifting and the effect of these shifts on economic fluctuations. The chapter introduces the multiplier and its relationship to autonomous spending. The chapter also explores how demand shocks prove simpler for policymakers to offset than do supply shocks.

How Well Do You Understand the Chapter?

Fill in the blanks using the terms below or circle the correct answer to complete the following statements. Terms may be used more than once. If you find yourself having difficulties, please refer to the appropriate section in the text.

aggregate output	fall	marginal propensity to save	positive supply shocks	short-run
aggregate price level	flexible	more	potential output	stabilization policies
autonomous change	higher price	movement along	price	stabilization policy
below	increase(s)	negative	purchasing power	stagflation
consumer spending	inflationary gap	negative demand shock	real GDP	increase demand shock
disposable income	interest rates	negative supply shocks	recession	supply shock
downward	left	no effect	reduces	unemployment
economic fluctuations	leftward	nominal wages	right	vertical
	less	positive	rightward	wages
	long-run	positive demand shock	self-correcting	wealth effect
	marginal propensity to consume		severity	zero
			shifts	

1. Deflation refers to a(n) _____ in the price level, while inflation refers to a(n) _____ in the price level. The term stagflation refers to a(n) _____ in the price level and at the same time, an increase in unemployment. The model of aggregate supply (*AS*) and aggregate demand (*AD*) can help us to understand economic fluctuations of _____ and price.

2. The *AS* curve illustrates the relationship between the _____ and aggregate output. In the short run, the *AS* curve is upward sloping. In the short run, there is a(n) _____ relationship between the amount of output producers are willing to supply and the aggregate price level. That is, holding everything else constant, in the short run as the price increases, the level of aggregate output _____. In the short run, the nominal _____ are "sticky" due to the existence of both formal and informal agreements. In the long run, the nominal _____ are completely _____.

3. The short-run *AS* curve _____ due to changes in input prices, nominal wages, and productivity. An increase in nominal wages results in a shift of the of the short run *AS* curve to the _____, while a decrease in nominal wages results in a shift of the short run *AS* curve to the _____. An increase in productivity shifts the short run *AS* curve to the _____. There will be a(n) _____ the *AS* curve with a change in the price level.

4. In the long run, _____ and prices are flexible and therefore in the long run, the aggregate price level has _____ on the quantity of aggregate output supplied. The *AS* curve in the long run is _____, where the level of aggregate output equals _____. If the level of potential output for an economy increases over time, then this implies that the long-run *AS* curve is shifting to the _____. These shifts represent economic growth.

5. The *AD* curve depicts the _____ relationship between the aggregate price level and the total quantity of aggregate output demanded by households, businesses, and government. A(n) _____, other things being constant, _____ the quantity of aggregate output demanded; a lower price, other things being constant, _____ the quantity of aggregate output demanded. A movement up or down the *AD* curve is due to changes in the _____ of all final goods and services.

6. *AD* curves are _____ sloping because of the wealth effect and the interest rate effect. When the aggregate price level changes, this affects the _____ of consumers' assets and hence consumers' wealth. We call this the _____. For example, a decrease in the aggregate price level increases the purchasing power of many assets and therefore leads to a(n) _____ in the quantity of aggregate output demanded. Interest rate effect is explained in the following way. When the aggregate price level changes, this affects the purchasing power of a given amount of money: for example, as the price level increases, people find they need _____ money to purchase the same basket of goods and services. Consumers bid up

_____ with their increased demand for money. As interest rates increase, this results in _____ investment spending and therefore a reduction in the quantity of aggregate output demanded. We call this the interest rate effect.

7. The *AD* curve shifts, holding everything else constant, due to changes in expectations, wealth, and changes in government fiscal or monetary policy. When consumers and firms become more optimistic, the *AD* curve shifts to the _____. A negative change in consumer or firm expectations shifts the *AD* curve to the _____. When the value of household assets increases, the *AD* curve shifts to the _____. Changes in government spending and taxes can cause the shifts of the *AD* curve. An increase in government spending or a decrease in taxes, holding everything else constant, shifts the *AD* curve to the _____. A decrease in government spending or an increase in taxes, holding everything else constant, shifts *AD* curve to the _____. A(n) _____ in the money supply reduces interest rates and increases investment spending. Thus, an increase in money supply shifts the *AD* curve to the _____, while a decrease in money supply shifts the *AD* curve to the _____.

8. There are two states of equilibrium the economy can be in: i) the economy can be in _____ equilibrium where *AD* equals the short-run *AS*; or ii) the economy can be in _____ equilibrium, where *AD* equals the long-run *AS* as well as the short-run *AS* and the aggregate output is equal to potential output. If the economy is in the first state, then, over time the short-run *AS* curve will shift, eventually bringing the economy into long-run equilibrium. In the short-run equilibrium, the _____ may be less than, equal to, or greater than potential output. If aggregate output is less than potential output, this implies recession and _____. Since jobs are scarce and workers are abundant, nominal wages will respond by falling over time and this will shift the short-run *AS* curve to the _____ leading output to expand. These rightward shifts of the *AS* curves will continue until the economy reaches the potential output. If aggregate output is greater than potential output, this implies unemployment is relatively low: since jobs are abundant and workers are scarce, _____ will increase over time leading the short-run *AS* curve to shift to the _____. This shift will reduce the equilibrium level of aggregate output, bringing it closer to the level of potential output.

9. The marginal propensity to consume (*MPC*) measures the change in consumer spending for every one dollar increase in _____. We can calculate the marginal propensity to consume as the change in _____ divided by the change in disposable income. The value of the marginal propensity to consume is always between _____ and one. The _____ is

the fraction of an additional dollar of aggregate disposable income that is saved. We can write the marginal propensity to save as one minus the marginal propensity to consume ($MPS = 1 - MPC$).

10. Aggregate spending is the sum of consumer spending, government spending, and investment spending. An increase or decrease in aggregate spending at any given level of real GDP is called a(n) _____ in aggregate spending. The multiplier is the ratio of the eventual change in _____ caused by a change in autonomous spending. The multiplier can be calculated using this formula:

$$\text{Multiplier} = 1/(1 - MPC).$$

The greater the _____, the greater is the multiplier. The smaller the _____, the smaller is the multiplier.

11. The *AS-AD* model is the basic model we use to understand _____. The short-run macroeconomic equilibrium is the intersection of the *AD* curve with the short-run *AS* curve. An event that shifts the short-run *AS* curve is called a _____. _____ shift the short-run *AS* curve to the left, while _____ shift the short-run *AS* curve to the right. A negative supply shock leads to _____ characterized by falling aggregate output (and rising unemployment) and increasing price level. A positive supply shock leads to rising aggregate output, falling unemployment, and a(n) _____ in the aggregate price level.

An event that shifts the *AD* curve is called a _____. A(n) _____ shifts the *AD* curve to the right, resulting in higher aggregate output and a higher aggregate price level. A(n) _____ shifts the *AD* curve to the left, resulting in lower aggregate output and a lower aggregate price level.

12. Short-run macroeconomic equilibrium aggregate output may be less than, equal to, or greater than potential output. Thus, the short-run macroeconomic equilibrium can represent an economy in an economic _____ or an economic expansion. Long-run macroeconomic equilibrium occurs when the short-run macroeconomic equilibrium is also a point on the long-run *AS* curve. Long-run macroeconomic equilibrium aggregate output is always equal to the _____. A recessionary gap occurs when the short-run macroeconomic equilibrium is _____ potential output. Recessionary gaps are hurtful due to the high levels of _____ and low levels of production associated with them. A(n) _____ occurs when the short-run

macroeconomic equilibrium is above potential output. In both the necessary gap and the inflationary gap, the economy is _____; given enough time the economy will adjust to economic shocks and eventually achieve potential output through adjustment in wages and prices, provided the government does not intervene with any activist policy.

13. Active _____ by the government can be used to offset demand shocks to the economy. This can reduce the _____ of recessions and can also diminish strong expansions in the presence of inflationary gaps. There are no easy _____ available to offset supply shocks. When policymakers try to offset supply shocks, they face a difficult trade-off: government can _____ aggregate output with _____ shift of the *AD* curve (leading to a further price hike), or the government can fight inflation by decreasing aggregate output by the _____ shift of the *AD* curve.

Learning Tips

TIP #1: It is important to distinguish between short-run and long-run *AS*.

In the short run, wages are sticky: this stickiness results in a short-run *AS* curve that is upward sloping. In the long run, wages are fully flexible, leading the economy to always produce its long-run equilibrium at the potential output level of real GDP. This is the output level the economy produces when all wages and prices are fully flexible. In the following graph, the short-run aggregate supply curve is *SRAS*, the aggregate demand curve is *AD*, the long-run aggregate supply curve is *LRAS*, and the potential output level, which represents the long-run equilibrium level of output, is *Y*. The economy in the short run may produce an aggregate output level that is greater than or less than the potential level of output *Y*. Figure 10.1, which follows, illustrates a situation where the short-run level of aggregate output Y_1 is less than the long-run level of output labeled *Y*.

Figure 10.1

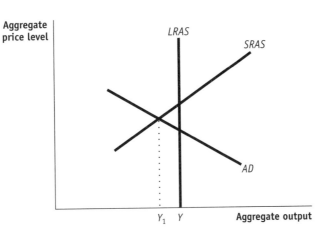

TIP #2: It is important to distinguish between a movement along the *AD* or *AS* curve and a shift of the *AD* or *AS* curve.

A change in the aggregate price level causes a movement along either curve (see Figures 10.2a and 10.2b, which follow), while a change in commodity prices, nominal wages, or productivity shifts the *AS* curve, and a change in expectations, wealth, physical capital, fiscal policy, or monetary policy shifts the *AD* curve (see Figures 10.2c and 10.2d, which follow).

Figure 10.2a

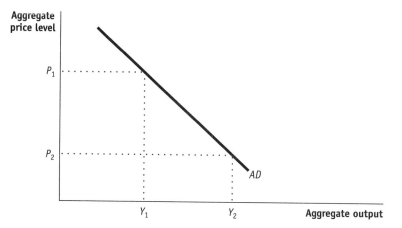

Figure 10.2b

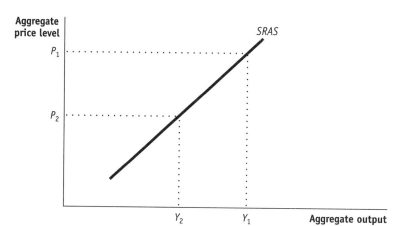

Figure 10.2c

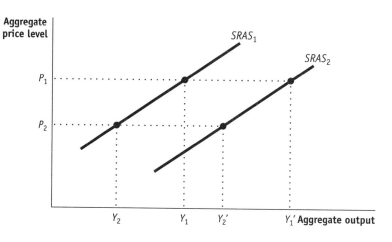

Figure 10.2d

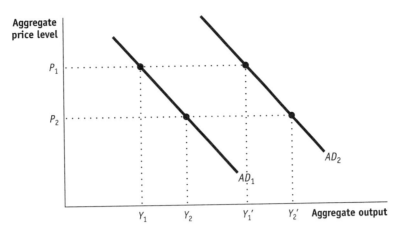

TIP #3: It is important to know the variables that shift *AS* and *AD*.

The text provides a list and an explanation for the variables that cause either the *AS* or *AD* curves to shift. It is crucial that you know these variables and that you understand the direction the curves shift with changes in these variables. (See the previous tip for a quick review of these variables.)

TIP #4: Changes in commodity prices have large impacts on production costs.

Understanding the impact of commodity prices on the *AS* curve will enhance your understanding of the impact of supply shocks in the *AS-AD* model.

TIP #5: The long-run *AS* curve is vertical, and its position represents the economy's potential output when all resources are fully employed.

It is important to understand why the long-run *AS* curve is vertical as well as the relevance of its position on the horizontal axis. Over time if an economy experiences economic growth the long-run *AS* curve shifts to the right, indicating the economy's potential output has increased.

TIP #6: It is important to understand why *AD* is downward sloping.

You need to review the wealth and interest rate effects and how they explain the inverse relationship between the aggregate price level and aggregate output.

TIP #7: It is important to understand the difference between short-run and long-run macroeconomic equilibrium and the relationship between these equilibria.

In long-run macroeconomic equilibrium, aggregate output equals potential output and the economy's *AD* equals both its short-run and long-run *AS* (see Figure 10.3a, which follows). In short-run macroeconomic equilibrium aggregate, output need not equal potential output, but the economy's *AD* must equal the short–run *AS*. Figure 10.3b, which follows, illustrates a short-run equilibrium with an inflationary gap where actual production, Y_2, is greater than *Y*. Figure 10.3c, which follows, illustrates a short-run equilibrium with a recessionary gap where actual production, Y_2, is less than *Y*. Over time the short-run *AS* adjusts through changes in the nominal wage to equate *AD* with the long-run *AS*.

Figure 10.3a

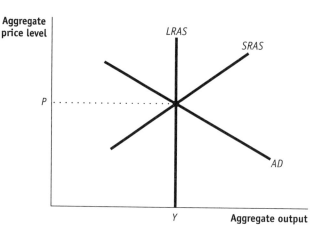

Figure 10.3b

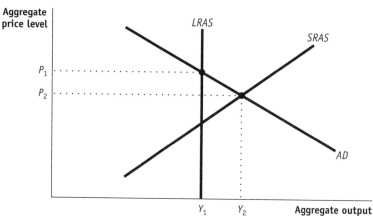

Figure 10.3c

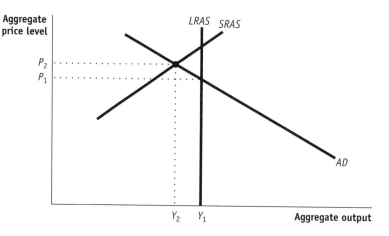

TIP #8: The multiplier concept is important to understand.

This chapter introduces the multiplier and uses it to illustrate the idea that a small change in one variable can lead to a big change in some other variable. The multiplier concept is an important idea in your study of macroeconomics.

Multiple-Choice Questions

1. In the short-run, a situation where the aggregate price level increases while the aggregate output level decreases is
   a. best explained as the result of a positive demand shock.
   b. stagflation.
   c. best explained as the result of a negative demand shock.
   d. Both a and b are correct.
   e. Both b and c are correct.

2. In the short-run, an increase in the aggregate price level due to a shift in *AD* first results in
   a. a rightward shift in the *AS* curve.
   b. a movement along the *AS* curve.
   c. no change in the level of aggregate production.
   d. a leftward shift in the *AS* curve.

3. Suppose the *AS* and *AD* model is initially in long-run equilibrium. Suppose there is an increase in wealth, holding everything else constant. Then, in the short run,
   a. there will be a movement along the *AD* curve.
   b. the economy will produce at its potential level of output.
   c. there will be a rightward shift in the *AD* curve.
   d. the aggregate level of production will increase while the aggregate price level will fall.

4. Nominal wages
   a. are often determined by contracts that were signed at some previous point in time.
   b. are slow to decrease in times of high unemployment, since employers may be reluctant to alter wages as a response to economic conditions.
   c. are fully flexible in both the short run and the long run.
   d. Both a and b are correct.
   e. The statements a, b, and c are correct.

5. Which of the following statements is true? In the short run, holding everything else constant,
   a. as production costs increase, profit per unit decreases, and this causes suppliers to increase their production.
   b. as production costs increase, profit per unit decreases, and this causes suppliers to reduce their production.
   c. as production costs decrease, profit per unit increases, and this causes suppliers to reduce their production.
   d. the *AS* curve is unaffected by changes in production costs.

6. Suppose there is an increase in the price of a commodity holding everything else constant. In the short-run,
   a. the producer will increase production since commodity prices have risen.
   b. the producer's profit per unit of output will decrease.
   c. the producer's price per unit of output will decrease.
   d. there will be a movement along the *AS* curve.
   e. both b and a are correct.

7. Which of the following will NOT make the *AS* curve shift to the left?
   a. an increase in the aggregate price level
   b. a decrease in commodity prices
   c. an increase in nominal wages
   d. None of the above cause the *AS* curve to shift to the left.
   e. Both a and b are correct.
   f. Both b and c are correct.

8. In comparing the short run with the long run, which of the following statements is true?
   a. In both the short run and the long run, the aggregate price level and the aggregate output level are positively related.
   b. In the short run, the economy never produces at the potential output level, while in the long run, the economy always produces at the potential output level.
   c. In the short run, nominal wages are slow to fully adjust to economic changes, while in the long run, nominal wages are completely flexible and make full adjustment to economic changes.
   d. All the above are correct.
   e. Both a and c are correct.
   f. Both b and c are correct.

9. In the long run, the aggregate price level increases. This
   a. is due to the short-run *AS* curve shifting to the right and the economy producing a level of aggregate output that is not equal to its potential output.
   b. is due to the *AD* curve shifting to the right.
   c. has no effect on the level of aggregate production in the economy.
   d. results in the economy moving to the level of production where aggregate output exceeds potential output.
   e. Both a and c are correct.
   f. Both b and c are correct.
   g. Both c and d are correct.

10. Suppose the economy is in short-run equilibrium and the level of aggregate output is less than potential output. Then, it must be true that
   a. unemployment in this economy is relatively low.
   b. over time the short-run *AS* curve will shift to the left.
   c. over time nominal wages will fall.
   d. the economy is also in long-run equilibrium.

11. *AD*
   a. depicts the relationship between the aggregate price level and the quantity of aggregate output demanded.
   b. is a positive relationship between the aggregate price level and the quantity of aggregate output demanded.
   c. is always equal to potential output, no matter what the aggregate price level is.
   d. increases, other things equal, as the aggregate price level increases.

12. As the aggregate price level increases, holding everything else constant,
   a. this reduces the purchasing power of many assets.
   b. this reduces the purchasing power of a given amount of money.
   c. the wealth and interest rate effects leads to a reduction in the quantity of aggregate output demanded.
   d. All of the above statements are true statements.

13. Holding everything else constant, the *AD* curve will shift to the right when
   a. the central bank decreases the money supply.
   b. household wealth increases.
   c. the government increases taxes paid by households.
   d. All of the above are correct.
   e. Both a and b are correct.
   f. Both b and c are correct.

14. Which of the following statements is true?
   a. The smaller the marginal propensity to save, the larger the multiplier.
   b. If the *MPC* equals .7, then the *MPS* equals 1.7.
   c. An increase in autonomous spending will lead to an equal increase in real GDP.
   d. The larger the marginal propensity to consume, the smaller the multiplier.

15. Suppose the marginal propensity to consume equals .75. Then an increase in government spending of $10 million will lead to an increase in real GDP of
   a. $4 million.
   b. $10 million.
   c. $40 million.
   d. $400 million.

   Answer the next two questions using the following information:

   Suppose Macroland is initially in long-run equilibrium. Then, suppose the central bank of Macroland increases the money supply.

16. In the short run, we know that this policy action
   a. will reduce interest rates and therefore stimulate investment spending.
   b. will lead to a reduction in unemployment and an increase in aggregate production.
   c. will lead to the short-run *AS* curve shifting to the right.
   d. All of the above are correct.
   e. Both a and b are correct.
   f. Both b and c are correct.
   g. Both a and c are correct.

17. In the long-run, Macroland will produce at
   a. the potential output level.
   b. a level of aggregate output greater than potential output.
   c. a level of aggregate output less than potential output.
   d. the same level of aggregate output as it did initially before the central bank increased the money supply, but with a lower aggregate price level than its initial level.

18. Which of the following statements is true?
   a. In a recessionary gap, aggregate output exceeds potential output.
   b. In an inflationary gap, aggregate output exceeds potential output.
   c. A recessionary gap is a long-run phenomenon that requires government policy action to eliminate.
   d. Recessionary gaps and inflationary gaps, if they exist, will be eliminated in the short run by the natural workings of the economy.

19. Suppose Funland is initially in long-run macroeconomic equilibrium. Then, there is a supply shock due to a severe increase in commodity prices. If Funland's policy-makers use active stabilization policy to offset this supply shock
   a. they can effectively eliminate the economic effects of the supply shock.
   b. they can either reduce the aggregate price level down to its initial equilibrium level, or they can increase aggregate output to its initial level.
   c. they can either increase the aggregate price level to its initial equilibrium level, or they can decrease aggregate output to its initial level.
   d. this will greatly reduce the economic fluctuations Funland experiences from this supply shock.

20. Which of the following statements is false?
   a. The long-run aggregate supply (*LRAS*) curve is vertical.
   b. The rightward shift of the *LRAS* is caused by economic growth.
   c. The aggregate demand (*AD*) curve is vertical in the long run.
   d. The short-run aggregate supply (*SRAS*) curve is positively sloped.

21. The effects of a decrease in the households' wealth can be illustrated by
   a. a leftward shift of the *AD* curve; recessionary gap in the short run; lower wages over time; rightward shifts of the *SRAS* curve over time, and no recessionary gap in the long run.
   b. a leftward shift of the *AD* curve; recessionary gap in the short run; lower wages over time; rightward shifts of the *AD* curve over time, and no recessionary gap in the long run.
   c. a leftward shift of the *AS* curve; recessionary gap in the short run; lower wages over time; rightward shifts of the *AD* curve over time, and no recessionary gap in the long run.
   d. a leftward shift of the *AS* curve; recessionary gap in the short run; lower wages over time; rightward shifts of the *AS* curve over time, and no inflationary gap in the long run.

22. A decrease in money supply and an increase in the wage rate will definitely lead to
   a. higher aggregate output in the short run.
   b. lower aggregate output in the short run.
   c. higher price in the short run.
   d. lower price in the short run.

23. An increase in taxes on households and a simultaneous increase of money supply due to expansionary monetary policy
   a. will lead to a leftward shift of the *AD* curve.
   b. will lead to a rightward of the *AD* curve.
   c. leads to no shifts in the *AD* curve.
   d. may cause a leftward shift or rightward shift or no shift of the *AD* curve.

24. When higher energy costs cause stagflation, the Bank of Canada can increase money supply to offset the recessionary gap, but it will cause
   a. further inflation.
   b. further deflation.
   c. favourable supply shocks.
   d. adverse demand shocks.

25. If disposable income decreases by 100 and consumption decreases by 80, then
   a. the MPS is minus 0.2.
   b. the MPC is minus 0.8.
   c. $(1 - MPS) = 0.8$.
   d. $(1 - MPS)$ is unknown.

Use the following to answer questions 26–27.

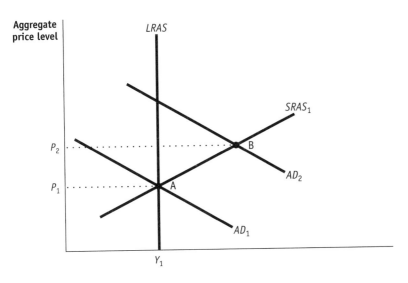

26. Which of the following statements is false?
   a. If we assume a reduction of taxes on households, it will explain the shift from point A to point B.
   b. Movement from point A to point B along the short-run aggregate supply curve shows higher supply prices and higher wage rates.
   c. Movement from point A to point B along the short-run aggregate supply curve shows a higher supply price, but input prices and wage rates are fixed.
   d. If the economy is at point B in the short run, it will lead to higher wage rates and a leftward shift of the AS curve, with the final equilibrium point lying where the AD_2 curve intersects the $LRAS$ curve.

27. Which of the following statements is false?
   a. At point A, there is neither a recessionary gap nor an inflationary gap.
   b. At point B, there is neither a recessionary gap nor an inflationary gap.
   c. The stabilization policy (for example, reduction of money supply) may dampen the inflationary gap.
   d. In the long run, the price is determined where the AD curve intersects the $LRAS$ curve.

28. If we take the multiplier as $1/(1 - MPC)$ and if the multiplier is 2.5, we can conclude that
a. the *MPC* is 0.75.
b. the *MPS* is 0.40.
c. $(1 - MPC) = 0.75$.
d. the *MPC* can take any value depending on the macro model we choose.

29. Consider an initial long-run equilibrium situation. If the economy encounters a negative demand shock, it will lead to
a. lower output and lower prices in the short run.
b. lower output and higher prices in the short run.
c. potential output eventually in the long run, but prices will return to the initial level.
d. less than potential output in the long run.

30. Consider an initial long-run equilibrium situation. If the economy encounters an adverse supply shock, it will lead to
a. lower output and lower prices in the short run.
b. lower output and higher prices in the short run.
c. potential output eventually in the long run, but prices will return to the initial level.
d. less than potential output in the long run.

Use the following to answer questions 31-32.

Real GDP (*Y*)	Taxes (*T*)	Consumption (*C*)
1,000	100	800
1,100	100	880
1,200	100	960
1,300	100	1,040
2,000	100	1,600

31. The *MPC* and *MPS* are ________________, respectively,
a. 0.8 and unknown
b. 0.8 and 0.2
c. unknown and 0.2
d. none of the above

32. Which of the following statements is false?
a. The *MPC* is 0.8 and the multiplier is 5.
b. The *MPS* is 0.2 and the multiplier is 5.
c. When $Y = 1{,}400$, the consumption is 1,120 and private saving is 280.
d. When $Y = 2{,}000$, the consumption is 1,600 and private saving is 300.

Problems and Exercises

1. Consider an economy that is initially in long-run equilibrium as drawn in the following graph where *LRAS* is the long-run *AS* curve, AD_1 is the aggregate demand curve, $SRAS_1$ is the short-run *AS* curve, Y_1 is potential output, and P_1 is the equilibrium aggregate price level.

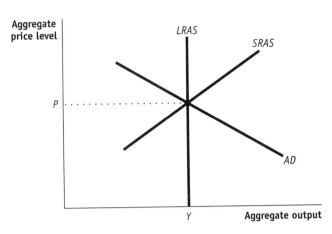

a. Draw a graph using the *AS-AD* model to illustrate the effect of each of the following separate changes to the model in the short run.
   1) The economy's central bank decreases the money supply.

   2) Productivity decreases in the economy.

   3) Consumer confidence in the economy increases.

   4) Commodity prices fall dramatically.

b. Identify verbally what happens to aggregate output and the aggregate price level relative to the initial long-run equilibrium for each of the scenarios.

c. For each of the scenarios determine whether the economy faces a short-run recessionary gap or an inflationary gap.

d. For each of the scenarios determine if there is an active stabilization policy that will offset the particular shock. If so, discuss what this active stabilization policy is. You may find it helpful to draw a graph illustrating the effects of your active policy prescription on the aggregate economy.

e. For each of the scenarios identify what happens in the long run to the aggregate price level and the aggregate output level if there is no active stabilization policy.

2. Consider an economy operating with an inflationary gap in the short run. Briefly describe what this short-run equilibrium looks like, making specific reference to potential output and then describe the process by which this economy moves from short-run to long-run macroeconomic equilibrium. Use a graph to illustrate your description.

3. Consider an economy operating with a recessionary gap in the short-run.
   a. Why does this represent a problem for this economy? Draw a graph illustrating your answer.

   b. What policies are available to policymakers to address this problem? Illustrate these policies using a graph.

   c. If policymakers do nothing, describe the mechanism by which this economy will return to long-run macroeconomic equilibrium. Draw a graph illustrating this long-run adjustment.

4. Suppose you are given the following information about Macroland, where Y is real GDP, T is taxes, and C is consumption spending.

Year	Y	T	C
1	100	50	40
2	150	50	80
3	300	50	200

   a. Fill in the following table using the information in the table.

Year	Disposable Income
1	
2	
3	

b. What is the *MPC* for this economy?

c. What is the *MPS* for this economy?

d. What is the value of the multiplier for this economy?

e. Given this information and the calculations you have made, compute the values for each of the various scenarios in the following table.

Scenario	Initial level of Y	Change in autonomous spending	Final level of Y after all changes in response to the change in autonomous spending
1) Government decreases spending by $20	$200		
2) Investment spending increases by $20	$300		
3) Consumption spending increases by $30	$400		

5. The *AS-AD* model is said to have a self-correcting mechanism. Explain what this means and how this self-correcting mechanism works. Use a graph to illustrate your answer.

6. Use a graph of the *AS-AD* model to illustrate long-run economic growth in an economy. Explain your graph and how it illustrates economic growth. Assume in your answer that *AD* does NOT change over time.

7. Consider the following table for a given economy.

Real GDP(Y)	Taxes(T)	Consumption (C)	Private Saving (SP)
1,000	100	800	
1,100	100		120
1,200	100	960	140
1,300	100	1,040	
1,600	100		
2,000	100	1,600	

a. Fill in the blanks.

b. What is the *MPC* of this economy? What is the *MPS*?

c. Find the equation for the consumption function.

d. What is autonomous consumption?

e. What is the multiplier?

8. a. If the economy's *MPC* is 0.75, then the economy's *MPS* is _____.

b. If the economy's multiplier is 2.5, then the economy's *MPC* is _____.

c. If the economy's multiplier is 3, then an increase in autonomous spending of 100 will increase real GDP by _____.

9. Consider the following shocks and indicate if it is a positive or negative demand or supply shock. Indicate whether the shock leads to higher or lower output and higher or lower price in the short run.

Type of shock	+ or –	demand or supply shock	Output	Price
↑ Taxes on income				
↑ G				
↑ oil price				
Lower wage rate				

10. Consider an economy's *AD* and *AS* curves in the following diagram.

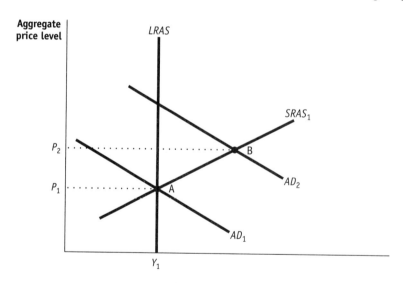

a. The long-run equilibrium output is _____.

b. If the *AD* curve shifts to the right from AD_1 to AD_2, there will be a recessionary or inflationary gap. Find the correct choice.

c. In the long run, the *AD* curve determines the price or output. Find the correct choice.

Answers to How Well Do You Understand the Chapter

1. fall, increase, increase, aggregate output

2. price, positive, increases, wages, wages, flexible

3. shifts, left, right, right, movement along

4. nominal wages, no effect, vertical, potential output, right

5. negative, higher price, reduces, increases, aggregate price level

6. downward, purchasing power, wealth effect, increase, more, interest rates, less

7. right, left, right, right, left, increase, right, left

8. short-run, long-run, aggregate output, unemployment, right, nominal wages, left

9. disposable income, consumer spending, zero, marginal propensity to save

10. autonomous change, real GDP, marginal propensity to consume, marginal propensity to consume

11. economic fluctuations, supply shock, Negative supply shocks, positive supply shocks, stagflation, decrease, demand shock, negative demand shock, positive demand shock

12. recession, potential output, below, unemployment, inflationary gap, self-correcting

13. stabilization policy, severity, stabilization policies, increase, rightward, leftward

Answers to Multiple-Choice Questions

1. Stagflation refers to the combination of rising inflation and decreasing aggregate production. When the *AS* curve shifts to the left (a negative supply shock), this causes the aggregate price level to increase and the aggregate level of output to decrease. **Answer: B.**

2. A change in the aggregate price level due to a shift in *AD* results in a movement along the *AS* curve. In the short run the *AS* curve is upward sloping, so an increase in the aggregate price level results in a higher level of aggregate production. **Answer: B.**

3. The economy produces at its potential level of output if it is at a long-run equilibrium. The increase in wealth will cause the *AD* curve to shift to the right, causing a movement along the *AS* curve, and an increase in aggregate production and the aggregate price level. **Answer: C.**

4. In the short run, nominal wages are "sticky" and take time to adjust to changes in economic conditions due to pre-existing contracts and employer reluctance to frequently alter wages. In the long run, nominal wages are fully flexible. **Answer: D.**

5. Production costs affect the level of aggregate production: as production costs increase, holding everything else constant, profit per unit decreases. Producers respond to this decrease in profit per unit by decreasing the quantity of goods and services they are willing to supply. **Answer: B.**

6. An increase in the price of a commodity, holding everything else constant, will cause the *AS* curve to shift to the left as aggregate production decreases at any given aggregate price level. Aggregate production decreases due to the decrease in producers' profit per unit, arising from the higher commodity price they must now pay. **Answer: B.**

7. An increase in the aggregate price level results in a movement along the *AS* curve and not a shift of the curve. A decrease in commodity prices results in a rightward shift of the *AS* curve. An increase in nominal wages causes the *AS* curve to shift to the left. **Answer: E.**

8. In the long run, the *AS* is vertical and not upward sloping as it is in the short run. It is possible for an economy to be in both long-run and short-run equilibrium simultaneously so that the economy is producing its potential level of output. In the short run, we assume nominal wages are constrained from full adjustment and are therefore sticky, while in the long run, nominal wages are assumed to be fully flexible. **Answer: C.**

9. In the long run, the economy by definition is already producing at the level of aggregate output we refer to as potential output. An increase in the aggregate price level in the long run can only be explained by a shift in the *AD* curve, and this shift will not affect aggregate output since the long-run *AS* curve is vertical. **Answer: F.**

10. Since the economy is producing at a level of aggregate output smaller than the level of potential output, the economy cannot be in long-run equilibrium. Since output is below potential output, we know that not all workers are being fully utilized: if all workers were fully employed this would result in higher levels of production. Therefore, unemployment must be relatively high, and this will lead to decreases in the nominal wage over time since jobs are scarce and workers are abundant. **Answer: C.**

11. The aggregate price level and the quantity of aggregate output demanded is the relationship captured by the *AD* curve. It is an inverse relationship: as the aggregate price level increases, other things equal, there is a decrease in the quantity of aggregate output demanded. **Answer: A.**

12. An increase in the aggregate price level, holding everything else constant, leads to a reduction in demand for aggregate output. This is due to the wealth effect and the interest rate effect. Answer (a) expresses how an increase in the aggregate price level affects people's wealth, while answer (b) expresses how this price change affects their purchasing power (via the interest rate effect). **Answer: D.**

13. The *AD* curve will shift to the left if the central bank decreases the money supply, since this policy action will increase interest rates, reduce investment spending, and therefore lead to lower *AD* at every aggregate price level. An increase in taxes reduces the disposable income households have and will therefore lead to lower *AD* at every aggregate price level (the *AD* curve will shift left). An increase in household wealth will shift the *AD* curve to the right, since households will increase their spending due to their increased wealth. **Answer: B.**

14. The multiplier is equal to $[1/(1 - MPC)]$, so as the *MPC* increases so too does the multiplier. Recall that an economy's marginal propensity to save plus its marginal propensity to consume must equal one. Thus, the smaller the marginal propensity to save, the larger will be the marginal propensity to consume and therefore the multiplier captures the idea that a single increase in autonomous spending leads to a change in real GDP that is a multiple of the size of that initial change in spending. **Answer: A.**

15. If the *MPC* equals .75, then the multiplier equals 4. Thus, a $10 million increase in government spending will increase real GDP by four times that amount or $40 million. **Answer: C.**

16. Since the economy is initially in long-run macroeconomic equilibrium, we know aggregate output is initially equal to potential output. The central bank's policy action will cause interest rates to fall and investment spending to increase. This will cause the *AD* curve to shift to the right, resulting in short-run aggregate output exceeding potential output. This increase in output will result in a decrease in unemployment. Over time this will lead nominal wages to increase, which will result in the short-run *AS* curve shifting to the left. **Answer: E.**

17. In the long run, macroeconomic equilibrium requires that the economy produce at that point where *AD* equals long-run *AS* as well as short-run *AS*. Short-run *AS* adjusts though changes in nominal wages to bring the equilibrium to this long-run equilibrium. When the central bank increases the money supply, this shifts the *AD* curve to the right. For a given long-run *AS* curve and this central bank action, it is possible to return to long-run macroeconomic equilibrium only if the short-run *AS* curve shifts to the left, resulting in a higher aggregate price level. **Answer: A.**

18. A recessionary gap is a situation in the short run where aggregate output is less than potential output. A recessionary gap is eliminated in the long run as the short-run *AS* curve adjusts to return the economy to potential output and long-run equilibrium. An inflationary gap is a situation in the short run where aggregate output is greater than potential output. As the economy moves to a long-run equilibrium, this inflationary gap will be eliminated and aggregate output will return to potential output. **Answer: B.**

19. Policymakers face a difficult tradeoff when they try to offset a supply shock. In this case, the supply shock reduces aggregate output and increases the aggregate price level. Active stabilization policy can shift *AD* to the right or to the left: if *AD* shifts to the right, this will stimulate aggregate output while simultaneously increasing the aggregate price level to even higher levels; and if AD shifts to the left, this will reduce the aggregate price level while simultaneously decreasing the aggregate output level to even lower levels. **Answer: B.**

20. The *AD* curve is downward sloping in both the short run and the long run. **Answer: C.**

21. The reduction of household wealth shifts the *AD* curve to the left. The new intersection point of the *AD* curve with the original *SRAS* curve will be below potential output; as a result, there will be a recessionary gap. This will cause lower wages over time and the *SRAS* curve will start shifting to the right. The process will continue until the recessionary gap is wiped out and the economy eventually restores the potential output. **Answer: A.**

22. A decrease in money supply will cause a leftward shift of the *AD* curve, and an increase in the wage rate will cause a leftward shift of the *SRAS* curve. The new intersection point of the *AD* with the *SRAS* will take place at a point where the output is less than the original output in the short run. We cannot predict the price, because we do not know the extent of the leftward shifts of the curves. **Answer: B.**

23. An increase in taxes on household will shift the *AD* to the left; an increase in money supply will cause a rightward shift of the *AD* curve. Since we do not know the extent of the above shifts, we cannot conclude whether the *AD* will finally shift to the left or to the right or stay the same. **Answer: D.**

24. The *SRAS* curve will shift to the left due to higher energy costs; if the Bank of Canada increases the money supply, it will cause a rightward shift of the *AD* curve. As a result, we will see higher prices and inflation. **Answer: A.**

25. Since $MPC = \Delta C/\Delta$ disposable income, we can find *MPC* as 0.8 and *MPS* as 0.2. **Answer: C.**

26. Reduction of taxes on households will cause the rightward shift of the *AD* curve: movement from point A to point B. Along a given supply curve (consider points A and B), the input prices and wages are constant. **Answer: B.**

27. At point B, we see an inflationary gap. **Answer: B.**

28. If the multiplier is 2.5, then $(1 - MPC) = MPS = 0.4$. **Answer: B.**

29. A negative demand shock shifts the *AD* curve to the left, and the new intersection point of the new *AD* curve with the old *SRAS* curve will take place at a point below the original output point leading to lower prices. **Answer: A.**

30. An adverse supply shock will shift the *SRAS* curve to the left. As a result, prices will increase and output will fall in the short run. **Answer: B.**

31. $MPC = 0.8$ and $MPS = 0.2$. **Answer: B.**

32. When $Y = 1{,}300$, $C = 1{,}040$. Since *MPC* is 0.8, we can see that increase of *Y* by 100 increases C by 80. Therefore, when $Y = 1{,}400$, $C = 1{,}120$; private saving $= 1{,}400 - 100 - 1{,}120 = 180$. **Answer: C.**

Answers to Problems and Exercises
(1)

1. a.

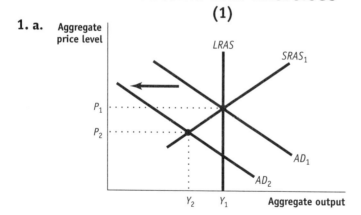

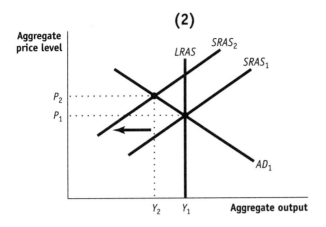

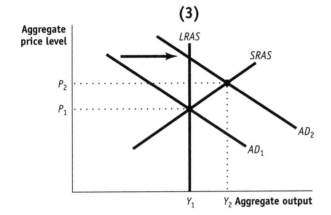

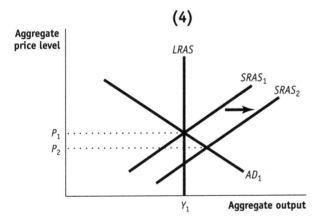

b. In scenario 1), the aggregate price level and the aggregate level of output both decrease relative to their initial levels. In scenario 2), the aggregate price level increases, while the aggregate level of output decreases relative to their initial levels. In scenario 3), the aggregate price level and the aggregate level of output both increase relative to their initial levels. In scenario 4), the aggregate price level falls, while the aggregate level of output increases relative to their initial levels.

c. A short-run recessionary gap is defined as a situation where the economy produces at a level of output that is less than potential output: scenarios 1) and 2) illustrate this situation. Scenarios 3) and 4) represent inflationary gaps since the level of aggregate output is greater than potential output.

d. For scenario 1), active stabilization policy can be used to bring the economy back to its initial aggregate price level and aggregate output level. This policy would need to shift AD to the right (back to its initial position) and could be accomplished by increasing government spending, decreasing taxes, or increasing the money supply.

For scenario 2), active stabilization policy cannot restore the economy to its initial equilibrium. A policy that shifts AD to the right would result in an increase in the aggregate price level relative to its initial level (P_3 versus P_1), and a return to the initial level of production, Y_1, for aggregate output. The following graph illustrates the implementation of an active stabilization policy that shifts AD to the right.

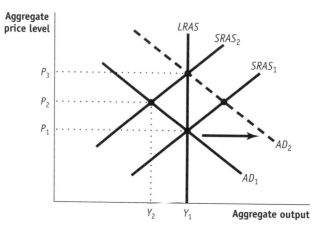

A policy that shifts AD to the left would result in a return to the initial aggregate price level of P_1, a decrease in the level of aggregate output relative to its initial position (Y_3 versus Y_1). The following graph illustrates this.

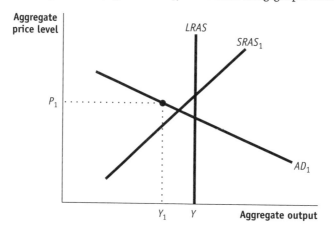

In scenario 3), active stabilization policy can be used to bring the economy back to its initial equilibrium. This policy would shift AD to the left and could be accomplished by decreasing government spending, increasing taxes, or decreasing the money supply.

In scenario 4), active stabilization policy cannot restore the economy to its initial equilibrium: shifting *AD* to the right restores the original price level to P_1, but increases the level of output above the initial level (Y_3 versus Y_1), thus, creating an inflationary gap. The following graph illustrates this.

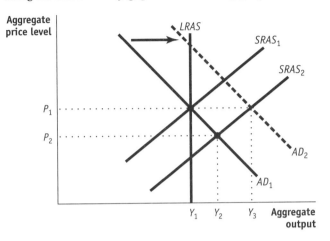

Shifting *AD* to the left restores output to its initial level Y_1, but the aggregate price level falls relative to its initial level (P_3 versus P_1). The following graph illustrates this.

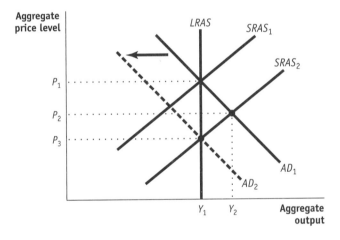

e. If there is no active stabilization policy implemented, then in scenario 1) the short-run *AS* curve will shift to the right as the nominal wage decreases in response to the recessionary gap. As the short-run *AS* curve shifts out, the economy will eventually reach long-run equilibrium where the aggregate output level returns to potential output, Y_1, while the aggregate price level falls to a lower long-run aggregate price level than the initial long-run P_1. In scenario 2), if there is no active stabilization policy implemented, the short-run *AS* curve will shift to the right, returning the economy back to its initial long-run macroeconomic equilibrium. In scenario 3), if there is no active stabilization policy implemented, the short-run *AS* curve will shift to the left, restoring the economy to the original level of aggregate output but a higher aggregate price level than the initial long-run P_1. In scenario 4), if there is no active stabilization policy implemented, the short-run *AS* curve will shift to the left, returning the economy to its initial equilibrium position.

2. An economy operating in the short run with an inflationary gap is producing a level of aggregate output, Y_1, that is greater than potential output, Y. This is illustrated in the following diagram.

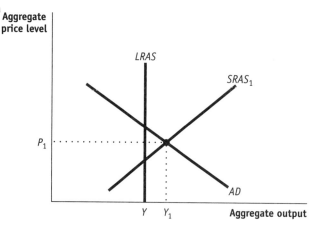

This implies that unemployment is relatively low and, therefore, workers are scarce and jobs are abundant. Over time this situation puts pressure on nominal wages to rise and this causes the short-run AS curve to shift to the left. As AS shifts to the left ($SRAS_2$), the level of aggregate production in the economy falls and this brings aggregate output closer to potential output. The nominal wage will continue to adjust until the short-run AS curve intersects the AD curve and the long-run AS curve at the same point. Then the economy will be in long-run macroeconomic equilibrium, where aggregate output equals potential output while the aggregate price level has risen to P_2 from P_1. This is illustrated in the following diagram.

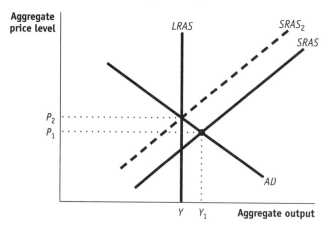

3. a. A recessionary gap for an economy is problematic, since it indicates that the economy is producing a lower level of aggregate output (Y_1) than its potential (Y): this lower output also signals that the economy faces higher unemployment than necessary. This is illustrated in the following graph.

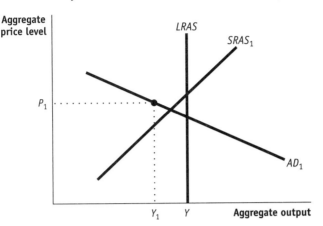

b. To offset a recessionary gap, active stabilization policy can be implemented that will return the economy to potential output. A recessionary gap caused by a leftward shift in AD is easily offset by using fiscal policy or monetary policy to shift AD to the right and returning the aggregate output to the level of potential output (Y). A recessionary gap caused by a leftward shift in AS is a more difficult problem: active stabilization policy that shifts AD to the right can bring the aggregate level of production back to potential output but only by raising the aggregate price level to a higher level. This is illustrated in the following diagram.

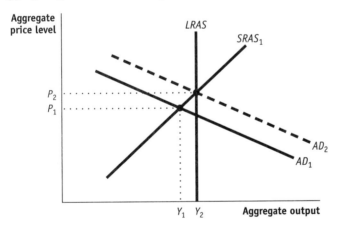

c. If policymakers do nothing, the economy will return to a long-run macroeconomic equilibrium over time through changes in the nominal wage and accompanying shifts in the short-run AS curve. If the recessionary gap is due to a leftward shift in AD, over time we can expect short-run AS to shift to the right, bringing the economy back to potential output and a lower aggregate price level than experienced during the recessionary gap. If the recessionary gap is due to a leftward shift in *AS*, over time we can expect short-run *AS* to shift back to the right, returning the economy to its potential output and a lower aggregate price level than it experienced during the recessionary gap. Both of these possibilities is illustrated in the following diagram.

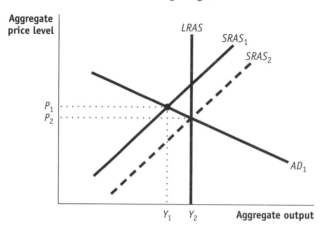

4. a.

Year	Disposable Income
1	50
2	100
3	250

b. The *MPC* is defined as the change in consumption spending divided by the change in disposable income. Using the information given to you and your calculations in (a), you can calculate the *MPC* as .8 (since the change in consumption from year 1 to year 2 is 40 and the change in disposable income from year 1 to year 2 is 50).

c. The *MPS* plus the *MPC* equals one. Since the *MPC* equals .8, this implies that the *MPS* equals .2.

d. The value of the multiplier for this economy equals $[1/(1 - MPC)]$ or 5.

e.

Scenario	Initial level of Y	Change in autonomous spending	Final level of Y after all changes in response to the change in autonomous spending
1) Government decreases spending by $20	$200	$20	Change in Y = Multiplier × (−20) = (40) = −$100, so final level of Y = $200 − $100 = $100
2) Investment spending increases by $20	$300	$20	Change in Y = Multiplier × (20) = $100, so final level of Y = $100 + $300 = $400
3) Consumption spending increases by $30	$400	$30	Change in Y = Multiplier × (30) = $150, so final level of Y = $150 + $400 = $550

5. The *AS-AD* model is self-correcting, since it will always return to long-run macro-economic equilibrium if given a sufficient amount of time for the short-run *AS* curve to adjust to economic changes through changes in the nominal wage. This adjustment process has been reviewed in several earlier problems: essentially, it is the idea that the short-run *AS* curve shifts due to changes in the nominal wage until that point where *AD* intersects both the short-run and the long-run *AS* curves at potential output. If this is still unclear to you, review questions 1) and 2) and the diagrams illustrating their answers.

6. Long-run economic growth is depicted in the *AS-AD* model as the long-run *AS* shifting to the right. Thus, your graph should depict several vertical *AS* curves, with each one farther to the right on the horizontal axis representing the ability of the economy to reach even higher levels of potential output. For a given *AD* curve, the level of aggregate output increases as the *LRAS* curve shifts to the right. The following graph illustrates this idea.

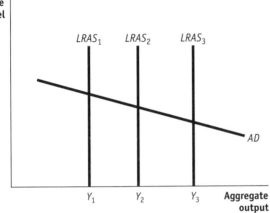

7. a.

Real GDP(Y)	Taxes(T)	Consumption (C)	Private Saving (SP)
1,000	100	800	**100**
1,100	100	**880**	120
1,200	100	960	140
1,300	100	1,040	**160**
1,600	100	**1,280**	220
2,000	100	1,600	**300**

   b. $MPC = 0.8$ and $MPC = 0.2$
   c. $C = 80 + 0.8(Y - T)$
   d. Autonomous consumption = 80.
   e. 5

8. a. $MPS = 0.25$
   b. $MPC = 0.6$
   c. 300

9.

Type of shock	+ or − demand or supply shock	Output	Price
↑ Taxes on income	− demand shock	lower	lower
↑ G	+ demand shock	higher	higher
↑ oil price	− supply shock	lower	higher
Lower wage rate	+ supply shock	higher	lower

10. a. The long run equilibrium output is Y_1.

    b. If the *AD* curve shifts to the right from AD_1 to AD_2, there will be an **inflationary gap**.

    c. In the long run, the *AD* curve determines the **price**.

chapter 11

Income and Expenditure

This chapter develops the consumption function and uses it to explain the relationship between disposable income and consumer spending. The chapter explores the effect of expected future income and aggregate wealth on consumer spending. In addition, the determinants of investment spending and the distinction between planned investment spending and unplanned inventory investment are discussed. The chapter explores the significance of the level of investment spending as an indicator of the future state of the economy. The chapter illustrates how the inventory adjustment process enables the economy to regain its equilibrium after a demand shock. The chapter uses the multiplier process to quantify the effect of a change in the consumption function or a change in planned investment on the income-expenditure equilibrium real GDP. The appendix explains the process for deriving the multiplier from the simple model presented in the chapter.

How Well Do You Understand the Chapter?

Fill in the blanks using the terms below or circle the correct answer to complete the following statements. Terms may be used more than once. If you find yourself having difficulties, please refer to the appropriate section in the text.

accelerator principle	decline	income	Keynesian cross diagram	recession(s)
added	decrease	income-expenditure	less	save
aggregate demand	disposable	income-expenditure equilibrium	less than	shift
autonomous	disposable income	increase	multiplier	short-run
change	down	intercept	negative	slope
closed	equilibrium	interest rate(s)	planned	stock
constant	firms	intersects	planned investment spending	sum
consumer	forty-five degree line	inventories	positively	taxes
consumer spending	GDP	inventory	productive	thrift
consumption function	greater	inversely	rate of return	unplanned
	growth	investment spending	real GDP	unpredicted
	horizontal			zero

1. Aggregate expenditure significantly impacts _____, which has been discussed in the previous chapter. The components of aggregate expenditure in the closed private sector economy are aggregate _____ spending and aggregate investment spending.

245

2. The consumption function is an equation that shows the relationship between a household's current _____ and its level of consumer spending. We can write the aggregate consumption function for an economy as $C = A + MPC \times YD$, where C is the aggregate _____ spending and A is the aggregate _____ spending, MPC is the marginal propensity to consume, and YD is aggregate _____ income. Autonomous spending (A) measures the level of consumer spending at zero disposable income; in other words, A depends on other determinants other than income. Both A and MPC are assumed to be _____. The MPC measures the change in consumer spending due to the change in the _____ income.

3. The aggregate _____ illustrates the relationship between the aggregate disposable income in an economy and the level of aggregate consumer spending. If we graph the aggregate _____, with disposable income on the horizontal axis and consumer spending on the vertical axis, then A is the _____ of the vertical line and the MPC is the _____ of the consumption function. Consumer spending and disposable income are _____ related to each other: as disposable income increases, consumer spending increases. We can write the aggregate _____ as $C = A + MPC \times YD$, where C is the aggregate _____, A is aggregate _____ consumer spending, MPC is the marginal propensity to consume, and YD is aggregate _____.

4. The two principal reasons behind shifts of the aggregate consumption function are changes in expected future disposable _____ and changes in wealth. The life-cycle hypothesis theorizes that consumers plan their spending over a lifetime and, as a result, try to smooth, or even out, their consumption spending over the course of their entire lives. A(n) _____ in expected future disposable income or wealth causes the vertical intercept A to increase (shift up), and this results in an upward _____ of the aggregate consumption function. Similarly, a(n) _____ in expected future disposable income or wealth causes the aggregate consumption function to shift _____.

5. The level of investment spending is a critical determinant of economic performance: most _____ result from a decrease in investment spending. In addition, declines in consumer spending are usually the result of a _____ in aggregate income (which is brought about by the multiplier process) due to a(n) _____ in investment spending. The two most important factors determining the level of investment spending are _____ and expected future _____.

6. The investment spending that firms bring in is not always the investment spending that they have _____. Planned investment spending refers to the investment spending _____ plan to make during a given time period and this depends primarily on the following: interest rate, the expected future level of real GDP, and the current level of _____ capacity.

7. The _____ in the loanable funds market equates the demand for funds to the supply of funds. Investment projects with a(n) _____ equal to or greater than the equilibrium interest rate will be funded, while those investment projects with a rate of return _____ the equilibrium interest rate will not be funded.

8. A(n) _____ in the market interest rate makes any given investment project less profitable, while a(n) _____ in the market interest rate makes any given investment project more profitable. Therefore, planned investment spending is _____ related to the interest rate.

9. The _____ is the idea that a higher rate of growth in real GDP leads to higher planned investment spending. The higher rate of growth in real GDP typically indicates rapid _____ in sales, leading businesses to quickly use up any excess productive capacity and resulting in higher _____.

10. Inventories are the _____ of goods that the firms hold in anticipation of future sales. Inventory investment refers to the _____ in total inventories held in the economy during a given period of time. Inventory investment may be positive, negative, or zero. Positive inventory investment indicates that the economy had _____ to its stock of inventories, while _____ inventory investment indicates that the level of inventories has decreased. Inventories fluctuate over time. Unintended changes in inventories (due to _____ fluctuations in sales) are referred as _____ inventory investment.

11. Thus, actual _____ in an economy in any given period is comprised of two parts: planned investment spending, $I_{planned}$, and unplanned inventory investment, $I_{Unplanned}$. Positive unplanned _____ investment typically occurs in a slowing economy where actual expenditure on goods and services is less than the _____ expenditure. Negative unplanned _____ investment occurs in a growing economy where actual expenditure exceeds _____ expenditure on goods and services. Inventories play a key role in the _____ macroeconomic models, and the behaviour of firms' _____ often signals the future state of the economy.

12. In a(n) _____ economy with no government, a fixed aggregate price level, and fixed interest rates, there are only two sources of AD: consumer spending and investment spending. In this economy, aggregate disposable income, $YD = Y$ minus _____; and $AE_{Planned}$, or the total amount of _____ expenditure in the economy is comprised of consumption spending C, and planned investment, $I_{Planned}$. The _____ of the $AE_{Planned}$ line in the closed no government economy equals the MPC. $AE_{Planned}$ may differ from _____ because of the influence of unplanned aggregate spending in the form of unplanned inventory investment. Over time the economy moves to that point where $AE_{Planned}$ equals GDP or the unplanned inventory investment is _____.

13. We can express these ideas using equations. We know GDP in this simple closed economy with no government sector, a fixed aggregate price level, and fixed interest rates can be written as $Y = C + I$, where Y is the _____. Furthermore, investment spending, I, can be written as the _____ of $I_{Planned}$ and $I_{Unplanned}$. Thus, $Y = C + I_{Planned} + I_{Unplanned}$. We also know that $AE_{Planned}$ is the sum of _____ plus planned investment, or $AE_{Planned} = C + I_{Planned}$. Thus, $GDP = AE + I_{Unplanned}$.

14. When GDP is _____ than $AE_{Planned}$, this implies that $I_{Unplanned}$ is positive; and this acts as a signal to firms to decrease their production; which over time moves the economy back to the _____. When GDP is _____ than $AE_{Planned}$, this implies that $I_{Unplanned}$ is negative; and this acts as a signal to firms to increase their production, which over time moves the economy toward the _____. When GDP equals $AE_{Planned}$, then the economy is in the _____ equilibrium. At this equilibrium, $I_{Unplanned}$ equals _____ and firms have no incentive to change their levels of production in the next period. We refer to this level of GDP as the income-expenditure equilibrium GDP.

15. We can make use of a _____ to help identify the income-expenditure equilibrium GDP. When we graph $AE_{Planned}$ on the vertical axis and _____ on the horizontal axis, the income-expenditure equilibrium GDP is that level of GDP, where the AE line _____ the forty-five degree line. This diagram is called the _____. The economy self-corrects when GDP is not equal to $AE_{Planned}$ through _____ adjustment.

16. The *AE* line, or $AE_{Planned}$, shifts in this simple model if there is a _____ in planned investment spending, $I_{Planned}$, or if there is a shift in the consumption function, *C*. Either shift triggers the _____ process, so for a change in either variable there will be an even bigger change in the _____ level of GDP. We can write this idea as the change in the income-expenditure equilibrium GDP. Recall that the _____ in this simple model equals $1/(1 - MPC)$.

17. Given a fixed aggregate price level, the multiplier effect causes the *AD* curve to _____ by an amount equal to the change in the equilibrium GDP. Our assumption of a fixed aggregate price level implies that the short-run *AS* curve is _____: thus, when *AD* shifts, this causes the equilibrium level of real GDP to change by the amount predicted by the _____ process.

18. The paradox of_____ refers to how individuals concerned about a potential economic downturn may worsen that economic downturn when they choose to act prudently and _____ their level of saving. It is a paradox, since what is "good" (households' _____ their income and spend less), produces a "bad"—an economy with more severe _____.

Learning Tips

TIP #1: A thorough understanding of the aggregate consumption function and the variables that shift the aggregate consumption function is essential.

Make sure you review the aggregate consumption function and understand the relationship between consumer spending and autonomous consumer spending, the marginal propensity to consume, and disposable income. The consumption function will shift upward with increases in wealth or expected future disposable income. Figure 11.1 is a representation of a consumption function: the slope of this function equals the *MPC*, and the *y*-intercept equals autonomous consumption spending, or *A*.

Figure 11.1

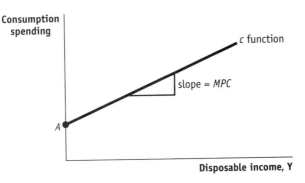

TIP #2: The forty-five degree line in the Keynesian cross diagram provides a help-ful visual tool for identifying the income-expenditure equilibrium GDP.

The Keynesian cross diagram illustrates the relationship between $AE_{Planned}$ and GDP: to the left of the point of intersection in the Keynesian cross, we know that AE is greater than GDP, inventories are falling, and firms will respond by increasing their production; to the right of the point of intersection in the Keynesian cross, we know that AE is less than GDP, inventories are rising, and firms will respond by decreasing their production. Figure 11.2, which follows, illustrates these points.

Figure 11.2

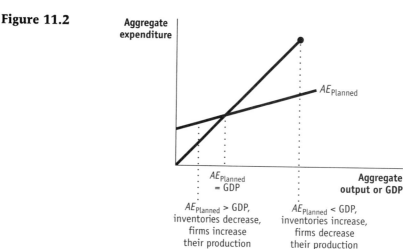

TIP #3: An understanding of investment spending and its components is a critical aspect of this chapter.

Make sure you can distinguish between planned investment spending and unplanned inventory investment. In the macroeconomic model presented in this chapter, the mech-anism that ensures the attainment of equilibrium is unplanned inventory adjustment. This concept is essential for understanding how this short-run model of the economy works. Figure 11.2 illustrates this inventory adjustment.

TIP #4: The model presented in this chapter has a number of simplifying assump-tions. You need to be familiar with these assumptions while understand-ing their implications.

The chapter builds a simple macroeconomic model that assumes a closed economy with no government. The assumption of no government eliminates the impact of taxes and transfers as well as government spending. The model also assumes a fixed aggregate price level and fixed interest rates. A fixed aggregate price level implies a horizontal short-run AS curve: with this AS curve we know that it is the location of the AD curve that deter-mines the equilibrium level of real GDP. In Figure 11.3, the aggregate price level is held constant at P, and we consider the effect of a shift in the AD on the level of aggregate production.

Figure 11.3

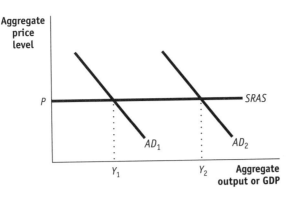

TIP #5: **This chapter continues the development of the multiplier from the previous chapter, and it then considers the impact of the multiplier on the macroeconomic model presented in this chapter.**

The text starts with a relatively simple economic model to develop important economic concepts like the multiplier. Review the definition of the multiplier, its calculation, and then practice using this concept in questions provided in the text and this study guide. Figure 11.4, which follows, illustrates this multiplier effect. The economy is initially producing Y_1. When there is an increase in autonomous spending, this causes $AD_{Planned}$ to shift up by an amount equal to this change in spending. This leads to a higher equilibrium level of output, Y_2. The multiplier equals the ratio of this change in aggregate output divided by the change in autonomous spending.

Figure 11.4

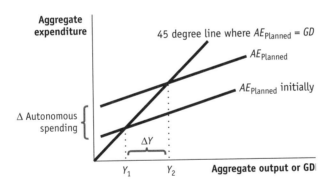

Multiple-Choice Questions

1. In a closed private sector economy, income-expenditure equilibrium is defined as

a. $Y = C + I$.
b. $Y = C + S$.
c. $Y = C + I + G$.
d. $Y = C + I + G + X - IM$.

2. Consumer spending
  a. usually accounts for two thirds of total spending on goods and services.
  b. will cause the AD curve to shift, if such spending changes.
  c. has a powerful impact on the economy's aggregate output and aggregate price level in the short run when it results in a shift in the AS curve.
  d. All of the above are correct.
  e. Both a and b are correct.

3. Consumer spending is affected by changes in
  a. current disposable income.
  b. expected future disposable income.
  c. wealth.
  d. All of the above affect consumer spending.

Use the following information to answer the next two questions.

Suppose aggregate consumer spending equals $5,000 when aggregate disposable income is zero. Furthermore, suppose that when disposable income increases from $300 to $400, consumer increases by $70 and that this relationship between a change in disposable income and its affect on consumer spending is predictable and constant.

4. What is the equation for the aggregate consumption function, given the previous information?
  a. $C = 5,000 + 70YD$
  b. $C = 500 + .7YD$
  c. $C = 5,000 + .7YD$
  d. $C = 5,000 + 7YD$

5. If aggregate disposable income equals $2,000, then what is the value of aggregate consumer spending?
  a. $7,000
  b. $19,000
  c. $6,400
  d. $5,140

6. Suppose aggregate wealth decreases in the economy due to the bursting of a housing price bubble. This will, holding everything else constant,
  a. reduce wealth and result in a decrease in autonomous consumer spending.
  b. cause the aggregate expenditure function to shift down.
  c. result in a lower level of consumer spending for any given level of disposable income.
  d. All of the above are correct.
  e. Both a and b are correct.

7. Which of the following statements is true?
  a. An increase in investment spending shifts the *AD* curve leftward, leading to an economic expansion.
  b. Most recessions start with a decrease in investment spending.
  c. Economists think decreases in consumer spending often follow decreases in investment spending.
  d. All of the above are true.
  e. Both b and c are true.

8. An increase in the market interest rate
  a. will make any given investment project less profitable.
  b. will cause companies to rely more heavily on financing their investment projects through retained earnings rather than borrowing.
  c. will reduce the rate of return for any given investment project.
  d. All of the above statements are true.

9. The accelerator principle
   a. helps to explain investment booms.
   b. refers to an increase in planned investment spending due to a higher rate of growth in real GDP.
   c. refers to an increase in government spending intended to stimulate the economy.
   d. All of the above are correct.
   e. Both a and b are correct.

10. Which of the following is NOT an assumption underlying the multiplier process for this chapter?
   a. Since this is a short-run process, the aggregate price level is sticky but not fixed.
   b. The interest rate is assumed to be fixed and unaffected by the factors analyzed in our model of the multiplier process.
   c. The multiplier process assumes a closed economy where government spending, taxes and transfers equal zero.
   d. In the short run, the economy always produces at the full employment level of output.

Use the following information to answer the next five questions.

Suppose Macroland is a closed economy with no government sector and therefore no government expenditure, taxes, or transfers. Furthermore, assume the aggregate price level and interest rate in Macroland is fixed. You are also told that the MPC in Macroland is constant. You are provided the following information about Macroland. (All numbers in the following table are dollar amounts.)

GDP	YD	C	$I_{Planned}$	$I_{Unplanned}$
100	100	150	50	−100
200			50	
400		300	50	

11. What is the consumption function for this economy?
   a. $C = 150 + .5YD$
   b. $C = 250 + .5YD$
   c. $C = 100 + .5YD$
   d. $C = 50 + .5YD$

12. When GDP equals 400, which of the following statements is true?
   a. Unplanned inventory investment is negative.
   b. Planned aggregate expenditure equals 400.
   c. Unplanned inventory investment is positive.
   d. The economy is in income-expenditure equilibrium when GDP equals 400.

13. What is the income-expenditure equilibrium GDP for Macroland?
   a. 200
   b. 300
   c. 500
   d. 600

14. Holding everything else constant, suppose wealth increases by 100. Which of the following statements is true?
   a. The *AD* curve shifts to the right.
   b. The *AE* line shifts upward.
   c. The income-expenditure equilibrium real GDP increases by more than 100.
   d. All of the above statements are true.
   e. Both a and b are true.

15. Given the change in wealth in question (14), the equilibrium level of GDP
   a. increases relative to its initial level.
   b. decreases relative to its initial level.
   c. is unaffected.
   d. may increase, decrease, or stay the same relative to its initial level.

16. According to the accelerator principle,
   a. higher rate of growth of real GDP brings higher inflation rate.
   b. higher rate of growth in real GDP leads to higher planned investment.
   c. higher rate of growth in real GDP leads to accelerated consumer spending.
   d. higher rate of growth in real GDP leads to accelerated national saving.

Consider a closed no-government private sector economy. Use the following table to answer questions 17–18.

Income	Consumption	Investment
500	500	200
1,000	900	200
1,500	1,300	200

17. Which of the following statements is false?
   a. The equilibrium Y is 1,500.
   b. At the equilibrium Y, the unplanned inventory investment is zero.
   c. The autonomous consumption is 200.
   d. The slope of the consumption function and aggregate expenditure function in the 45-degree diagram is 0.8.

18. Which of the following statements is false?
   a. The multiplier is 5.
   b. If planned investment increases by 100 and we take into account all the multiplier effects, then the AD curve (with constant price assumption) will shift by 500.
   c. If planned investment increases by 100, then the new income-expenditure equilibrium will be 2,000.
   d. If planned investment increases by 100, then the intercept of the new aggregate expenditure (AE) line in the 45-degree diagram will be 300.

Answer questions 19–20 on the basis of the following no-government closed economy constant price macro model.
$Y = AE$
$AE = C + I$
$C = 100 + 0.75Y$
$I = 200$

19. Use the previous model and find the incorrect answer from the following
   a. The equilibrium Y is 1,200 and the multiplier is 4.
   b. The equilibrium Y is 1,200 and private saving is 200.
   c. The equilibrium Y is 1,200 and the autonomous consumption expenditure is 200.
   d. If autonomous consumption increases by 100 due to an increase of wealth, the equilibrium Y will increase by 400.

20. If households become more thrifty and save 40% of the aggregate income, while autonomous consumption remains constant at 100 and autonomous investment remains constant at 200, then
 a. the new equilibrium Y will be 750, and the private saving will be 200.
 b. the equilibrium Y will be higher than the previous level of 1,200, and new private saving will be higher than the previous level of 200.
 c. Y will remain at the same level of 1,200, but new private saving will be higher than the previous level of 200.
 d. More saving means more investment and more investment means more income, and at the same time we observe higher multiplier.

Use the following table to answer question 21.

Investment project	Rate of return
Project A	11%
Project B	9%
Project C	7%
Project D	5%
Project E	4%

21. Which of the following statements is false?
 a. If the market interest rate is 6%, then only the investment Project A will be funded.
 b. If the market interest rate increases to 12%, none of the investment projects will be funded.
 c. If the market interest rate drops to 3%, all the investment projects will be funded.
 d. If the market interest rate increases to 10% from 3%, investments will decrease and income-expenditure equilibrium GDP will decrease.

Use the following Keynesian-cross diagram to answer questions 22–25.

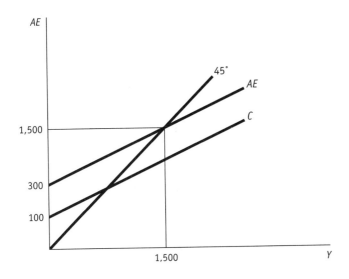

22. The aggregate consumption function is _____ and aggregate private saving (S_P) function is _____.
a. $C = 100 + 0.8Y$ and $S_P = 100 + 0.2Y$
b. $C = 100 + 0.8Y$ and $S_P = -100 + 0.2Y$
c. $C = 300 + 0.8Y$ and $S_P = -300 + 0.2Y$
d. $C = 300 + 0.8Y$ and $S_P = 100 + 0.2Y$

23. Which of the following statements is true?
a. The autonomous consumption spending is 100; an increase in the autonomous consumption spending may increase or decrease the MPC.
b. The autonomous consumption spending is 300; an increase in the autonomous consumption spending may increase or decrease the MPS.
c. The autonomous consumption spending is 100; an increase in the autonomous consumption spending has no effect on MPC or MPS.
d. The autonomous consumption spending is 300; an increase in the autonomous consumption spending has no effect on MPC, but it may increase MPS.

24. Find the incorrect answer from the following solutions.
a. The autonomous expenditure is 300; the multiplier is 5, and the equilibrium Y is 1,500, which is equal to 5 times 300.
b. The multiplier is 5; if investment decreases by 100, it will cause a leftward shift of the AD curve by 100.
c. The multiplier is 5; if investment decreases by 100, it will cause a leftward shift of the AD curve by 500.
d. If autonomous expenditure remains constant, but the MPC increases to 0.9, the intersection of the aggregate expenditure line with the 45-degree line will take place where Y = 3,000.

25. If the AE line shifts down by 100, then Y will
a. decrease by 100.
b. decrease by 250.
c. decrease by 500.
d. Y may increase or decrease, even if we assume a constant price closed economy private sector model.

Problems and Exercises

1. Econoland analyzes its aggregate consumer spending and aggregate disposable income and finds the following data. All numbers in the table are dollar amounts.

YD	C
0	100
100	180
200	260
300	340
500	500

Assume Econoland is a closed economy with no government spending, no taxes, and no transfers. Furthermore, assume the aggregate price level and interest rate are fixed in Econoland.
a. What does autonomous consumer spending equal in this economy?

b. What is the value of the *MPC* for Econoland?

c. Use the following graph to graph the data given in the previous table. Label the consumption function you construct with a *C*.

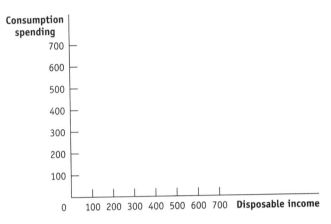

d. What is the slope of the consumption function you graphed in part (c)?

e. What is the relationship between the slope of the consumption function and the *MPC*? Explain your answer.

f. Suppose future expected disposable income increases in Econoland. How will this affect autonomous consumer spending, the *MPC*, and the consumption function?

2. Use the following data to answer this question for Funland, a closed economy with no government sector, a fixed aggregate price level, and a fixed interest rate. All numbers in the table are dollar amounts.

GDP	YD	C	$I_{Planned}$	$AE_{Planned}$	$I_{Unplanned}$
	20	22	20		
	50		20		−10
80			20		2
100		70	20		

a. Fill in the missing values in the previous table.

b. What is the value of autonomous consumer spending?

c. What is the *MPC* for Funland?

d. Graph the above information using a Keynesian cross diagram. Label the income-expenditure equilibrium GDP.

e. What is the income-expenditure equilibrium real GDP for Funland? (Hint: the table does not include the income-expenditure equilibrium GDP, but the table does provide the information necessary to find this equilibrium.)

f. Suppose $I_{Planned}$ increases by 20, holding everything else constant. Fill in the following table given this change.

GDP′	YD′	C′	I′$_{Planned}$	AE′$_{Planned}$	I′$_{Unplanned}$
	20	22	40		
	50		40	80	
80			40	98	
100		70	40		

g. Given the change in (f), what is the new equilibrium level of real GDP for Funland?

h. Explain the relationship between the multiplier and the answer you gave for (f).

3. Outlandia's planned aggregate expenditure line is depicted in the following graph, where the vertical axis measures planned aggregate expenditure and the horizontal axis measures real GDP.

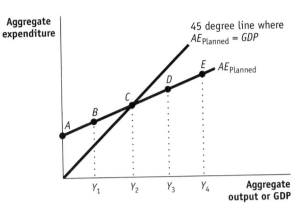

a. The previous graph is referred to as a Keynesian cross diagram. Interpret the information provided in the graph.

Suppose Outlandia's economy currently is operating at point B.
b. Is this an income-expenditure equilibrium for Outlandia? Explain your answer.

c. At point B, describe what is happening to inventories and production in Outlandia.

d. What level of GDP will this economy produce once it is at an income-expenditure equilibrium?

e. At what levels of labeled GDP on the previous graph is unplanned inventory investment positive? Explain your answer.

f. At what levels of labeled GDP on the previous graph is planned aggregate expenditure greater than income? Explain your answer.

g. Explain the significance of point C in the previous graph.

4. Suppose Inlandia's autonomous consumer spending equals 500 and that consumer spending increases by $50 for every $100 increase in aggregate disposable income. Assume Inlandia is a closed economy with no government sector, a fixed aggregate price level, and fixed interest rates.

a. Use the following graph to plot Inlandia's consumption function.

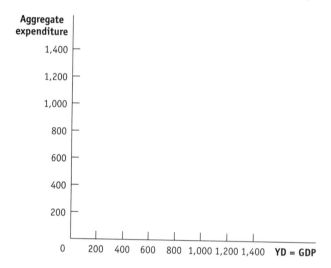

b. Suppose you are told that planned investment spending equals $100, no matter what the level of income in the economy. Graph this information in the previous graph and label the line you draw $I_{Planned}$.

c. On the previous graph, graph the $AE_{Planned}$ line and label it $AE_{Planned}$.

d. What is the income-expenditure equilibrium real GDP for Inlandia?

e. Sketch a diagram showing the relationship between $AE_{Planned}$, $I_{Planned}$, the consumption function, and the forty-five degree line.

f. What is the value of the multiplier for this economy?

g. What will be the change in the income-expenditure equilibrium level of real GDP if autonomous consumption decreases by $50?

5. The Project Analyst in your firm has studied the cost and revenue estimates of the following projects.

Investment project	Rate of return
Project #1:	15%
Project #2:	10%
Project #3:	7%
Project #4:	6%
Project #5:	5%
Project #6:	4%

a. If the market interest rate is 9%, which investment projects will be undertaken?
b. If the interest rate drops to 5%, which investment projects will be undertaken?
c. What is the relationship (positive or negative) between investment and interest rate?
d. If $I = 2{,}000 - 5{,}000r$, where I is the investment and r is the interest rate, find the investment when I is 10% and when r is 8%.

6. Consider a no-government private-sector closed economy.
$Y = AE$
$AE = C + I$
$C = 80 + 0.8Y$
$I = 300$

a. Find equilibrium Y, C, and private saving.

b. Find the multiplier. What is the change in Y if autonomous investment increases by 100?

c. What is the multiplier if MPC is 0.75?

7. Consider a no-government private-sector closed economy. The consumption and investment schedules of this economy follow:

Income	Consumption	Investment	Aggregate expenditure	Unplanned inventory
0	100	400		
500	500	400		
1,000	900	400		
1,500	1,300	400		
2,000	1,700	400		
2,500	2,100	400		
3,000	2,500	400		

a. Fill in the last two columns of the accompanying table.

b. The autonomous expenditure is _____. The autonomous consumption is _____. The MPC is _____. The slope of the AE line is _____. The equilibrium Y is

_____.

c. The multiplier is _____. If I decreases by 100, Y will decrease by

_____.

8. Use the accompanying graph to answer the following questions:

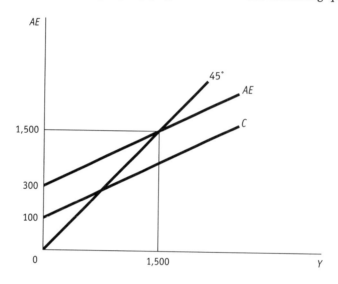

a. The slope of the AE line is _____. The steeper the slope is, the higher/lower (circle the correct choice) the multiplier is.

b. If autonomous expenditure increases by 500, What is ΔY?

Answers to How Well Do You Understand the Chapter

1. aggregate demand, consumer

2. disposable income, consumer, autonomous, disposable, constant, disposable

3. consumption function, consumption function, intercept, slope, positively, consumption function, consumer spending, autonomous, disposable income

4. income, increase, shift, decrease, down

5. recessions, decrease, decline, interest rates, real GDP

6. planned, firms, productive

7. interest rate, rate of return, less than

8. increase, decrease, inversely

9. accelerator principle, growth, planned investment spending

10. stock, change, added, negative, unpredicted, unplanned

11. investment spending, inventory, planned, inventory, planned, short-run, inventories

12. closed, taxes, planned, slope, GDP, zero

13. real GDP, sum, consumer spending

14. greater, income-expenditure equilibrium, less, income-expenditure equilibrium, income-expenditure, zero

15. forty-five degree line, GDP, intersects, Keynesian cross diagram, inventory

16. change, multiplier, equilibrium, multiplier

17. shift, horizontal, multiplier

18. thrift, increase, save, recession

Answers to Multiple-Choice Questions

1. In a closed private sector model, we ignore G, T, X, and IM. **Answer: A.**

2. Consumer spending affects the level of AE on goods and services and therefore shifts the AD curve, not the AS curve. Typically, consumer spending comprises two thirds of total spending on goods and services. **Answer: E.**

3. All three of these variables affect the level of consumer spending. **Answer: D.**

4. The basic equation for the aggregate consumption function is $C = A + MPC \times YD$, and from the information we know, A, the aggregate autonomous consumer spending, equals \$5,000 and the MPC can be calculated as the change in consumer spending divided by the change in aggregate disposable income, or 70/100, which equals .7. So, $C = 5,000 + .7YD$. **Answer: C.**

5. Using the equation from question (4), substitute \$2,000 for YD and solve for C. In this case, C equals $5,000 + .7(2,000)$, or \$6,400. **Answer: C.**

6. When the housing price bubble bursts, this reduces households' wealth and causes them to reduce their level of consumption spending, including autonomous consumption spending, at every level of disposable income. This downward shift in the consumption function results in a downward shift of the aggregate expenditure function and a decrease in the value of autonomous consumer spending. **Answer: D.**

7. An increase in investment spending increases AE for goods and services, which shifts the AD curve to the right and leads to a higher level of aggregate output (an economic expansion) and a higher aggregate price level for a given short-run upward sloping AS curve (and no change in the aggregate price level, if we assume a fixed aggregate price level and therefore a horizontal short-run AS curve). Studies of recessions indicate that most recessions follow a drop in investment spending, and this drop in investment spending results in a fall in consumer spending. **Answer: E.**

8. A change in the market interest rate does not affect the rate of return for any given investment project. It does, however, affect the opportunity cost of borrowing and as the market interest rate increases, this makes any given investment project less profitable due to the relationship between the market interest rate and the project's rate of return. Firms, whether they use retained earnings or borrow, recognize that the market interest rate reflects the opportunity cost of using or acquiring funds. **Answer: A.**

9. The accelerator principle states that a higher rate of growth in real GDP leads to higher planned investment spending. This results in a boom in investment spending. Government spending intended to stimulate the economy is expansionary fiscal policy. **Answer: E.**

10. Both answers (b) and (c) are assumptions in our model of the multiplier process in this chapter. This model allows the level of aggregate output to vary in the short-run (answer d). Answer (a) is not true. **Answer: A.**

11. We know the general equation for the consumption function is $C = A + MPC \times YD$. We need to find the values for A and the MPC. From the table and the assumptions underlying Macroland's economy, we know GDP equals YD. The MPC is the change in consumption divided by the change in disposable income: from the table, we can calculate that the change in consumption from 150 to 300 equals 150 and that the change in YD from 100 to 400 equals 300: thus, the MPC equals .5. We can now write $C = A + .5YD$ and use one of the combinations of consumption and disposable income from the table to solve for A; for example, when consumption equals 150, YD equals 100 and A can be computed as 100. **Answer: C.**

12. When GDP equals 400, we can calculate $AE_{Planned}$ by summing C plus $I_{Planned}$. $AE_{Planned}$ equals 350, so income (GDP) is greater than expenditure, and therefore unplanned inventory investment is positive. **Answer: C.**

13. To find the income-expenditure equilibrium level of real GDP, we need to identify where $AE_{Planned}$ equals GDP. Recall that $AE_{Planned} = C + I_{Planned} = 100 + .5YD + 50 = 150 + .5YD$. Since GDP equals YD for Macroland, this gives us GDP $= 150 + .5YD = 150 + .5GDP$. Solving for GDP we get 300. When YD equals GDP at 300, $AE_{Planned}$ also equals 300. **Answer: B.**

14. An increase in wealth, holding everything else constant, increases autonomous consumer spending and results in the consumption function and the planned aggregate expenditure line shifting upward. This in turn leads to a rightward shift in the AD curve. Due to the multiplier effect, we know that an increase in wealth of 100 will result in real GDP increasing by more than 100. **Answer: D.**

15. A change in wealth of 100 will cause the equilibrium level of real GDP to increase, since the increase in wealth causes the planned aggregate expenditure line to shift up. **Answer: A.**

16. Higher rate of growth in real GDP indicates rapid growth in sales and business use, which increase planned investment spending. **Answer: B.**

17. $Y = C + I = 1,500$. The consumption function is $C = A + 0.8Y$. If $Y = 1,000$ and $C = 900$ and $0.8Y = 900$, then A = autonomous consumption = 100. **Answer: C.**

18. Since autonomous consumption is 100 and since the investment now stands at 300, the total autonomous expenditure is 400. **Answer: D.**

19. All solutions are correct. The autonomous consumption expenditure is 100. **Answer: C.**

20. This question deals with the paradox of thrift. If MPS increases to 0.4 and the new MPC is 0.6, then the new Y drops to 750 (derived from $Y = 300 + 0.6Y$) with savings at the old level of 200. **Answer: A.**

21. An investment project is funded if the rate of return is greater than (or equal to) the market interest rate. If the interest rate is 6%, three investment projects will be funded. All other options are true. **Answer: A.**

22. Since Y equals disposable income and since private saving equals $(Y - C)$, we can derive $C = 100 + 0.8Y$ and $S_P = -100 + 0.2Y$. **Answer: B.**

23. The autonomous consumption is 100, and changes in the autonomous consumption will have no effect on MPC and MPS. **Answer: C.**

24. The $AE = 300 + 0.8Y$; the autonomous expenditure is 300 and the equilibrium Y is 1,500. If investment increases by 100, Y will increase by 500 and the AD curve at a given price will shift by 500. **Answer: B.**

25. Since the multiplier is 5, Y will decrease by 500 due to a shift of the AE line by 100. **Answer: C.**

Answers to Problems and Exercises

1. a. Autonomous consumer spending refers to the level of consumer spending that occurs when disposable income equals zero. In the data given, when disposable income equals zero, consumer spending equals 100: autonomous consumer spending therefore equals 100.

b. The *MPC* equals the change in consumption divided by the change in disposable income. For any two data points (consumption and disposable income combinations), the *MPC* = 8.

c.

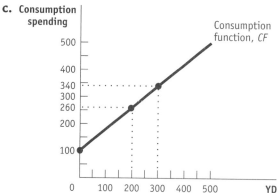

d. The slope of the consumption function equals the *MPC*, or .8.

e. They are equal. It indicates there is a positive relationship between changes in disposable income and changes in consumption. The *MPC* tells us the change in consumer spending for a dollar increase in disposable income. In this problem, the *MPC* equals .8, so we know that when disposable income increases by $1, then consumer spending will increase by $.80.

f. An increase in future expected disposable income will increase autonomous consumption, according to the life-cycle hypothesis. This will cause the consumption function to shift upward by the amount of the change in autonomous consumer spending. There will be no change in the *MPC*.

2. a.

GDP	YD	C	$I_{Planned}$	$AE_{Planned}$	$I_{Unplanned}$
20	20	22	20	42	−22
50	50	40	20	60	−10
80	80	58	20	78	2
100	100	70	20	90	10

b. We know $C = A + MPC \times YD$. We can calculate the *MPC* as the change in consumer spending divided by the change in disposable income: for example, the *MPC* equals $(40 - 22)/(50 - 20) = .6$. Plugging this value for the *MPC* back into our equation for the consumption function yields $C = A + .6YD$. We can choose a consumption spending and disposable income level like (22, 20), substitute these values into this equation, and solve for A. Doing this, we find A equals 10.

c. The *MPC* equals the change in consumption divided by the change in disposable income, or in this case, .6. See explanation in part (b).

d.

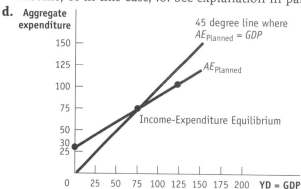

e. To find the income-expenditure equilibrium real GDP in Funland, set $AE_{Planned}$ equal to GDP, since at the income-expenditure equilibrium these two variables are equal. $AE_{Planned}$ equals consumption spending plus planned investment spending. So, GDP = $C + I_{Planned}$ or GDP = 10 + .6YD + 20. Recall that GDP equals YD in this simple model with no government sector, so we can rewrite this equation as GDP = 10 + .6GDP + 20 and then solve for GDP to get 75 for our equilibrium real GDP.

f.

GDP'	YD'	C'	$I'_{Planned}$	$AE'_{Planned}$	$I'_{Unplanned}$
20	20	22	40	62	−42
50	50	40	40	80	−30
80	80	58	40	98	−18
100	100	70	40	110	−10

g. The old equilibrium level of real GDP from part (d) was 75. We have a change in investment spending of 20, and this change will be magnified by the multiplier process. The multiplier in this example equals 2.5, so the change in real GDP equals 2.5 times the $20 change in investment spending. The new equilibrium is the original 75 plus the 2.5(20) or 50, for a total new equilibrium of 125. We could also find the equilibrium by equating GDP' = $AE'_{Planned}$ where $AE'_{Planned}$ = 10 + .6YD + 40. Recalling that GDP equals YD in this simple model, we can rewrite this relationship as GDP = 50 + .6GDP. Solving for GDP, we get 125 as the new equilibrium GDP. The following graph illustrates this.

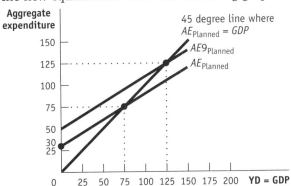

h. We can use the multiplier to see the effect of a change in investment spending on the change in the equilibrium level of real GDP.

3. a. This is a graph of the Keynesian cross which depicts the planned aggregate expenditure line: this line illustrates the positive relationship between GDP and the level of planned expenditure in the economy. The cross is made by this line and the forty-five degree reference line. The point of intersection of these two lines identifies the income-expenditure equilibrium where GDP equals $AE_{Planned}$. When Y is less than Y_2, planned aggregate expenditure is greater than GDP, inventories are falling, and this change in inventories acts as a signal to producers to increase their production. When Y is greater than Y_2, planned aggregate expenditure is less than GDP, inventories are rising, and this change in inventories acts as a signal to producers to decrease their production.

b. No, the income-expenditure equilibrium is at point C on the graph. At point B, $AE_{Planned}$ is greater than GDP, or income. This causes inventories to fall, and firms view this as a signal that they should increase their production from Y_1 towards Y_2, the income-expenditure equilibrium real GDP.

c. See the answer in part (b).

d. This economy, holding everything else constant, will produce GDP equal to Y_2 when it is in income-expenditure equilibrium.

e. Unplanned inventory investment is positive wherever GDP is greater than $AE_{Planned}$: GDP output levels Y_3 and Y_4 represent two output levels where unplanned inventory investment is positive. So, at any output level greater than Y_2, unplanned inventory investment is positive.

f. This is true for any level of GDP less than Y_2. For example, at points A and B, $AE_{Planned}$ exceeds GDP.

g. Point C represents the income-expenditure equilibrium level of real GDP where $AE_{Planned}$ equals GDP.

4. a. (see answer at part (c))

b. (see answer at part (c))

c.

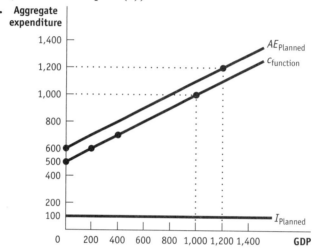

d. Solving for the income-expenditure requires us to know the consumption function $(C = 500 + .5YD)$ and the level of planned investment spending (100). We know $AE_{Planned}$ equals GDP in equilibrium and that $AE_{Planned}$ is the sum of consumption spending plus planned investment spending. So, GDP = $AE_{Planned}$ = C + $I_{Planned}$ = 500 + .5YD + 100. We also know in our simple model that GDP equals YD. So, GDP = 600 + .5GDP, and solving for GDP we find it is equal to 1,200.

e.

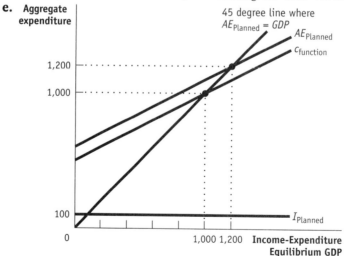

f. We calculate the multiplier as $1/(1 - MPC)$: if the MPC equals .5, then the multiplier equals 2.

g. The change in equilibrium real GDP equals the multiplier times the change in autonomous consumption or $(2)(-50)$ or -100. Equilibrium real GDP will fall by 100 with this change in autonomous consumption.

5. a. Project #1 and Project #2.
  b. All investment projects, except project #6, will be undertaken.
  c. negative
  d. $I = 1,500$ when r is 10%. $I = 1,600$, when $r = 8\%$

6. a. $Y = 1,900$, $C = 1,600$, private saving = 300.
  b. The multiplier is 5. The change in Y is 500.
  c. 4

7. a.

Income	Consumption	Investment	Aggregate expenditure	Unplanned inventory
0	100	400	500	−500
500	500	400	900	−400
1,000	900	400	1,300	−300
1,500	1,300	400	1,700	−200
2,000	1,700	400	2,100	−100
2,500	2,100	400	2,500	0
3,000	2,500	400	2,900	+100

  b. 500; 100; 0.8; 0.8; 2,500
  c. 5; 500

8. a. 0.8; higher
  b. 2,500

chapter 12

Fiscal Policy

This chapter focuses on fiscal policy—government spending and taxation—and its use as an economic tool for managing economic fluctuations. The chapter discusses expansionary fiscal policy, or the use of government spending and/or taxation policy to stimulate the economy, as well as contractionary fiscal policy, or the use of government spending and/or taxation policy to slow down the economy. In addition, the chapter explores the multiplier effect of fiscal policy as well as the affect of automatic stabilizers on the size of the multiplier. The chapter continues with the development of the budget balance and how economic fluctuations affect this budget balance. The chapter also discusses the long-run consequences of public debt and the significance of the government's implicit liabilities.

How Well Do You Understand the Chapter?

Fill in the blanks using the terms below or circle the correct answer to complete the following statements. Terms may be used more than once. If you find yourself having difficulties, please refer to the appropriate section in the text.

automatic stabilizers	economic	inflationary gap	recessionary gap
autonomous aggregate spending	equally	interest payments	reduces
	faster	investment spending	right
autonomous change	fiscal	left	saving
balanced budget	fiscal policy	less	shift
borrows	future growth rate	long-run	slower
debt	GDP	minus	spending
debt-GDP ratio	government	more	surplus
decrease(s)	government debt	multiplier	taxes and transfers
deficit	implicit liabilities	multiplier effect	T – G – TR
direct	income tax	potential	time
disposable income	increase(s)	potential output	transfer payments

1. Discretionary _____ refers to the use of government spending or tax or both to manage aggregate demand (*AD*). In Canada, the government spending as a percentage of _____ was 41.7% in 2003, and for the same year, the government tax revenue was 43.4% of GDP. In 2004, about 31% of government revenue came from personal income tax in Canada. The three most important programs in government _____ in Canada are health, _____, and social insurance programs. Canada's social insurance programs are intended to protect families against _____ hardships.

2. The government _____ is defined as $(T - G - TR)$. The basic equation of national income accounting, $GDP = C + I + G + X - IM$, reminds us that government's purchases of goods and services (G) have direct impacts on the total spending of the economy. The government also affects consumption (C) through changes in _____ and _____, and it may also affect investment through government policy.

3. Increases in taxes, holding everything else constant, reduce _____ and consumer spending. When taxes go down, they lead to _____ in disposable income and consumer spending. Increases in government transfer payments, holding everything else constant, _____ disposable income and consumer spending. _____ in government transfer payments, holding everything else constant, decrease disposable income and _____ consumer spending. Government can impact the incentives to engage in _____ through changes in tax policy.

4. The government can use changes in taxes or government spending to shift the *AD* curve. Expansionary fiscal policy in the form of increases in government spending, decreases in taxes, or increases in government transfers will shift the *AD* curve to the _____. The *AD* curve shifts to the _____ with decreases in government spending, increases in taxes, or _____ in government transfers. When the economy faces a _____, the aggregate output is more than _____: an expansionary fiscal policy can be used to _____ the *AD* curve to the _____ to help eliminate the recessionary gap. When the economy faces a(n) _____, the aggregate output is _____ than potential output: the government can use contractionary fiscal policy, which will _____ the *AD* curve to the _____ to help eliminate the inflationary gap.

5. Important lags exist in the use of fiscal or monetary policy. These lags include the _____ necessary for _____ to realize the need for policy intervention, the time necessary to develop policy, and the time necessary for the government to implement the policy and have it take effect. The existence of lags makes the use of _____ and monetary policy to correct economics fluctuations _____ challenging than our analysis suggests.

6. A change in government spending is an example of a(n) _____ in the aggregate spending. Holding the price level constant, this change in autonomous aggregate spending will change the real GDP by an amount equal to the _____ times the change in the _____. Recall that the _____ in our simple model equals $1/(1 - MPC)$.

7. If we assume that the change in *G* equals the change in *T*, the absolute change in the *AD* will be less with respect to *T*. A decrease in taxes or increase in transfers will _____ GDP by $MPC/(1 - MPC)$ times the change in taxes or transfers; an increase in taxes or decrease in transfers will _____ GDP by $MPC/(1 - MPC)$ times the change in government spending. Note that $[MPC/(1 - MPC)]$ is _____ than $[1/(1 - MPC)$.

8. In considering income tax, we can see that when GDP increases, the government tax revenue automatically _____. The effect of this automatic increase in government tax revenue when GDP rises, is to dampen the size of the multiplier. When the economy slows down (and the GDP falls), the GDP falls less because the multiplier effect is smaller with income tax. When the economy expands (and the GDP increases), the GDP increases less because the _____ is smaller with _____. Therefore, income tax is a(n) _____. Other examples of automatic stabilizers include income transfers, unemployment insurance benefits, healthcare, and social welfare payments. _____ as well as taxes can act as automatic stabilizers. Discretionary fiscal policy refers to fiscal policy that is the _____ result of policy action by policymakers. It does not refer to automatic adjustment in the economy that occurs because of _____. The multiplier effect of discretionary fiscal policy is dampened in the presence of income tax. The multiplier effect is further dampened if we take into account import as a function of our GDP.

9. Recall that the budget balance equals tax revenue _____ government spending on goods and services minus government transfers. We can write the budget balance, $S_{Government}$, symbolically as $S_{Government}$ = _____. A positive budget balance indicates a budget _____, while a negative budget balance indicates a budget _____. Holding everything else constant, discretionary expansionary fiscal policy _____ the budget balance, while discretionary contractionary fiscal policy _____ the budget balance. Equal size changes in government spending or taxes impact the budget balance _____, but have very different impacts on *AD* due to the fact that the multiplier effect of a change in government spending is greater than the _____ of an equal size change in government taxes or transfers.

10. The cyclically-adjusted budget balance estimates the size of the budget balance if real GDP was exactly equal to _____ output. It effectively eliminates the impact of recessionary or inflationary gaps on budget balance. Most economists do not endorse legislation requiring that the government maintain a(n) _____, since this type of rule would undermine the role of taxes and transfers as automatic stabilizers and it would also undermine the role of discretionary fiscal policy. When the government's spending exceeds tax revenue,

it usually _____ funds from the loanable fund market. Governments that run persistent deficits find they have a rising government _____. A government deficit is the difference between the amount of money a government spends and the amount of money it receives in taxes. _____ is the sum of money a government owes at a particular point in time.

11. When the government runs persistent budget _____ it competes with firms that plan to borrow funds for investment spending. The government borrowing may "crowd out" private _____ and lead to a reduction in the economy's _____. When the government runs persistent budget deficits this leads to financial pressure on future budgets due to the increasing size of the interest payments on the accumulated _____. Holding everything else constant, a government that owes large amounts in _____, must raise more revenue from taxes or spend less.

12. Governments that print money to pay their bills find that this leads to _____. The _____ effects of persistent budget deficits suggest that governments should run a budget that is approximately balanced over time.

13. The _____ is a measure used to assess the ability of governments to pay their debt. This measures government debt as a percentage of _____. When GDP grows at a(n) _____ rate than the rate of growth of the government's debt, then the burden of paying the debt falls relative to the government's ability to collect tax revenue. The debt-GDP ratio can fall even when debt is rising provided that GDP grows _____ than debt. The debt-GDP ratio will rise when debt is rising if GDP grows _____ than debt.

14. _____ are promises made by governments that represent debt but are not included in the government's _____ statistics. The current capital value of Canada's total liabilities in 2004 was $1.1 trillion.

15. Taxing income at a constant tax rate t allows us to model a macroeconomy where tax revenues increase as the level of aggregate output increases. The inclusion of this income tax rate alters the _____ for a change in autonomous spending from $1/(1 - MPC)$ to $1/[1 - MPC(1 - t)]$. This new multiplier will be _____ than the original multiplier for a given MPC.

Learning Tips

TIP #1: This chapter contains some new vocabulary. In the context of fiscal policy, you need to be familiar with these concepts, including the government deficit, government debt, implicit liabilities, the debt-GDP ratio, and budget balance.

As in the other chapters it is essential that you learn and understand any new terms that are introduced. Many of the terms in this chapter represent complicated concepts or relationships.

TIP #2: Discretionary fiscal policy affects aggregate spending and causes shifts of the *AD*.

Expansionary fiscal policy increases aggregate expenditure and shifts the *AD* curve to the right. Contractionary fiscal policy decreases aggregate expenditure and shifts the *AD* curve to the left. Since consumption depends on disposable income, an increase in taxes reduces disposable income and reduces consumer spending.

TIP #3: When the economy has a recessionary gap, an expansionary fiscal policy can be used to eliminate the recessionary gap. When the economy has an inflationary gap, a contractionary fiscal policy can be used to eliminate the inflationary gap.

TIP #4: Lags in fiscal policy and the crowding-out effect lessen the effectiveness of fiscal policy.

TIP #5: Two multipliers are presented and used in this chapter: the multiplier for a change in government spending and the multiplier for a change in taxes.

The multiplier for a change in government spending equals $1/(1 - MPC)$, while the multiplier for a change in taxes equals $[-MPC/(1 - MPC)]$. For example if the *MPC* equals .8, then the multiplier for a change in government spending is equal to 5, while the multiplier for a change in taxes is equal to -4. A \$1 increase in government spending will increase aggregate output by \$5 holding everything else constant, while a \$1 increase in taxes will decrease aggregate output by \$4 holding everything else constant. Make sure you work some problems using these multipliers and that you understand why they do not have equivalent values. Also, spend time thinking about why the multiplier for government spending is positive while the multiplier for a change in taxes is negative. An increase in government spending represents an increase in the level of spending in the economy and will stimulate aggregate production, while an increase in taxes reduces the level of spending in the economy and will therefore contract aggregate production.

TIP #6: Review the distinction between fiscal policy that is discretionary versus fiscal policy that reflects the impact of automatic stabilizers.

TIP #7: The use of the multiplier thus far in our models presumes a horizontal *SRAS*. If the *SRAS* is upward sloping, then the impact on aggregate output will be smaller than that predicted by the multiplier.

Essentially this tip should remind you that a horizontal *SRAS* implies a fixed price level, while an upward sloping *SRAS* implies that prices are not fixed. A shift in *AD* due to a change in autonomous spending or taxes will cause a larger change in aggregate output (and a change equal to the amount predicted by the multiplier effect) if prices are held constant then if prices vary. Let's look at a diagram of this represented in Figure 12.1.

Figure 12.1

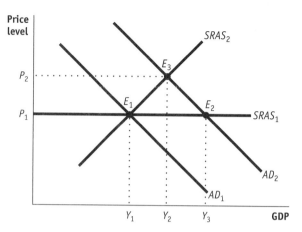

AD_1 is our initial AD curve; $SRAS_1$ is the short-run aggregate supply curve if prices are held constant, and $SRAS_2$ is the short-run aggregate supply curve if prices vary. Initially the economy is at point E_1, producing Y_1 at a price level P_1. When autonomous aggregate spending increases this shifts AD_1 to AD_2, and the horizontal distance Y_1 to Y_3 measures the multiplier effect on aggregate output (point E_2). However, given $SRAS_2$ a rightward shift in AD from AD_1 to AD_2, increases output from Y_1 to Y_2 while simultaneously increasing the price level from P_1 to P_2 (point E_3).

TIP #8: You will want to understand what the cyclically adjusted budget balance is and how it relates to the budget balance and to potential GDP. The cyclically adjusted budget balance is an estimate of what the budget balance would be if real GDP were exactly equal to potential GDP.

This measure takes into account the extra tax revenue the government would receive and the smaller level of transfer payments it would make if the recessionary gap were eliminated or the tax revenue the government would lose and the extra transfer payments it would make if the inflationary gap were eliminated. The cyclically adjusted budget balance fluctuates less than the actual budget deficit, because years with a large budget deficit are typically associated with large recessionary gaps.

Multiple-Choice Questions

1. Which of the following statements is true?
   a. Sweden's government sector is relatively large, representing nearly 60% of Sweden's GDP.
   b. In Canada, taxes on personal income and corporate income accounted for 40% of total government revenue in 2004.
   c. In Canada, consumption taxes (such as general sales taxes and specific taxes on goods like alcohol, tobacco, and fuel) accounted for 21% of total government revenue in 2004.
   d. All of the above statements are true.
   e. All of the above statements are false.

2. Total government spending differs from government expenditure because it
   a. refers to the purchase of goods and services and does not include transfers since this represents a transfer of income from one individual to another.
   b. refers to the purchase of goods and services as well as expenditures on transfers.
   c. includes, in the United States government, transfers such as spending on Social Security, Medicare, and Medicaid.
   d. Both (a) and (c) are correct.
   e. Both (b) and (c) are correct.

3. Contractionary fiscal policy
   a. is most helpful for restoring an economy to the potential output level of production when there is a recessionary gap.
   b. shifts the *AD* curve to the right, restoring the equilibrium level of output to the potential output level for the economy.
   c. often causes inflation or an increase in the aggregate price level.
   d. if effective, shifts *AD* to the left, resulting in a reduction in the aggregate output and the aggregate price level for a given short-run aggregate supply curve (*SRAS*).

4. Which of the following statements is true? Holding everything else constant,
   a. an economy can eliminate an inflationary gap by increasing government spending.
   b. expansionary fiscal policy refers to an increase in taxes.
   c. when potential output is greater than actual aggregate output, the economy faces a recessionary gap.
   d. when *SRAS* intersects *AD* to the right of the long-run aggregate supply (*LRAS*) curve, the economy faces a recessionary gap.

5. Monetary and fiscal policy
   a. affect the economy in predictable ways and with relatively short time lags.
   b. involve significant time lags with regard to their implementation and effect on the economy.
   c. take so long to implement in the economy that they prove to be useless policies.
   d. when implemented always worsen economic fluctuations because of the lags involved in their implementation.

6. Japan during the 1990s
   a. implemented expansionary fiscal policy.
   b. relied on large-scale government spending on goods and services to stimulate *AD*.
   c. found that expansionary monetary policy could not be utilized since short-term interest rates were already approximately equal to zero.
   d. All of the above statements are true.

7. Holding everything else constant, the multiplier effect for taxes or transfers
   a. is the same as the multiplier effect for changes in autonomous aggregate spending.
   b. is smaller than the multiplier effect for changes in autonomous aggregate spending.
   c. is larger than the multiplier effect for changes in autonomous aggregate spending.
   d. may be smaller, larger, or equal to the multiplier effect for changes in autonomous aggregate spending.

8. Which of the following statements is true?
   a. Automatic stabilizers act like automatic expansionary fiscal policy when the economy is in a recession.
   b. Automatic stabilizers refer to government spending and taxation rules that cause fiscal policy to be expansionary when the economy expands and contractionary when the economy contracts.
   c. Automatic stabilizers reduce the size of the multiplier.
   d. All of the above are true statements.
   e. Both (a) and (c) are true.

9. Discretionary fiscal policy refers to
   a. the effect of automatic stabilizers on the economy.
   b. a situation in which citizens can choose to participate or not participate in government programs.
   c. fiscal policy that is the direct result of deliberate decisions made by policymakers.
   d. fiscal policy that is either the direct result of deliberate decisions made by policymakers or the result of the impact of automatic stabilizers on the economy.

10. Holding everything else constant, the government's budget balance
    a. tends to increase during a recession.
    b. tends to increase during an expansion.
    c. will increase if the government pursues expansionary fiscal policy.
    d. Both (a) and (c) are correct.
    e. Both (b) and (c) are correct.

11. Which of the following statements is true?
    a. Two different changes in fiscal policy that have equal effects on the budget balance will always have equal effects on *AD*.
    b. A change in taxes or transfers will have a larger effect on *AD* than an equal size change in government purchases of goods and services.
    c. The budget deficit almost always falls when unemployment rises.
    d. The cyclically-adjusted budget balance provides an estimate of the budget balance assuming real GDP is equal to potential output.

12. When a government decides to spend more than it collects in tax revenue
    a. it usually borrows the necessary funds.
    b. the budget balance increases.
    c. it runs a budget deficit but reduces its overall level of government debt.
    d. it is forced to sell valuable assets to finance its spending.

13. Which of the following statements is true?
    a. The fiscal year 2006 runs from October 1, 2006 through September 30, 2007.
    b. Public debt is that amount of government debt held by individuals and institutions outside of the government.
    c. The government's total debt includes the public debt as well as the debt owed by one part of the government to another part of the government (for example, the Social Security trust funds).
    d. All of the above statements are true statements.
    e. Both (b) and (c) are true.

14. Which of the following statements is false?
    a. In the fiscal year of 2004, the federal government of Canada paid about 5% of GDP in interests on its debt.
    b. In Canada, the federal government's net debt at the end of 2004 was $523 billion.
    c. The government debt as a percentage of GDP in Canada was about 43% in 2004.
    d. The government debt as a percentage of GDP in Italy was about 96% in 2004.

15. The government debt is
   a. an alternative, but equivalent term for the government deficit.
   b. the difference between the amount of money government spends and the amount of tax revenue the government collects during a given period of time.
   c. the amount of money the government owes at a particular point in time.
   d. best measured over a given period of time.

16. Suppose the government of Macroland repeatedly finds itself running a deficit. This may
   a. result in less private investment spending as government borrowing "crowds out" this spending.
   b. result in lower long-run economic growth if the deficit reduces private investment spending.
   c. cause the government of Macroland to have less budgetary flexibility in the future due to the diversion of tax revenue to pay interest on the debt.
   d. All of the above statements are possible effects of repeatedly running a deficit.

17. The debt-GDP ratio
   a. provides a measure of government debt as a percent of GDP.
   b. provides a measure of government debt relative to the potential ability of the government to collect taxes to cover that debt.
   c. can fall, even if the level of government debt is rising, provided that GDP grows faster than the debt.
   d. All of the above statements are true statements.

18. Which of the following statements is false?
   a. Implicit liabilities are usually included in the debt statistics in Canada.
   b. According to Robson, the current capital value of implicit liabilities in Canada is $1.1 trillion; this is, 84% of the 2004 GDP.
   c. According to Robson, unless growth is better than 3.9%, taxes have to rise as a share of GDP to keep spending programs at their current per capita levels.
   d. Implicit liabilities are not included in the calculation of debt-GDP ratio in Canada.

19. Which of the following statements is false?
   a. The composition of the total Canadian government spending in 2004 included debt charges and protection of persons and property.
   b. Health care, education, and social services accounted for about 61% of the total Canadian government spending in 2004.
   c. If we omit debt charges, the total spending on health care, education, and social services accounted for about 70% of the Canadian government's spending in 2004.
   d. Debt charges peaked at around 18% of total government spending in 2004 in Canada.

20. Suppose the *MPC* equals .5 and the tax rate is .1 for an economy. Holding everything else constant, when government spending increases by $10 billion, what is the total change in aggregate output?
   a. $10 billion
   b. $20 billion
   c. $18.2 billion
   d. $10.5 billion

21. Which of the following statements is true?
   a. When the government "captures" a fraction t of any increase in GDP in the form of taxes, this produces a larger multiplier effect.
   b. If the tax rate is .05 and the *MPC* is .4, then the multiplier for a change in autonomous spending equals 1.6.
   c. If the tax rate is .1 and GDP increases by $1.2 billion, then the government will collect an additional $.12 billion during the given time period.
   d. All of the above statements are true.
   e. Both (b) and (c) are true.

22. When we consider the government spending and tax revenues as a percentage of GDP in 2003 for selected countries (as presented in the textbook), we can conclude that
   a. France has the highest percentage.
   b. Sweden has the highest percentage.
   c. Canada has the highest percentage.
   d. Japan has the highest percentage.

23. When we consider the composition of government spending and the composition of tax revenues in Canada for the fiscal year of 2004 (as presented in the textbook), we can conclude all of the following, except
   a. Personal income tax and corporate income tax account for 51% of the tax revenues.
   b. Personal income tax, consumption tax (such as GST and specific tax on alcohol, tobacco, fuel, etc) account for about 52% of the tax revenues.
   c. Social services and health care account for 46% of the total government spending.
   d. Debt services account for less than 15% of the total government spending.

24. When we consider the government debt-GDP ratio in 2004 for selected countries (as presented in the textbook), we can conclude all of the following, except
   a. The United States has the highest debt-GDP ratio.
   b. Italy has a debt-GDP ratio of over 90%.
   c. Denmark has the lowest debt-GDP ratio.
   d. Canada's debt-GDP ratio is around 43%.

25. Which of the following statements is false?
   a. If the growth of real GDP is greater than the growth of deficit, the debt-GDP ratio will decrease.
   b. Even if the government keeps a balanced budget every year, the debt-GDP ratio can increase.
   c. If we cut government spending, we must see a reduction in the debt-GDP ratio.
   d. The debt-GDP ratio depends on the growth of GDP and the growth of deficit.

26. Consider a short-run equilibrium with an inflationary gap. The government can use which one of the following policy options to close the inflationary gap?
   a. Make equal increases in both taxes and government expenditures.
   b. Increase taxes and/or reduce government expenditures.
   c. Decrease taxes and/or increase government expenditures.
   d. Increase government expenditures.

27. Consider a short-run equilibrium with a recessionary gap. The government can use which one of the following policy-options to close the inflationary gap?
   a. Make equal reductions in both taxes and government expenditures.
   b. Increase taxes and/or reduce government expenditures.
   c. Decrease taxes and/or increase government expenditures.
   d. Decrease government expenditures.

28. Consider a short-run equilibrium with constant price. An increase in government expenditure where $\Delta G = 100$ caused the *AD* curve to shift by 400. We can definitely conclude that
   a. *MPC* = 0.75.
   b. *MPS* = 0.25.
   c. the government expenditure multiplier is 4.
   d. the tax multiplier is 4.

29. Consider a closed model with no income tax and a constant price level. The government expenditure multiplier is given as 4. We can definitely conclude all of the following except:
   a. *MPC* = 0.75.
   b. *MPS* = 0.25.
   c. the tax multiplier = −3.
   d. when $\Delta G = 100$, it will cause the *AD* curve to shift to the left by 400.

30. Consider a closed model with a constant price level. Assume that the income tax rate is 20%. The government expenditure multiplier is 2.5. We can conclude
   a. *MPS* = 0.40.
   b. *MPC* = 0.60.
   c. *MPC* = 0.75.
   d. *MPS* = 0.20.

31. Consider a closed model with a constant price level. Assume that the income tax rate is 25%. The tax multiplier is −2. We can conclude
   a. *MPS* = 0.4.
   b. *MPC* = 0.6.
   c. *MPC* = 0.75.
   d. *MPS* is none of the above.

32. Consider a closed model with a constant price level. Assume that the income tax rate is 25%. The government expenditure multiplier is 2.5. We can conclude
   a. the tax multiplier is −2.
   b. the tax multiplier is more than 2.5.
   c. the tax multiplier is +2.
   d. the tax multiplier cannot be solved.

33. A reduction in consumer confidence is likely to lead to all of the following except
   a. a reduction in autonomous private saving.
   b. a reduction in autonomous consumption.
   c. a reduction in aggregate expenditure
   d. a leftward shift of the *AD* curve.

Answer questions 34–36 on the basis of the following.

The equation of aggregate demand for output is
$Y = 1,000 - 0.75T + 1.25G + 500/P$, where *Y* is real GDP, *P* is price level, *T* is taxes, and *G* is government expenditure. Assume a horizontal aggregate supply curve.

34. If $P = 1$ and $G = T = 200$, then the demand for real GDP (output) is
   a. 1,550.
   b. 1,650.
   c. 1,700.
   d. none of the above.

35. If both G and T increase by 100, then the aggregate demand curve will shift to the right by
   a. 200.
   b. 100.
   c. 50.
   d. none of the above.

36. If we use $\Delta Y/\Delta T$ as the tax multiplier and $\Delta Y/\Delta G$ as the government expenditure multiplier, we can conclude that the tax multiplier is _____ and the government expenditure multiplier is _____.
   a. 0.75; 1.25
   b. –0.75; 1.25
   c. 2; 2
   d. –1.5; 2.5

Answer questions 37–38 on the basis of the following macro model.

$Y = AE$	[Equilibrium condition]
$AE = C + I + G$	[Aggregate expenditure]
$C = 80 + 0.8(Y - T)$	[Consumption function]
$Y_D = Y - T$	[Disposable Income]
$T = 100$	[Tax]
$G = 200$	[Government expenditure]
$I = 100$	[Investment]

37. The equilibrium Y is _____ and the national saving is _____.
   a. 1,500; 200
   b. 1,500; 100
   c. 800; 300
   d. 750; 100

38. The government expenditure multiplier is _____ and the tax multiplier is _____.
   a. 5; –4
   b. 5; 5
   c. 2.5; –2
   d. 2.5; 2.5

Answer questions 39–40 on the basis of the following macro model.

$Y = AE$	[Equilibrium condition]
$AE = C + I + G$	[Aggregate expenditure]
$C = 80 + 0.8(Y - T)$	[Consumption function]
$T = 100 + 0.25Y$	[Tax]
$G = 200$	[Government expenditure]
$I = 100$	[Investment]

39. The equilibrium Y is _____ and the national saving is _____.
   a. 1,500; 200
   b. 1,500; 100
   c. 800; 200
   d. 750; 100

40. The government expenditure multiplier is _____ and the tax multiplier is _____.
a. 5; −4
b. 5; 5
c. 2.5; −2
d. 2.5; 2.5

Problems and Exercises

1. For each of the following situations identify whether it is an example of expansionary discretionary fiscal policy, contractionary discretionary fiscal policy, or fiscal
policy in the form of an automatic stabilizer.
a. During 2002, tax revenue for Macrovia falls as the economy enters a recession.

b. During 2002, in light of projected deficiencies in *AD*, Macrovia's legislature authorizes an expenditure of $200 million in order to build a new hydroelectric dam.

c. In 2005, fearing a too-rapidly expanding economy, Macrovia adopts a budget
that calls for 10% spending cuts in all government departments for the following
fiscal year.

d. In 2004, unemployment benefits rise 5% in response to rising unemployment in
Macrovia.

2. The following graph depicts the economy of Macroland's short-run aggregate supply curve (*SRAS*), its long-run aggregate supply curve (*LRAS*), and its aggregate
demand curve (*AD*). Macroland is currently producing at point *E*.

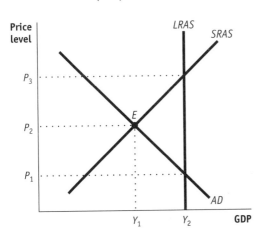

a. Is potential GDP for Macroland equal to Y_1 or Y_2? Describe Macroland's current production relative to its potential production.

reccessionary

b. Does Macroland have a recessionary gap or an inflationary gap? Explain your answer.

recssionary below potential

c. Suppose Macroland wishes to produce at its potential output level. Holding everything else constant, identify which of the following policy initiatives might help it reach this goal and how these policy initiatives would help.
  i. The government initiates policies that encourage private investment spending.

  shift AD →

  ii. The government increases the amount of money it borrows in the loanable funds market in order to increase its level of government spending in the economy.

  shift AD →

  iii. The government increases taxes on consumers and corporations.

  AD←

  iv. The government authorizes new spending programs.

  AD →

d. What is the current price level in Macroland? If Macroland successfully engages in expansionary fiscal policy so that *AD* shifts and actual output equals potential output, what will happen to the price level?

P ↑

3. Funlandia's economists estimate that its potential level of output is $100 in year 1 and this level of potential output grows 5% per year. Assume Funlandia is a closed economy.

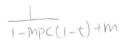

$$\frac{1}{1 - MPC(1-t) + m}$$

a. Fill in the following table for Funlandia given the above information.

Year	Potential output
Year 1	$100
Year 2	105
Year 3	110.25
Year 4	

Suppose Funlandia's economists provide you with the following table of data. All numbers in the table are in dollars.

Year	Potential output	Actual output	T	YD	C	I	G
Year 1	100	100	10	90	55	30	15
Year 2		104	10			30	17
Year 3		115	10			30	22.5
Year 4			10	108	64	30	24

b. What is the consumption function for this economy?

$a + mpc \cdot DI$

$C = (0.5)YD + 10$

c. Fill in the missing values for the same table using the information you have been given or that you computed in parts (a) and (b).

d. Fill in the following table for Funlandia.

Year	Recessionary gap	Inflationary gap	Actual output equals potential output
Year 1	No	No	Yes
Year 2			
Year 3			
Year 4			

e. Suppose Funlandia maintains a policy of using discretionary fiscal policy to insure that actual output equals potential output. Summarize the recommended discretionary fiscal policy necessary to achieve this goal in the following table.

Year	Discretionary fiscal policy
Year 1	
Year 2	
Year 3	
Year 4	

4. Suppose Uplandia is a closed economy where the level of planned investment spending equals $100 and is unaffected by the level of aggregate spending. Furthermore, suppose consumers consume 60% of any increase in their disposable income and autonomous consumer spending equals $20. Uplandia currently has a zero budget balance, with taxes and transfers equal to $50 and government spending on goods and services also equal to $50. Furthermore, assume the price level is fixed in Uplandia in the short run.

a. What is Uplandia's consumption function?

$C = a + mpc \cdot DI$

$C = a + mpc$

$C = 20 + mpc$

b. What is the income-expenditure equilibrium for Uplandia?

$$Y = C + I + G$$
$$Y = 20 + 0.6(Y - 50) + 100 + 50$$

c. Suppose Uplandia wants output to equal $400, the potential level of output. Does Uplandia have an inflationary gap or a recessionary gap? Explain your answer.

d. What is the change in government spending needed to enable this economy to reach its potential output, holding everything else constant?

e. Instead of a change in government spending, Uplandia decides to pursue a change in taxes in order to reach its potential output. Holding everything else constant, what is the change in taxes needed to enable this economy to reach its potential output?

f. Suppose the government decides it wants to maintain a zero budget balance. This implies that any increase in government spending, G, must be accompanied by an equivalent increase in taxes, T. Suppose Uplandia chooses to reach its potential output level while maintaining a zero budget balance. What will the change in G and T need to be in order to accomplish this goal?

g. In your answers to (d), (e) and (f), you use different multipliers to reach potential output in Uplandia. If your only criterion for choosing policy is getting the most "bang for the buck" or, in other words, getting the largest change in aggregate output for a given dollar change in government spending or taxation, which is the best policy? Explain your answer.

h. Relate your answer in part (g) to the debate over the wisdom of a balanced-budget rule for the federal government.

5. Uplandia is concerned about its debt-GDP ratio and the projections about this ratio over the next five years. The following table gives data about Uplandia's real GDP for this year (Year 1) and its projected real GDP for the next five years. Real GDP is projected to grow 3% per year over the next five years as is the government deficit.

Year	Real GDP (millions of dollars)	Debt (millions of dollars)	Budget deficit (millions of dollars)	Debt (percent of real GDP)	Budget deficit (percent of real GDP)
Year 1	800	200	20	25%	2.5%
Year 2	824	206	20.6	25.75	
Year 3					
Year 4					
Year 5					
Year 6					

a. Fill in the missing cells in the table.
b. Describe in words what is happening to the government's debt-GDP ratio and deficit-GDP ratio when real GDP and the government deficit grow at the same rate.

Suppose Uplandia decides to reduce government spending over the next five years. This results in the government deficit growing 1% per year over the next five years while real GDP continues to grow 3% per year.
c. Fill in the table below based on these projections.

Year	Real GDP (millions of dollars)	Debt (millions of dollars)	Budget deficit (millions of dollars)	Debt (percent of real GDP)	Budget deficit (percent of real GDP)
Year 1	800	200	20	25%	2.5%
Year 2					
Year 3					
Year 4					
Year 5					
Year 6					

d. Describe in words what is happening to the government's debt-GDP ratio and deficit-GDP ratio when real GDP grows at 3% per year while the deficit grows at 1% per year.

Suppose Uplandia, buoyed by its projected real GDP growth rate, passes legislation reducing its taxes while simultaneously deciding to go to war. Its economists project real GDP will continue to grow at 3% per year but now, due to these policy decisions, the government deficit is projected to grow at 10% per year. The results of these changes is shown in the following table.

Year	Real GDP (millions of dollars)	Debt (millions of dollars)	Budget deficit (millions of dollars)	Debt (percent of real GDP)	Budget deficit (percent of real GDP)
Year 1	800	200	20	25%	2.5%
Year 2	824	222	22	26.94%	2.67%
Year 3	848.72	246.2	24.2	29.01%	2.85%
Year 4	874.18	272.82	26.62	31.21%	3.05%
Year 5	900.41	302.10	29.38	33.55%	3.25%
Year 6	927.42	334.30	32.2	36.05%	3.47%

e. Describe in words what is happening to the government's debt-GDP ratio and deficit-GDP ratio when real GDP grows at 3% per year while the deficit grows at 10% per year.

f. Can you generalize your findings from this exercise? What general principles does this exercise present?

6. Suppose you are given the following set of equations to describe the closed economy of Fantasia.

$$C = A + MPC\ (Y - T)$$
$$T = tY \text{ where } t \text{ is the tax rate}$$

Furthermore, suppose the price level in Fantasia is fixed in the short run.

a. Using the previous equation, derive an expression for the multiplier for this economy.

You are given some additional information about Fantasia's economy. You are told

$$C = 10 + .5\ (Y - T)$$
$$T = .1Y$$
$$I_{Planned} = \$50 \text{ million}$$
$$G = \$50 \text{ million}$$

b. What is the income-expenditure equilibrium in Fantasia?

c. What is the value of the multiplier for changes in autonomous spending in Fantasia?

Suppose you are told that the potential output level in Fantasia is $180 million.

d. Given your answer in (b), is Fantasia operating with a recessionary or an inflationary gap?

e. The government in Fantasia decides to engage in discretionary fiscal policy to make Fantasia's level of aggregate output equal to its potential output. As Fantasia's chief economist, what change in the level of government spending is necessary to restore the economy to potential output?

7. Calculate ΔG to close the recessionary or inflationary gaps in the following cases. Assume a closed economy along with a horizontal aggregate supply curve. All figures are in billion dollars.

a. Potential GDP is 200, while the actual real GDP is 160. The MPC (out of disposable income) is 0.8 and the income tax rate is 25%.

b. Potential GDP is 200, while the actual real GDP is 260. The MPC (out of disposable income) is 0.75 and the government collects one-third of real GDP as taxes. In other words, the MPC is $\frac{3}{4}$ of disposable income and disposable income is $\frac{2}{3}$ of income.

8. Use the accompanying closed economy model and answer the following questions.

$Y = AE$ [Real GDP = Aggregate Expenditure]

$AE = C + I + G$ [Aggregate expenditure]

$C = 80 + 0.8(Y - T)$ [Consumption function]

$Y_D = (Y - T)$ [Disposable income

$T = 100$ [Tax]

$G = 200$ [Government expenditure]

$I = 300$ [Investment]

a. Find Y, Y_D, C, private saving and government saving.

b. Assume an increase of G by 100 and find Y. What is the value of the multiplier?

c. Keep the G at the original level, but reduce T by 100. Find Y and the multiplier.

d. What will be ΔY, if $\Delta G = \Delta T = 100$?

9. Use the accompanying closed economy model and answer the following questions.

$Y = AE$	[Real GDP = Aggregate Expenditure]
$AE = C + I + G$	[Aggregate expenditure]
$C = 80 + 0.8(Y - T)$	[Consumption function]
$Y_D = (Y - T)$	[Disposable income
$T = 100 + 0.20Y$	[Tax]
$G = 200$	[Government expenditure]
$I = 300$	[Investment]

a. Find Y, T, Y_D, C, private saving and government saving.

b. Assume an increase of G by 100 and find Y. What is the value of the multiplier?

c. Keep the G at the original level, but reduce autonomous taxes by 100. In other words, write the new tax function as $T = 0.25Y$. Find Y and the multiplier.

d. If both autonomous G and autonomous taxes increase by 100, what will be the change in Y?

10. Use the accompanying closed economy model and answer the following questions.

$Y = AE$	[Real GDP = Aggregate Expenditure]
$AE = C + I + G$	[Aggregate expenditure]
$C = 80 + 0.8(Y - T)$	[Consumption function]
$Y_D = (Y - T)$	[Disposable income]
$T = 100 + 0.25Y$	[Tax]
$G = 1,300$	[Government expenditure]
$I = 300$	[Investment]

a. Suppose, the potential real GDP = 4,400. What will be the actual budget deficit and the structural budget deficit?

b. Calculate the change in G that will close the recessionary gap. What will be the structural budget deficit after the change in G?

Answers to How Well Do You Understand the Chapter

1. fiscal, GDP, spending, education, economic

2. saving, taxes, transfers

3. disposable income, increases, increases, decrease, investment spending

4. right, left, decreases, recessionary gap, less, shift, right, inflationary gap, potential output, shift, left

5. time, government, fiscal policy, more

6. autonomous change, multiplier, autonomous aggregate spending, multiplier

7. increase, decrease, less

8. increases, multiplier effect, income tax, automatic stabilizer, transfer payments, direct, automatic stabilizers

9. minus, $T - G - TR$, surplus, deficit, reduces, increases, equally, multiplier effect

10. potential, balanced budget, borrows, debt, Government debt

11. deficit, investment spending, future growth rate, debt, interest payments

12. inflation, long-run

13. debt-GDP ratio, GDP, faster, faster, slower

14. Implicit liabilities, debt

15. multiplier, less

Answers to Multiple-Choice Questions

1. This question is a review of facts presented in the chapter. Each statement is factual. **Answer: D.**

2. Total government spending includes the government's purchases of goods and services as well as the expenditures the government makes in the form of transfer payments. The three primary transfer programs in terms of dollar cost in the United States are Social Security, Medicare, and Medicaid. **Answer: E.**

3. Contractionary fiscal policy is a reduction in government spending or an increase in taxes aimed at shifting *AD* to the left. For a given *SRAS*, this leftward shift in *AD* will lead to a lower level of equilibrium aggregate output and a reduction in the aggregate price level. Contractionary fiscal policy is implemented when the economy produces a level of output in excess of potential output: contractionary fiscal policy is used to offset an inflationary gap. **Answer: D.**

4. When *SRAS* intersects *AD* to the right of *LRAS*, the economy faces an inflationary gap. This inflationary gap can be eliminated through a decrease in government spending or an increase in taxes, since either policy will cause *AD* to shift to the left holding everything else equal. A decrease in government spending or an increase in taxes are examples of contractionary fiscal policy. By definition, when potential output is greater than actual aggregate output, the economy is operating with a recessionary gap. **Answer: C.**

5. There are significant lags involved in the implementation of fiscal and monetary policy. These lags can result in a situation where the implemented policy actually worsens the economic situation (for example, using expansionary fiscal policy to counteract a recessionary gap that has turned into an inflationary gap by the time the fiscal policy takes effect). **Answer: B.**

6. Answers (a), (b) and (c) all describe Japan's economy during the 1990s. Japan found itself pursuing aggressive expansionary fiscal policy to prop up *AD* and, at the same time, found monetary policy to be ineffective since interest rates could not fall any lower. **Answer: D.**

7. In our simple model, the multiplier effect for changes in taxes or transfers equals (in absolute value) $MPC/(1 − MPC)$, while the multiplier effect for changes in autonomous aggregate spending equals $1/(1 − MPC)$. The multiplier effect of changes in taxes and transfers is smaller than the multiplier effect of changes in autonomous aggregate spending. **Answer: B.**

8. Automatic stabilizers act to automatically lessen the economic consequences of recessions and expansions. They do this by providing an automatic fiscal policy response that stimulates a contractionary economy and slows down, or contracts, an expansionary economy. This activity effectively lessens the multiplier process and therefore reduces the size of the multiplier. **Answer: E.**

9. Discretionary fiscal policy refers to fiscal policy that is implemented at the discretion of policymakers. It is therefore the direct result of deliberate actions taken by policymakers. **Answer: C.**

10. The budget balance, $S_{Government}$, is defined by the equation $S_{Government} = T − G − TR$. In an expansion, tax revenue increases and transfers decrease (both of these changes are the result of automatic stabilizers): for a given level of government spending, the budget balance increases. If the government pursues expansionary fiscal policy while holding everything else constant, this will decrease the budget balance. **Answer: B.**

11. Answers (a), (b), and (c) are all incorrect. The multiplier effect from a change in taxes and transfers is smaller than the multiplier effect from a change in government spending and therefore the effect of a change in taxes and transfers on *AD* will be smaller than an equal change in government spending. When unemployment rises, this leads to lower tax revenue (as income falls in the economy, tax revenue also decreases) and higher expenditures on transfer programs like unemployment compensation: thus, the budget deficit almost always rises when unemployment rises. Answer (d) provides a straightforward definition of the cyclically-adjusted budget balance. **Answer: D.**

12. When the government spends more than it collects in tax revenue, the government runs a deficit and must acquire additional funds: typically it does this by borrowing the necessary funds. When the government's deficit increases, this adds to the value of the government debt. It is unusual for governments to sell valuable assets to finance their spending programs. When the government spends more than it collects in tax revenue, this causes the budget balance to decrease (recall the budget balance is defined in equation form as $S_{Government} = T − G − TR$). **Answer: A.**

13. The fiscal year runs from October 1 through September 30th: so, for example, if the fiscal year runs from October 1, 2005 through September 30, 2005, it is considered fiscal year 2005 (and <u>not</u> fiscal year 2004). Public debt is defined as given in answer (b), and the total government debt includes not only the public debt but also the debt that one part of government owes to another part of government. **Answer: E.**

14. All of the statements are true, except the first statement. In the fiscal year of 2004, the Federal Government of Canada paid about 1.8% of GDP in interests on its debt. **Answer: A.**

15. The government debt is not the same as the government deficit. The government deficit is the difference between the amount of money a government spends and the amount of money it collects in tax revenue during a given period of time. The government debt, in contrast, is the total amount of money a government owes at a particular point in time. **Answer: C.**

16. Answers (a), (b), and (c) are all possibilities. When the government runs a deficit, it will typically borrow funds. When the government borrows funds, it competes with firms in the financial markets for those funds. This competition may "crowd out" private investment spending and therefore lead to lower long-run rates of economic growth. In addition, as the deficits persist the government will find that increasing amounts of its tax revenue must be dedicated to paying the interest expense of the debt, and this means the government must either reduce its spending in other areas or raise more revenue from taxes. **Answer: D.**

17. The debt-GDP ratio provides a measure of the size of the government debt relative to the size of the economy: this is a helpful comparison, since the size of the economy provides a measure of the potential tax revenue that can be raised by the government. If the government debt is increasing at the same time that GDP is also increasing, it is possible that the debt-GDP ratio is actually falling, provided that GDP is growing at a faster rate than debt. **Answer: D.**

18. Implicit liabilities are not included in the debt statistics in Canada. All other statements are based on facts presented in the chapter. **Answer: A.**

19. All the statements, except the last statement, are correct. The last statement is false, because debt services accounted for 11% of the total spending in the fiscal year of 2004. **Answer: D.**

20. To find this answer we need to use the multiplier presented in the appendix: $1/[1 - MPC(1 - t)]$. In this example this multiplier equals 1.82, so the $10 billion increase in government spending leads to aggregate output increasing by (1.82)($10 billion) or $18.2 billion. **Answer: C.**

21. From the appendix we know that the inclusion of a tax rate in our model, holding everything else constant, reduces the size of the multiplier. Using the formula for this multiplier, $1/[1 - MPC(1 - t)]$, and substituting in the given information, we find that answer (b) is correct. Answer (c) is a simple, and an accurate, mathematical computation. **Answer: E.**

22. Given the statistical data in the textbook, Sweden has the highest percentage. **Answer: B.**

23. Personal income tax and corporate income tax account for 40% of the tax revenue. **Answer: A.**

24. The United States does not have the highest debt-GDP ratio. **Answer: A.**

25. Even if government spending is cut, we may see an increase in debt-GDP ratio if *FDP* falls at a greater rate than occurs if government spending is reduced. **Answer: C.**

26. Contractionary fiscal policy is required to close the inflationary gap and the option of "increase taxes and/or reduce government expenditures" is a contractionary fiscal policy that will help close the inflationary gap. **Answer: B.**

27. Expansionary fiscal policy is required to close the recessionary gap and the option of "decrease taxes and/or increase government expenditures" is an expansionary fiscal policy that will help close the recessionary gap. **Answer: C.**

28. The multiplier is $\Delta Y/\Delta G = 4$. However, we can't predict the MPC out of disposable income, since we don't know if the there is any income tax. If we assume that there is no income tax, then the MPC will be 0.75 and MPS will be 0.25. With income tax, the MPC will not be 0.75. **Answer: C.**

29. The government expenditure multiplier is $1/[1 - MPC]$, which is equal to 4. We can solve $[1 - MPC] = 0.25$, $MPC = 0.75$ and tax multiplier $= -MPC/[1 - MPC] = -3$. When $\Delta G = 100$, the AD curve should shift to the *right* by 400. **Answer: D.**

30. The government expenditure multiplier is $1/[1 - MPC(1 - t)]$, which is equal to 2.5. Since $t = 0.2$, we can re-write $1/[1 - MPC(0.8)] = 2.5$ and solve $MPC = 0.75$. **Answer: C.**

31. The tax multiplier is $-MPC/[1 - MPC(1 - t)]$, which is equal to -2. Since $t = 0.25$, we can re-write the tax-multiplier as $-MPC/[1 - MPC(0.75)] = -2$ and solve $MPC = 0.8$ and $MPS = 0.2$. **Answer: D.**

32. The government expenditure multiplier is $1/[1 - MPC(1 - t)]$, which is equal to 2.5. Since $t = 0.25$, we can re-write $1/[1 - MPC(0.75)] = 2.5$ and solve $MPC = 0.80$. Since the tax multiplier is $-MPC/[1 - MPC(1 - t)]$, we can solve the tax multiplier as $-0.8/0.4 = 2$. **Answer: C.**

33. A reduction in consumer confidence will cause a reduction in autonomous consumption and an increase in autonomous private saving. As a result, aggregate expenditure will fall and the AD curve will shift to the left. **Answer: A.**

34. $Y = 1,000 - 0.75(200) + 1.25(200) + 500 = 1,600$. **Answer: D.**

35. $\Delta Y = (-0.75 \Delta T) + (1.25\Delta G) = 50$. **Answer: C.**

36. With other variables constant, we can see that $\Delta Y = (-0.75 \Delta T)$. Therefore, $\Delta Y/\Delta T$ = tax multiplier $= -0.75$. With other variables constant, we can see that $\Delta Y = (1.25 \Delta G)$. Therefore, $\Delta Y/\Delta G$ = government expenditure multiplier $= 1.25$. **Answer: B.**

37. We can derive $Y = 300 + 0.8Y$ and solve $Y = 1,500$, $Y_D = 1,400$, $C = 1,200$, private saving $= 200$, government saving $= 100 - 200 = -100$, and national saving $= 200 - 100 = 100$. Note that in the closed model, national saving equals investment. **Answer: B.**

38. The government expenditure multiplier is $1/[1 - MPC] = 1/0.2 = 5$, and the tax multiplier is $-MPC/[1 - MPC] = -0.8/0.2 = -4$. **Answer: A.**

39. We can derive $Y = 300 + 0.8(1 - 0.25)Y$; or $Y = 300 + 0.6Y$ and solve $Y = 750$, $T = 100 + 0.25(750) = 287.5$, $Y_D = 462.5$, $C = 450$, private saving $= 12.5$, government saving $= 287.5 - 200 = 87.5$, and national saving $= 12.5 + 87.5 = 100$. Note that in the closed model, national saving equals investment. **Answer: D.**

40. The government expenditure multiplier is $1/[1 - MPC(1 - t)] = 1/0.4 = 2.5$, and the tax multiplier is $-MPC/[1 - MPC(1 - t)] = -0.8/0.4 = -2$. **Answer: C.**

Answers to Problems and Exercises

1. a. This is an example of an automatic stabilizer: as GDP in Macrovia falls, this leads automatically to smaller tax collections for a given tax rate.

  b. This is an example of expansionary discretionary fiscal policy: the additional government expenditure will stimulate AD.

c. This is an example of contractionary discretionary fiscal policy: Macrovia moves to cut government spending which will reduce AD and slow down the economic expansion.

d. This is an example of an automatic stabilizer: as unemployment rises, this leads to less AD. But the payment of unemployment benefits lessens this fall in aggregate spending and results in a smaller overall impact on AD.

2. a. The potential output level for Macroland is Y_2 where $LRAS$ equals $SRAS$ equals AD. Currently, Macroland is producing Y_1 at price level P_2: this represents a recessionary situation, or a recessionary gap, since Macroland has the potential to produce a higher level of output than it is currently producing.

b. Macroland has a recessionary gap since their current level of production, Y_1, is less than their potential level of production, Y_2.

c. Any policy initiative that shifts AD to the right will help Macroland move toward its potential output level. Items (i) and (iv) will both shift AD to the right: government policies which stimulate private investment spending lead to higher levels of aggregate spending and a rightward shift in AD; and new spending by government will also lead to higher levels of aggregate spending and a rightward shift in AD. Items (ii) and (iii) will cause AD to shift to the left: item (ii) will lead to higher interest rates which will "crowd out" some private investment spending; and item (iii) will reduce disposable income and lead to lower levels of aggregate spending.

d. The current price level in Macroland is P_2. If the government engages in fiscal policy that results in the economy returning to the potential level of output, this will lead to increases in the price level from P_2 to P_3.

3. a.

Year	Potential output
Year 1	$100
Year 2	105
Year 3	110.25
Year 4	115.76

b. The consumption function can be written as $C = A + MPC (Y - T)$. From the table we can compute the MPC as the change in consumption divided by the change in disposable income, or 9/18, which equals .5. To find A, we need to use one of the consumption and disposable income combinations from the table. For example, when disposable income equals 90, consumption equals 55. So, $C = A + .5 (Y - T)$ can be rewritten as $55 = A + .5(90)$ and solving for A, we find A equals 10. Thus, the consumption function for this economy is $C = 10 + .5 (Y - T)$.

c.

Year	Potential output	Actual output	T	YD	C	I	G
Year 1	100	100	10	90	55	30	15
Year 2	105	104	10	94	57	30	17
Year 3	110.25	115	10	105	62.5	30	22.5
Year 4	115.76	118	10	108	64	30	24

d.

Year	Expansionary gap	Inflationary gap	Actual output equals potential output
Year 1	No	No	Yes
Year 2	Yes	No	No
Year 3	No	Yes	No
Year 4	No	Yes	No

e.

Year	Discretionary fiscal policy
Year 1	No policy necessary
Year 2	Increase government spending or decrease taxation
Year 3	Decrease government spending or increase taxation
Year 4	Decrease government spending or increase taxation

4. a. To find the consumption function first recall the general form: $C = A + MPC$ $(Y - T)$. From the given information we know A equals $20 and the MPC equals .6. Thus, $C = 20 + .6(Y - T)$.

b. To find the income-expenditure equilibrium, solve the equation $Y = C + I + G$. We know C can be written as $20 + .6(Y - T)$; I equals $100; and G equals $50. We also know T, taxes, equals $50. So, $Y = 20 + .6(Y - 50) + 100 + 50$, or Y equals $350.

c. Uplandia is currently producing with a recessionary gap, since its current output of $350 is less than its potential output of $400.

d. The multiplier for a change in aggregate spending equals $1/(1 - MPC)$. We know that the change in aggregate production equals the multiplier times the change (in this case) in government spending. In this problem, we want output to increase by $50, our multiplier value is 2.5, and thus government spending must increase by $20 in order for this economy to produce its potential output of $400.

e. The multiplier for a change in taxes equals $- MPC/(1 - MPC)$, or in this case -1.5, since the MPC equals .6. Recall that the change in aggregate output equals the multiplier times the change in the level of taxes. We want output to increase by $50, the multiplier's value is -1.5, and, thus, taxes must decrease by $33.33. Here you need to remember that aggregate output increases as taxes fall, holding everything else constant, and aggregate output decreases as taxes increase, holding everything else constant.

f. We can find our answer by recognizing that we have two multiplier effects occurring simultaneously it the government chooses to maintain a zero budget balance. We could write this as the change in aggregate output equals the multiplier effect from the change in government spending plus the multiplier effect from the change in taxes. Note, though, that the change in government spending equals the change in taxes. Thus, the change in aggregate output equals $1/(1 - MPC)$ times the change in government spending plus $[-MPC/(1 - MPC)]$ times the change in government spending. Since the desired change in aggregate output equals $50, we can solve this equation and find that the change in government spending and in taxes must both equal $50.

g. The most "bang for the buck" comes from a change in government spending since the multiplier has a value of 2.5. A change in taxes is multiplied by the smaller (in absolute value) multiplier of 1.5 and the balanced budget scenario has an even smaller multiplier value of 1.

h. A balanced budget rule for the federal government would restrict the government's ability to engage in discretionary fiscal policy in times of economic need. It would also prove costly, since for any given change in aggregate output, a balanced budget rule forces the federal government to spend more than it would if the government were free to pursue discretionary fiscal policy without regard to its budgetary consequences.

5. a.

Year	Real GDP (millions of dollars)	Debt (millions of dollars)	Budget deficit (millions of dollars)	Debt (percent of real GDP)	Budget deficit (percent of real GDP)
Year 1	800	200	20	25%	2.5%
Year 2	824	220.6	20.6	26.77%	2.5%
Year 3	848.72	241.82	21.22	28.49%	2.5%
Year 4	874.18	263.68	21.86	30.16%	2.5%
Year 5	900.41	286.2	22.52	31.79%	2.5%
Year 6	927.42	309.4	23.2	33.36%	2.5%

b. When the real GDP and the government deficit grow at the same rate, the deficit-to-GDP ratio stays constant at 2.5%, while the debt-to-GDP ratio increases from 25% to 33.36% in five years.

c.

Year	Real GDP (millions of dollars)	Debt (millions of dollars)	Budget deficit (millions of dollars)	Debt (percent of real GDP)	Budget deficit (percent of real GDP)
Year 1	800	200	20	25%	2.5%
Year 2	824	220.2	20.2	26.72%	2.45%
Year 3	848.72	240.6	20.4	28.35%	2.40%
Year 4	874.18	261.2	20.6	29.88%	2.36%
Year 5	900.41	282.0	20.8	31.32%	2.31%
Year 6	927.42	303.0	21	32.67%	2.26%

d. When the real GDP grows at 3% per year and the government deficit grows at 1% per year, the deficit-to-GDP ratio falls from 2.5% to 2.26% in five years, while the debt-to-GDP ratio increases from 25% to 32.67% in five years.

e. When real GDP grows at 3% per year and the deficit grows at 10% per year, the deficit-to-GDP ratio increases from 2.5% to 3.47% over five years while the debt-to-GDP ration increases from 25% to 36.05% over five years.

f. The rate of growth of both real GDP and the deficit each year are important when considering what happens to the debt-to-GDP ratio and the deficit-to-GDP ratio. If GDP grows at a faster rate than the deficit, the deficit-to-GDP ratio will decline while the debt-to-GDP ratio may continue to increase, but at a slower rate than would occur if the deficit and GDP grew at the same rate.

6. a. To find the multiplier, start by recalling the equilibrium condition where aggregate expenditure equals aggregate income. We can write this as $Y = C + I + G$ for the closed economy of Fantasia. We can substitute A for C and get $Y = A + MPC(Y - T) + I + G$. We can also substitute tY for T and have $Y = A + MPC(Y - tY) + I + G$. Rearranging terms we have $Y - MPC(1 - t)Y = A + I + G$ or $Y[1 - MPC(1 - t)] = A + I + G$. We can solve this equation for Y and have $Y = [1/(1 - MPC(1 - t))](A + I + G)$. The multiplier is $[1/(1 - MPC(1 - t))]$.

b. Use the equation $Y = C + I + G$ and substitute in the data you have to get $Y = 10 + .5(Y - .1Y) + 100$. Solving for Y, the income-expenditure equilibrium equals $200.

c. The value of the multiplier, $[1/(1 - MPC(1 - t))]$, equals 1.818, or approximately 1.82.

d. Fantasia is operating with an inflationary gap since actual output of $200 exceeds potential output of $180 million.

e. Since aggregate output needs to fall by $20 million and the multiplier equals 1.82, that implies that government spending must decrease by $10.98 million.

7. a. Recessionary gap = 40. The government expenditure multiplier is $1/[1 - MPC(1 - t)] = 1/[1 - 8(.75)]1/0.4 = 2.5$. Therefore, $\Delta G = +16$.

b. Inflationary gap = 60. The government expenditure multiplier is

$$\frac{1}{1 - \frac{3}{4}\left(\frac{2}{3}\right)} = 2$$

Therefore, $\Delta G = -30$.

8. $Y = AE$　　　　　　　　[Real GDP = Aggregate Expenditure]
$AE = C + I + G$　　　　　　[Aggregate expenditure]
$C = 80 + 0.8(Y - T)$　　　[Consumption function]
$Y_D = (Y - T)$　　　　　　　[Disposable income]
$T = 100$　　　　　　　　　　[Tax]
$G = 200$　　　　　　　　　　[Government expenditure]
$I = 300$　　　　　　　　　　[Investment]

a. $Y = C + I + G$
$Y = 80 + 0.8(Y - 100) + 300 + 200$
$Y = 500 + 0.8Y$
$0.2Y = 500$
$Y = 2,500$
$Y_D = 2,500 - 100 = \textbf{2,400}$
$C = 80 + 0.8(2,400) = \textbf{2,000}$
Private saving = $2,400 - 2,000 = \textbf{400}$
Government saving = $100 - 200 = \textbf{-100}$
National saving = $400 - 100 = 300$

b. $Y = 600 + 0.8Y$
$Y = 3,000$
Multiplier = $1/[1 - MPC] = \textbf{5}$

c. $Y = 580 + 0.8Y$
$Y = 2,900$
Multiplier = $-MPC/[1 - MPC] = \textbf{-4}$

d. $\Delta G = 100 \rightarrow \Delta Y = 500$
$\Delta T = 100 \rightarrow \Delta Y = -400$
Therefore, the net change is $Y = 100$.

9. $Y = AE$　　　　　　　　[Real GDP = Aggregate Expenditure]
$AE = C + I + G$　　　　　　[Aggregate expenditure]
$C = 80 + 0.8(Y - T)$　　　[Consumption function]
$Y_D = (Y - T)$　　　　　　　[Disposable income
$T = 100 + 0.25Y$　　　　　[Tax]
$G = 200$　　　　　　　　　　[Government expenditure]
$I = 300$　　　　　　　　　　[Investment]

a. $Y = C + I + G$
$Y = 80 + 0.8[Y - (100 + 0.25Y)] + 300 + 200$
$Y = 500 + 0.8[0.75]Y$
$Y = 500 + 0.6Y$
$0.4Y = 500$
$Y = 1,250$
$T = 100 + 0.25(1,200)$
$T = \mathbf{412.5}$
$Y_D = 1,250 - 412.5 = \mathbf{837.5}$
$C = 80 + 0.8(837.5) = \mathbf{750}$
Private saving $= 837.5 - 750 = \mathbf{87.5}$
Government saving $= 412.5 - 200 = \mathbf{212.5}$
National saving $= 87.5 + 212.5 = 300$

b. $Y = 600 + 0.6Y$
$Y = \mathbf{1,500}$
Multiplier $= 1/[1 - MPC(1 - t)] = \mathbf{2.5}$

c. $Y = 80 + 0.8[Y - 0.25Y)] + 300 + 200$
$Y = 580 + 0.6Y$
$Y = \mathbf{1,450}$
Multiplier $= -MPC/[1 - MPC(1 - t)] = \mathbf{-2}$

d. $\Delta G = 100 \rightarrow \Delta Y = 250$
$\Delta T = 100 \rightarrow \Delta Y = -200$
Therefore, the net change is $Y = 50$.

10. a. We can solve $Y = 4,000$ and $T = 1,100$.
Actual budget deficit $= G - T = 1,300 - 1,100 = \mathbf{200}$.
If $Y = 4,400$, T at the potential Y would have been $T = 100 + 0.25(4,400) = 1,200$, and structural budget deficit would be equal to $(1,300 - 1,200) = 100$.

b. The recessionary gap is 400. Since the multiplier is 2.5, we will need $\Delta G = 160$. In other words, G will increase to 1,460. Given the new G, the structural deficit will be $[1,460 - 1,200] = 260$.

chapter 13

Money, Banking, and the Bank of Canada

What is money? How money supply is measured? How the Bank of Canada conducts its monetary policy in Canada? To answer these questions, this chapter begins with various functions of money and measurements of money supply. How banks create money through loan and deposit operations, what is the relation between monetary base and money supply, and how the money multiplier works are also analyzed in this chapter. We then see various functions of the Bank of Canada and examine the kind of monetary policy tools used by the Bank of Canada.

How Well Do You Understand the Chapter?

accounts	deposit insurance	highly	monetary policy	required reserve ratio
appreciation	deposit switch-ing	increase	money multiplier	requirements
assets		interest	money supply	reserves
Bank of Canada	deposits	intervene	money-creation	run
bank rate	depreciation	intrinsic value	most liquid	savings accounts
circulation	desired reserve ratio	least liquid	open market operations	sum
commodity money	direct effect	liabilities	overnight rate	target
commodity-backed money	excess reserves	liability	purchases	unit of account
credit cards	fiat money	liquid	purchases of goods and services	value
currency	fixed	liquidity		
decrease	Governor	loans		
		medium		
		monetary base		

1. Money is an asset that can easily be used to make _____ of goods and services. Money includes cash, which is _____, plus other assets that are _____ liquid. Currency in _____ consists of cash in the hands of the public. Chequable bank deposits are bank accounts that provide cheque writing privileges to the holders of these _____ _____. The _____ is the total value of financial assets in the economy that are considered money. There are multiple definitions of the money supply based on the degree of _____ of the assets. Debit cards are used to transfer funds from his or her bank accounts. _____ access funds, that can be borrowed by their users, create a _____ for the user, and therefore, are not included in the calculation of the money supply.

301

2. Money acts as _____ of exchange, a store of _____, and a(n) _____. An asset that is used to make serves as a medium of exchange. Money acts as a store of _____ due to its ability to maintain its purchasing power over time, provided there is little inflation. Money is a measure people use to set prices and make economic calculations: we refer to this role for money as the _____.

3. The types of money fall into three broad categories. _____ refers to the use of an asset as a medium of exchange that has useful value independent of its role as a medium of exchange. Gold is a good example of commodity money. _____ (or gold-back money) refers to items used as a medium of exchange that have no _____ (for example, paper currency), but whose ultimate value rests on the promise that they could be exchanged for goods (or gold). _____ refers to money whose value derives strictly from the government's decree (law) that it be accepted as a means of payment.

4. The _____ uses three measures of the money supply. These monetary aggregates are: M1, M2, and M3. The M1 defines money (most narrowly defined) as the _____ of currency in circulation, travelers' cheques, and chequable bank deposits. The M2 is comprised of M1 plus _____. The M3 includes all the assets in M2 plus term _____. The M1 is the _____ measure of money, while M3 is the _____.

5. A T-account is a type of financial spreadsheet that displays an institution's financial position. The left-hand side of the T-account represents the institution's _____, and the right-hand side of the T-account is the institution's _____. Banks hold _____ in order to meet the demand for funds from their depositors. Bank _____ are composed of the currency in the banks' vaults and the bank deposits held by the Bank of Canada in each bank's own account. The _____ is the fraction of bank deposits a bank holds as reserves. In Canada, individual banks maintain whatever reserve ratios they think are appropriate. Running of cash could trigger a banking panic or a _____. Most countries minimize the risk of a bank run by deposit insurance, capital requirements, and reserve requirements. In Canada, the Canadian Deposit Insurance Corporation (CDIC) provides _____, a guarantee by the federal government that depositors will be paid up to a designated maximum amount per account even if the bank fails. Capital _____ ensures that the banks hold more assets than the value of their bank deposits. There is no legal reserve requirement policy in Canada.

6. Banks receive deposits of funds from their customers and then use these funds to make interest-earning financial transactions. For example, banks make

_____ to customers and purchase Treasury bills; both financial transactions provide income in the form of _____ to the banks.

7. Banks affect the _____ in two ways. First, they remove some money from circulation by holding currency in their bank vaults and in their reserve accounts at the Bank of Canada. Second, banks create deposits and money when they make loans. Loan-creation is deposit-creation and deposit-creation is

_____.

8. _____ are those held by a bank that exceed the level of desired reserves. In a simplified model, banks lend out all their _____; the increase in bank deposits from lending out the excess reserves equals the excess reserves divided by the _____. We can, therefore, write the _____ as 1/*rr*, where *rr* is the desired reserve ratio. In the real world, the _____ is smaller than the one in our simplified model.

9. The _____ equals the sum of currency in circulation and reserves held by the bank. This is controlled by the monetary authorities. The _____ equals currency in circulation plus bank deposits. The _____ is the ratio of the money supply to the monetary base.

10. The Central Banks oversee and regulate the banking system, and they control the monetary base. In Canada, the central bank is the _____. The main functions of the Bank of Canada are the following ones: the Bank of Canada is the banker of other commercial banks; the Bank of Canada is the banker of the Federal Government of Canada; the Bank of Canada is the issuer of _____ in Canada, and the Bank of Canada conducts _____ in Canada.

11. The Governor of the Bank of Canada, along with five Deputy Governors, forms the _Governing Council,_ and this _Council_ implements Canada's monetary policy. All the operations of the _____ are overseen by a Board of Directors consisting of the Governor, Senior Deputy Governor, Deputy Minister of Finance, and 12 outside Directors. This Board also appoints the _____ of the Bank of Canada.

12. The policy tools of the Bank of Canada are the Bank Rate, _____, and government deposit switching. The _____ is the interest rate the Bank of Canada charges on loans to other banks. The Bank of Canada rate is one quarter of a percentage point above the _____ for the overnight rate. Banks lend money to each other in the overnight funds market, a financial market that allows banks to borrow reserves (usually just overnight), from banks that have excess reserves. The interest rate in this market is called the _____. If the Bank of Canada reduces the _____ of the overnight rate, it will encourage other banks to increase loans and thereby _____ money supply.

13. Open-market operations occur whenever the Bank of Canada enters the bond market and buys or sells bonds. This has a _____ on the monetary base. Open-market purchase of bonds will lead to excess reserves, which in turn will _____ loan-creation, deposit-creation, and money supply. Open-market sale of bonds will _____ money supply.

14. Instead of buying (or selling) bonds, the Bank of Canada can buy or sell foreign _____. When the Bank of Canada buys foreign currency, it increases the supply of Canadian dollar, which causes _____ of Canadian dollar. When the Bank of Canada sells foreign currency, it decreases the supply of Canadian dollar, which causes _____ of Canadian dollar. A country can conduct a floating (flexible) exchange rate system with no intervention from the Central Bank. The opposite of the floating exchange rate is the _____ exchange rate system. Under the fixed exchange rate system, the Central Bank must continuously _____ in the foreign exchange market (by buying or selling foreign currency) to maintain the fixed exchange rate.

15. The process of shifting government accounts from the Bank of Canada to the chartered banks (or in the other directions) is called _____. This can also affect bank reserves and the money supply. Transfer of government deposits from the Bank of Canada to chartered banks will _____ the money supply; a switch of government deposits away from the chartered banks depletes their reserves, and it will _____ the money supply.

Learning Tips

TIP #1: It is important to understand the definition and the distinction between the monetary base, the money supply, and reserves.

The money supply is the value of financial assets in the economy that are considered money: this would include cash in the hands of the public, checkable bank deposits, and traveler's checks, using the narrow definition of the money supply given by the monetary aggregate M1. Bank reserves are composed of the currency banks hold in their vaults plus their deposits at the Bank of Canada. The monetary base is the sum of currency in circulation and bank reserves. The monetary base is not equal to the money supply: the money supply is larger than the monetary base.

TIP #2: It is important to understand the distinction between assets and liabilities.

Make sure you clearly understand what an asset and a liability are and then recognize that any financial instrument represents both an asset and a liability. For example, a mortgage represents a liability for the borrower and an asset for the lender; a checking account deposit represents a liability for the bank providing the check service and an asset to the individual depositing the funds.

TIP #3: For any T-account, clearly identify whose perspective is represented in the T-account.

T-accounts represent the assets and liabilities of an institution or an individual. When making a T-account, consider whose T-account it represents: this will help you more clearly identify whether the financial instruments you include are assets or liabilities. For example, bank reserves are a liability in the Bank of Canada T-account and an asset in a bank's T-account.

TIP #4: Each T-account must always balance: that is, total assets must equal total liabilities where total liabilities include capital.

If your T-account does not balance, check your entries to find your error.

TIP #5: Understand the meaning of desired reserves and excess reserves; and how lending of excess reserves increase money supply.

The money multiplier is the inverse of the reserve ratio (rr) when we don't hold any cash. The actual money multiplier is less than this. Remember that loan-creation means deposit-creation.

TIP #6: The three tools of monetary policy are the Bank of Canada rate, open-market operations, and deposit switching.

When the Bank of Canada rate goes down, it increases loan creations; and when the Bank of Canada rate goes up, it decreases loan creations. When the Bank of Canada buys bonds, it increases loan-creation, deposit-creation, and money supply. When the Bank of Canada sells bonds, the money supply goes down. Deposit-switching, in the form of transfer of government deposits from the Bank of Canada to the chartered banks, increases banks' ability to increase loans and increase money supply. Deposit-switching, in the form of transfer of government deposits away from the chartered banks toward the Bank of Canada reduces banks' ability to increase loans and, as a result, money supply goes down.

TIP #7: By buying or selling foreign currency, the Bank of Canada can cause appreciation or depreciation of the Canadian dollar in the foreign exchange market.

Multiple-Choice Questions

1. Which of the following statements is true?
   a. The definition of money includes all forms of wealth.
   b. Money is an asset that can be easily used to purchase goods and services.
   c. Money consists of cash, which is liquid, plus other assets that are relatively illiquid.
   d. All of the above statements are true statements.
   e. Both (a) and (b) are true.
   f. Both (b) and (c) are true.

2. Credit cards
   a. are just another name for debit cards that allow users to access funds in their bank account.
   b. create an asset for users since the use of credit cards enables people to purchase goods and services.
   c. provide a means of borrowing funds, thus creating a liability, in order to make purchases of goods and services.
   d. Both (a) and (b) are correct.
   e. (a) and (c) are correct.

3. Money
   a. increases welfare since it increases gains from trade.
   b. eliminates the need for a "double coincidence of wants" between trading partners.
   c. includes currency in circulation plus checkable deposits.
   d. All of the above statements are true statements.
   e. Both (b) and (c) are true.

Use the following statements to answer the next question.
   I. The price of bananas is quoted in dollars rather than in units of apples, and the price of apples is quoted in dollars rather than in units of bananas.
   II. The $100 Sue saved this year will have $100 worth of purchasing power five years from now, provided there is no inflation.
   III. The building contractor said the new roof for our house would cost $6,000.

4. Money has three roles in an economy. Statement _____ illustrates the use of money as a medium of exchange; statement _____ illustrates the use of money as a unit of account; and statement _____ illustrates the use of money as a store of value.
   a. III; I; II
   b. I; III; II
   c. III; II; I
   d. II; III; I

5. Which of the following statements is true?
   a. Fiat money is paper currency issued by the government and redeemable in a valuable asset like gold.
   b. Fiat money is money issued by a ruler and thus is found only in countries with a monarchy.
   c. Commodity money is poor type of money, since it cannot be used in trade even though it is a valuable commodity.
   d. None of the above statements is true.

6. M1 includes
   a. currency in circulation, savings account deposits, and checkable bank deposits.
   b. currency in circulation, travelers' checks, and other near-monies, including checkable bank deposits.
   c. currency in circulation, travelers' checks, and checkable bank deposits.
   d. currency in circulation, travelers' checks, checkable bank deposits, and saving account deposits.

7. In a bank's T-account,
   a. Joe's checking account deposit is treated as an asset.
   b. Ellen's car loan is counted as a liability.
   c. bank deposits at the Bank of Canada are an asset for the bank.
   d. assets exactly equal liabilities when there are positive capital requirements.

Use the following T-account for a bank to answer the next three questions. T-bill refers to Treasury bills.

Assets		Liabilities	
Required reserves	$100	Deposits	$1,000
Loans	$400		
Treasury bills	$800		

8. Given this T-account and assuming the bank holds no excess reserves, what is the required reserve ratio?
   a. 10%
   b. 40%
   c. 80%
   d. 1%

9. Given this T-account, how much capital does this bank currently hold?
   a. zero
   b. $300
   c. $400
   d. $500
   e. $1,300

10. Suppose this is the only bank in the banking system. Furthermore, suppose all money is held in this bank and the bank holds no excess reserves. If the Bank of Canada makes an open-market sale of $50 worth of T-bills to this bank, what will happen to the money supply after all adjustments are made?
   a. The money supply will increase by $50.
   b. The money supply will decrease by $50.
   c. The money supply will increase by $500.
   d. The money supply will decrease by $500.

11. Bank runs
   a. can be reduced by providing deposit insurance, requiring banks to hold significant amounts of capital, and by mandating required reserves.
   b. are often caused by rumor and the fear that other people will withdraw their funds.
   c. when rumored, may significantly impact the prices banks receive when they sell assets to increase their liquidity.
   d. All of the above are true statements.

12. Banks affect the money supply
   a. when they take deposited currency out of circulation and deposit it in their bank vaults.
   b. when they lend their excess reserves to their customers.
   c. when a customer from one bank writes a check to a customer of another bank who deposits that check into his or her checking account.
   d. All of the above statements are true.
   e. Both (a) and (b) are true.

13. The monetary base consists of
   a. currency in circulation plus bank deposits.
   b. bank deposits plus bank reserves.
   c. bank deposits, bank reserves, and currency in circulation.
   d. currency in circulation plus bank reserves.

14. In a simple banking system, where banks hold no excess reserves and all funds are kept as bank deposits, then
   a. the money multiplier equals 1 divided by the required reserve ratio.
   b. total deposits will equal reserves multiplied by the reciprocal of the required reserve ratio.
   c. $1 increase in excess reserves will increase deposits by an amount equal to 1 divided by the required reserve ratio.
   d. All of the above statements are true.

15. Holding everything else constant, in our simple banking model, the greater the required reserve ratio, the
   a. greater the effect on the monetary base.
   b. greater the effect on the money supply for any given change in the monetary base.
   c. greater the money multiplier.
   d. smaller the money multiplier.
   e. Both (a) and (c) are correct.

16. Suppose the required reserve ratio initially is 10% of bank deposits and is increased by the Bank of Canada to 20% of bank deposits. Holding everything else constant, this will
   a. reduce the size of the money multiplier.
   b. cause the banking system to contract the level of bank deposits in the banking system.
   c. change the value of the money multiplier from 10 to 5.
   d. All of the above statements are true.

17. Prima withdrew $100 from her chequing account and deposited this $100 in her savings account. As a result,
   a. M1 decreased and M2 increased.
   b. M1 decreased and M2 stayed unchanged.
   c. M1 stayed unchanged and M2 increased.
   d. M1 stayed unchanged and M2 decreased.

18. Fiat money
   a. has intrinsic value.
   b. is an example of commodity-backed money.
   c. is accepted due to the government decree that it should accepted as a means of payment.
   d. has a very low liquidity

19. The excess reserves in the banking system are $100 million. If the money multiplier is 4, then the total deposit creation, after all the multiplier processes have taken place, will be
   a. $100 million.
   b. $300 million.
   c. $400 million.
   d. none of the above.

20. Currently, the banking system's desired reserve ratio (rr) is 0.30 with money multiplier being (1/rr); the total reserves of the banking system stand at $240 with zero excess reserves. If the desired reserve ratio (rr) decreases to 0.20, the banking system can increase deposits by
   a. $500.
   b. $400.
   c. $240.
   d. $120.

21. Which of the following statements is false?
   a. If the Bank of Canada conducts an open-market purchase of bonds and at the same time increases the bank rate, the money supply will increase.
   b. If the Bank of Canada conducts an open-market purchase of bonds and at the same time increases the bank rate, the money supply will decrease.
   c. If the Bank of Canada conducts an open-market purchase of bonds and at the same time increases the bank rate, the money supply will not change.
   d. If the Bank of Canada conducts an open-market purchase of bonds and at the same time increases the bank rate, the money supply may increase, decrease, or stay the same.

22. Which of the following statements is false?
   a. Under a fixed-exchange rate system, the Central bank must continuously intervene in the foreign exchange market (by buying or selling foreign currency) to maintain the fixed exchange rate.
   b. By selling U.S. dollars in the open market, the Bank of Canada can increase the value of the Canadian dollar in the foreign exchange market.
   c. By buying U.S. dollars in the open market, the Bank of Canada can increase the value of the Canadian dollar in the foreign exchange market.
   d. The value of the Canadian dollar may go down if the Bank of Canada decreases its bank rate.

23. (Assume that the money multiplier is 2.5 and the banking system has zero excess reserves). The Bank of Canada withdraws $100 million from the Bank of Montreal. As a result, the banking system in Canada will experience
   a. an increase of money supply of $250 million.
   b. a decrease of money supply of $250 million.
   c. an increase of money supply of $150 million.
   d. a decrease of money supply of $150 million.

24. The money multiplier is 3 and the money supply is $300 billion. Therefore, the monetary base is
   a. $900 billion.
   b. $300 billion.
   c. $100 billion.
   d. $3 billion.

25. The money multiplier is 3 and the monetary base is $300 billion. Therefore, the money supply is
   a. $900 billion.
   b. $300 billion.
   c. $100 billion.
   d. $3 billion.

Answer questions 26–27 on the basis of the following information. The desired reserve ratio is 20%, and the public does not hold any cash. For your benefit, you can formulate a T-account with the following data pertaining to the banking system in Canada.

Assets		Liabilities	
Reserves	$10 million	Deposits	$50 million
Loans	$30 million		
Bonds	$10 million		

26. The Bank of Canada conducts an open-market operation and buys $10 million worth of bonds from the banking system. Assuming that all the multiplier effects have taken place, the total deposits and the total loans in the banking system in Canada will be _____ and _____, respectively.
    a. $100 million; $80 million
    b. $100 million; $70 million
    c. $50 million; $40 million
    d. $50 million; $50 million

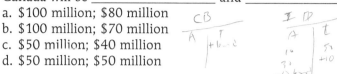

27. The Bank of Canada conducts an open market operation and buys $10 million worth of bonds from the non-bank public. Assuming that all the multiplier effects have taken place, the total deposits and the total loans in the banking system in Canada will be _____ and _____, respectively.
    a. $100 million; $80 million
    b. $100 million; $70 million
    c. $50 million; $40 million
    d. $50 million; $50 million

28. The Bank of Canada performs all the following functions, except
    a. the Bank of Canada is the banker of chartered banks.
    b. the Bank of Canada advises the Government of Canada in its tax-expenditure decisions.
    c. the Bank of Canada is the banker of the Federal Government of Canada.
    d. the Bank of Canada conducts the monetary policy in Canada.

29. Which of the following statements is false?
    a. The money multiplier will go down if there is a decline in the public's confidence in the banking system.
    b. The money multiplier will go down if there is a decline in the desired reserve ratio.
    c. The money multiplier will go up if the public decides to hold less and less cash.
    d. If we keep zero cash and the desired reserve ratio is also zero, then the money multiplier is infinity.

30. Which of the following statements is false?
    a. If the non-bank public keeps zero cash and the desired reserve ratio of banks is 100%, then the money multiplier is one.
    b. The lower the money-supply/monetary-base ratio is, the lower the money multiplier is.
    c. The quantity of monetary base can't be greater than the quantity of the money supply.
    d. If the non-bank public keeps zero cash and banks' desired reserve ratio is 100%, then the money multiplier is zero.

31. Assume that the Royal Bank is the only bank (monopoly bank) in our economy. The desired reserve ratio is 40%, and the public in our economy does not hold any cash. If an additional $100 is deposited and all the multiplier effects are taken into consideration, it will lead to an increase of loans by
    a. $100.
    b. $140.
    c. $250.
    d. none of the above.

32. Assume that the reserve ratio is 25% and that non-bank public does not keep any cash. At present, the banking system's total deposits are $400 million. The banking system wants to increase total deposits by $100 million. Therefore, the banking system should
  a. increase the reserve ratio to 100%.
  b. reduce the reserve ratio to 20%.
  c. increase the reserve ratio by 5%.
  d. reduce loans.

Problems and Exercises

1. Consider the following three lists of assets.

List A	List B	List C
$50 in cash	A car	A boat
A six-month CD worth $50,000, redeemable without penalty six months from today's date	A checking account deposit	The coins you collect in a jar
A share of stock	A treasury bond issued by the government	A savings account deposit
A savings account deposit		

  a. Rank each of these lists of assets from the most liquid asset to the least liquid asset.

  b. For each list, identify any item that is included in M1.
       checking acc

  c. For each list, identify any item that is included in M2.

       Sav account

  d. For each list, identify any item that is included in M3.

  e. Why is money not equivalent to wealth?

2000   ·10000
8000

2. Suppose Fantasia has a single bank that initially has $10,000 of deposits, reserves of $2,000, and loans of $8,000. To simplify our example, we will assume that bank capital equals zero. Furthermore, Fantasia's central bank has a required reserve of 10% of deposits. All monetary transactions are made by check: no one in Fantasia uses currency.

a. Construct a T-account depicting the initial situation in Fantasia. In your T-account, make sure you differentiate between required and excess reserves and that your T-account's assets equal its liabilities.

b. Explain how you calculated the level of excess reserves in Fantasia.

c. Suppose the bank in Fantasia loans these excess reserves (the amount of excess reserves you calculated in (b)) until it reaches the point where its excess reserves equal zero. How does this change the T-account?

d. Did the money supply in Fantasia change when the bank loaned out the excess reserves? Explain your answer.

e. What is the value of the money multiplier in Fantasia? Using the money multiplier, compute the change in deposits.

3. You are provided the following T-accounts for the central bank of Economia and the only commercial bank in Economia. In Economia, all financial transactions occur within the banking system: no one holds currency. The required reserve ratio imposed by the central bank is 20% of deposits.

Central bank of Economia

Assets		Liabilities	
Treasury bills	$20,000	Reserves	$20,000
Total assets	$20,000	Total liabilities	$20,000

Commercial bank of Economia

Assets		Liabilities	
Required reserves	$20,000	Deposits	$100,000
Loans	$70,000	Capital	$20,000
Treasury bills	$30,000		
Total assets $120,000		Total liabilities and capital	$120,000

Suppose the central bank in Economia purchases $2,000 of Treasury bills from the commercial bank.

a. Provide a T-account for both the central bank and the commercial bank showing the immediate effect of this transaction. Be sure to differentiate between required and excess reserves for the commercial bank.

b. Provide a T-account for the commercial bank once the commercial bank loans out its excess reserves and all adjustments have been made through the money multiplier process.

c. What happens to the money supply when the central bank purchases $2,000 of Treasury bills from the commercial bank?

d. Relate the change in the money supply to the money multiplier.

e. What was the monetary base initially?

f. What is the monetary base after all adjustments to the central bank's monetary policy have taken effect?

4. The following T-accounts are for the central bank of Macropedia and its sole commercial bank. In Macropedia, citizens always hold $1,000 in currency and the reserve requirement equals 10%. The commercial bank adheres to a strict policy of always lending out its excess reserves.

Central bank of Macropedia

Assets		Liabilities	
Treasury bills	$11,000	Reserves	$10,000
		Currency in circulation	$1,000
Total assets	$11,000	Total liabilities	$11,000

Commercial bank of Macropedia

Assets		Liabilities	
Reserves	$10,000	Deposits	$100,000
Loans	$80,000	Capital	$0
Treasury bills	$10,000		
Total assets	$100,000	Total liabilities and capital	$100,000

a. Does the commercial bank initially satisfy the required reserve? Explain your answer.

Suppose the central bank sells $5,000 in Treasury bills to the commercial bank.

b. Provide a T-account for both the central bank and the commercial bank showing the immediate effect of this transaction.

c. Given your answer in (b), describe the commercial bank's problem. Be specific in your answer and identify what options the commercial bank has for resolving its problem.

d. Provide a T-account for the commercial bank after it fully adjusts to the central bank's selling of $5,000 in Treasury bills.

e. What happens to the monetary base in this problem?

f. What happens to the money supply?

5. Use the following information about Macroland to answer this question.

Bank deposits at the central bank	$100 million
Currency in bank vaults	$50 million
Currency held by the public	$75 million
Checkable deposits	$600 million
Traveler's checks	$5 million

a. What are bank reserves equal to in Macroland?

b. Suppose banks hold no excess reserves in Macroland. What is the required reserve ratio given the information in this table?

c. If the public does not change its currency holdings, what will happen to the level of checkable deposits in Macroland, relative to their initial level, if the central bank of Macroland purchases $10 million Treasury bills in the open market? Explain your answer and provide a numerical answer.

d. If the public does not change its currency holdings, what will happen to the level of checkable deposits in Macroland, relative to their initial level, if the central bank of Macroland sells $5 million Treasury bills in the open market? Explain your answer and provide a numerical answer.

6. The following T-accounts show the assets and liabilities of all banks in Canada. The reserve ratio is 10%. All financial transactions occur within the banking system: no one holds cash.

Assets		Liabilities	
Actual reserves	$200 million	Deposits	$1,000 million
Loans	$700 million		
Bonds	$100 million		

a. What is the amount of total desired reserves? What is the amount of excess reserves?

b. What will be the final T-account after all the excess reserves are loaned out?

c. After all the multiplier processes have taken place, ΔLoans will be

_____.

7. The following table shows assets and liabilities of all banks in Canada. The reserve ratio is 10%. The non-bank public holds 10% of deposits as cash.

Assets		Liabilities
Actual reserves	$100 million	Deposits $1,000 million
Loans	$900 million	
Bonds	zero	

    a. What is the amount of total desired reserves? What is the amount of excess reserves? What is the monetary base? What is the money supply? What is the money multiplier?

    b. Assume that the Bank of Canada purchases $100 worth of bonds from the non-bank public and all the multiplier processes have taken place. What is the amount of total deposits? What is the amount of total reserves? What is the monetary base now? What is the money supply now? What is the money multiplier?

8. Consider the following balance sheet of the banking system, where the reserve ratio is 20% and the cash-deposit ratio is 20%. The banks do not keep excess reserves.

    a. Fill in the blanks that follow:

Assets		Liabilities	
Reserves	$1,000 million	Deposits	$5,000 million
Loans	$4,000 million		
Total	$5,000 million	Total	$5,000 million

The money supply = _____.

The monetary base = _____.

The money multiplier = _____.

    b. Suppose the Bank of Canada deposits $200 million of government deposits in the banking system. Reconsider the final balance sheet and answer the following questions.

Assume that all the multiplier effects have taken place and banks do not have excess reserves. Fill in the following blanks:

The total monetary base = _____.

The money supply = _____.

The total deposits = _____.

The total reserves = _____.

The total currency holdings with public = _____.

The money multiplier = _____.

Answers to How Well Do You Understand the Chapter

1. purchases, liquid, highly, circulation, accounts, money supply, liquidity, credit cards, liability

2. medium, value, unit of account, value, unit of account

3. commodity money, commodity-backed money, intrinsic value, fiat money

4. Bank of Canada, sum, savings accounts, deposits, most liquid, least liquid

5. assets, liabilities, reserves, reserves, desired reserve ratio, run, deposit insurance, requirements

6. loans, interest

7. money supply, money-creation

8. excess reserves, excess reserves, required reserve ratio, money multiplier

9. monetary base, money supply, money multiplier

10. Bank of Canada, currency, monetary policy

11. Bank of Canada, Governor

12. open market operations, bank rate, target, overnight rate, target, increase

13. direct effect, increase, decrease

14. currency, depreciation, appreciation, fixed, intervene

15. deposit switching, increase, decrease

Answers to Multiple-Choice Questions

1. Answer (b) provides a straightforward definition of money. Money includes cash plus other assets that are highly liquid like checking accounts. Money does not include all forms of wealth since some forms of wealth are highly illiquid. **Answer: B.**

2. Credit cards and debit cards are not equivalent: credit cards allow the user to borrow funds, and this borrowing represents a liability for the user since the funds must be repaid. **Answer: C.**

3. Answers (a), (b), and (c) are factual statements about money that are all discussed in the text. **Answer: D.**

4. Statement I is an example of money used as a unit of account since it provides a standard measure for the prices of all goods and services in an economy. Statement II is an example of money's role as a store of value: we value money because of its ability to represent purchasing power over time. Statement III provides an example of money as a medium of exchange: the building contractor gives us a price for a particular item. **Answer: A.**

5. Each of these statements is incorrect. Fiat money is money whose value derives entirely from its official status as a means of exchange: this is not limited to countries with monarchies. Fiat money is not redeemable in some other commodity. Commodity money is a more limited form of money than commodity-backed money or fiat money, since it ties up more of an economy's resources to facilitate making transactions rather than using those resources for more productive uses. **Answer: D.**

6. M1 is the narrowest definition of money and includes only currency in circulation, travelers' checks, and checkable bank deposits. **Answer: C.**

7. Joe's checking account balance is an asset from Joe's perspective but a liability from the bank's perspective since the bank is liable, or owes money, to Joe. Ellen's car loan is a liability for Ellen since it represents something she owes to someone else, while it represents an asset to the bank since it represents a promise to pay the bank a certain amount of money. When the bank deposits funds at the Bank of Canada, this deposit is an asset for the bank and a liability for the Bank of Canada. If there are positive capital requirements, then assets are greater than liabilities. **Answer: C.**

8. The required reserve ratio is equal to required reserves divided by checkable deposits: in this example, this bank holds 10% of its checkable deposits as required reserves. **Answer: A.**

9. The bank's capital is the difference between its total assets and total liabilities. In this case, the bank's assets sum to $1,300 while the liabilities total $1,000. The difference, $300, is the bank's capital. **Answer: B.**

10. When the Bank of Canada sells $50 worth of T-bills, it debits the reserve account of the bank that sells the T-bills to the Bank of Canada. This results in the bank having insufficient reserves to support their current level of deposits. The bank will contract the loans it holds until the deposits in the bank are the amount that can be supported by the new level of reserves. The new reserves in this problem equal $50 (the initial $100 minus the $50 spent on the T-bills): $50 in reserves can support $500 in deposits when the required reserve ratio equals 10. So the money supply will decrease from $1,000 to $500, or a decrease of $500. **Answer: D.**

11. Even the rumor of a potential bank run can result in dramatic decreases in the value of a bank's assets. Rumor and fear can combine to create a self-fulfilling prophecy: depositors fear that the behavior of other depositors will drive even a financially stable bank into instability. The potential for bank runs can be eliminated through effective regulation that provides deposit insurance while requiring bank capital and a designated reserve ratio. **Answer: D.**

12. Banks affect the money supply, or the sum of currency in circulation plus bank deposits when they hold currency in their bank vaults, thus reducing the total amount of currency in circulation. Banks also affect the money supply when they loan out their excess reserves and create additional bank deposits. Check writing and check cashing do not affect the money supply since they do not change the overall level of currency in circulation plus bank deposits. **Answer: E.**

13. The monetary base consists of currency in circulation and bank reserves, while the money supply equals currency in circulation plus bank deposits. **Answer: D.**

14. All of the statements restate the relationship between excess reserves and the required reserve ratio and their impact on the level of bank deposits. We can write this relationship as the change in bank deposits equals excess reserves times ($1/rr$). Recall that $1/rr$ is simply the reciprocal of the required reserve ratio. **Answer: D.**

15. Since the money multiplier is defined as $1/rr$, when the required reserve ratio increases, the money multiplier decreases holding everything else constant. The required reserve ratio does not affect the monetary base; but, for a given change in the monetary base, the larger the required reserve ratio the smaller the effect of the change in the monetary base on the money supply. **Answer: D.**

16. When the required reserve ratio increases, the money multiplier, defined as $1/rr$, must necessarily decrease. If the required reserve ratio equals 10%, the money multiplier equals 10; and if the required reserve ratio equals 20%, the money multiplier equals 5. When the reserve requirement increases, banks find that their reserves' ability to support bank deposits decreases, and this leads banks to contract the level of bank deposits in the banking system. **Answer: D.**

17. M1 decreased, but M2 stayed unchanged. **Answer: C.**

18. Fiat money has no intrinsic value; it is not backed by any gold or commodity. **Answer: C.**

19. Δdeposits = $100 million times 4 = $400 million. **Answer: C.**

20. Δdeposits = Excess reserves times the multiplier = $80 times 5 = $400. **Answer: B.**

21. Money supply will increases after open-market purchase of bonds by the Bank of Canada; money supply will go down when the Bank rate increases. Without knowing the effects and extent of the previously mentioned changes, we cannot determine if the money supply will decrease, increase, or stay the same. **Answer: D.**

22. When the Bank of Canada buys U.S. dollars, the supply of Canadian dollar in the foreign exchange market increases. As result, the value of the Canadian dollar will decrease. The statement in part c is the only false statement. **Answer: C.**

23. Bank deposits will go down and the money supply will decrease by $250 million. **Answer: B.**

24. Money multiplier = (Money supply)/(monetary base). Since the money multiplier is 3 and the money supply is $300 billion, the monetary base must $100 billion. **Answer: C.**

25. Money multiplier = (Money supply)/(monetary base). Since the money multiplier is 3 and the monetary base is $300 billion, the money supply must be $900 billion. **Answer: A.**

26. After the multiplier effects, the balance sheet will look like the following one:

Assets		Liabilities	
Reserves	$20 million	Deposits	$100 million
Loans	$80 million		
Bonds	zero		

Answer: A.

27. After the multiplier effects, the balance sheet will look like the following one:

Assets		Liabilities	
Reserves	$20 million	Deposits	$100 million
Loans	$70 million		
Bonds	$10 million		

Answer: B.

28. The Bank of Canada does not advise the government regarding tax-expenditure policies of the government. **Answer: B.**

29. All statements in this question are correct with one exception. The money multiplier will go up if the desired reserve ratio goes down. **Answer: B.**

30. All statements in this question are correct with one exception. The correct statement is: if the non-bank public keeps zero cash and banks' desired reserve ratio is 100%, then the money multiplier is one, not zero. **Answer: D.**

31. Deposits will increase by $250 million; loans will increase by $ 150 million. **Answer: D.**

32. With the reserve ratio of 25%, the total reserves equal $100 million and the total deposits equal $400 million. The banking system can support $500 million deposits, if it decreases the reserve ratio to 29%. **Answer: B.**

Answers to Problems and Exercises

1. a. List A: $50 in cash, a savings account deposit, a share of stock, a six-month CD redeemable without penalty six months from today's date

List B: The checking account deposit, a Treasury bond issued by the government, a car

List C: The coins you collect in a jar, a savings account deposit, a boat

b. In List A, the $50 in cash is included in M1; in List B, the checking account deposit is included in M1; and in List C, the coins in a jar are included in M1.

c. M2 includes any item in M1 plus the savings account deposit (List A) and (List C), and the six-month CD (List A).

d. M3 includes any item in M2.

e. Wealth includes all assets, physical or financial, that an individual owns at a particular point in time. Although these assets may be quite valuable, they may not all possess the characteristic of liquidity. Money possesses this characteristic, and thus, includes only those items that can easily be used to purchase goods and services. In this question, the bonds, stock, and boat are assets and therefore part of the owner's wealth, but they are not considered money.

2. a.

Assets		Liabilities	
Required reserves	$1,000	Deposits	$10,000
Excess reserves	$1,000		
Loans	$8,000		
Total assets	$10,000	Total liabilities	$10,000

b. Excess reserves are equal to total reserves minus required reserves, or $1,000. To find required reserves, multiply deposits by the required reserve ratio [($10,000)(.1) = $1,000].

c.

Assets		Liabilities	
Required reserves	$2,000	Deposits	$20,000
Excess reserves	$0		
Loans	$18,000		
Total assets	$20,000	Total liabilities	$20,000

d. Yes, since the money supply is defined as bank deposits plus currency in circulation. Since Fantasia has no currency in circulation, we need only consider what happens to bank deposits. Initially, bank deposits equaled $10,000 and after the loaning out of all the excess reserves, bank deposits equal $20,000. Thus, the money supply increased by $10,000.

e. The money multiplier equals $1/rr$, or 10 in this example, since no one holds currency and the bank does not hold excess reserves. The change in deposits equals the money multiplier times the change in reserves or, in this case, the change in deposits equals $(1/.1)(\$1,000)$ or $10,000.

3. a.

Central bank of Economia

Assets		Liabilities	
Treasury bills	$22,000	Reserves	$22,000
Total assets	$22,000	Total liabilities	$22,000

Commercial bank of Economia

Assets		Liabilities	
Required reserves	$20,000	Deposits	$100,000
		Capital	$20,000
Excess reserves	$2,000		
Loans	$70,000		
Treasury bills	$28,000		
Total assets	$120,000	Total liabilities and capital	$120,000

b.

Commercial bank of Economia

Assets		Liabilities	
Required reserves	$22,000	Deposits	$110,000
		Capital	$20,000
Loans	$80,000		
Treasury bills	$28,000		
Total assets	$130,000	Total liabilities and capital	$130,000

c. The money supply increases from $100,000 to $110,000. Recall that the money supply equals checkable deposits plus currency in circulation: since Economia has no currency in circulation, the money supply equals the level of deposits.

d. The change in the money supply equals the money multiplier times the change in the monetary base. In this problem, the money multiplier equals 5, and the change in the monetary base is the $2,000 increase in reserves that occurs when the central bank purchases the Treasury bills.

e. The monetary base equals reserves plus currency in circulation. In Economia, currency in circulation equals zero, so the monetary base is equivalent to reserves. Initially the monetary base is $20,000.

f. The monetary base increases to $22,000.

4. a. Yes, the commercial bank has reserves of $10,000 and deposits of $100,000: reserves equal 10% of deposits which satisfies the required reserve ratio.

b.

Central bank of Macropedia

Assets		Liabilities	
Treasury bills	$6,000	Reserves	$5,000
		Currency in circulation	$1,000
Total assets	$6,000	Total liabilities	$6,000

Commercial bank of Macropedia

Assets		Liabilities	
Reserves	$5,000	Deposits	$100,000
Loans	$80,000	Capital	$0
Treasury bills	$15,000		
Total assets	$100,000	Total liabilities	$100,000

c. The commercial bank has insufficient reserves to meet the required reserve ratio: when its deposits equal $100,000, it needs $10,000 in required reserves. With reserves of $5,000, it can only support $50,000 of deposits. In the short term, it can borrow reserves from the central bank of Macropedia. Since there is only one commercial bank in Macropedia, it can not borrow from the federal funds market since there is no federal funds market. Over time the commercial bank will find it needs to decrease its outstanding loans and therefore, deposits, until its reserves are sufficient to meet the required reserve ratio.

d.

Commercial bank of Macropedia

Assets		Liabilities	
Reserves	$5,000	Deposits	$50,000
Loans	$30,000	Capital	$0
Treasury bills	$15,000		
Total assets	$50,000	Total liabilities	$50,000

e. The monetary base is initially equal to $11,000 ($10,000 in reserves plus $1,000 in currency in circulation). After the central bank's activity, the monetary base is $6000 ($5000 in reserves plus $1000 in currency in circulation).

f. The money supply is initially $101,000 ($100,000 in checkable bank deposits plus $1000 in currency in circulation). After the central bank's actions and full adjustment, the money supply is $51,000 ($50,000 in checkable bank deposits plus $1,000 in currency in circulation). The money supply decreases by $50,000, or the amount predicted by the money multiplier process.

5. a. Bank reserves equal currency in bank vaults plus bank deposits at the central bank, or $150 million.

b. We can calculate the required reserve ratio, rr, as the ratio of required reserves to checkable deposits. Since there are no excess reserves in Macroland, the bank reserves calculated in part (a) equal the required reserves: thus, $150 million/$600 million equals a required reserve ratio of .25.

c. When the central bank of Macroland purchases $10 million in Treasury bills, this increases the level of reserves in the banking system by $10 million. This increase in reserves starts the multiplier process: the change in the money supply is calculated as the increase in reserves times the money multiplier or ($10 million)(4) = $40 million. Thus, the money supply increases by $40 million when the Central Bank purchases Treasury bills on the open market.

d. Using the concept explained in part (c), this sale of Treasury bills by the central bank will decrease the money supply by $20 million. We can see this by recalling that the change in the money supply equals the change in reserves times the money multiplier or (−$5 million)(4), or −$20 million.

6. a. desired reserves = $100 million; excess reserves = $100 million

b.

Assets		Liabilities	
Actual reserves	$200 million	Deposits	$2,000 million
Loans	$1,700 million		
Bonds	$100 million		

c. ΔLoans = $1,000 million

7. a. (All numbers are in millions.) Total desired reserves = $100, excess reserves = zero, monetary base = $100 + $100 = $200, money supply = $100 + $1,000 = $1,100, multiplier = 5.5

b. Total deposits = $1,500, total reserves = $150, monetary base = $150 + $150 = $300
money supply = $1,650

8. a. (All numbers are in millions.) Money supply = $5,000 + $1,000 = $6,000
Monetary base = $1,000 + $1,000 = $2,000
Money multiplier = $6,000/$2,000 = 3

b. The total monetary base = $2,000 + $200 = $2,200.
The money supply = $6,600.
The total deposits = $5,500.
The total reserves = $1,100.
The total currency holdings with public = $1,100.
The money multiplier = 3.

chapter 14

Monetary Policy

This chapter explains money demand and then uses this concept to develop the liquidity preference model of interest rate determination. The chapter considers the Bank of Canada's ability to move interest rates and explores the effect of monetary policy on short-run economic performance. The chapter also discusses monetary neutrality, or the idea that monetary policy in the long-run does not affect real aggregate output but does affect the price level.

How Well Do You Understand the Chapter?

Fill in the blanks using the terms below or circle the correct answer to complete the following statements. Terms may be used more than once. If you find yourself having difficulties, please refer to the appropriate section in the text.

assets	expansion	net exports	short run
Bank of Canada	future	no effect	smaller
buying	greater	nominal GDP	spending
decrease(s)	higher	potential	targeting
demand	increase(s)	price level	the same as
demand for	left	proportional	together
double	less than	real demand for money	transmission
down-sloping	loanable fund market	real variables	velocity of money
downward		right	vertical
equal to	lower		
equalize	money demand	severe	
equilibrium	money neutrality	shift	

1. Money is held by individuals and firms in order to facilitate making transactions. The opportunity cost of holding money is the lost interest income. The higher the interest rate, the _____ is the opportunity cost of holding money: people reduce their holding of money as the interest rate _____. This implies that the demand curve for money slopes _____.

2. Short-term interest rates are interest rates on financial _____ that mature within six months or less. All short-term interest rates on all short-term assets tend to move _____ since they are in effect competing for the same business. A short-term asset that offers a lower-than-average interest rate will be sold by investors. When these assets are sold, this forces the interest rate on these assets to increase, since new buyers must be rewarded with a(n) _____ rate in order to be willing to buy the asset. This reasoning

implies that short-term interest rates will tend to _____ across the financial assets found in the short-term interest rate market. Long-term interest rates are interest rates paid on financial assets that mature a number of years into the _____. Long-term interest rates may differ from short-term interest rates. In this chapter's discussion of interest rates, we will simplify our discussion and assume that there is only one interest rate.

3. The _____ curve illustrates the relationship between the nominal quantity of money demanded and the interest rate. It is a downward-sloping curve. For a given interest rate, a(n) _____ in the price level causes the demand curve for money to shift to the right, while a _____ in the price level causes the demand curve for money to shift to the left.

4. The nominal quantity of money, M, is proportional to the _____. Other things being constant, if the aggregate price level doubles, then the nominal quantity of money will _____. In other words, holding everything else constant, the real quantity of money demanded after an aggregate price level change (M_2/P_2) is _____ the real quantity of money demanded before the aggregate price level change (M_1/P_1).

5. There are a number of factors that _____ the real money demand curve (RMD), including changes in the level of real aggregate _____, changes in banking technology, and changes in banking institutions that alter people's real demand for money. Holding everything else constant, an increase in real aggregate spending will shift the real money demand curve to the _____, while a decrease in real aggregate spending will shift the real money demand curve to the _____. Holding everything else constant, advances in information technology tend to shift the real money demand curve to the _____, since these advances make it easier for the public to make transactions while holding _____ amounts of money. Changes in institutions can increase or decrease the _____ money by changing the opportunity cost of holding money.

6. The _____, (V), equals nominal GDP, ($P \times Y$), divided by the nominal quantity of money, (M). Thus, $V = PY/M$. We can rearrange this equation to get the quantity equation: $MV = PY$. The quantity equation states that the nominal quantity of money multiplied by the velocity of money equals _____. The velocity approach provides a special case of the real money demand curve. We can rewrite the quantity equation, solving for real money demand to get $M/P = (1/V)Y$. This equation tells us that the _____, M/P, is proportional to Y (real GDP), where the constant of proportionality is $1/V$. If this equation is true, then it implies that if V increases, people will need less money; and the real money demand curve at a given Y will shift to the _____.

7. The _____ sets a target interest rate and uses the Bank of Canada's monetary instruments (for example, open-market operation) to achieve the target. The liquidity preference model of the interest rate illustrates the determination of the interest rate by the supply and demand for money. The _____ interest rate is determined by the intersection of the money supply curve and the money demand curve. The money supply curve is a(n) _____ line whose location is controlled by the Bank of Canada through its monetary control instruments. The money demand curve is a(n) _____ line.

8. If the nominal market interest rate is lower than the equilibrium level, then the quantity of money demanded will be _____ than the quantity of money supplied. People will want to _____ their money holdings by selling other financial assets to achieve this goal: in order to sell these financial assets, they will have to offer a(n) _____ interest rate to attract buyers. This will lead the nominal interest rate to _____, bringing about equilibrium between the demand and supply of money.

9. If the nominal market interest rate is greater than the equilibrium level, then the quantity of money demanded will be _____ than the quantity of money supplied. People will want to decrease their money holdings, and they will do so by _____ other financial assets. Due to increased _____ for these interest-bearing financial assets, sellers of these assets will find that they can offer them at a lower nominal interest rate and still find willing buyers. As a result, the nominal interest rate will _____, thereby restoring the money market equilibrium, where the supply of money equals the demand for money.

10. When the Bank of Canada purchases Treasury bills in the open market, this _____ the money supply causing the money supply curve to shift to the _____. For a given money demand curve, this increase in the supply of money will result in a _____ equilibrium interest rate. Thus, if the _____ sets a target interest rate _____ than the prevailing interest rate, it can reach this target by engaging in open-market purchases. When the Bank of Canada sells Treasury bills in the open market, this will _____ the money supply, and the money supply curve will shift to the _____. For a given money demand curve, this decrease in the supply of money will result in a _____ equilibrium interest rate.

11. Monetary _____ in the short run can increase aggregate output; the process by money supply affects aggregate demand is called _____ mechanism. If money supply is increased, it will cause _____ interest rate, which in turn will increase aggregate demand through two channels: direct

and indirect. The direct channel is through _____ investment spending and _____ consumption spending if we assume that consumption is negatively related to the interest rate. The indirect channel is through the exchange rate and _____.

12. Consider a short-run situation when the economy is facing a recessionary gap. To offset the recessionary gap, the Bank of Canada can increase money supply; as a result, the *AD* curve will shift to the _____ and in the short run, *Y* will increase. With an inflationary gap, the Bank of Canada can _____ the money supply; the *AD* curve will shift to the _____ and *Y* will decrease.

13. The Bank of Canada has adopted a formal inflation _____ to guide monetary policy decisions. We have seen that an adverse aggregate demand shock will shift the *AD* curve to the _____, and both price and output will go down (causing a recessionary gap); the Bank of Canada can _____ the money supply and reduce interest rate to reach the pre-shock price level and inflation rate at the target level. In the face of inflationary gaps, the Bank of Canada will _____ the money supply and raise the interest rate to reach the original target inflation. Inflation targeting works with demand shocks, but when the economy faces adverse supply shocks, inflation targeting may make a recession more _____.

14. In the long run, the changes in the money supply do not affect aggregate output, since aggregate output in the long run is always _____ potential output. Thus, a monetary expansion in the long run raises the aggregate price level and wage rates while having _____ on real GDP.

15. A change in the money supply leads to a(n) _____ change in the aggregate price level in the long-run. That is, if an economy is initially in long-run equilibrium and the nominal money supply increases, long-run equilibrium can only be restored when all _____ return to their original levels. Since the nominal money supply increased, the real money supply can only return to its initial level with a proportionate _____ in the aggregate price level. _____ refers to the idea that changes in the money supply have no real effects on the economy. An increase in the money supply causes only an equal percentage increase in the aggregate price level in the long run.

16. Monetary policy does have powerful real effects in the _____ and can be used to ward off recessions or slow an expanding economy. In the long run, the equilibrium interest rate is determined in the _____, and this interest rate is the one that arises when the economy produces at _____ output.

Learning Tips

TIP #1: The interest rate is the price of money, because the interest rate provides a measure of the opportunity cost of holding money.

As the interest rate increases, the quantity of money demanded decreases since the opportunity cost of holding money rises with increases in the interest rate. This relationship implies that the demand for money is downward sloping: the quantity of money demanded is inversely related to the interest rate. This relationship is illustrated in Figure 14.1: when the interest rate is r_1, the quantity of money demanded is M_1; when the interest rate rises to r_2, the quantity of money demanded decreases to M_2.

Figure 14.1

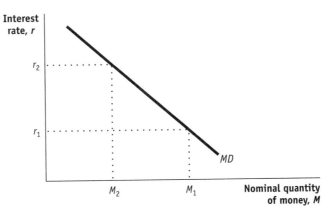

TIP #2: It is important to understand what causes a movement along the money demand curve and what factors cause a shift in the money demand curve.

As with other demand curves, a change in the price of money—the interest rate—causes a movement along the demand curve (see Figure 14.1). A change in the aggregate price level shifts the nominal money demand curve: when the aggregate price level increases, the nominal money demand curve shifts to the right since people will now demand a greater amount of nominal money at every interest rate due to the higher aggregate price level; when the aggregate price level decreases, the nominal money demand curve shifts to the left since people will now demand a smaller amount of nominal money at every interest rate due to the lower aggregate price level. Money demand (real or nominal) also shifts with changes in real aggregate spending, changes in banking technology, and changes in banking institutions. We can summarize these change in the following table.

Change	Effect on money demand
Increase in interest rate	Movement along money demand curve and decrease in quantity of money demanded
Decrease in interest rate	Movement along money demand curve and increase in quantity of money demanded
Increase in aggregate price level	Money demand shifts to the right
Decrease in aggregate price level	Money demand shifts to the left
Increase in real aggregate spending	Money demand shifts to the right
Decrease in real aggregate spending	Money demand shifts to the left
Advance in bank technology	Money demand shifts to the left
Changes in institutions	Money demand shifts to the left or right, depending on the institutional change

TIP #3: Equilibrium in the money market equates the demand for money with the supply of money at the equilibrium interest rate.

Figure 14.2

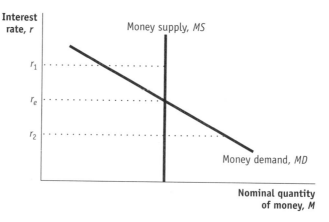

If the interest rate (r_1 in Figure 14.2) is greater than the equilibrium interest rate (r_e), the quantity of money supplied is greater than the quantity of money demanded at that interest rate. Investors will drive the interest rate down to the equilibrium level r_e by shifting their assets out of money holdings and into nonmonetary interest-bearing financial assets. This will cause the interest rate to decrease toward r_e.

If the interest rate (r_2 in Figure 14.2) is less than the equilibrium interest rate (r_e), the quantity of money supplied is less than the quantity of money demanded at that interest rate. Investors will drive the interest rate up to the equilibrium level r_e by shifting their assets out of nonmonetary interest-bearing financial assets and into money holdings. This will cause the interest rate to increase toward r_e.

TIP #4: It is important to understand how the Bank of Canada through its open-market operations effectively controls interest rates in the economy.

When the Bank of Canada purchases Treasury bills in the open market, this injects new reserves into the banking system and leads to an expansion in the money supply from MS_1 to MS_2. For a given money demand curve MD, this results in a decrease in the interest rate from r_1 to r_2. Figure 14.3 below illustrates the effect of an open-market purchase by the Bank of Canada.

Figure 14.3

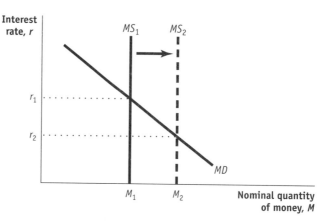

When the Bank of Canada sells Treasury bills in the open market, this removes reserves from the banking system and effectively shifts the money supply curve to the left. For a given money demand curve, this action by the Bank of Canada results in an increase in the interest rate.

TIP #5: **The quantity equation expresses the relationship between the nominal quantity of money and nominal GDP. From this equation we can see that any increase in the quantity of money will cause a proportionate increase in the aggregate price level in the long run.**

The quantity theory of money states that the quantity of money, *M*, times the velocity of money, *V*, equals the aggregate price level, *P*, times the aggregate real output, *Y*. In equation form we have

$$MV = PY$$

In the long run, aggregate real output equals potential output. If *V* is assumed to be constant, then this implies that an increase in the quantity of money must result in a proportionate increase in the aggregate price level. For example, if the quantity of money doubles, then the aggregate price level will also double for a given velocity and a given level of aggregate real output.

TIP #6: **It is important to distinguish between the short-run and long-run effects of monetary policy.**

In the short run, monetary policy can be used to stimulate *AD* and shift it to the right, resulting in an increase in aggregate real output, or monetary policy can be used to contract *AD*, thereby shifting it to the left and leading to a decrease in the level of aggregate real output. In the long run, monetary policy has no effect on aggregate real output since aggregate real output in the long run will always equal potential output. Economists refer to this as monetary neutrality: money is neutral in its effect on aggregate real output in the long run, since it cannot affect the level of aggregate real output.

TIP #7: **The monetary transmission mechanism works through two channels.**

$$M^S \uparrow \rightarrow r \downarrow \rightarrow \text{investment and consumption} \uparrow \rightarrow AE \uparrow \rightarrow AD \uparrow$$
$$r \downarrow \rightarrow \text{value of Canadian dollar} \downarrow \rightarrow \text{net export} \uparrow \rightarrow AE \uparrow \rightarrow AD \uparrow$$

TIP #8: **The Bank of Canada follows an inflation targeting policy.**

Multiple-Choice Questions

1. People choose to hold money because
   a. it has little or no opportunity cost since money does not earn interest.
   b. it facilitates making transactions.
   c. it yields a lower rate of return than non-monetary assets.
   d. Both (b) and (c) are correct.

2. The opportunity cost of holding money
   a. is always greater than the short-term interest rate.
   b. is equal to the difference between the interest rate on assets that are not money and the interest rate on assets that are money.
   c. is equal to the long-term interest rate.
   d. is always equal to zero since it costs you nothing to hold money.

3. Which of the following statements is true?
   a. The nominal demand for money is proportional to the real demand for money.
   b. All short-term interest rates tend to move together.
   c. The higher the short-term interest rate, the lower the opportunity cost of holding money.
   d. The quantity of money demanded is positively related to the interest rate.

4. Which of the following statements is true?
   a. The real quantity of money is equal to the nominal amount of money divided by the aggregate price level.
   b. The real quantity of money measures the purchasing power of the nominal quantity of money.
   c. The real quantity of money is proportional to the nominal quantity of money for any given interest rate.
   d. All of the above statements are true.
   e. Both (a) and (b) are true.

5. If the price level doubles holding everything else constant, we know that
   a. the nominal quantity of money demanded also doubled.
   b. the real quantity of money demanded also doubled.
   c. the interest rate also doubled.
   d. Both (a) and (b) are correct.

6. For a given interest rate, when money demand is greater than money supply, then
   a. interest rates will increase.
   b. interest rates will decrease.
   c. people will sell nonmonetary assets.
   d. people will buy nonmonetary assets.
   e. Both (a) and (c) are correct.

7. The Bank of Canada sets a target interest rate and can achieve that interest rate through
   a. open-market purchases, if the federal funds rate is initially less than the target rate.
   b. open-market sales, if the federal funds rate is initially less than the target rate.
   c. legislative action that decrees the level of the discount rate and thus the federal funds rate.
   d. stimulating the demand for money, if the initial interest rate is less than the target rate.

8. The liquidity preference model of interest rate determination states that
   a. interest rates are determined solely by the Bank of Canada.
   b. interest rates are determined by the supply of and demand for money.
   c. people always prefer liquidity and do not consider the opportunity cost of holding money when they decide how much money they wish to hold at any given point in time.
   d. interest rates are determined in the market for nonmonetary assets and not the market for money.

9. The money supply curve in the liquidity preference model is drawn as a vertical line since
   a. there is only one level of money supply that will enable an economy to produce at the full employment level of output and the appropriate aggregate price level.
   b. Parliament sets by law the level of the money supply in the economy.
   c. the Bank of Canada chooses the level of the money supply through its open-market operations.
   d. the money supply curve is unimportant in determining the equilibrium level of interest rates in the liquidity preference model.

10. When people offering to sell nonmonetary financial assets find that they must increase the interest rate these assets pay in order to sell them, this tells us that
   a. the demand for money is less than the supply of money.
   b. the supply of money equals the demand for money.
   c. the demand for money is greater than the supply of money.
   d. we cannot know anything about the relationship between the demand for money and the supply of money from this information.

11. Which of the following statements is true?
   a. Short-term interest rates tend to move independently of one another.
   b. Long-term interest rates tend to move together, and they tend to mimic short-term interest rates.
   c. Open-market purchases by the Bank of Canada result in the interest rate decreasing.
   d. Open-market sales by the Bank of Canada increase the money supply and cause a movement along the money demand curve.

Use the following graph to answer the next two questions.

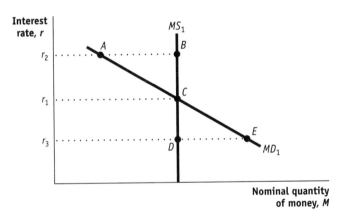

12. The economy is currently operating at its potential output level. Which point in the graph here is most likely to represent this long-run situation in the money market? Point
   a. *A*, since high interest rates encourage people to save more leading to levels of investment.
   b. *B*, since the Bank of Canada controls the money supply we know we must be on the money supply curve in the long-run.
   c. *C*, since at this point the money market is in equilibrium.
   d. *D*, since low interest rates encourage business investment which leads to higher economic growth.
   e. *E*, since low interest rates reduce inflationary pressures in the economy.

13. In the graph, which point most likely represents a possible new short-run equilibrium if the Bank of Canada conducts an open market sale? Point
   a. *A*
   b. *B*
   c. *C*
   d. *D*
   e. *E*

14. Which of the following statements is true?
  a. In the long run, an increase in the nominal money supply increases the potential output level.
  b. In the long run, an increase in the nominal money supply will have no effect on real variables, including the aggregate price level.
  c. In the long run, an increase in the nominal money supply will lead to a proportionate increase in the aggregate price level.
  d. Both (a) and (b) are correct.
  e. Answers (a), (b), and (c) are correct.

15. Which of the following statements is true?
  a. As the interest rate increases, the opportunity cost of holding money increases and people tend to increase their holdings of money.
  b. All short-term interest rates on financial assets that mature in six months or less tend to be equal to each other.
  c. As the interest rate decreases, the opportunity cost of holding money increases and people tend to increase their holdings of money.
  d. As the interest rate increases, the price of bonds increases.

16. Consider a real money demand curve and determine which of the following statements is true.
  a. As the interest rate increases, the opportunity cost of holding money increases and people tend to hold more balances.
  b. The real money demand curve will shift to the right if the velocity of money increases at a given level of income.
  c. The real money demand curve will shift to the left if the velocity of money increases at a given level of income.
  d. As the real money demand curve becomes more interest-sensitive, the real demand curve becomes steeper.

17. Which of the following factors will not cause a shift of the real money demand curve?
  a. changes in the banking technology
  b. changes in the interest rate
  c. changes in aggregate spending
  d. changes in the velocity of money

18. If $V = 10$ and $Y = 1,000$, the real money demand is _____. If V increases to 20 (while Y and other variables remain constant), the real money demand will be _____.
  a. 10,000; 20,000
  b. 1,000; 2,000
  c. 1,00; 50
  d. 100; 200

Answer questions 19–20 on the basis of the following table. Assume that price level (P) stays constant at one.

Interest rate	Money supply	Money demand
1%	$10,000	$19,000
5%	10,000	15,000
8%	10,000	12,000
10%	10,000	10,000
15%	10,000	5,000

19. Which of the following statements is false?
   a. The equilibrium interest rate is 10%.
   b. When the interest rate is 5%, there is an excess demand for money, which will cause a decrease (shift) of the money demand curve.
   c. Along the money demand schedule at various interest rates, the real GDP (Y), the velocity of money (V), and other variables that cause the shift of the money demand curve remain constant.
   d. The money supply remains constant at each and every level of interest rates. If the money multiplier is 2, we can conclude that the monetary base is $5,000.

20. Assume that the monetary base is $5,000 and the money multiplier is 2. Assume further that Y and V (and other variables that cause the shift of the money demand curve) remain constant. If the Bank of Canada increases the monetary base by 20%, we can conclude all of the following statements except
   a. The equilibrium interest rate will decrease to 8%.
   b. The equilibrium interest rate will increase to a level above 10%.
   c. The equilibrium level of money demand will be $12,000.
   d. At the equilibrium point, money supply = money demand = $12,000.

21. Consider an economy with a recessionary gap. To fight this recessionary gap, the Bank of Canada can _____ monetary base; as a result, the *AD* curve will shift to the _____.
   a. increase; right
   b. increase; left
   c. decrease; right
   d. decrease; left

22. The effectiveness of expansionary monetary policy will increase if the money demand curve becomes _____ interest-sensitive and the investment function is _____ interest-sensitive.
   a. less; more
   b. more; more
   c. less; less
   d. more; less

23. Consider an economy with an inflationary gap. To fight this inflationary gap, the Bank of Canada can _____ money supply; as a result, the *AD* curve will shift to the _____.
   a. increase; right
   b. increase; left
   c. decrease; right
   d. decrease; left

24. According to monetary transmission mechanism, an increase in money supply will cause
   a. a lower interest rate, more investment, more aggregate spending, and a rightward shift of the *AD* curve.
   b. a lower interest rate, lower money demand, more investment, more aggregate spending, and a rightward shift of the *AD* curve.
   c. higher interest rate, more investment, more aggregate spending, and a rightward shift of the *AD* curve.
   d. a lower interest rate, a lower value of domestic currency, less investment, less aggregate spending, and a leftward shift of the *AD* curve.

25. Monetary neutrality implies all the following except
   a. A change in the money supply has no effect on price, output, and employment in the long run.
   b. A change in the money supply by 25% will increase price by 25% in the long run.
   c. Changes in monetary variables have no effects on the real variables in the long run.
   d. If monetary neutrality holds in the long run, then any change in M will have no effect on M/P, real GDP and real wage rate.

26. The effects of a decrease in money supply in the short run are all the following except
   a. higher interest rates, lower value of domestic currency in the foreign exchange market, lower investment, and a leftward shift of the AD curve.
   b. higher interest rates, higher value of domestic currency in the foreign exchange market, lower net exports, and a leftward shift of the AD curve.
   c. higher interest rates, lower investment, lower aggregate spending, and a leftward shift of the AD curve.
   d. higher interest rates, lower investment, lower net exports due to higher value of Domestic currency in the foreign exchange market, and a leftward shift of the AD curve.

Problems and Exercises

1. The following figure illustrates the relationship between the nominal quantity of money, M, and the interest rate, r.

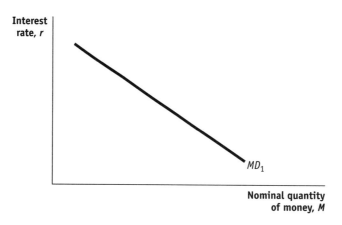

For each of the following situations, use the previous graph for reference.
   a. Holding everything else constant, the interest rate increases from r_1 to r_2. Graph this in the following figure.

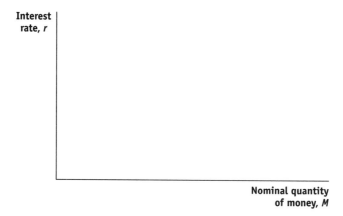

b. Holding everything else constant, the level of aggregate real income decreases. Graph this in the following figure.

Interest
rate, *r*

Nominal quantity
of money, *M*

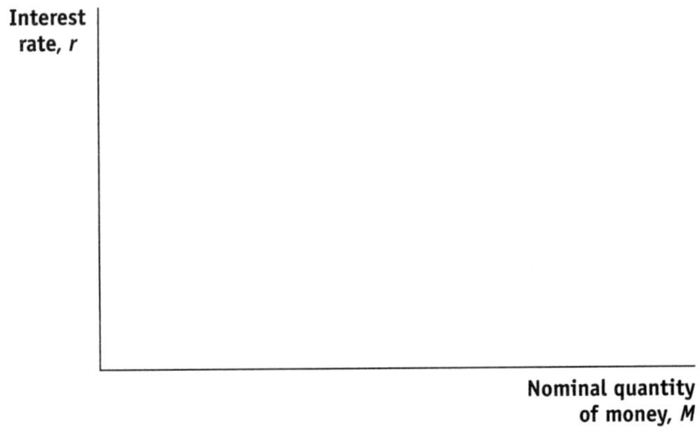

c. Holding everything else constant, there is an increase in the aggregate price level. Graph this in the following figure.

Interest
rate, *r*

Nominal quantity
of money, *M*

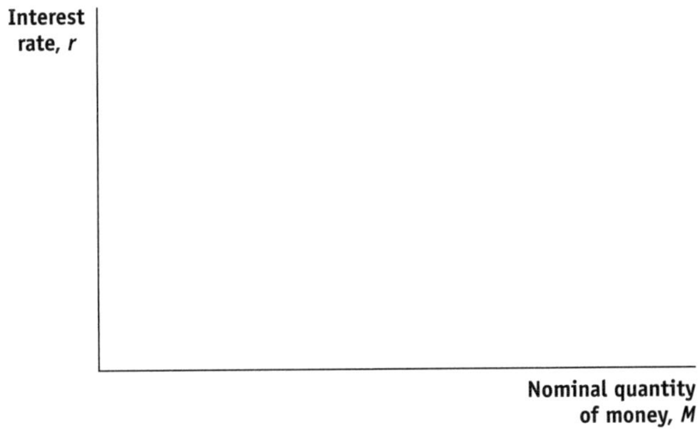

d. Holding everything else constant, individuals in a community are now able to use Internet banking for their money and financial assets accounts. Graph this in the following figure.

Interest
rate, *r*

Nominal quantity
of money, *M*

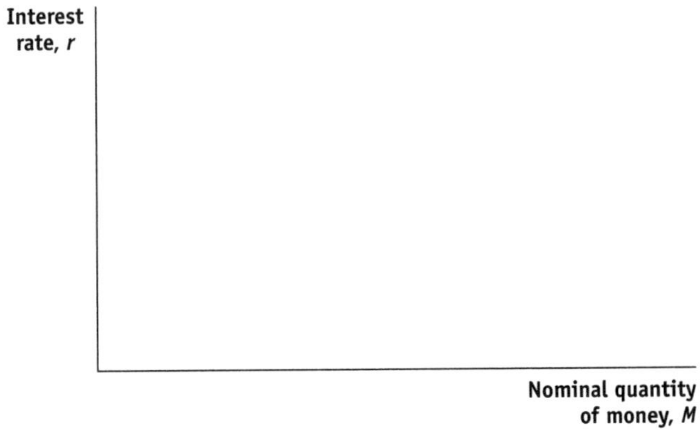

2. Consider two assets: both Asset A and Asset B are one-month bonds issued by different companies that have the same amount of risk. Asset A initially earns a higher interest rate for its holder than does Asset B. Explain why you would expect this interest rate differential to disappear. Explain the process that leads Assets A and B to have approximately the same interest rate.

3. Use the following table to answer this question.

Change	Effect on nominal money demand	Effect on real money demand
Decrease in aggregate price level		
Increase in interest rate		
Change in regulation so that interest is now allowed on checking accounts		

   a. On the table, enter how each scenario will affect nominal money demand and real money demand.
   b. Explain why a change in the aggregate price level affects the nominal demand curve differently than it does the real money demand curve.

4. Use the following figure of the nominal money demand and money supply curves to answer this question. Assume this market is initially in equilibrium with the nominal quantity of money equal to M_1 and the interest rate equal to r_1.

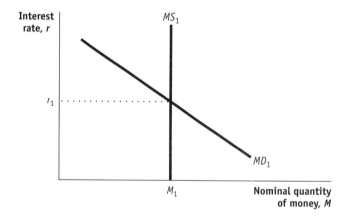

a. Suppose the Bank of Canada engages in an open-market purchase of Treasury bills. Holding everything else constant, what happens to the equilibrium quantity of money and the equilibrium interest rate? Sketch a graph illustrating these changes.

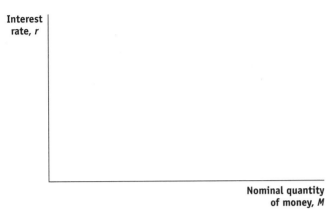

b. Suppose the Bank of Canada engages in an open-market sale of Treasury bills. Holding everything else constant, what happens to the equilibrium quantity of money and the equilibrium interest rate? Sketch a graph illustrating these changes.

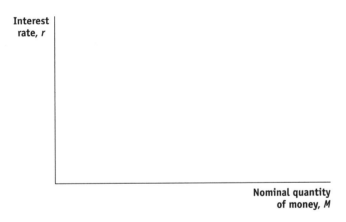

c. Suppose the aggregate price level increases. Holding everything else constant, what happens to the equilibrium quantity of money and the equilibrium interest rate? Sketch a graph illustrating these changes.

Interest
rate, *r*

Nominal quantity
of money, *M*

5. Use the *AS-AD* model to answer this question.
  i) Scenario I

   The economy of Macroland is initially in long-run equilibrium. Then the Bank of Macroland decides to reduce interest rates through an open market operation.

   a. Draw a graph representing the initial situation in Macroland. In your graph, be sure to include the short-run aggregate supply curve (*SRAS*), the long-run aggregate supply curve (*LRAS*), and the aggregate demand curve (*AD*). On your graph mark the equilibrium aggregate price level and the aggregate output level as well as potential output.

Aggregate
price
level, *P*

Real GDP

   b. Draw a graph of the money market showing its initial situation before the Bank of Macroland engages in monetary policy and showing as well as the effect of the Bank of Macroland monetary policy actions. Be sure to indicate the initial equilibrium as well as the equilibrium after the monetary policy.

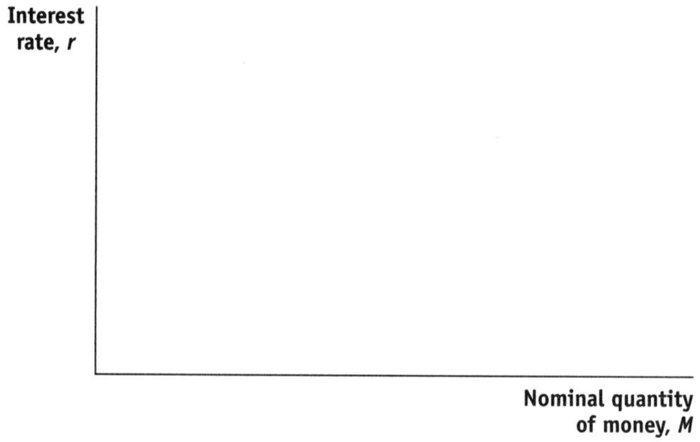

Interest
rate, *r*

Nominal quantity
of money, *M*

c. How does this monetary policy action affect the aggregate economy in the short run? Explain your answer verbally while also including a graph of the *AS-AD* model to illustrate your answer.

d. How does this monetary policy action affect the aggregate economy in the long run?

ii) Scenario II

Econoland is currently operating with a recessionary gap.

e. Draw a graph representing Econoland's economic situation using an *AS-AD* model. Be sure to indicate in your graph *SRAS, LRAS, AD*, the short-run equilibrium aggregate price level (P_1), the short-run equilibrium aggregate output level (Y_1), and the potential output level (Y_E).

f. What monetary policy would you suggest the Bank of Econoland pursue if its only goal is to restore production in Econoland to the potential output level? Explain how this monetary policy would achieve this goal.

g. Is there a potential drawback to the implementation of this particular monetary policy? Explain your answer.

iii) Scenario III

Upland is currently operating with an inflationary gap.

h. Draw a graph representing Upland's economic situation using an *AS-AD* model. Be sure to indicate in your graph *SRAS, LRAS, AD*, the short-run equilibrium aggregate price level (P_1), the short-run equilibrium aggregate output level (Y_1), and the potential output level (Y_E).

i. What monetary policy would you suggest the Bank of Upland pursue if its only goal is to restore production in Upland to the potential output level? Explain how this monetary policy would achieve this goal.

    j. Is there a potential drawback to the implementation of this particular monetary policy? Explain your answer.

6. Suppose that when the Bank of Macroland reduces the interest rate by 1 percentage point it increases the level of investment spending by $500 million in Macroland. If the marginal propensity to save equals .25, what will be the total rise in real GDP, assuming the aggregate price level is held constant? Explain your answer.

7. Consider the following table.

Interest rate	Money supply	Money demand
0.01	$12,000	$19,000
0.05	12,000	15,000
0.08	12,000	12,000
0.10	12,000	10,000
0.15	12,000	5,000

    a. If we plot the money supply curve with interest rate in the vertical axis, the money supply curve will be a _____ line.

    b. If the accompanying table corresponds to a money multiplier of 2 in the banking system, then the monetary base is equal to _____.

    c. (Assume that $P = 1$) If the money demand function is written as $M^D = 0.5Y - 100,000r$, where Y is real GDP and r is the interest rate, then the corresponding Y in the above table is _____.

    d. The equilibrium interest rate is _____, and the equilibrium quantity of M is _____.

    e. If Y increases to 44,000, the new equilibrium interest rate will be _____.

    f. If Y stays constant at 40,000 and M increases to $15,000, the new equilibrium interest rate will be _____.

8. Trace the effects (write either increase, decrease, or remain constant) when we consider the following in the short run.

    a. The effects of open-market purchases of bonds by the Bank of Canada:

        Money supply will _____.

        Monetary base will _____.

        Interest rate will _____.

        Investment spending will _____.

        The value of domestic currency in the foreign exchange market will _____.

        Net exports will _____.

        Aggregate expenditure will _____.

        The *AD* curve (at given price levels) will _____.

b. The effects of an increase in the Bank of Canada's overnight rate:

a. The effects of open-market purchases of bonds by the Bank of Canada:

Money supply will _____.

Monetary base will _____.

Interest rate will _____.

Investment spending will _____.

The value of domestic currency in the foreign exchange market will

_____.

Net exports will _____.

Aggregate expenditure will _____.

The *AD* curve (at given price levels) will _____.

9. a. Assume that the Bank of Canada has increased the money supply and this has resulted in a reduction in the interest rate by 1%, which has increased investment by 100. If we consider that the *MPC* is 0.6, then the *AD* curve will shift to the right/left (circle the correct choice) by _____.

b. Assume that the Bank of Canada has increased the money supply and this has resulted in a reduction in the interest rate by 1%, which has increased investment by 200. If we consider that the *MPC* is 0.6, then the *AD* curve will shift to the right/left (circle the correct choice) by _____.

c. We can conclude that the higher the interest-sensitivity of investment is, the larger/smaller (circle the correct choice) the shift of the *AD* curve is.

10. a. If $MV = PY$ is true and if M increases by 5%, V by 3%, and Y by 2%, then P will increase by _____.

b. If $MV = PY$ is true and if M increases by 5%, V by 3%, and P by 7%, then the % change in Y will be _____.

Answers to How Well Do You Understand the Chapter

1. higher, increases, downward

2. assets, together, higher, equalize, future

3. money demand, increase, decrease

4. price level, double, the same as

5. shift, spending, right, left, left, smaller, demand for

6. velocity of money, nominal GDP, real demand for money, left

7. Bank of Canada, equilibrium, vertical, down-sloping

8. greater, increase, higher, increase

9. less than, buying, demand, decrease

10. increases, right, lower, Bank of Canada, lower, decrease, left, higher

11. expansion, transmission, lower, higher, higher, net exports

12. right, decrease, left

13. targeting, left, increase, decrease, severe

14. equal to, no effect

15. proportional, real variables, increase, Money neutrality

16. short run, loanable fund market, potential

Answers to Multiple-Choice Questions

1. Although money typically does yield a lower rate of return than nonmonetary assets, this is not the reason people choose to hold money. Rather, they choose to hold money because money facilitates making transactions. There is an opportunity cost of holding money: when holding money you forego the higher rate of return you could earn by holding nonmonetary assets. **Answer: B.**

2. The opportunity cost of holding money is measured by what is lost when holding money: this is calculated as the difference between the rate of return you could earn by holding nonmonetary assets minus the rate of return on monetary assets. **Answer: B.**

3. The nominal demand for money is proportional to the aggregate price level. The higher the short-term interest rate, the greater the opportunity cost of holding money since you could be earning this higher short-term interest rate if you chose to hold nonmonetary assets. The quantity of money demanded is inversely, or negatively, related to the interest rate: as the interest rate increases, the quantity of money demanded decreases. Short-term interest rates do move together since if there is a difference in the rate of return on short-term financial assets, there will be movement toward the asset that pays the higher return and away from the asset that pays the lower return. As the market adjusts to this movement, there will be a tendency for the rate of returns for both assets to move toward one another: short-term interest rates will therefore tend to move together. **Answer: B.**

4. The first two statements are factual statements that are true by definition. The real quantity of money is not proportional to the nominal quantity of money. However, the nominal quantity of money demanded is proportional to the aggregate price level. **Answer: E.**

5. To maintain the same level of purchasing power as was initially had, when the aggregate price level doubles, the nominal quantity of money demanded will also double. However, a doubling of prices will have no effect on the real quantity of money demanded since this real money demand is, by definition, the amount of money that holds purchasing power constant. Holding everything else constant, assumes that a doubling of the price level will have no impact on the interest rate. **Answer: A.**

6. When money demand is greater than money supply, people wish to increase their money holdings. This will cause them to sell their nonmonetary assets: as the supply of these nonmonetary assets increases, people will find they must offer higher interest rates on these assets in order to sell them. Thus, interest rates will increase. **Answer: E.**

7. If the target interest rate is greater than the federal funds rate, then the Bank of Canada needs to engage in monetary policy that will shift the money supply curve to the left, resulting in an increase in interest rates for a given money demand curve. The Bank of Canada, therefore, will engage in open-market sales of Treasury bills. The Bank of Canada does not set the discount rate, and the Bank of Canada's monetary policy affects the money supply curve and not the money demand curve. **Answer: B.**

8. The liquidity preference model uses the interaction between the demand for money and the supply of money to analyze the determination of interest rates. Interest rates are impacted by the Bank of Canada's policy and its effect on the money supply curve. People consider the opportunity cost of holding money when making their decisions about the level of money they wish to hold. One can model interest rate determination in either the framework of money demand and supply or the framework of demand and supply of loanable funds. **Answer: B.**

9. The Bank of Canada controls the money supply through open-market operations. We know that the determination of interest rates depends not only on the demand for money but also on the supply of money. Parliament does not have the authority to determine the country's money supply. Different levels of money supply are compatible with the full-employment level of output, since interest rate determination depends on both the money supply and the money demand. **Answer: C.**

10. When interest rates must rise, this implies they are initially too low: in the money market, this would imply that the interest rate is initially below the equilibrium interest rate or where money demand is greater than money supply. **Answer: C.**

11. Short-term interest rates tend to move together, while long-term interest rates may or may not mimic short-term interest rates. When the Bank of Canada makes an open-market purchase, this increases the level of reserves in the banking system which leads to an expansion in the money supply. **Answer: C.**

12. In the long run, the economy is in equilibrium, including the money market where the demand for money must equal the supply of money. This is only true at point C in the graph. **Answer: C.**

13. When the Bank of Canada conducts an open-market sale, this causes the money supply to shift to the left and, for a given demand curve, results in the interest rate increasing. Only point A illustrates this scenario. **Answer: A.**

14. In the long run, the economy will operate at the potential output level: any increase in the money supply will not affect the real value of aggregate output, but will lead to a proportionate increase in the aggregate price level. **Answer: C.**

15. As the interest rate increases, the opportunity costs of holding money increases and people tend to hold less money. We also know that the price of bonds and the interest rate are inversely related. All short-term rates are equal to each other. **Answer: B.**

16. The true statement is: the real money demand curve will shift to the left if the velocity of money increases at a given level of income. We have seen that as the interest rate increases, the opportunity costs of holding money increases and people tend to hold less money. When we draw the money demand curve, the money demand curve becomes flatter as money demand becomes more interest-sensitive. **Answer: C.**

17. The movement along a given real money demand curve is caused by interest rate changes. All other factors, like changes in the banking technology, changes in the aggregate spending and changes in the velocity of money, will cause shifts of a real money demand curve. **Answer: B.**

18. Since real money demand $(M/P) = (1/V)Y$, we can use the numbers given in the question and solve M/P as 100 (when $Y = 1,000$ and $V = 10$) and solve M/P as 50 (when $Y = 1,000$ and $V = 20$). **Answer: C.**

19. The equilibrium interest rate is found with the condition that money-supply equals money-demand; therefore, the equilibrium interest rate in 10%, where the excess demand or excess supply of money is zero. Since the money supply is equal to the monetary base times the money multiplier, the monetary base is $5,000 given a money supply at $10,000 and a multiplier at 2. Along a money demand curve, all other factors other than the interest rate are constant. **Answer: B.**

20. The equilibrium interest rate is found with the condition that money-supply equals money demand; therefore, the equilibrium interest rate in 8%, where the money demand = money supply = $12,000. **Answer: B.**

21. To fight a recessionary gap, the Bank of Canada can increase money supply through an increase in the monetary base. This will cause the *AD* curve to shift to the right. **Answer: A.**

22. The effectiveness of the money demand curve depends on the following: the extent of the change in the interest rate due to monetary expansion, the extent of the change in investment due to change in the interest rate, and the extent of the change in the *AD* curve. If the money demand curve is less-interest sensitive, a very small increase in the money supply will be required to cause a reduction in the interest rate; this reduction in the interest rate will cause a sizeable change in the investment, if the investment is very interest-sensitive. The greater the change is in investment, the greater will be the rightward shift of the *AD* curve, given $[1/(1 - MPC)]$. **Answer: A.**

23. To fight an inflationary gap, the Bank of Canada can decrease the money supply through a reduction in the monetary base. This will cause the *AD* curve to shift to the left. **Answer: D.**

24. The monetary transmission mechanism shows how changes in the money supply can affect aggregate spending in the short run via changes in the interest rates. With an increase in money supply, the interest rate goes down, investment spending (I) increases, and consumption spending (C) may also increase if we assume that consumption spending is inversely related to interest rate increases; lower interest rate can also lead to a lower value of domestic currency, which will increase net exports (NX). Increases in I, C, and NX will lead to the rightward shift of the *AD* curve. **Answer: A.**

25. In the long run, a change in money supply has no effect on output and employment; it causes a proportionate change in price. According to monetary neutrality in the long run, the nominal or monetary variables have no effect on real variables, like M/P, real GDP, real wage rates, relative prices, etc. **Answer: A.**

26. The effects of a decrease in money supply in the short run are: lower business investment due to a higher interest rate, lower consumption spending due to a higher interest rate, higher value of domestic currency (causing lower net exports) due to a higher interest rate, lower aggregate expenditure, and a leftward shift of the *AD* curve. **Answer: A.**

Answers to Problems and Exercises

1. a. An increase in the interest rate causes a movement along the money demand curve as illustrated in the following figure.

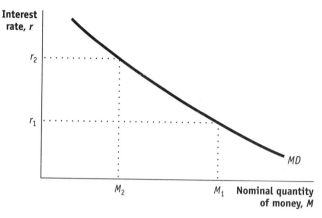

b. As the level of aggregate real income decreases, this causes the money demand curve to shift to the left as individuals demand less money at every interest rate. This is illustrated in the following figure.

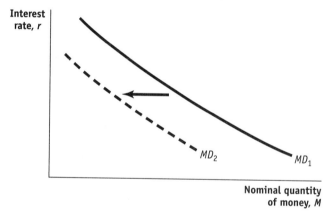

c. An increase in the aggregate price level causes the money demand curve to shift to the right, as individuals demand more money at every interest rate to facilitate making their transactions at the new higher price levels. This is illustrated in the following figure.

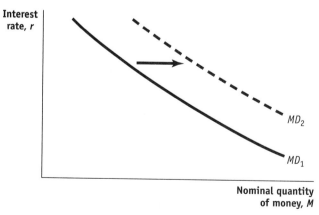

d. With new technology for managing money and financial assets, people will decrease their demand for money at every interest rate. This will cause money demand to shift to the left, as illustrated in the figure from part b of this answer.

2. Since both Asset A and Asset B are short-term financial assets, we anticipate that the interest rate paid on both assets should be roughly equivalent. If the returns differ, investors will sell the asset offering the lower return: to find a buyer for this asset, they must offer a higher rate on it. This buying and selling of assets will lead the returns on these short-term financial assets to move toward approximately the same return.

3. a.

Change	Effect on nominal money demand	Effect on real money demand
Decrease in aggregate price level	Shifts the nominal money demand curve to the left	Has no effect
Increase in interest rate	Causes a movement along the nominal money demand curve	Causes a movement along the real money demand curve
Change in regulation, so interest is now allowed on checking accounts	Shifts the nominal money demand curve to the right	Shifts the real money demand curve to the right

b. When the aggregate price level changes, the nominal money demand curve does not automatically take into account the effect of this change in prices on the nominal demand for money. For example, as the aggregate price level rises, people will find that, due to the increase in the aggregate price level, they need to hold greater amounts of money in order to make their transactions. This causes the nominal money demand curve to shift to the right: people demand a greater quantity of nominal money at every interest rate. In contrast, the real money demand curve automatically takes into account any change in the aggregate price level: a change in the aggregate price level requires a proportionately equal change in the nominal quantity of money in order that the real quantity of money is unchanged.

4. a. When the Bank of Canada increases the money supply through an open-market purchase of Treasury bills, this shifts the money supply curve from MS_1 to MS_2 and results in a decrease in the equilibrium interest rate from r_1 to r_2 and an increase in the equilibrium quantity of money from M_1 to M_2. The following figure illustrates these changes.

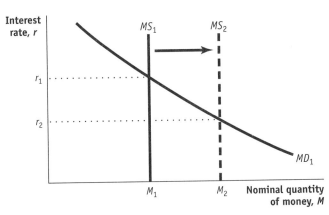

b. When the Bank of Canada decreases the money supply through an open-market sale of Treasury bills, the money supply curve shifts from MS_1 to MS_2. This causes the equilibrium interest rate to increase from r_1 to r_2, while the equilibrium quantity of money decreases from M_1 to M_2. These changes are illustrated in the following figure.

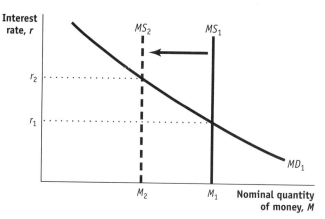

c. An increase in the aggregate price level shifts the nominal money demand curve to the right from MD_1 to MD_2. This causes the equilibrium interest rate to increase from r_1 to r_2, while the equilibrium quantity of money is unchanged. The following figure illustrates this situation.

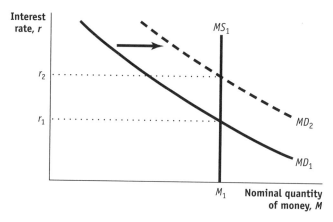

5. a.

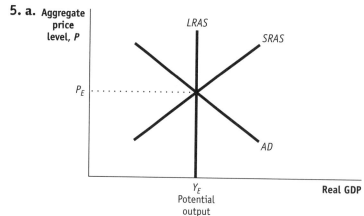

b.

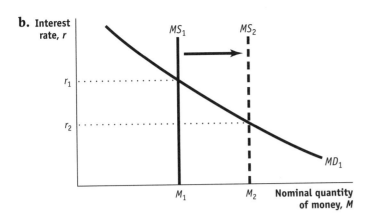

c. When the Bank of Macroland reduces interest rates through an open-market purchase of Treasury bills, this increases aggregate demand and causes the *AD* curve to shift to the right to AD_2. In the short run, this causes aggregate real output to increase to Y_2 and the aggregate price level to increase to P_2. This is illustrated in the following figure.

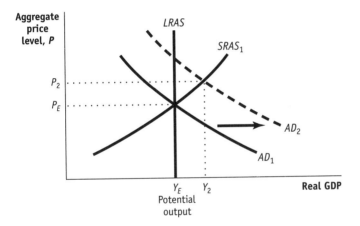

d. In the long run, the economy must return to producing its potential output Y_E. This economic adjustment will occur as the SRAS curve shifts to the left as nominal wages rise. As the *SRAS* curve shifts back to $SRAS_3$, this will eliminate the inflationary gap, restore the economy to its potential output level, and lead to an even higher aggregate price level, P_3. The following figure illustrates this long-run adjustment.

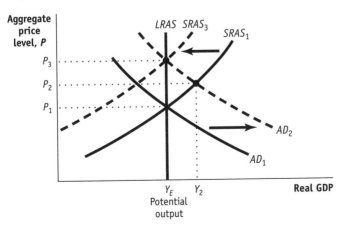

e.

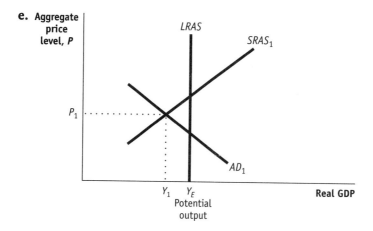

f. If the Bank of Macroland expands the money supply through open-market purchases, this will reduce interest rates and stimulate investment spending and, therefore, aggregate demand. As AD shifts to the right from AD_1 to AD_2, this will cause real GDP to increase to Y_E and prices to rise to P_2. The following figure illustrates this situation.

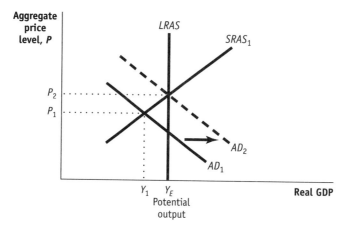

g. If the Bank of Macroland engages in activist monetary policy, this will cause the aggregate price level to increase. Alternatively, policymakers could do nothing and wait for the SRAS to shift to the right as nominal wages fall. In the long run, aggregate output would return to Y_E and the aggregate price level would fall below its initial level of P_1.

h.

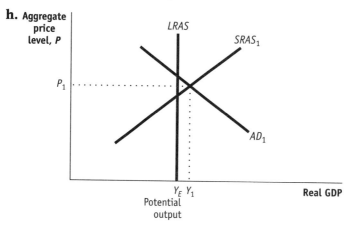

i. The Bank of Macroland should decrease the money supply and thereby increase the interest rate through open-market sales of Treasury bills. This action by the FOMC will cause the *AD* to shift to the left, restoring the economy to its potential output level at a lower aggregate price level than P_1.

j. No, this policy restores the economy to its long-run position without raising the aggregate price level.

6. The action by the Bank of Macroland effectively creates a change in autonomous investment spending of $500 million. This change in autonomous investment spending will cause real GDP to increase by a larger, multiplied amount due to the multiplier process. Since the multiplier equals $1/(1 - MPC)$ or, in this case, 4, we can compute the total change in real GDP as 4 ($500 million) or $2 billion.

7. a. vertical
 b. $6,000
 c. $40,000
 d. 0.08 or 8%; $12,000
 e. 0.10 or 10%
 f. 0.05 or 5%

8. a. increase; increase; decrease; increase; decrease; increase; increase, increase
 b. decrease; decrease; increase; decrease; increase, decrease, decrease; decrease

9. a. $\Delta Y = \Delta I[1/(1 - MPC)] = 250$
 b. $\Delta Y = \Delta I[1/(1 - MPC)] = 500$
 c. larger

10. a. Since $MY = PY$, we can write the following:
 % change in M + % change in V = % change in P and % change in Y
 5% + 3% = % change in P and 2%.
 Therefore, the % change in P will be 6%.
 b. Since $MY = PY$, we can write the following:
 % change in M + % change in V = % change in P and % change in Y
 5% + 3% = 7% change in P and % change in Y.
 Therefore, the % change in Y will be 1%.

chapter 15

Labour Markets, Unemployment, and Inflation

This chapter develops the idea of the natural rate of unemployment and explores why its value is not equal to zero. The chapter also considers the cyclical unemployment rate and its relationship to the business cycle. The chapter explores structural unemployment and the effect of minimum wages and efficiency wages on the level of structural unemployment found in an economy. The chapter considers why the actual rate of unemployment may differ from the natural rate of unemployment over time. The chapter explores the Phillips curve which expresses the short-run relationship between unemployment and inflation and discusses why this relationship does not continue into the long run. In addition, the chapter considers the nonaccelerating inflation rate of unemployment, or NAIRU, and its policy implications.

How Well Do You Understand the Chapter?

accelerating inflation	falling	inflationary	NAIRU	structural
collective bargaining	fluctuations	job search	negatively	structural unemploy-ment
cycles	frictional	labour strike	Okun's law	substantial
decrease(s)	future	labour-contracts	output	sum
discouraged	greater	laid-off	output gap	surplus
disequilibrium	half	less	rise	vertical
efficiency wages	high	long-run	rising	wage staggering
expected inflation rate	higher	low	shocks	zero
	increase(s)	lower	short-run	
	inflation	matching	slow	
	inflation rate	more	slowly	

1. Even when the economy is at full employment, it does not mean that the unemployment rate is _____. The economy can have a(n) _____ amount of unemployment due to individual workers leaving jobs for a variety of reasons, including personal reasons, technological change, changes in consumers' tastes, and the decline of some businesses. The natural rate of unemployment is composed of frictional unemployment, _____ and seasonal unemployment. Frictional unemployment is the unemployment due to the time workers spend in their _____. Frictional unemployment occurs because of the constant process of job creation and job destruction and due

to the entry of new workers into the job market. Frictional unemployment is not a signal of a labour _____.

2. Structural unemployment is unemployment that results when there are _____ people seeking jobs in a labour market than there are jobs available at the prevailing wage. Structural unemployment exists when the supply of labour is _____ than the demand for labour at the current wage rate. At the equilibrium wage rate there will be _____ structural unemployment, but there will still be some frictional unemployment since there will always be some workers who are looking for work, even though the number of jobs available is equal to the number of workers seeking jobs. Structural unemployment exists when the wage rate is _____ than the equilibrium wage: this may be due to the existence of minimum wages, labour unions, hysteresis, and efficiency wages

3. An effective or binding minimum wage creates _____ employment, since at the minimum wage the quantity of labour supplied is _____ than the quantity of labour demanded.

4. Labour unions through _____ can often win higher wages from employers than the market would have provided. Unionized workers can threaten a(n) _____, a collective refusal to work, more effectively than can a single labourer. Effective labour unions are able to earn wages in excess of the equilibrium wage rate: this creates a situation of _____ unemployment, where the quantity of labour supplied exceeds the quantity of labour demanded. Labour unions may also contribute to _____ unemployment through their negotiated labour contracts: with long-term contracts, the employers lose the ability to _____ wages under conditions of decreasing labour demand. _____ refers to firms having different timetables for negotiating their labour contracts. This leads the labour market to adjust _____ from one equilibrium to another when the demand for labour changes.

5. According to the hysteresis hypothesis, _____ (due to recessions, for example) in output around the potential output might influence the potential output. A deep recession can cause long-term unemployment for some workers and lead to _____ natural rate of unemployment. Hystersis can also be linked to "inside-outside" theory. If unionized workers are laid off in a recession, the longer they are unemployed, the _____ influence they have on union negotiations. In effect, the _____ workers become "outsiders", and the union attempts to maximize the wages of the new and smaller group of "insiders". Hence, they bargain wage adjustments upward, and the outsiders become long-term unemployed, and as a result, the natural rate of unemployment _____.

6. When employers choose to pay wages _____ than the equilibrium wage, this can result in structural unemployment. This practice of paying _____ acts as an incentive for better worker performance and lower worker turnover, but it can also lead to _____ unemployment, since a(n) _____ wage rate will attract a larger pool of workers looking for high-paying jobs. Public policy designed to help unemployed workers may also create incentives that will slow an unemployed worker's return to work.

7. The natural rate of unemployment is the rate of unemployment around which the unemployment rate in the economy fluctuates. This rate of unemployment is the _____ of frictional and structural unemployment and seasonal unemployment. The cyclical unemployment rate measures the deviation in the unemployment rate from the natural unemployment rate. Cyclical unemployment arises from the business _____. Actual unemployment is the _____ of the natural unemployment rate plus cyclical unemployment.

8. The natural rate of unemployment changes over time due to changes in the characteristics of the labour force, changes in labour market institutions, changes in government policies, and changes in productivity. The natural rate of unemployment _____ when there is an increase in the number of new workers, since new workers are more likely to add to the number of _____ unemployment. Changes in labour market institutions can also affect the natural rate of unemployment. Temporary employment agencies can help to _____ the natural rate of unemployment, as they reduce frictional unemployment by _____ workers to jobs. Technological change can increase structural unemployment, which in turn will _____ natural rate of unemployment.

9. Government policy may _____ the natural rate of unemployment by increasing both structural and frictional unemployment. For example, generous unemployment benefits or a binding-high minimum wage may result in _____ levels of structural and frictional unemployment. Other government policies may reduce the natural rate of unemployment through their effect on structural and frictional unemployment. For example, employment subsidies and job-training programs both aim to _____ the natural rate of unemployment.

10. _____ in the labour productivity growth can reduce the natural rate of unemployment, while _____ in labour productivity growth lead to increases in the natural rate of unemployment.

11. In an economy, actual output fluctuates around potential output in the _____: a(n) _____ gap occurs when actual output is less than potential output, and a(n) _____ gap occurs when actual output is greater than potential output. The percentage difference between the actual level of real GDP and the potential output is called the _____. A negative output gap is associated with an unusually _____ unemployment rate, while a positive output gap is associated with an unusually _____ unemployment rate.

12. _____ provides an estimate of the negative relationship between the output gap and the unemployment rate. According to _____, each additional percentage point of output gap reduces the unemployment rate by less than 1 percentage point. According to Okun, the unemployment rate is equal to the natural rate of unemployment times _____ the output gap or in equation form: Unemployment Rate = Natural rate of unemployment − (0.5 × Output gap).

13. The relationship between the output gap and the unemployment rate is _____ than one-to-one for several reasons. First, firms meet changes in demand for their products by changing the number of hours their existing workers work rather than changing the number of workers they hire. Second, the number of workers looking for work is affected by the availability of jobs: as the number of jobs fall, some workers will become _____ and stop looking for work. This will cause the unemployment rate to rise _____ than what it would be if these workers were to continue their job search.

14. The labour market is in _____ when the actual rate of unemployment is not equal to the natural rate of unemployment. The labour market may remain out of equilibrium for long periods of time, because wages, unlike the prices of many goods and services, adjust _____ to surpluses or shortages of labour.

15. Wages adjust _____ to surpluses or shortages of labour because of misperceptions by workers as well as by firms about the equilibrium wage rate. Market-clearing wages are constantly changing as demand conditions change, and firms and workers may be _____ to recognize these conditions. Wages may also be _____ to adjust because they are sticky: wages may also be sticky because firms are slow to reduce wages when there is a _____ of labour. Wages may prove sticky because of the existence of long-term _____ or because of workers' focus on relative wages. Wages seem to be stickier when equilibrium wages are _____ than when they are _____, since workers are apt to put pressure on employers to pay _____ wages. Prices may also be _____ to adjust to changing market conditions due to menu costs, which are the small costs associated with the act of changing prices.

16. Economic data suggests that when the unemployment rate is _____, the wage rate tends to fall and when the unemployment rate is low, the wage rate tends to _____. There is a similar pattern in the relation between the unemployment rate and the rate of inflation: in the short-run, the rate of inflation is _____ related to the unemployment rate. The short-run Phillips curve represents this negative relationship between the unemployment rate and the _____.

17. In the short run, a(n) _____ in the aggregate price level due to shifts in *AD* results in increases in real GDP, which in turn leads to _____ unemployment rates. Thus, aggregate price increases occur as unemployment _____.

18. The most important factor affecting inflation rates other than the unemployment rate is the _____. The expected inflation rate is the rate of inflation that employers and workers expect in the near _____. The expected inflation rate affects the short-run Phillips curve. When the expected inflation rate _____, this causes the short-run Phillips curve to shift up by the amount of the expected inflation at every unemployment rate. In general, people base their expectations about inflation on past _____. If the inflation rate has been 5%, then people will expect the inflation rate to continue to be around 5%. The _____ Phillips curve worked in the 1960s but seemed to break down in the 1970s, as the economy experienced both high unemployment and high inflation. This stagflation is believed to be the result of supply _____ (for example, the energy crisis in the 1070s) and a buildup of expectations about inflation.

19. The long-run Phillips curve is a _____ line at an unemployment level high enough that the actual inflation rate equals the expected inflation rate. This unemployment rate is called the non-accelerating inflation rate of unemployment, or _____, since it is the level of unemployment that equates the actual rate of inflation with the expected inflation rate. An economy operating at levels of unemployment below the NAIRU will experience _____. That is, an unemployment rate below NAIRU cannot be maintained in the _____, because wages and prices will increase to lead the economy to the potential output.

Learning Tips

TIP #1: The distinction between frictional, structural, and cyclical unemployment is important.

All economies experience frictional unemployment: jobs are created and destroyed and new workers are constantly entering the labour market: these events make some unemployment inevitable. Structural unemployment occurs because there is a mismatch between the supply of labour and the demand for labour: this mismatch is the result of the current wage exceeding the wage rate that would equate the supply of labour to the demand for labour. Cyclical unemployment is the unemployment that occurs due to fluctuations in economic production due to the business cycle.

TIP #2: It is important to fully understand the concept of the natural rate of unemployment, or the NAIRU.

The NAIRU provides a measure of the unemployment rate that corresponds to the economy operating at its potential output level without any inflationary pressures. Economies that adopt policies in order to reduce their unemployment rate below this natural rate will experience inflation: persistent adoption of these policies will generate accelerating inflation.

TIP #3: It is important to understand the short-run Phillips curve (*SRPC*) and how the expected inflation rate affects it as well as why the long-run Phillips curve (*LRPC*) is a vertical line at the NAIRU.

The *SRPC* illustrates the negative relationship between the inflation rate and the unemployment rate. The *SRPC* is drawn with a given level of expected inflation. If expected inflation increases, this will shift the *SRPC* upward by the change in the expected inflation rate. In the long run the economy, no matter what the expected inflation rate, will settle at an unemployment rate equal to the NAIRU. Figure 15.1 depicts three *SRPC*: $SRPC_0$ is drawn with expected inflation equal to 0%; $SRPC_1$ is drawn with expected inflation equal to 1%; and $SRPC_2$ is drawn with expected inflation equal to 3%. On the graph we see that this economy operates at its natural rate of unemployment (point *A*) when the unemployment rate equals 4%, the inflation rate equals 0%, and the expected inflation rate equals 0%. If the expected inflation rate increases to 1%, then the natural rate of unemployment of 4% is only possible with an inflation rate of 1% (point *B* on the graph). If the expected inflation rate rises to 3%, this shifts the *SRPC* to $SRPC_2$ and the natural rate of unemployment of 4% is only possible with an inflation rate of 3% (point *C*). The economy in the long run will gravitate back to the vertical line representing the natural rate of unemployment and its independence in the long run from the inflation rate.

Figure 15.1

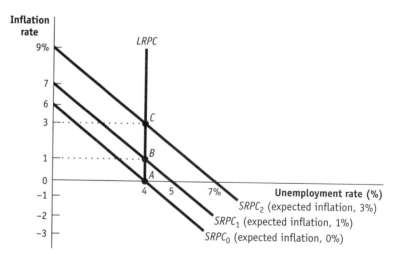

TIP #4: It is important to understand how Okun's Law works and the relationship between the natural rate of unemployment, the level of aggregate production in the economy, and the actual rate of unemployment expressed by Okun's Law.

A modern version of Okun's Law can be stated as

Unemployment rate = Natural rate of unemployment − (0.5 × Output gap)

This equation depicts the relationship between the output gap (the difference between actual output and potential output measured in percentage terms) and the unemployment rate. When the output gap equals zero, this implies actual output equals potential output and, therefore, the unemployment rate equals the natural rate of unemployment. When an economy has a negative output gap, this implies actual output is less than potential output and the economy faces a recessionary gap. Okun's Law indicates that this negative output gap will result in the unemployment rate exceeding the natural rate of unemployment. When an economy has a positive output gap, this implies actual output is greater than potential output and the economy faces an inflationary gap. Okun's Law indicates that this positive output gap will result in the unemployment rate falling below the natural rate of unemployment.

Multiple-Choice Questions

1. Which of the following statements is true?
   a. The natural rate of unemployment equals a country's unemployment rate during a recession.
   b. The natural rate of unemployment equals a country's unemployment rate during an expansion.
   c. The natural rate of unemployment is the sum of frictional and structural unemployment.
   d. The natural rate of unemployment is the sum of frictional and cyclical unemployment.

2. Job creation and job destruction is
   a. a natural occurrence in a labour market.
   b. only a problem during an economic recession.
   c. a primary reason for why there is unemployment even when the economy is at full employment.
   d. all of the above are true statements.
   e. Both (a) and (c).

3. Which of the following statements is true?
   a. The duration of unemployment for a majority of unemployed workers is fourteen weeks or less.
   b. There is always frictional unemployment since there are always new workers entering the job market.
   c. Even small amounts of frictional unemployment are harmful to an economy.
   d. All of the above statements are true.
   e. Both (a) and (b).
   f. Both (b) and (c).

4. Which of the following statements is true?
   a. Structural unemployment refers to the unemployment that occurs when there are more employers demanding labour than there are employees supplying labour.
   b. Structural unemployment refers to a situation when the market wage rate is lower than the equilibrium wage rate.
   c. Structural unemployment occurs when there is a surplus of labour at the current wage rate.
   d. When there is structural unemployment, frictional unemployment equals zero.

5. A minimum wage in order to be binding must
   a. be equal to or less than the equilibrium wage rate.
   b. be greater than the equilibrium wage rate.
   c. be set so that there is a persistent surplus in the labour market.
   d. be set so that there is a persistent shortage in the labour market.
   e. Both (a) and (d).
   f. Both (b) and (c).

6. Which of the following statements is true?
   a. Strong labour unions and an effective minimum wage reduce the level of structural unemployment in an economy.
   b. Strong labour unions and an effective minimum wage benefit all workers equally.
   c. Workers acting collectively through a union may find that they have more power than if they acted individually.
   d. All of the above statements are true.
   e. Both (b) and (c).

7. Efficiency wages
   a. are wages negotiated by unions.
   b. are always less than the minimum wage.
   c. are wages paid by employers that exceed the equilibrium wage rate and that are offered as an incentive for better performance.
   d. are a means for employers to retain employees while providing incentives for greater work effort.
   e. are (b), (c), and (d).
   f. are both (c) and (d).

8. The natural rate of unemployment is
   a. equal to 0% in every economy, since this is the level of unemployment that every economy should naturally want to achieve.
   b. is the sum of frictional and cyclical unemployment.
   c. equal to cyclical unemployment when the economy is producing at the full employment level of aggregate output.
   d. Both (b) and (c).
   e. None of the above.

9. The natural rate of unemployment
   a. is constant and does not change over time.
   b. changes when there are changes in labour force characteristics.
   c. may change due to changes in labour market institutions like unions, temporary employment agencies, and technological change.
   d. increases with increases in the minimum wage level.
   e. All of the above statements are true statements.
   f. Answers (b), (c) and (d) are true.

10. Hysteresis hypothesis refers to
   a. the trend of the cyclical unemployment over time.
   b. the trend of actual rate of unemployment over time.
   c. the situations where long-term unemployment for some workers (caused by deep recession) may lead to a higher natural rate of unemployment.
   d. the reduction of the natural rate of unemployment.

11. Which of the following statements is true?
  a. When actual output is equal to potential output, the natural rate of unemployment equals the actual rate of employment.
  b. During an inflationary gap, the unemployment rate is greater than the natural rate of unemployment.
  c. During a recessionary gap, the unemployment rate is greater than the natural rate of unemployment.
  d. Actual output fluctuates around potential output in the long run.

12. Cyclical unemployment and the output gap
  a. move together, but cyclical unemployment fluctuates more than the output gap.
  b. have a relationship with one another that can be quantified through Okun's Law.
  c. are negatively related to one another: when the cyclical unemployment rate increases by 1%, this leads to a decrease of ½% in the output gap.
  d. All of the above statements are true.

13. The relationship between changes in the output gap and changes in the unemployment rate is less than one-to-one because
  a. companies often meet changes in the demand for their product by changing the number of hours their current workers work.
  b. the availability of jobs affects the number of people who are looking for jobs.
  c. the rate of growth in labour productivity tends to accelerate during times of economic prosperity and decelerate during times of economic adversity.
  d. All of the above statements are true.

14. A jobless recovery
  a. occurs when the output gap becomes less positive.
  b. occurs when real GDP is growing faster than potential GDP.
  c. occurs when real GDP is growing slower than potential GDP.
  d. occurs when the output gap is widening.

15. The labour market may be in disequilibrium for long stretches of time since
  a. workers may have misperceptions about what the actual equilibrium wage is.
  b. employees' wages have been set by long-term contracts.
  c. the menu costs of changing wages may be sufficiently high to discourage frequent changes in the wage rate.
  d. All of the above statements are true.

16. The term sticky wages refers to the fact that
  a. Firms are slow to reduce wages even when there is a shortage of labour.
  b. Employees are slow to accept lower wages even when their current wage rate is lower than the equilibrium wage rate in the labour market.
  c. Wages are slow to adjust downward even if there is a surplus of labour.
  d. Wages are quick to adjust since workers only care about their relative wage, and so if someone earns a higher wage, other wage rates will quickly adjust to this new level.

17. Which of the following statements is true?
  a. The short-run Phillips curve is a vertical line with the horizontal intercept equaling the NAIRU.
  b. The short-run Phillips curve depicts the negative relationship between the unemployment rate and the inflation rate.
  c. An economy with a low rate of unemployment is an economy that has a shortage of labour and other resources, and this leads to falling prices.
  d. Both (a) and (c).
  e. Both (b) and (c).

18. Expected inflation

    a. does not impact the short-run or the long-run Phillips curve.

    b. is the rate of inflation that workers and employers expect in the near future.

    c. and the unemployment rate are the most significant factors affecting the rate of inflation in an economy.

    d. Both (b) and (c) are true.

    e. All of the above statements are true statements about expected inflation.

Use the following graph to answer the next three questions. In this graph $SRPC_1$ is the short-run Phillips curve for this economy when the expected inflation rate equals 0%.

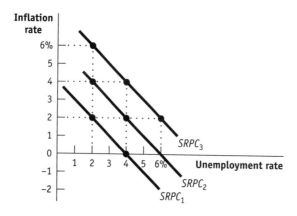

19. Using the previous graph, we know that the short-run Phillips curve ($SRPC$) equals $SRPC_2$ when the expected inflation rate equals

    a. 0%.

    b. 2%.

    c. 4%.

    d. 6%.

20. Suppose the inflation rate is 4% and this economy finds that its unemployment rate equals 3%. What is the NAIRU for this economy, given this information?

    a. 0%

    b. 2%

    c. 3%

    d. 4%

21. Suppose the policymakers for the economy depicted in the previous graph decide to pursue an unemployment rate of 2%. This will

    a. cause accelerating inflation in the long run.

    b. lead to rightward shifts of the $SRPC$, with each shift reflecting the expected inflation rate.

    c. cause equilibrium wage rates to fall.

    d. All of the above are true statements.

    e. Both (a) and (b) are true.

22. Efficiency wages are set _____ the equilibrium wage rate, and this causes _____ unemployment

    a. above; structural

    b. above; cyclical

    c. below; structural

    d. below; cyclical

23. (Assume that the minimum wage sets the wage for unskilled workers.) The minimum wage is set _____ the equilibrium wage, and it will _____ the total labour income of the unskilled workers.
   a. above; decrease
   b. above; increase
   c. below; decrease
   d. below; increase

24. Which of the following factors does not have a significant impact on the structural rate of unemployment?
   a. hysteresis
   b. falling aggregate demand
   c. labour unions
   d. minimum wages
   e. efficiency wages

25. In 2005, the unemployment rate in Canada was 7% and the largest contributing factors was
   a. seasonal unemployment.
   b. frictional unemployment.
   c. structural unemployment.
   d. cyclical unemployment.

26. Which of the following statements is false?
   a. Positive output gap occurs when the actual GDP is greater than the potential GDP.
   b. Negative output gap occurs when the actual GDP is less than the potential GDP.
   c. Positive output gap occurs when the actual GDP is less than the potential GDP.
   d. When the output gap is zero, the actual GDP is equal to the potential GDP.

27. Which of the following statements is false?
   a. With a positive output gap, the actual unemployment rate is less than the natural rate of unemployment.
   b. With a positive output gap, the actual unemployment rate is greater than the natural rate of unemployment.
   c. With a negative output gap, the actual unemployment rate is greater than the natural rate of unemployment.
   d. With a zero output gap, the actual unemployment rate is equal to the natural rate of unemployment.

28. Okun's Law shows
   a. the effect of an additional structural unemployment rate on the loss of GDP.
   b. the relationship between positive GDP gap and an extra unemployment rate above the natural rate.
   c. the relationship between negative GDP gap and an extra unemployment rate above the natural rate.
   d. the relationship between zero GDP gap and an extra unemployment rate above the natural rate.

Answer Questions 29–30 on the basis of the following five assumptions.
1. The natural rate of unemployment is 6%.
2. The expectational inflation is zero.
3. If 1% deflation occurs due to falling aggregate demand, it will lead to a 2% cyclical unemployment rate.
4. If 1% inflation occurs due to the policy-induced increase in aggregate demand, it will lead to an unemployment rate 2% below the natural rate.
5. With a 1% cyclical unemployment rate, the GDP gap is minus 2%.

29. Which of the following statements is false?
  a. With 5% deflation, the loss of GDP (below potential GDP) is 5%.
  b. With 5% deflation, the loss of GDP (below potential GDP) is 10%.
  c. With 5% deflation, the loss of GDP (below potential GDP) is 20%.
  d. With zero deflation, the loss of GDP (below potential GDP) is zero.

30. Which of the following statements is false?
  a. The slope of the short Phillips curve is minus 0.5.
  b. If deflation is 2%, then the actual unemployment rate is 8%.
  c. If deflation is 2%, then the actual unemployment rate is 10%.
  d. With 2% inflation, we will observe the actual unemployment rate to be at 2%.
  e. If the actual unemployment is 16%, then the cyclical unemployment is 10% and the deflation is 5%.

Problems and Exercises

1. Use the following graph to answer this question.

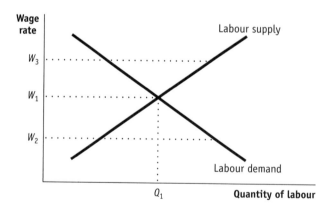

  a. What is the equilibrium wage and quantity of labour in this labour market?

  b. At the equilibrium wage rate, what is the structural unemployment rate? Explain your answer.

c. If the structural unemployment rate is a positive number, what do you know must be true about the current wage in this labour market? Explain your answer.

d. Suppose the government passes minimum wage legislation setting the minimum wage at W_2, where W_2 is less than W_1. Explain the effect of this legislation on this labour market.

e. Suppose the government passes minimum wage legislation setting the minimum wage at W_3, where W_3 is greater than W_1. Explain the effect of this legislation on this labour market.

2. Economists believe that the natural rate of unemployment is greater than zero. Assuming structural unemployment and cyclical unemployment are both zero, how do you explain this insistence that the natural rate of unemployment must still be a positive number? Explain your answer fully.

3. The text considers the effects of minimum wage legislation and union power on the workings of the labour market. Compare and contrast the effects of minimum wage legislation and union power on the labour market, noting how they are similar in their impact on the labour market as well as how they differ in their impact on the labour market.

4. Many European countries are plagued by a condition economists have called "Eurosclerosis" in which the natural rate of unemployment is higher than the natural rate of unemployment found in other industrialized countries. What policies and economic changes could help countries suffering from this condition effectively reduce their natural rate of unemployment?

5. Use the following graph to answer this question.

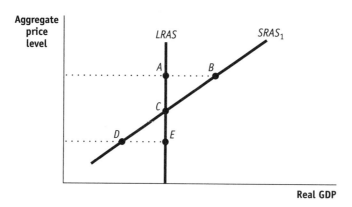

a. On the graph, which point best represents a recessionary gap for this economy in the short run? Explain your answer.

b. Given the graph, how would you explain this economy's recessionary gap? Using Okun's Law, what are the consequences of a recessionary gap on a country's unemployment rate?

c. What is the level of actual unemployment relative to the natural rate of unemployment when this economy operates in the short run with a recessionary gap? Explain your answer and be sure to indicate what type of unemployment would cause these two rates to be different from one another.

d. At what point(s) on the graph is the actual unemployment rate equal to the natural rate of unemployment? Explain your answer.

e. On the graph, which point best represents an inflationary gap for this economy in the short run? Explain your answer.

f. Given the graph, how would you explain this economy's inflationary gap? Using Okun's Law, what are the consequences of an inflationary gap on a country's unemployment rate?

g. What is the level of actual unemployment relative to the natural rate of unemployment when this economy operates in the short run with an inflationary gap? Explain your answer.

6. Suppose the natural rate of unemployment in Macroland equals 5% and that the economy of Macroland is currently producing at its potential output level of real GDP.

a. If the level of real GDP increases by 2% from its potential output level, then what happens to the unemployment rate in Macroland according to Okun's Law?

b. If the level of real GDP decreases by 3% from its potential output level, then what happens to the unemployment rate in Macroland according to Okun's Law?

c. Suppose that the level of real GDP initially in Macroland equals $100 million. If real GDP increases to $105 million, what will the new unemployment rate equal according to Okun's Law?

7. Suppose you are given the following information about the economy of Funland.

Unemployment rate	Inflation rate	Expected inflation rate
1%	6%	2%
2	5	2
3	4	2
4	3	2

a. Draw a graph with the unemployment rate on the horizontal axis and the inflation rate on the vertical axis. On this graph represent the above short-run Phillips curve (*SRPC*) based on expected inflation of 2%. Label this $SRPC_1$.

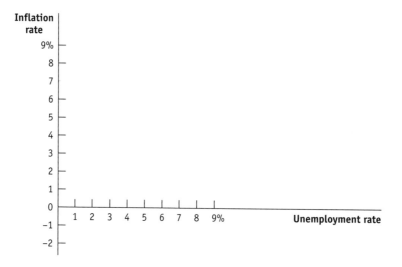

b. Given $SRPC_1$, at what rate of unemployment will inflation equal 0% for this economy? If expected inflation is 2%, then how will this economy adjust over time to this expected inflation rate? Illustrate this short-run adjustment on a graph and then explain your answer.

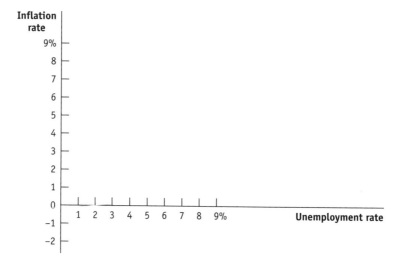

c. If policymakers could effectively change inflationary expectations to where people expected inflation to be 0%, then what would be this economy's NAIRU? Illustrate this on a graph labeling all new information clearly. Explain your answer.

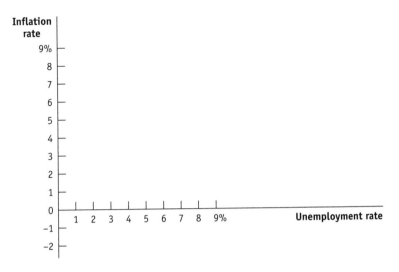

d. For the economy of Funland, what will the long-run Phillips curve (*LRPC*) look like and where will it be located? Explain your answer using a graph to illustrate your answer.

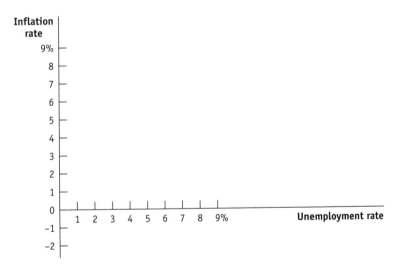

8. Consider the following short-run Phillips curve (*SRPC*) with zero expected inflation.

Assume that the natural rate of unemployment is 6%.

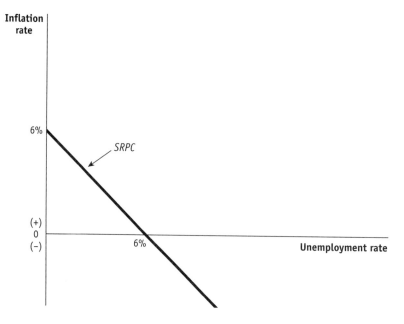

a. The slope of the short-run Phillips curve (*SRPC*) is _____.

b. With zero inflation, the actual unemployment is _____ and the cyclical unemployment is _____.

c. With 4% inflation rate, the unemployment rate will go down to _____.

d. With 4% deflation rate, the unemployment rate will increase to _____ and the cyclical unemployment will be _____.

e. With 2% expected inflation, the *SRPC* in the accompanying figure will shift up by _____.

f. In the long-run, the Phillips curve will be a _____ line.

9. Answer the following questions on the basis of the following five assumptions.
  1. The natural rate of unemployment is 6%.
  2. The expectational inflation is zero.
  3. If 1% deflation occurs due to falling aggregate demand, it will lead to a 2% cyclical unemployment rate.
  4. If 1% inflation occurs due to the policy-induced increase in aggregate demand, it will lead to an unemployment rate 2% below the natural rate.
  5. With a 1% cyclical unemployment rate, the GDP gap is minus 2%.

  a. With zero inflation, the actual unemployment rate is _____;

  cyclical unemployment is _____, and the GDP gap is

  _____.

  b. With 2% inflation rate, the actual unemployment rate is _____

  and the GDP gap is _____.

  c. With 4% deflation, the actual unemployment rate is _____ and

  the GDP gap is _____.

  d. With 10% deflation, the actual unemployment rate is _____ and

  the GDP gap is _____.

10. Fill in the blanks in the following table and indicate in the 3rd line the proper arrow:

U^N stands for the natural rate of unemployment.

Year	U^N	% of youth in labour force	% of women in labour force
1970	4.5%		
2005	7%		
Direction	↑		

Answers to How Well Do You Understand the Chapter

1. zero, substantial, structural unemployment, job search, surplus

2. more, greater, zero, greater

3. structural, greater

4. collective bargaining, labour strike, structural, structural, decrease, Wage staggering, slowly

5. fluctuations, higher, less, laid-off, increases

6. higher, efficiency wages, structural, higher

7. sum, cycles, sum

8. increases, frictional, lower, matching, increases

9. increase, higher, decrease

10. Increases, decreases

11. short-run, recessionary, inflationary, output gap, high, low

12. Okun's law, Okun's law, half

13. less, discouraged, less

14. disequilibrium, slowly

15. slowly, slow, slow, surplus, labour-contracts, falling, rising, higher, slow

16. high, rise, negatively, inflation rate

17. increase, lower, decreases

18. expected inflation rate, future, increases, inflation, short-run, shocks

19. vertical, NAIRU, accelerating inflation, long-run

Answers to Multiple-Choice Questions

1. The natural unemployment rate is defined as the sum of frictional and structural unemployment. It is the unemployment rate that occurs when there is no cyclical unemployment, which is that unemployment directly tied to economic business cycles. **Answer: C.**

2. Job creation and job destruction naturally occur in an economy, and it is this natural process that leads to economies always having some unemployment even if the economy is producing at full employment. We can think about how there are always people in our economy that are entering the labour force and looking for work, and there are always people whose jobs are ending and are in need of finding new work. This process occurs during both economic expansions and recessions. **Answer: E.**

3. Referring to figure 15-1 we can see that 77% of the unemployed are unemployed for fourteen weeks or less. Frictional unemployment occurs because of job creation and job destruction and because there are always new workers entering the job market. Frictional unemployment can be beneficial to an economy, since the economy may be more productive if workers take the time to find jobs that are well matched to their skills. **Answer: E.**

4. Structural unemployment occurs when there is an excess supply of labour in a labour market. This occurs when the wage rate is greater than the equilibrium wage rate in the market. Every economy has frictional unemployment due to job creation and job destruction as well as the entry of new workers into the job market. **Answer: C.**

5. A minimum wage to be effective, and therefore binding, must be set at a level in excess of the equilibrium wage rate. This will result in the supply of labour exceeding the demand for labour and thus a surplus of labour. **Answer: F.**

6. Strong labour unions and an effective minimum wage act to increase the level of structural unemployment in an economy, since they both tend to create a surplus of labour in the labour market. It is true though that workers acting collectively may possess greater negotiating power in an industry than would those workers acting individually. Strong unions and an effective minimum wage benefit those people who continue to work, but hurt those who become unemployed when the wage rate rises above the equilibrium wage rate in the labour market. **Answer: C.**

7. Efficiency wages are wages paid by employers in excess of the equilibrium wage rate. They are offered to improve employee work effort while also providing an incentive for workers to stay with their current employer. Efficiency wages may be equal to or greater than the minimum wage. **Answer: F.**

8. The natural rate of unemployment is equal to the sum of frictional and structural unemployment. It will always be greater than zero, since there will always be new workers entering the job market and workers moving from one job to another. The cyclical unemployment rate is equal to zero when the economy produces at the full employment level of aggregate output, but at this level of output there is still frictional unemployment. **Answer: E.**

9. The natural rate of unemployment is affected by changes in labour force characteristics and by changes in labour market institutions. In addition, the natural rate of unemployment will increase whenever the government mandates more generous benefits for workers (for example, an increase in the minimum wage rate). **Answer: F.**

10. Hysteresis refers to the trend of the natural rate of unemployment. The increase in the natural of unemployment can be caused by many factors. In some cases, cyclical unemployment due to deep recession may lead to a rate higher than the natural rate of unemployment. **Answer: C.**

11. When actual output equals potential output, the unemployment rate equals the natural rate of unemployment and not the natural rate of employment. During an inflationary gap the unemployment rate is less than the natural rate of unemployment, since when the economy is producing an output level greater than its potential output level, it is temporarily using resources at more than the normal rate. Thus, during a recessionary gap the unemployment rate will be greater than the natural rate of unemployment, since there is a negative output gap and this is associated with unusually high unemployment. Actual output fluctuates around potential output in the short run: in the long run, actual output equals potential output due to full price adjustment. **Answer: C.**

12. Cyclical unemployment and the output gap are inversely related to each other, and this relationship can be quantified by Okun's Law, which estimates that for a 1% increase in the output gap there will be a reduction in the unemployment rate of ½ of a percentage point. Thus, a 1% increase in the unemployment rate would be associated with a 2% decrease in the output gap. **Answer: B.**

13. The relationship between changes in the output gap and changes in the unemployment rate is estimated by Okun's Law, which finds that a rise in the output gap of 1 percentage point reduces the unemployment rate by about ½ of a percentage point. The reasons for this being less than a one-to-one relationship relate to how firms react to changes in the demand for their product, how workers respond to changes in economic conditions, and how the growth rate of labour productivity is affected by economic conditions. The text reviews each of these factors and their effect on the relationship between changes in the output gap and changes in the unemployment rate. **Answer: D.**

14. A jobless recovery refers to a situation where the economy is expanding but the unemployment rate continues to rise. This occurs when the output gap becomes more positive, which corresponds to a situation where real GDP is growing at a slower rate than the rate of growth of potential GDP. **Answer: C.**

15. All of the above statements are true and come from the text. **Answer: D.**

16. Sticky wages occur when employers are slow to reduce wages in the face of a surplus of labour. **Answer: C.**

17. The short-run Phillips curve is downward sloping and depicts the relationship between the unemployment rate and the inflation rate. It is not vertical: the long-run Phillips curve is vertical and intersects the horizontal axis at the NAIRU. An economy that has a low unemployment rate will typically see rising prices due to shortages of labour and other resources. **Answer: B.**

18. Expected inflation and the unemployment rate are the most significant factors affecting the inflation rate in an economy. Expected inflation is that rate of inflation that workers and employers expect in the near future. Changes in expected inflation cause the short-run Phillips curve to shift: increases in the expected inflation rate cause the short-run Phillips curve to shift up, while decreases in the expected inflation rate cause the short-run Phillips curve to shift down. **Answer: D.**

19. $SRPC_2$ reflects a short-run Phillips curve drawn with expected inflation of 2%. We know this since this curve has shifted up by 2% at every unemployment rate from the short-run Phillips curve that is drawn with an expected inflation rate of 0% ($SRPC_1$). **Answer: B.**

20. The NAIRU is the nonaccelerating-inflation rate of unemployment for the economy, or that level of unemployment where the inflation rate matches inflationary expectations. An unemployment rate below 4% requires ever-accelerating inflation. **Answer: D.**

21. The unemployment rate of 2% is below the unemployment rate that this economy can maintain while still avoiding inflation. If this economy tries to pursue an inflation rate of 2%, it will initially be accompanied by 2% inflation: this inflation rate will then be built into inflationary expectations and the $SRPC$ will shift to the right. But, again if policymakers persist in trying to achieve 2% unemployment, this will cause even higher inflationary expectations to be built into the $SRPC$, shifting the curve further to the right. Thus, trying to achieve an unemployment level of 2% for this economy will lead to accelerating inflation in the long run along with shifts in the $SRPC$ in the short run. We can also expect wages to rise with expectations of higher inflation and with higher actual inflation rates. **Answer: E.**

22. Efficiency wages are set above the equilibrium wage, and this leads to structural unemployment. **Answer: A.**

23. The minimum wage is set above the equilibrium wage. It will increase the total labour income. **Answer: B.**

24. Falling aggregate demand brings cyclical unemployment. Structural unemployment is caused by hysteresis, trade union's wage settlements, the minimum wage, and the efficiency wage. **Answer: B.**

25. In 2005, there was a 7% unemployment rate, and structural unemployment was close to 5.6%. **Answer: C.**

26. Positive output gap occurs when the actual GDP is greater than the potential GDP, and negative output gap occurs when the actual GDP is less than the potential GDP. When the output gap is zero, the actual GDP is equal to the potential GDP. **Answer: C.**

27. With a positive output-gap, the actual unemployment rate is less than the natural rate of unemployment. With a negative output-gap, the actual unemployment rate is greater than the natural rate of unemployment. With zero output-gap, the actual unemployment rate is equal to the natural rate of unemployment. **Answer: B.**

28. According to Okun's law, output loss is caused by the unemployment rate; in other words, it shows the relationship between negative GDP gap and extra unemployment rate above the natural rate. As the negative GDP-gap becomes larger, cyclical unemployment becomes larger. **Answer: C.**

29. With 5% deflation, we see 10% cyclical unemployment, which in turns leads to a 20% loss of GDP. **Answer: C.**

30. Given the assumptions, a 2% deflation brings 4% cyclical unemployment. Since the natural rate of unemployment is 6%, the actual unemployment is 10%. **Answer: B.**

Answers to Problems and Exercises

1. **a.** The equilibrium wages rate is W_1 and the equilibrium quantity of labour is Q_1, where the supply of labour equals the demand for labour.
   b. At the equilibrium wage rate, the structural unemployment rate equals zero since the number of people seeking jobs in the labour market equals the number of jobs available at that equilibrium, or current, wage rate.
   c. If the structural unemployment rate is a positive number, then the wage rate must be greater than the equilibrium wage rate and the supply of labour must exceed the demand for labour, resulting in a surplus of labour.
   d. For a minimum wage to have any impact on the market, it must be set above the equilibrium wage rate. The minimum wage is just a specific example of a price floor, and price floors only impact markets when they are set above the equilibrium price.
   e. When the government sets the minimum wage above the equilibrium wage rate, it affects the market by preventing the wage rate from adjusting to that point where the demand for labour equals the supply of labour. Thus, an effective minimum wage will create a surplus of labour and, hence, a positive structural unemployment rate.

2. Even when the economy produces at its potential output and the unemployment rate equals the natural rate, there will be people entering the job market as well as workers moving between jobs. This frictional unemployment is a natural part of the working of the labour market: hence, even when the economy is at its natural rate of unemployment, there will still be positive frictional unemployment.

3. Labour unions and effective minimum wage legislation both affect the labour market by working to raise the current wage above the equilibrium wage rate and creating barriers to prevent the wage from adjusting back to the equilibrium level. Both labour unions and minimum wage legislation have the potential to create structural unemployment through their ability to create a situation where the supply of labour is greater than the demand for labour. Labour unions, through collective bargaining, often result in workers securing higher wages than the market would have provided if workers bargained individually. Labour unions often negotiate for long-term contracts, and these contracts may lead to structural unemployment due to the wage rigidity they introduce into the labour market.

4. Eurosclerosis refers to the high natural rate of unemployment experienced in many European countries. These high natural rates are thought to be the result of policies enacted to help workers. The reduction of unemployment benefits and legislative action to limit the power of unions would help to reduce the natural rate of unemployment. In addition, changes in labour force characteristics, changes in labour market institutions, and changes in productivity could help reduce the natural rate of unemployment.

5. a. This Point D best represents a recessionary gap in this economy since, at point D, actual real GDP is less than the potential level of real GDP.

   b. The economy would produce at point D if there was a negative demand shock that caused the AD curve to shift to the left so that it intersected the $SRAS$ at point D. This is illustrated in the following graph.

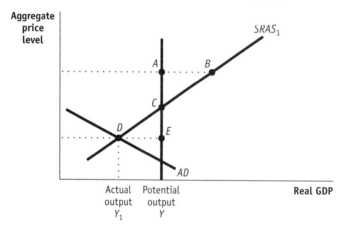

When a country produces a level of real GDP corresponding to a recessionary gap (Y_1 versus Y in the graph), this creates a negative output gap. According to Okun's Law, a negative output gap will increase the unemployment rate above the natural rate of unemployment.

   c. The level of actual unemployment exceeds the natural rate of unemployment due to the existence of both structural and cyclical unemployment.

   d. At points A, C, and E, the natural rate of unemployment and the actual rate of unemployment rate are equal. We know this because the economy is producing at its potential output level, which is the level of output where the unemployment rate equals the natural rate.

   e. Point B best represents an inflationary gap, since actual output at point B is greater than the potential output level of real GDP.

f. The economy would produce at point B in the short run, given the *SRAS* curve if there was a positive *AD* shock that shifted the *AD* curve to the right where it intersects the *SRAS* curve at point B. This is illustrated in the following figure.

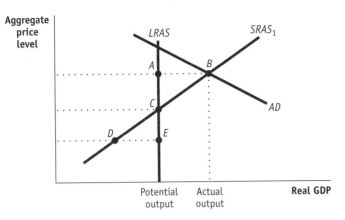

If the economy produces with an inflationary gap, this creates an positive output gap. According to Okun's Law, a positive output gap will decrease the actual unemployment rate below the natural rate of unemployment.

g. The rate of actual unemployment is less than the natural rate of unemployment, since the economy will need to employ more workers in order to increase production beyond the potential output level of real GDP.

6. a. If the level of real GDP increases by 2%, then the unemployment rate will fall by 1% to an unemployment rate of 4%. We can see this using formula 15-1: Unemployment rate = Natural rate of unemployment − (0.5 × Output gap) = 5% − (0.5 × 2%) = 4%.

b. If the level of real GDP decreases by 3%, then the unemployment rate will rise by 1.5%, for an unemployment rate of 6.5%. To see this, use the formula given in part (a) and substitute in the relevant values.

c. If the level of real GDP is initially $100 million, then an increase of real GDP to $105 million represents a 5% increase in output from its potential output level. Using the formula given in part (a), we can then calculate the new unemployment rate as 2.5% : as the level of real GDP increases, the economy will see its unemployment rate fall.

7. a.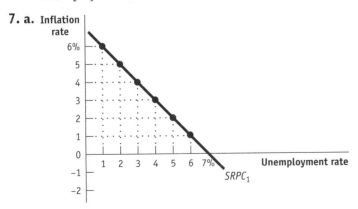

b. Given $SRPC_1$, inflation equals 0% when the unemployment rate equals 7%. Over time people will come to expect inflation of 2%, and this will cause the $SRPC$ to shift up by this amount and people's expectations of inflation to rise to 4%. The new $SRPC$ will be $SRPC_2$, as illustrated in the following graph.

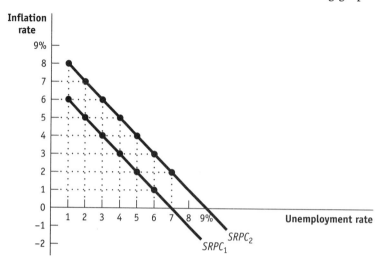

Of course, over time this will cause $SRPC_2$ to shift up reflecting higher inflationary expectations.

c. This country's NAIRU would be 5%. Effectively, we are looking for the $SRPC$ that has inflationary expectations of 0%, which we can illustrate as a downward shift of $SRPC_1$ where at any given unemployment rate, the inflation rate is reduced by 2%. We can illustrate this in the following figure as $SRPC_0$.

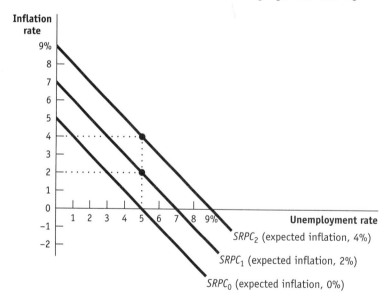

d. For Funland the *LRPC* will be a vertical line at a 5% unemployment rate. This is illustrated in the following figure.

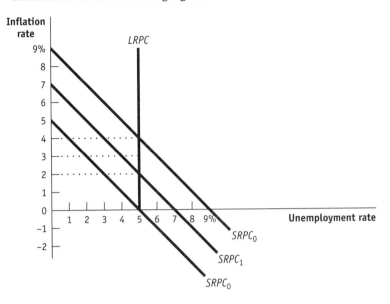

8. Consider the following short-run Phillips curve (*SRPC*) with zero expected inflation.

Assume that the natural rate of unemployment is 6%.

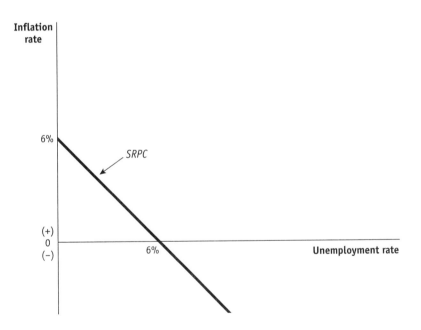

a. The slope of the short-run Phillips curve (SRPC) is minus one.
b. With zero inflation, the actual unemployment is 6% and the cyclical unemployment is zero.
c. With a 4% inflation rate, the unemployment rate will go down to 2%.
d. With a 4% deflation rate, the unemployment rate will increase to 10% and the cyclical unemployment will be 4%.
e. With 2% expected inflation, the *SRPC* in the accompanying figure will shift up by 2%.
f. In the long run, the Phillips curve will be a vertical line.

9. Answer the following questions on the basis of the following five assumptions
1. The natural rate of unemployment is 6%.
2. The expectational inflation is zero.
3. If 1% deflation occurs due to falling aggregate demand, it will lead to a 2% cyclical unemployment rate.
4. If 1% inflation occurs due to the policy-induced increase in aggregate demand, it will lead to an unemployment rate 2% below the natural rate.
5. With a 1% cyclical unemployment rate, the GDP gap is minus 2%.
a. With zero inflation, the actual unemployment rate is 6%; cyclical unemployment is zero, and the GDP gap is zero.
b. With 2% inflation rate, the actual unemployment rate is 2% and the GDP gap is + 8%.
c. With 4% deflation, the actual unemployment rate is 14% and the GDP gap is 16%.
d. With 10% deflation, the actual unemployment rate is 26% and the GDP gap is 40%.

10. Fill in the blanks in the following table and indicate on the 3rd line the correct arrow:

U^N stands for the natural rate of unemployment.

Year	U^N	% of youth in labour force	% of women in labour force
1970	4.5%	22%	31%
2005	7%	16%	46%
Direction	↑	↓	↓

chapter 16

Inflation, Disinflation, and Deflation

This chapter analyzes the underlying causes of inflation as well as the costs of inflation. The chapter explores the relationship between the rate of growth of the money supply and the inflation rate: economies that collect an inflation tax by printing money find that this practice can lead to high rates of inflation. The chapter also discusses the relationship between high inflation and hyperinflation. In the chapter, the costs of inflation as well as the costs of disinflation are discussed along with the debate about the optimal rate of inflation. In addition, the chapter discusses why even moderate rates of inflation may be difficult to eliminate and why deflation presents a problem for economic policy.

How Well Do You Understand the Chapter?

Fill in the blanks using the terms below or circle the correct answer to complete the following statements. Terms may be used more than once. If you find yourself having difficulties, please refer to the appropriate section in the text.

above	*hurt*	*poor*
accelerate	*increase(s)*	*price-stability*
anticipated	*inflation*	*printing*
benefit(s)	*inflation tax*	*real*
benefits	*large*	*real GDP*
debt-deflation	*left*	*real interest rate*
decrease(s)	*liquidity trap*	*recession*
deflation	*low*	*reduce*
difficult	*lower*	*reduction*
disinflation	*LRAS*	*right*
equals	*measurement*	*rise*
fall	*monetary*	*seigniorage*
Fiat money	*nominal*	*shoe-leather costs*
high	*nominal interest rate*	*unchanged*
higher	*plus*	*zero bound*

1. The classical model of the price level shows that any increase in the money supply does not change the level of real GDP, but it does result in a(n) _____ in the overall price level. An increase in the nominal money supply (*M*) leads to an increase in the aggregate price level (*P*) in the long run and leaves the real money supply (*M/P*) _____.

2. The classical model of the price level assumes that the economy moves from one long-run equilibrium to another equilibrium because wages and prices are flexible: in this model, the economy always produces at a point on its _____ curve.

3. Consider an initial long-run equilibrium situation with the *AD* curve and the *SRAS* curve intersecting at a point where the *LRAS* curve lies. An increase in money supply will shift the *AD* curve to the _____. At the new short-run equilibrium, the new price is _____ than the original price. In the long run, the nominal wages will _____ and the *SRAS* curve will shift to the _____, and the process will continue until the *SRAS* curve intersects the *AD* curve at the point where the *LRAS* lies. The price flexibility assumption seems to work well in periods of _____ inflation since in periods of high inflation wage and price stickiness seem to disappear. The price flexibility assumption is a(n) _____ assumption during periods of low inflation.

4. _____ is money that has no intrinsic value, and in modern economies this reliance on the use of flat money means that governments can choose to simply _____ money and use this to pay some of their bills.

5. Sources of revenue for the government include the right to print money, or _____. When governments run _____ deficits and are unwilling to _____ taxes or decrease spending, they often turn to printing money to finance their deficit and this leads to large _____ in the aggregate price level. This action imposes a(n) _____ on those people who currently hold money. We can calculate inflation tax as inflation rate times (nominal money supply). In real terms, real inflation tax = inflation rate × real money supply. This real inflation tax represents the _____ value of goods and services that are lost due to inflation tax.

6. In the face of high inflation, people will try to avoid holding money and hold other goods instead of money. In other words, the public will _____ the level of real money it holds. This _____ in real money holding forces the government to generate a higher rate of inflation in order to collect the same amount of real inflation tax: this action causes the inflation rate to _____, and at some point inflation rate explodes into hyperinflation.

7. Before we consider the effects of inflation, we should distinguish anticipated (expected) inflation from unanticipated (unexpected) inflation. Moderate anticipated _____ does not affect the level of real GDP and real income, but it does hurt some people while helping other people. Unanticipated _____ can impose real costs on the economy and, if it is sufficiently high, it can reduce _____ and, therefore, real income.

8. Inflation can hurt some people while benefiting others primarily because contracts that extend over a period of time are typically specified in _____ terms. Thus, if the inflation rate is _____ than expected, then the borrower will find they are paying back dollars with less purchasing power than they expected: The borrower will _____ from the unexpectedly high inflation, while the lender is _____. If the inflation rate is _____ than expected, then the borrower will be paying back dollars with greater purchasing power than the borrower anticipated: the lender will _____ from the unexpectedly high inflation, while the borrower is _____. If the actual inflation rate _____ the antici- pated rate, then the inflation does not benefit either the borrower or the lender.

9. The _____ interest rate is the interest rate expressed in money terms, while the _____ interest rate is the interest rate adjusted for the inflation rate. We can write an equation expressing the relationship between the nominal interest rate and the real interest rate: the nominal interest rate equals the real interest rate _____ the rate of inflation.

10. Real interest rate = Nominal interest rate – Inflation rate. People should decide whether they should borrow funds based on their expectation about the _____ and not the nominal rate of interest. Like borrowers, lenders should also be concerned with the real interest rate rather than the _____.

11. The expected inflation rate impacts the nominal rate of interest: if the expected inflation rate increases, the nominal interest rate will _____ by the same amount. The Fisher effect states that the expected real interest rate is unaffect- ed by the change in expected inflation. That is, both lenders and borrowers base their decisions on the _____ rate of interest. As long as the inflation is _____, it will not affect the equilibrium quantity of loanable funds or the real interest rate, but it will affect the equilibrium nominal interest rate.

12. Anticipated _____ can impose real costs on the economy in the form of shoe-leather costs, and unit-of-account costs. An economy with _____ levels of anticipated inflation expends some of its resources on coping with the inflation and this diverts these resources from more productive uses: this causes _____ in the economy and, therefore, real income, to fall. The increased costs of transactions due to inflation are referred to as _____; these are the increased costs people incur as they expend energy to avoid the inflation tax. Menu costs, or the cost of changing listed prices, _____ during periods of inflation. The unit-of-account costs of inflation are costs that arise from the way inflation makes money a less reliable unit of _____.

13. Most central banks aim for _____. The Bank of Canada has an inflation target of 1% to 3%. Economies will experience moderate inflation if they pursue economic policies that target an unemployment rate that is _____ than the natural rate of unemployment. Governments may purposefully pursue such targets prior to an election in order to achieve _____ rates of unemployment at the time of the election.

14. _____ refers to the process of bringing down inflation when the inflation has become embedded in expectations. An economy trying to _____ inflation that is built into expectations will fund this a(n) _____ task; policymakers will need to keep the unemployment rate _____ the natural rate for an extended period of time on order to bring down this kind of inflation.

15. Moderate inflation may also be the result of supply shocks to the economy. If the short-run *AS* curve shifts to the _____, this brings a _____ level of aggregate prices while reducing the level of real GDP. Policymakers find it difficult to pursue anti-inflationary policy when there is a negative supply shock, since this will produce even _____ _____ levels of unemployment. The great disinflation of the 1980s in Canada illustrates this problem: disinflation was achieved by pushing the economy into the worst _____ since the Great Depression.

16. _____ refers to a falling aggregate price level. Unexpected deflation _____ lenders who are owed money, because the real value of the payments they receive from borrowers _____ during deflation; unexpected deflation hurts borrowers who owe money, because the real value of the payments they make to lenders _____ during deflation. During a period of deflation, borrowers must cut their spending when the burden of their debt increases due to the deflation: this leads to a sharp _____ in aggregate demand which worsens the economic slump. The effect of deflation in reducing aggregate demand is known as _____ theory.

17. During a period of deflation, people will expect inflation to _____; these expectations will lead to a reduction in the aggregate price level. There is a limit however to how far the _____ interest rate can fall: this is called the _____, a situation in which the nominal interest rate cannot fall below zero. This zero bound means that the central bank can find itself in a situation where it cannot effectively use _____ policy to stimulate the economy: if the nominal interest rate is already zero, the central bank cannot cut the nominal interest rate any further. This situation is called the _____, where monetary policy is useless as a means of stimulating aggregate demand because the nominal interest rate simply cannot _____ any further. Most central banks seek a positive inflation rate of 2% to 2.5% rather than 0% inflation, because they do not want to experience _____ where monetary policy no longer can be used to stimulate a slumping economy.

Learning Tips

TIP #1: The chapter introduces new vocabulary that you will want to learn and understand. In particular, you will want to be able to define and distinguish between anticipated and unanticipated inflation; real and nominal interest rates; and deflation and disinflation. You will also want to understand the concept of debt deflation.

Unanticipated inflation is inflation that is not expected: this type of inflation does not affect the level of real GDP, but it hurts some people while helping others. Anticipated inflation is inflation that is expected: this type of inflation can lead to reductions in real GDP and, therefore, reductions in real income. The nominal interest rate is the interest rate expressed in money terms, while the real interest rate is the interest rate adjusted for inflation. The real interest rate is equal to the nominal interest rate minus the inflation rate. Deflation refers to a fall in the aggregate price level, and disinflation refers to a decrease in the inflation rate reflecting policymakers' decisions that the economy has built-in inflationary expectations that need to be reduced. The chapter also discusses debt deflation: deflation makes existent loan contracts more costly for borrowers: and, as the real burden of their debt increases, borrowers will decrease their spending. This reduction in aggregate spending is referred to as debt deflation.

TIP #2: It is important to understand the distinction between inflation and hyperinflation and their causes.

Inflation refers to an increase in the general price level in the economy and may be due to positive demand shocks or negative supply shocks. Figure 16.1 illustrates a positive demand shock while Figure 16.2 illustrates a negative supply shock: both types of shocks lead to higher aggregate price levels.

Figure 16.1

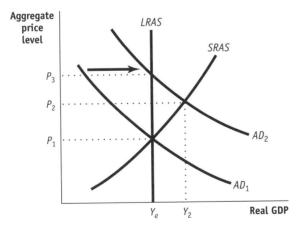

Figure 16.2

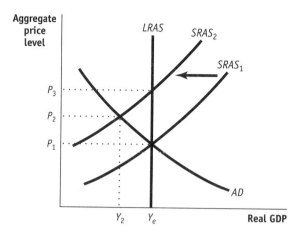

Hyperinflation refers to inflation in excess of 50% per-month: hyperinflation in an economy is caused by the government printing money to finance its government deficits.

TIP #3: Nominal Interest Rate = Real Interest + Inflation Rate.

If the expected inflation rate increases, nominal interest rate will increase by the same amount, because both lenders and borrowers base their decisions on real interest rates, not nominal interest rates. As long as inflation is anticipated, it will not affect the equilibrium quantity of loanable funds or the real interest rate.

TIP #4: You will want to review the concept of the liquidity trap and the zero bound for nominal interest rates.

The zero bound refers to the lower limit for the nominal interest rate: nominal interest rates cannot fall below zero percent. When an economy finds that its nominal interest rate has fallen to zero, it will no longer be able to use monetary policy to stimulate the economy: the monetary policy will be unable to stimulate aggregate spending through decreases in the nominal interest rate. This situation is referred to as a liquidity trap: increasing the money supply, an increase in liquidity, does nothing for the economy since the economy is "trapped" by the inability of the nominal interest rate to fall further.

Multiple-Choice Questions

1. Which of the following statements is true?
   a. High inflation and hyperinflation are equivalent terms: both refer to an inflation rate in excess of 50% per-month.
   b. During periods of high inflation, people are eager to hold large sums of money since these sums of money grow in value, the higher the inflation rate.
   c. In the long run, an increase in the money supply does not change real GDP.
   d. All of the above are true statements.
   e. Both (a) and (b).
   f. Both (a) and (c).

2. The classical model of the price level
   a. reflects the work of John Maynard Keynes.
   b. ignores the short-run movements of the economy in response to a change in the money supply.
   c. works well particularly for periods in which inflation is low.
   d. All of the above statements are true.
   e. Both (a) and (b) are true.
   f. Both (a) and (c) are true.
   g. Both (b) and (c) are true.

3. In periods of high inflation,
   a. the short-run *AS* curve adjusts quickly by shifting to the right.
   b. the short-run *AS* curve adjusts slowly, if at all, and will eventually shift to the left.
   c. the short-run *AS* curve is insensitive to the high inflation and is therefore unaffected by the high inflation.
   d. the short-run *AS* curve adjusts swiftly and shifts to the left due to rising nominal wages.
   e. None of the above statements is true.

4. The Bank of Canada monetizes the government's debt when it
   a. sells Treasury bills on the open market.
   b. purchases Treasury bills on the open market.
   c. mandates the use of fiat money as a medium of exchange.
   d. Both (a) and (c) are correct.
   e. Both (b) and (c) are correct.

5. Seigniorage is the term
   a. used to describe open-market operations.
   b. that dates back to the Middle Ages and refers to the government's right to issue coins and to charge, and therefore, collect a fee for issuing these coins.
   c. that economists use to refer to the government's right to print money.
   d. All of the above statements are true statements.
   e. Both (a) and (b) are true.
   f. Both (a) and (c) are true.
   g. Both (b) and (c) are true.

6. An inflation tax
   a. is a tax that is levied on the Bank of Canada when it increases the money supply.
   b. is a tax on those who hold money that occurs when the inflation erodes the purchasing power of their money.
   c. occurs when the government prints money to cover its budget deficit.
   d. All of the above are true statements.
   e. Both (a) and (b) are true.
   f. Both (a) and (c) are true.
   g. Both (b) and (c) are true.

7. For a given inflation rate, an increase in the real money supply
   a. does not affect the real inflation tax.
   b. increases the real inflation tax.
   c. decreases the real inflation tax.
   d. may increase, decrease, or have no effect on the real inflation tax.

8. When there is unexpected inflation in an economy, then
   a. real GDP will decrease in the economy in the long run.
   b. real income will decrease in the economy in the long run.
   c. borrowers benefit while lenders lose.
   d. lenders benefit while borrowers lose.
   e. Answers (a), (b), and (c) are true.
   f. Answers (a), (b), and (d) are true.

9. Which of the following statements is true?
   a. Most contracts that extend over a period of time are expressed in real terms so that borrowers and lenders can fully understand the consequences of their economic agreement.
   b. The nominal interest rate is equal to the real interest rate minus the inflation-rate.
   c. When the actual inflation equals the anticipated inflation rate, borrowers are better off.
   d. Anticipated inflation can inflict real costs on the economy.

10. Mary expects the inflation rate to be 5%, and she is willing to pay a real interest rate of 3%. Joe expects the inflation rate to be 5%, and he is willing to loan money if he receives a real interest rate of 3%. If the actual inflation rate is 6% and the loan contract specifies a nominal interest rate of 8%, then
   a. Joe is glad he lent out funds even though his real interest rate has fallen.
   b. Joe is sorry he lent out funds since his real interest rate is now 9%.
   c. Mary is glad she borrowed the funds because her real interest rate has fallen.
   d. Mary is sorry she borrowed funds since her real interest rate is now 9%.

11. According to the Fisher effect, changes in the expected inflation rate will
   a. have little or no effect on the nominal interest rate.
   b. cause both the demand and supply of loanable funds curves to shift in the same direction.
   c. cause both the demand and supply of loanable funds curves to shift, but in opposite directions.
   d. have no effect on the equilibrium quantity of loanable funds.
   e. Answers (a), (b), and (c) are true.
   f. Answers (a), (b), and (d) are true.
   g. Both (c) and (d) are true.
   h. Both (b) and (d) are true.

12. Which of the following statements is true?
   a. The Fisher effect states that the expected real interest rate is unaffected by the change in expected inflation.
   b. Borrowers and lenders should base their decisions on the real rate of interest and not the nominal rate of interest.
   c. Anticipated inflation can impose real costs on the economy.
   d. All of the above statements are true.
   e. Both (a) and (b).
   f. Both (a) and (c).
   g. Both (b) and (c).

13. Disinflation in an economy, which has grown to expect inflation, is
   a. easy to achieve and does not affect actual output.
   b. difficult to accomplish and invariably results in an increase in the natural rate of unemployment.
   c. possible only if policymakers are willing to accept higher rates of unemployment and a negative output gap.
   d. Both (a) and (c).
   e. Both (b) and (c).

14. Which of the following statements is true?
   a. Moderate inflation may be the result of politicians pursuing too low an unemployment rate for the economy prior to an election.
   b. Moderate inflation may be the result of an aggregate supply shock to the economy.
   c. Moderate inflation is easily brought under control through a process called disinflation.
   d. All of the above are true statements.
   e. Both (a) and (b).
   f. Both (a) and (c).
   g. Both (b) and (c).

15. In a period of unexpected deflation,
   a. borrowers find that it is easier for them to make their loan payments, since prices are falling.
   b. lenders benefit, since there are more people eager to borrow money during a period of deflation.
   c. lenders benefit, since they are repaid dollars with greater real value than they anticipated when signing the loan contract.
   d. All of the above are true statements.

16. Debt deflation
   a. occurs when there is deflation, and the value of the borrower's debt is reduced due to the falling aggregate price level.
   b. occurs when borrowers reduce their aggregate spending, because the deflation increases the debt burden that borrowers experience.
   c. reduces the impact of the deflation on the level of aggregate demand, thus restoring the economy to its potential level of output in a timely manner.
   d. affects only lenders and not borrowers.

17. An economy will experience a liquidity trap when
   a. the Bank of Canada refuses to expand the money supply, even though there is an increased demand for money in the economy.
   b. the Bank of Canada refuses to expand the money supply in order to raise nominal interest rates to an acceptable level.
   c. the Bank of Canada finds that it cannot reduce nominal interest rates, even if it engages in open-market purchases of Treasury bills.
   d. the Bank of Canada adopts a target inflation rate of 0%, and successfully achieves this target.

18. When the central bank finds that it cannot use monetary policy to reduce the nominal interest rate, it must be the case that
   a. the economy is operating in a liquidity trap.
   b. the central bank has reached the zero bound.
   c. the money market is in disequilibrium.
   d. All of the above statements are true statements.
   e. Both (a) and (b) are true.
   f. Both (a) and (c) are true.
   g. Both (b) and (c) are true.

19. Which of the following statements is true?
  a. The classical model assumes that prices are flexible, but wages are not flexible.
  b. Monetary expansion will shift the *AD* curve to the right to maintain greater than full-employment output in the long run.
  c. If money supply doubles, price doubles; therefore, the quantity theory of money is a valid hypothesis of the classical model.
  d. According to the classical model, an increase in money supply (*M*) will increase real money balance (*M/P*).

20. Which of the following statements is false?
  a. Fiat money has some intrinsic value.
  b. When large fiscal deficits are financed by printing money, it causes large increases in the aggregate price level.
  c. Inflation tax = Inflation rate × nominal money supply.
  d. Real inflation tax = Inflation rate × Real money supply.

21. Which of the following statements is true?
  a. The cost of anticipated inflation is zero.
  b. The cost of unanticipated inflation is zero.
  c. Real interest rate = Nominal interest rate + Inflation rate.
  d. Real interest rate = Nominal interest rate − Inflation rate.

22. Which of the following statements is false?
  a. Unanticipated inflation benefits lenders and hurts borrowers.
  b. With unanticipated inflation, lenders lose and borrowers gain.
  c. With unanticipated deflation, lenders gain and borrowers lose.
  d. Moderate anticipated inflation does not affect the real GDP (or real income).

23. Disinflation policy conducted by the Bank of Canada will lead to
  a. lower real wage and lower output in the short run.
  b. lower price and lower output and higher unemployment in the short run.
  c. higher price and lower output and higher unemployment in the short run.
  d. lower real wage, lower price and lower output and higher unemployment in the short run.

24. Consider the following:
  Real interest rate = Nominal interest rate − Inflation rate.
  a. If the nominal interest rate decreases by 1% and the inflation rate decreases by 2% (i.e., the deflation rate is 2%), then the real interest rate will increase by 1%.
  b. If the nominal interest rate decreases by 1% and the inflation rate decreases by 2% (i.e., the deflation rate is 2%), then the real interest rate will decrease by 1%.
  c. If the nominal interest rate decreases by 1% and the inflation rate decreases by 2% (i.e., the deflation rate is 2%), then the real interest rate will increase by 3%.
  d. If the nominal interest rate decreases by 1% and the inflation rate decreases by 1% (i.e., the deflation rate is 1%), then the real interest rate will increase by 1%.

25. Which of the following statements is true when we consider debt-deflation theory?
  a. With unexpected deflation, the lenders earn extra income, while borrowers lose income. Since there are more borrowers then lenders, the net effect is less aggregate spending and a decrease in aggregate demand.
  b. With unexpected inflation, lenders earn extra income, while borrowers lose income. Since there are more borrowers then lenders, the net effect is less aggregate spending and a decrease in aggregate demand.
  c. With unexpected inflation, borrowers earn extra income, while lenders lose income. The net effect is less aggregate spending and a decrease in aggregate demand.
  d. With unexpected deflation, borrowers earn extra income, while lenders lose income. The net effect is more aggregate spending and an increase in aggregate demand.

Problems and Exercises

1. Use the following table to answer this question.

Real inflation tax	Inflation rate	Real money supply
$5 million	5%	$100 million
	5	120 million
12.80 million		160 million
14 million	7	
20 million		200 million

a. We know that the real inflation tax is equal to the inflation rate times the real money supply. Use this information to fill in the missing entries in the table.

b. For a given level of the real money supply, what happens to the real inflation tax if the inflation rate increases?

c. For a given level of the real money supply, if the real inflation tax is decreasing, what must be true about the inflation rate?

d. For a given real inflation tax, what happens to the real money supply if the inflation rate increases?

2. Suppose you live in an economy that is currently experiencing hyperinflation. At the start of the year, the cost of a loaf of bread is $2.00.

a. If the inflation rate is 100% a month, what will be the price of the loaf of bread in twelve months? You might find it helpful to organize your answer in a table giving the month of the year and the price of the bread for that month.

b. What is the total price increase in percentage terms for the year?

3. Joe loans Mary $1,000 for the year. They agree that Mary will repay the full $1,000 at the end of the year and in addition, they agree that Mary will pay Joe $50 in interest payments.

   a. What is the nominal interest rate that Mary and Joe have agreed to in this contract?

   b. If Joe and Mary both anticipate that inflation will be 3% for the year, what real interest rate are each of them trying to achieve in their loan contract?

   c. Suppose the actual inflation rate for the year is 2%. Who benefits the most from this inflation rate, and why do you think they benefit the most? Explain your answer.

   d. Suppose the actual inflation rate for the year is 4%. Who benefits the most from this inflation rate, and why do you think they benefit the most? Explain your answer.

   e. If the actual inflation rate equals the nominal interest rate, how does this affect the outcome of this loan contract?

   f. If you knew what the actual inflation rate was going to be, and it happened to equal the nominal interest rate, would you be willing to be a lender? Why or why not? Explain your answer.

4. Suppose that both borrowers and lenders anticipate correctly that the inflation rate will increase by 5 percentage points over the next year.

   a. What do you know will happen to the real interest rate?

   b. What do you know will happen to the nominal interest rate?

c. Describe the effects of this anticipated inflation on the demand for loanable funds curve and the supply of loanable funds curve. Use the following graph to illustrate your answer.

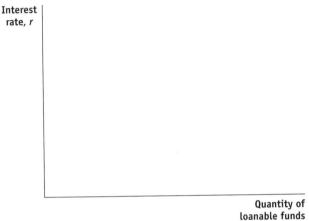

5. This chapter describes both disinflation and deflation: write a brief essay contrasting and comparing these two terms. How are these terms similar and how are they dissimilar?

6. Expansionary monetary policy typically reduces the nominal interest rate, and this in turn acts as a stimulus for aggregate demand. Why does this not work in the case of a liquidity trap? In your answer, make sure you identify what a liquidity trap is and why it prevents monetary policy from stimulating the economy. Use the following graph to illustrate your answer.

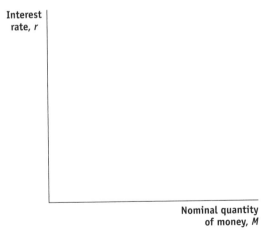

7. Explain why during a period of deflation the debt burden increases and how this relates to debt deflation.

8. Assume that the economy is initially at point A. Consider the following graph and answer the following questions.

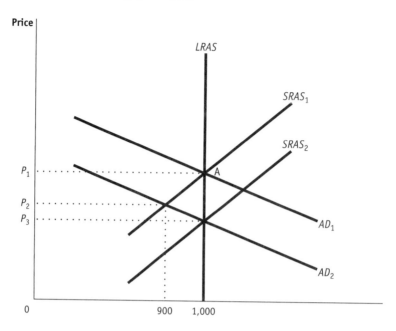

a. Consider an unexpected once-for-all reduction of money supply; as a result, the AD_1 curve shifted left to the AD_2 curve. What is the new equilibrium output in the short run? What is the percentage GDP gap?

b. Suppose a 1% additional unemployment rate causes a 2% loss in real GDP. What will be the additional unemployment, given your answer in part a?

c. In the long run, what will be the equilibrium price and output? What brings this new long-run equilibrium outcome? What is the relevant *SRAS* curve?

9. Assume that Nominal interest rate = Real interest rate + Inflation rate. Fill in the blanks or circle the correct choice.
   a. If the inflation rate is zero and the real interest rate is 5%, the nominal interest rate is _____.

b. Assume that the anticipated inflation rate is zero and the nominal interest rate is 5%. If the nominal interest rate is constant, but the actual (unanticipated) inflation rate is 2%, then borrowers gain/lose and lenders gain/lose.

c. If anticipated inflation rate is 3%, the nominal interest will increase by _____ and the amount of loanable funds will increase/decrease/remain constant.

10. Explain whether the following statement is true or false:

"When the economy experiences a liquidity trap, the Bank of Canada can increase money supply by buying bonds in the open market; but this money supply increase has no effect on investment or aggregate demand".

11. Explain whether the following statement is true or false:

"In a liquidity trap, the monetary policy is not effective, but the fiscal policy is effective".

Answers to How Well Do You Understand the Chapter

1. increase, unchanged

2. *LRAS*

3. right, higher, increase, left, high, poor

4. Fiat money, printing

5. seigniorage, large, increase, increases, inflation tax, real

6. reduce, reduction, accelerate

7. inflation, inflation, real GDP

8. nominal, higher, benefit, hurt, lower, benefit, hurt, equals

9. nominal, real, plus

10. real interest rate, nominal interest rate

11. increase, real, anticipated

12. inflation, high, real GDP, shoe-leather costs, rise, measurement

13. price-stability, lower, low

14. disinflation, reduce, difficult, above

15. left, higher, higher, recession

16. deflation, benefits, increases, increase, decrease, debt-deflation

17. fall, nominal, zero bound, monetary, liquidity trap, fall, liquidity trap

Answers to Multiple-Choice Questions

1. High inflation is not the same as hyperinflation: economists distinguish between the two terms, calling any inflation rate in excess of 50%-per-month a hyperinflation. During periods of high inflation, people reduce their money holdings since the purchasing power of their money holdings falls due to the inflation. In the long run, the economy will produce at its potential level of output no matter what the level of the money supply. **Answer: C.**

2. The classical model of the price level was used by the "classical" economists who wrote before the work of John Maynard Keynes. It is a model that ignores the short-run movements of the economy in response to a change in the money supply and instead focuses on the long-run adjustment process. It is a model that works particularly well when analyzing periods with high inflation, since these long-run adjustments are apt to be quicker than the economic adjustment that occurs when the inflation rate is relatively low. **Answer: B.**

3. In periods of high inflation, the short-run *AS* curve adjusts quickly through wage and price adjustment: this causes the short-run *AS* curve to shift to the left due to the higher nominal costs associated with the high inflation in order to move the economy toward its long-run equilibrium. **Answer: D.**

4. The Bank of Canada monetizes the government's debt when it purchases Treasury bills on the open market: this purchase has the effect of increasing the money supply in circulation in the economy. The adoption of fiat money by an economy does not lead to monetization of the debt: it is the actual use of this money issued by the government to purchase the debt that monetizes the debt. **Answer: B.**

5. This term is covered in the text: it is a term dating from the Middle Ages that referred to the right to stamp gold and silver into coins and then charge a fee for making the coins: this right belonged to the medieval lords, or seigneurs. Today the term is used by economists to describe the government's right to print money. The government, through the Bank of Canada, engages in seignorage when it makes an open-market purchase (which is a type of open-market operation) of Treasury bills. **Answer: G.**

6. An inflation tax is the reduction in purchasing power that occurs during inflation. This inflation tax occurs when the government spends more than its revenue and turns to printing money to cover its deficit. This printing of money, by expanding the money supply, leads to inflation and a loss of purchasing power for people who hold money. **Answer: G.**

7. The real inflation tax is equal to the inflation rate multiplied by the real money supply. Thus, for a given inflation rate if the real money supply increases, this must necessarily result in an increase in the real inflation tax. **Answer: B.**

8. Unexpected inflation has no effect on real GDP and real income in the economy in the long run: the economy will return to its potential output level. However, the unexpected inflation will hurt some people while benefiting other people: borrowers will find that they are paying back dollars with less purchasing power. Hence, borrowers will benefit from the unexpected inflation while lenders will be hurt. **Answer: C.**

9. Most contracts that extend over time are expressed in nominal terms and not real terms. The nominal interest rate equals the real interest rate plus the inflation rate. When the actual inflation equals the anticipated inflation rate, the inflation rate does not create winners or losers in loan contracts, since both parties to the contract have used accurate expectations of inflation to anticipate the inflation rate and they have both agreed to the real rate they actually receive when the contract is honored. Anticipated inflation diverts resources from productive uses to less productive uses: resources are used to avoid the inflation tax. **Answer: D.**

10. Both Mary and Joe would like to negotiate a contract where the real interest rate is 3%, and they both anticipate the expected inflation rate will be 5%. Thus, the nominal rate in the contract will equal the real interest rate plus the expected inflation rate, or 8%. When the actual inflation rate is 6%, this means that the dollars paid back have less purchasing power than anticipated: Mary will find this beneficial to her as the borrower, while Joe will find this hurts him since the dollars he receives in payment for the loan have less purchasing power than the dollars he loaned out. **Answer: C.**

11. When the expected inflation rate changes, this causes both the demand and supply curves for loanable funds to shift in the same direction (see figure 16–4 in the text). The equilibrium quantity of loanable funds will be unaffected by this change, but the nominal interest rate will change by the change in the expected inflation rate. **Answer: H.**

12. All three statements are straightforward statements found in your text. **Answer: D.**

13. Disinflation in an economy where inflationary expectations are embedded is possible only if policymakers are willing to push the economy into a recession and thereby reduce inflationary expectations. This will necessarily result in an increase in the unemployment rate and an output gap, since actual output will be less than potential output. This policy does not affect the natural rate of unemployment. **Answer: C.**

14. Moderate inflation may be caused by politicians pursuing too low an unemployment rate; due to using a target rate of unemployment that is lower than the natural rate of unemployment; or because of aggregate supply shocks to the economy. Eliminating moderate inflation through disinflation is a costly procedure, since it requires accepting a higher than normal unemployment rate in order to reduce inflationary expectations. **Answer: E.**

15. In a period of unexpected deflation, borrowers will find that the real value of the loan payments they make has risen in value and thus, borrowers will be hurt by the unexpected deflation. Lenders will benefit because the loan payments they receive will have greater real value due to the deflation. Borrowers, due to the increased economic burden of their debt, will typically reduce their overall spending and will choose therefore to borrow less during a period of deflation. **Answer: C.**

16. Debt deflation is the reduction in aggregate demand caused by deflation. A borrower's existent debt is not reduced due to deflation: the borrower's real debt is increased during a period of deflation, since the deflation increases the real burden of the borrower's debt. Debt deflation reduces spending and therefore worsens the economic slump: the economy does not move quickly to its potential output level. **Answer: B.**

17. The liquidity trap is a situation in which monetary policy cannot be used because nominal interest rates must stay at zero or above. Monetary policy is ineffective when the economy operates in a liquidity trap, since the nominal interest rate cannot fall below zero. The Bank of Canada could adopt a target inflation rate of 0% and not necessarily run into the liquidity trap: however, the Bank of Canada would likely choose a higher inflation target, since it allows them more room to adjust nominal interest rates as a way of stimulating aggregate demand. **Answer: C.**

18. When the central bank cannot effectively use monetary policy to stimulate the economy, it must be at the zero bound, or the nominal interest rate must equal zero. When the nominal interest rate is at zero, then the economy is operating in a liquidity trap—a situation where monetary policy is ineffective. The money market can still be in equilibrium, even though monetary policy cannot be used to stimulate the economy. **Answer: E.**

19. The classical model assumes that prices and wages are flexible. The quantity theory of money is consistent with the classical model, because increases in nominal money supply increases prices at the same rate and, as a result, all real variables including M/P stay unchanged. **Answer: C.**

20. Fiat money has no intrinsic value. **Answer: A.**

21. Real interest rate = Nominal interest rate - inflation rate. **Answer: D.**

22. All the statements are true except one, which is statement a. Unanticipated inflation hurts lenders and benefits borrowers. **Answer: A.**

23. Disinflation policy by the Bank of Canada will lead to the leftward shift of the *AD* curve and price will decrease. In the short run, the real wage will increase, output will decrease, and unemployment will increase. **Answer: B.**

24. Percentage change in real interest rate = percentage change in nominal interest rate – percentage increase in inflation rate.

In part a, we get – 1% – (–2%) = 1%.
In part b, we get +1%, not –1%.
In part c, we should get – 1% – (–2%) = 1%, not 3%.
In part d, we get no change in real interest rate because – 1% – (–1%) = zero.

Answer: A.

25. According to debt-deflation theory, deflation brings reduction in aggregate spending and aggregate demand. **Answer: A.**

Answers to Problems and Exercises

1. a.

Real inflation tax	Inflation rate	Real money supply
$5 million	5%	$100 million
6 million	5	120 million
12.80 million	8	160 million
14 million	7	200 million
20 million	10	200 million

b. The real inflation tax will increase. When the inflation rate increases, then the purchasing power of the money supply is reduced: this is equivalent to a tax on the value of all money held by the public. In the table shown here in part (a) you can see this illustrated when the real money supply equals $200 million: when the inflation rate is 7%, the real inflation tax is $14 million, and when the inflation rate is 10%, the real inflation tax is $20 million.

c. If the real inflation rate is falling, this indicates that the purchasing power of the money supply is being eroded more slowly. This can only be true if the inflation rate is lower than its previous levels. Again, this is illustrated in the table shown here.

d. There is a trade-off between the inflation rate and the money supply for a given constant level of real inflation tax: the real inflation tax can be constant with an increasing inflation rate only if the real money supply is decreasing.

2. a. To calculate the price of the bread in twelve months let's use the following table to organize our answer.

Month of the year	Price of a loaf of bread
1	$4.00
2	8.00
3	16.00
4	32.00
5	64.00
6	128.00
7	256.00
8	512.00
9	1,024.00
10	2,048.00
11	4,096.00
12	8,192.00

b. To calculate the total increase in price for the period, we use the formula: percentage change in price equals (the current price – the base price) × 100/(the base price) or the percentage change in price equals (8,192 – 2) × 100/2 equals 459,500%.

3. a. The nominal interest rate the Mary and Joe have agreed to in this contract is 5%, since the $50 interest payment represents 5% of the $1,000 loan.

b. We can calculate the real interest rate as the nominal interest rate minus the expected inflation rate: in this case, the nominal interest rate is 5% and the expected inflation rate is 3%, giving us a real interest rate of 2%.

c. If the actual inflation rate is 2%, then the real rate of interest that is paid on the loan is 3%, which is higher than the real interest rate that Mary and Joe thought they were agreeing to when they signed their loan contract. For Joe, the lender, this means that he is earning more than he anticipated from the loan. For Mary, the borrower, this means that she is paying back more dollars in real terms than she planned on when she signed the contract.

d. If the actual inflation rate is 4%, then the real rate of interest that is paid on the loan is 1%, which is lower than the real interest rate that Mary and Joe thought they were agreeing to when they signed their loan contract. For Joe, the lender, this means that he is earning less than he anticipated from the loan. For Mary, the borrower, this means that she is paying back fewer dollars in real terms than she planned on when she signed the contract.

e. If the actual inflation rate equals the nominal rate of interest, then the real interest rate is zero. When the real rate of interest equals zero, this represents a situation where the lender earns no real return on the money he or she has lent out, while the borrower is paying no real cost for the use of the money. The borrower wins, while the lender is hurt under this scenario.

f. No, if you knew what the actual inflation rate was going to be and it equaled the nominal interest rate for the loan, you would refuse to be a lender since the real return you would earn on the loan would be zero. If you made the loan, you would be giving up the use of your funds for the period of the loan without receiving any real compensation for the use of those funds.

4. a. The real interest rate will be unaffected by this anticipated inflation rate, since both demanders and suppliers in the loanable funds market will take this anticipated inflation into account.

b. The nominal interest rate will increase by 5 percentage points due to the increase in the anticipated rate of inflation of 5 percentage points.

c. Both the demand and the supply curves in the loanable funds market will shift upward by the amount of the anticipated inflation rate: this will leave the equilibrium quantity of loanable funds unchanged in the market while increasing the nominal interest rate by the amount of the anticipated inflation. The following figure illustrates this.

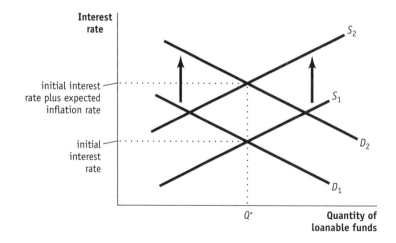

5. Disinflation refers to the deliberate pursuit by policymakers to bring down inflation that has become embedded in expectations. Here, policymakers pursue policy aimed at reducing inflationary expectations in order to reduce the increase in the aggregate price level. Disinflation may be very expensive economically, since it may result in significant decreases in real GDP in order to remove inflationary expectations from the economy. Deflation, on the other hand, refers to a fall in the aggregate price level. This deflation is not the result of conscious policymaking activity, but may prove difficult to remedy through policy if the economy is operating in a liquidity trap where nominal interest rates are equal to zero. In such a situation, monetary policy cannot be used to stimulate aggregate demand through lower nominal interest rates. So, even though disinflation and deflation both are concerned with either slowing down inflation or a direct fall in the aggregate price level, they represent different challenges to the policymaker.

6. In the case of a liquidity trap, the nominal interest rate initially is equal to zero and thus cannot fall any lower despite expansionary monetary policy. The following graph illustrates a liquidity trap, where *MS* is the nominal money supply, *MD* is the nominal money demand, and *r* is the nominal interest rate.

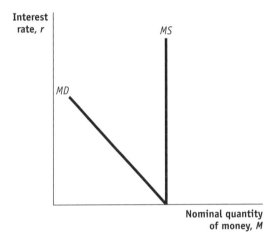

In the graph, when the central bank pursues expansionary monetary policy to shift the *MS* to the right, this will have no effect on the nominal interest rate since it is already at its minimal level of zero. Monetary policy cannot be used to stimulate the economy if the economy faces a liquidity trap.

7. When there is a deflation, prices in an economy fall. The effect of this fall in prices is to increase the economic burden of any pre-existing debt, since the borrower's payments are not adjusted downward to reflect the deflation. Borrowers lose from deflation due to the increased real burden of their debt: this increased debt burden may lead them to be short of cash and force them to cut their spending sharply when their debt burden rises. Thus, deflation reduces aggregate demand, which deepens the economic slump that may, in turn, lead to further deflation. This reduction in aggregate demand due to the effect of deflation is referred to as debt deflation.

8. a. Real GDP = 900 and GDP gap = −10%.
  b. 5%
  c. Long run equilibrium price = P_3 and real GDP = 1,000.
  Lower wages (shift the *SRAS* to the right) and lower prices
  $SRAS_2$.

9. a. 5%
  b. Borrowers gain and lenders lose.
  c. 3%; constant.

10. The statement is true. Money supply will increase with an open-market purchase of bonds by the Bank of Canada, but this will not lower the interest rate any further. As a result, neither investments will change nor the aggregate demand.

11. Monetary policy will be ineffective in a liquidity trap, because the interest rate cannot be brought down any (further through money supply increases) to stimulate aggregate demand and income. Expansionary fiscal policy with an increase in government spending will increase aggregate spending as well as aggregate income. Since the interest rate is constant in a liquidity trap, there will be no crowding-out effect and, as a result, fiscal policy will have maximal effect on the economy's income in a recessionary situation.

chapter 17

The Making of Modern Macroeconomics

This chapter discusses the limitations of the classical macroeconomics model and how it was not adequate for the economic problems posed by the Great Depression. The chapter also develops the primary ideas underlying Keynesian economics and presents an overview of the modifications of Keynesian economics that occurred in response to criticisms of this approach. The chapter then discusses the new classical macroeconomics and the elements of modern macroeconomic consensus, before addressing the main areas of dispute among macroeconomic theorists today.

How Well Do You Understand the Chapter?

Fill in the blanks using the terms below or circle the correct answer to complete the following statements. Terms may be used more than once. If you find yourself having difficulties, please refer to the appropriate section in the text.

activist	*expectation*	*ineffective*	*monetary policy*	*short-run*
aggregate demand	*fiscal policy*	*inflation target*	*more*	*slump*
asset prices	*flexibility*	*information*	*natural rate of unemployment*	*smooth out*
broad	*flexible*	*instability*		*stable*
business confidence	*high*	*key*	*political*	*steadily*
business cycle	*higher*	*limit*	*political business cycle*	*technical*
constant	*inadequate*	*long-run*		*unchanged*
contraction	*increase*	*lower*	*ratio*	*vertical*
counterproductive	*increasing*	*M1*	*rational expectation*	*what*
cutting	*independent*	*macroeconomic policies*	*recovery*	*World War II*
erratically	*industrial*	*macroeconomic policy activism*	*result*	*zero*
	industrial society			

1. The term macroeconomics was first used in 1933. Prior to the 1930s, the classical model of the price level dominated economic thinking about monetary policy. This model, based on the assumption of _____ prices, held that a(n) _____ in the monetary supply, holding other things equal, would lead to an equal proportional rise in the aggregate price level and the level of real aggregate output will remain _____. This model focused on _____ economic adjustments while regarding _____ economic adjustment as unimportant. By the 1930s, the measurement of business cycles was well advanced even though there was no generally accepted theory of

business cycles. The Great Depression demonstrated, once and for all, that economists cannot ignore the _____. The Great Depression provided a strong incentive for economists to develop theories that could provide rationale for _____ in the face of business-cycle fluctuations.

2. The modern business cycle probably originated in the home of the _____ Revolution, Britain, which was already a largely industrial and urban society by 1820. There was a British recession in 1846-1847. We don't know for sure when Canada experienced its first business cycle. There are two reasons for this. We only have GDP data from 1926 and output by industry data from 1919. The second reason is: modern business cycles depend on having a predominantly _____; but Canada was overwhelmingly a rural agricultural society throughout the 19th century. In the United States, the modern business cycle could not have occurred much before 1880.

3. Keynesian economics mainly reflects two innovations: first, it emphasized _____ effects of shifts in aggregate demand and their impact on aggregate output rather than the long-run determination of the aggregate price level; and second, it argued that changes in _____ were the primary cause of business cycles. Keynes's economic ideas have been accepted across a broad part of the political spectrum. The main practical consequence of Keynes's work was the justification of _____: Keynes's work indicated that monetary and fiscal policy could be used to _____ business-cycle fluctuations.

4. Keynes's work suggested that economic _____ requires aggressive fiscal expansion: this deficit spending creates jobs. In the 1930s, the modest increases in deficit spending were _____ to end the Great Depression. In 1937, Roosevelt gave in to advice from non-Keynesian economists who urged him to balance the budget and raise the interest rate. The result was a renewed _____. The massive expansionary fiscal policy that occurred as a result of _____ was sufficient to create jobs in the short run and to prove that aggressive fiscal policy could result in economic recovery.

5. Keynes suggested that monetary policy would be _____ in depression conditions due to the liquidity trap where interest rates cannot fall below _____. Although this is true, Friedman and Schwartz with their 1963 publication of *A Monetary History of the United States, 1867–1960* persuaded many economists that the Great Depression could have been avoided if the U.S. Federal Reserve had acted to prevent a monetary _____. Over time, economists came to believe that monetary policy should play a _____ role in economic management. If the government tries to stimulate the economy by _____ taxes, it must decide which taxes to

cut; if the government decides to stimulate the economy with government spending, it must decide _____ to spend money on. Monetary policy, in contrast, does not involve such choices: when the central bank cuts interest rates to fight a recession, it cuts everyone's interest rate at the same time. Economic management of the economy through monetary policy instead of fiscal policy makes macroeconomics a more _____, and less _____ issue.

6. Monetarism asserts that GDP will grow _____ if the money supply grows steadily. The monetarist policy prescription was to have the Central bank target a _____ growth of money supply, such as 3% per year, and maintain that target regardless of any fluctuations in the economy. Monetarists believed that a steady growth rate of the money supply would prove to be _____ effective in smoothing out business cycle fluctuations than active policy intervention, since active policy intervention encounters lags in its implementation and effectiveness. Friedman believed that if the money supply is kept fixed, while the government pursues an expansionary fiscal policy, it will crowd out investment (due to a(n) _____ interest rate) and, as a result, it will _____ the effect on aggregate demand. A higher interest rate will also cause an appreciation of the Canadian dollar and, as a result, it will _____ net exports and limit the effect of the fiscal expansion on aggregate demand. Friedman did not favour discretionary monetary policy; he argued that the central bank should follow a _____ rule. Friedman believed that the *velocity of money* is _____. The velocity of money in Canada, as measured by the _____ of nominal GDP to M1, was stable during the period of 1967–1981 and after 1981, the velocity of money began to fall and move somewhat _____. Between 1975 and 1982, the Bank of Canada flirted with monetarism, instead of targeting interest rates. In November 1982, the Bank of Canada announced that the recorded _____ series was not a useful guide to policy at the time. Despite this experience, economists believe that the much or too little discretion in monetary policy is

_____.

7. In 1968 Friedman and Phelps proposed the _____, or NAIRU. The natural rate hypothesis gives a more limited role to macroeconomic policy than did earlier ideas. They claimed that the apparent trade-off between unemployment and inflation (short-run Phillips curve) would not survive an extended period of time with _____ prices: that is, the existence of inflationary expectations would cause the economy to continue to have inflation even with _____ levels of unemployment.

8. The _____ results when politicians use macroeconomic policy to serve political ends. This can result in unnecessary economic _____.

9. New classical macroeconomics returned to the classical view that shifts in the

_____ curve causes changes in the aggregate price level only, but not the aggregate output level. This approach challenged the Keynesian idea that the short-run aggregate supply curve is upward sloping and instead argued that the supply curve was _____. This position was based on two concepts: _____ and real business cycle theory.

10. Rational _____ is the view that individuals and firms make decisions optimally, using all available information. If this is true then people will form their expectations about inflation not only by considering historical data, but also by taking into account any available _____ about government intentions with regard to trading off higher inflation for lower unemployment. The implication of this logic is that _____ can change the level of unemployment only if it comes as a surprise to the public.

11. Real _____ theory argues that fluctuations in the rate of growth of total factor productivity cause the business cycle. Some economists argue that declining productivity during a recession is a(n) _____, not a cause, of the recession.

12. Among macroeconomists there is _____ agreement that monetary policy is an effective policy tool for stabilizing the economy, but that it cannot successfully reduce the unemployment rate below the _____. In addition, most macroeconomists agree that discretionary fiscal policy should be avoided, except in the exceptional cases that call for activist government intervention in the form of _____.

13. There is _____ agreement among macroeconomists that central banks should be politically _____, but these macroeconomists debate whether central banks should pursue formally stated inflation targets, what the level of formal _____ should be if the central bank adopts such a policy, and whether central banks should intervene to prevent extreme movements in asset prices. At present, _____ rate of the Bank of Canada is 2% (the midpoint of 1% and 3% band). This target inflation rate is due for revision in 2006. The European Central Bank's rules say that it should seek price-stability, which is defined as 0% – 1% inflation. The U.S. Federal Reserve believes that the absence of specific guidelines gives the central bank more _____ in coping with economic events. There is a long-standing debate whether the central bank restricts its concerns to inflation and possibly unemployment, or should also prevent extreme movements in _____.

Learning Tips

TIP #1: This chapter requires you to be able to compare and contrast different macroeconomic theories.

The following table provides a summary of these models. You will want to review each model and think about the focus of each model, and how the models differ with regard to their underlying assumptions and their policy implications.

	Classical macro	Keynesian macro	Monetarism	Modern consensus
Focus of model	Long-run determination of the aggregate price level	Short-run determination of the aggregate output level and the effects of shifts in *AD* on that level of aggregate output	Effect of money supply growth on the level of short-run aggregate output in the economy	Summarizing points of agreement among modern-day macroeconomists
Prices	Flexible in the short run and the long run	Flexible in the long run, but sticky in the short run	Flexible in the long run, but sticky in the short run	Flexible in the long run, but sticky in the short run
Unemployment	Model does not worry about unemployment: assumes that economy will produce at potential output level in both the short run and the long run, due to price flexibility	Unemployment possible in the short run due to leftward shifts in aggregate demand that lead to decreases in output and aggregate production less than the potential output level for the economy	Unemployment possible in the short run due to leftward shifts in aggregate demand that lead to decreases in output and aggregate production less than the potential output level for the economy	Unemployment possible in the short run due to leftward shifts in aggregate demand that lead to decreases in output and aggregate production less than the potential output level for the economy
Aggregate supply curve	Vertical in both the short run and long run, thus shifts in aggregate demand have no effect on the level of aggregate output	*SRAS* is upward sloping, so shifts in aggregate demand affect aggregate output and thus employment	*SRAS* is upward sloping, so shifts in aggregate demand affect aggregate output and thus employment	*SRAS* is upward sloping, so shifts in aggregate demand affect aggregate output and thus employment; *LRAS* is vertical at the potential output level for the economy
Shifts in aggregate demand	Focus on changes in money supply and how this shifts the aggregate demand cure and raises the aggregate price level	Changes in "animal spirits," or business confidence, cause shifts in aggregate demand; model emphasizes the importance of demand shocks	Shift in aggregate demand because of fiscal policy changes will have no effect on aggregate output due to crowding out effect; shifts in aggregate demand affect aggregate output only if driven by changes in the money supply	Shift in aggregate demand possible because of changes in fiscal policy or the money supply

	Classical macro	**Keynesian macro**	**Monetarism**	**Modern consensus**
Effect of monetary policy	Increase in money supply leads to an equal and proportionate rise in the aggregate price level and no effect on aggregate output in the long run	Not particularly effective in depression conditions	Plays key role in economic management; GDP will grow steadily if the money supply grows steadily (a monetary policy rule)	Can be used to shift aggregate demand curve and to reduce economic instability
Policy ramifications	Economy in long run is at potential output: simply be patient for that result to occur	Legitimized macroeconomic policy activism: the use of monetary and fiscal policy to smooth out business cycles	Expansionary fiscal policy with a fixed money supply leads to crowding out: importance of monetary policy	Fiscal and monetary policy can shift the aggregate demand curve

TIP #2: A key issue underlying this chapter is the shape of the short-run aggregate supply curve.

The classical macroeconomists thought the short-run aggregate supply curve was vertical; hence, shifts in aggregate demand could cause changes in the aggregate price level, but not changes in the level of aggregate output. Figure 17.1 illustrates this idea.

Figure 17.1

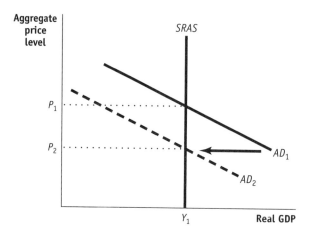

The Keynesian approach emphasized that the short-run aggregate supply curve is upward sloping and thus, shifts in aggregate demand, would cause both the aggregate price level as well as the aggregate output level to change. Figure 17.2 illustrates this idea.

Figure 17.2

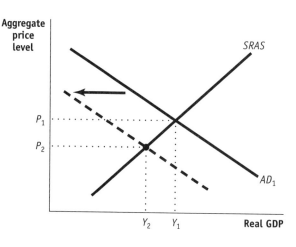

The monetarist approach concurred with the Keynesians that the short-run aggregate supply is upward sloping, but emphasized that fiscal policy would be relatively ineffective if the money supply was held constant due to the crowding out effect. In addition, this approach favored the implementation of a monetary policy rule, thereby effectively reducing the scope of monetary policy.

The new classical macroeconomics returned briefly to the classical view that the short-run aggregate supply curve is vertical, but eventually found that economic data supports an upward-sloping aggregate supply curve rather than a vertical aggregate supply curve.

TIP #3: You will want to closely review the description of the modern consensus and be able to explain what this term means and how the modern consensus answers the five questions found in Table 17-1.

The text provides a concise summary of these four approaches in the table provided on page 429: reviewing this table and the one given under the first tip in this section will help to reinforce the similarities and distinctions between these different approaches.

Multiple-Choice Questions

1. Which of the following statements is true?
   a. Macroeconomists believe the use of expansionary monetary policy is always an ineffective method for reducing economic recessions.
   b. Herbert Hoover was essentially a Keynesian macroeconomist at heart.
   c. The classical model of the price level holds that prices are flexible, and therefore the long-run aggregate supply curve is horizontal.
   d. All of the above statements are true.
   e. All of the above statements are false.
   f. Both (a) and (b) are true.
   g. Both (a) and (c) are true.
   h. Both (b) and (c) are true.

2. The Great Depression
   a. re-enforced prevailing economic views of the day that it was only long-run economic performance that was important.
   b. threatened both economic and political stability.
   c. illustrated that market economies produced consistently at the potential output level.
   d. All of the above statements are true.
   e. Both (b) and (c) are true.

3. Which of the following statements is true about Keynes's contributions to economic theory?
   a. In the long run, fluctuations in aggregate output are primarily due to fluctuations in aggregate demand.
   b. In the short run, the aggregate supply curve is upward sloping, and therefore shifts in aggregate demand will cause fluctuations in aggregate output.
   c. Shifts in the aggregate demand curve in the short run are primarily due to changes in the money supply.
   d. "Animal spirits" primarily affect aggregate supply in the long run.

4. Macroeconomic policy activism refers to
   a. the use of expansionary monetary policy to fight economic expansions.
   b. the use of monetary and fiscal policy to smooth out business cycle fluctuations.
   c. the idea that running large government deficits is never an acceptable means of eliminating business cycle fluctuations.
   d. Both (b) and (c).

5. Which of the following statements is true?
   a. In a liquidity trap, expansionary monetary policy can effectively raise interest rates.
   b. Friedman and Schwartz's work helped to prove the effectiveness of fiscal policy as a way of managing the economy.
   c. Friedman and Schwartz's work helped make macroeconomics a more technical, and less political, issue.
   d. Keynes made other economists aware of the limitations of macroeconomic policy activism.

6. Monetarism
   a. states that there is no relationship between the rate of growth of the money supply and the level of aggregate output in an economy.
   b. has nothing in common with Keynesian ideas.
   c. includes a strong belief in the efficacy of discretionary fiscal policy.
   d. maintains that most efforts of policymakers to reduce economic fluctuation actually result in greater economic instability.

7. When the central bank pursues a formula that determines its actions, this is called
   a. monetarism.
   b. a monetary policy rule.
   c. discretionary monetary policy.
   d. discretionary fiscal policy.

8. The NAIRU
   a. is equivalent to the natural rate of unemployment.
   b. hypothesis states that inflation eventually gets built into expectations, so that any attempt to keep the unemployment rate above the natural rate will lead to an ever-rising inflation rate.
   c. states that once inflation is embedded in the public's expectations, it would continue even in the face of high unemployment.
   d. All of the above statements are true statements.
   e. Both (a) and (b) are true.
   f. Both (a) and (c) are true.
   g. Both (b) and (c) are true.

9. Which of the following statements is true?
   a. Activist macroeconomic policy lends itself to political manipulation.
   b. Adoption of a monetary policy rule by the central bank lends itself to political manipulation.
   c. Political business cycles reduce economic instability in an economy.
   d. Velocity, after 1980, was predictable and steady in the Canadian economy.

10. New classical macroeconomics
   a. held that shifts in aggregate demand affected the aggregate output level and not the aggregate price level.
   b. incorporates rational expectations, the belief that individuals and firms make their decisions optimally using all available information.
   c. provides a logical argument that suggests monetary policy is ineffective as a method for stabilizing the economy.
   d. All of the above statements are true statements.
   e. Both (a) and (b) are true.
   f. Both (a) and (c) are true.
   g. Both (b) and (c) are true.

11. Real business cycle theory
   a. states that the correlation between total factor productivity and the business cycle is the result of the effect of the business cycle on productivity.
   b. states that fluctuations in the rate of growth of factor productivity cause the business cycle.
   c. states that fluctuations in the business cycle cause changes in the rate of growth of factor productivity.
   d. is a widely-held view among macroeconomists today.

12. Expansionary monetary policy is helpful in fighting recessions, provided the economy is not operating in a liquidity trap, according to
   a. classical macroeconomics.
   b. monetarism.
   c. the modern consensus among macroeconomists.
   d. All of the above are true statements.
   d. Both (a) and (c).
   f. Both (b) and (c).

13. Which of the following statements is true?
   a. According to the Keynesians, fiscal policy is ineffective in fighting recessions.
   b. According to the monetarists, fiscal policy is ineffective in fighting recessions.
   c. The modern consensus holds that discretionary fiscal policy is always acceptable.
   d. According to the classical macroeconomists, discretionary monetary policy is always acceptable.

14. The classical macroeconomics explained
   a. why there is a prolonged and sustained GDP gap from the potential output.
   a. how wage-price flexibility corrects any deviation from full-employment output.
   b. explains the need for macroeconomic policies to fight recession.
   c. explains how aggregate demand affects real GDP and unemployment.

15. Classical macroeconomics prior to 1930 believed in all the following statements except
   a. if the money supply increases, the price level will increase at the same rate.
   b. GDP gaps are corrected through wage-price flexibility and, as a result, the aggregate supply curve is a vertical line at the full-employment output point.
   c. aggregate demand determines supply of output, employment, and unemployment.
   d. aggregate demand determines price-level without any effect on the changes in output, employment, and unemployment.

16. The Great Depression
- a. can be explained by the classical macro model.
- b. provided the rationale for Keynesian macroeconomics with a strong emphasis on fiscal policy to fight the Great Depression.
- c. provided the rationale for Keynesian macroeconomics with a strong emphasis on long-term growth policy to fight the Great Depression.
- d. provided the rationale for Keynesian macroeconomics with a strong emphasis on monetary policy to fight the Great Depression.

17. Keynes argued for all the following except
- a. given the liquidity trap with very low interest rate, expansionary monetary policy rather than expansionary fiscal policy will stimulate economic recovery.
- b. given the liquidity trap with very low interest rates, expansionary fiscal policy rather than expansionary monetary policy will stimulate economic recovery.
- c. the falling (leftward shift) of the *AD* curve is the cause of prolonged recession.
- d. to offset falling aggregate demand, the government should increase government expenditure.

18. Which of the following statements is false?
- a. World War II demonstrated that expansionary fiscal policy can, in fact, create jobs in the short run.
- b. The main practical consequence of Keynes's work was that it legitimized macroeconomic policy activism.
- c. Keynes was a socialist and he can be labeled as a leftist economist.
- d. According to Keynesian economics, the economy is not inherently competitive and stable; price and wage adjustments are very painfully slow in severe recession.

19. Which of the following statements is false?
- a. Velocity of money is $V = PY/M$.
- b. According to monetarists, V is constant and any fluctuation of money supply will explain fluctuation of nominal GDP.
- c. Statistical data in Canada for the last 50 years proved that velocity of money is constant.
- d. According to monetarists, discretionary monetary policy is counterproductive.

20. If the hypothesis of the NAIRU is true,
- a. activist monetary policy will be successful to reduce unemployment rate.
- b. there is no inflationary expectation.
- c there is no trade-off between inflation and unemployment.
- d. the Phillips curve is a down-sloping line.

21. According to the rational expectation hypothesis, all the following statements are true except
- a. anticipated monetary policy can reduce the unemployment rate.
- b. policy multipliers are zero.
- c. it is possible to have disinflation without recession.
- d. the aggregate supply curve will be vertical in the long run.

22. According to the real business cycle theory, all the following statements are true except
   a. fluctuations in the rate of growth of total factor productivity cause the business cycle.
   b. fluctuations in aggregate demand cause business-cycle fluctuations.
   c. aggregate demand policy cannot fight recessions.
   d. aggregate demand fluctuations are temporary, and the market will eventually correct for them.

23. According to modern consensus, all of the following statements are true except
   a. monetary policy can be used to shift the aggregate demand curve.
   b. discretionary monetary policy can be used to fight recession.
   c fiscal policy can be used to shift the aggregate demand curve.
   d. the long-run aggregate supply curve is a vertical line.

Problems and Exercises

1. Why did Keynes respond to the classical viewpoint by claiming that in the long run, "we are all dead"? Explain how his economic thinking about the macroeconomy represented a departure from the prevailing economic thought of the day.

2. How did the Great Depression provide an incentive for economists to develop new theories and new positions with regard to the efficacy of policy as a means of reducing business cycle fluctuations?

3. Briefly describe the two primary innovations in Keynesian economics. How did Keynes's work legitimize macroeconomic policy activism? Use the following graph to help illustrate your answer, and be sure in your answer to compare the Keynesian viewpoint with the classical viewpoint.

4. The new classical macroeconomics, developed in the 1970s and 1980s, challenged the Keynesian macroeconomic view that the short-run aggregate supply curve is upward sloping. What did the new classical macroeconomists propose with regard to the short-run aggregate supply curve, and what reasons did they give for ascribing to this viewpoint?

5. Although most macroeconomists agree that fiscal policy can affect the level of aggregate output in the short run, many macroeconomists do not support the use of discretionary fiscal policy as a method for smoothing business cycle fluctuations. Why, if fiscal policy is potentially effective, do these macroeconomists reject it as a policy tool? Is there any time that these macroeconomists would advocate the use of discretionary fiscal policy?

6. Why is it essential that central banks be politically independent?

7. Suppose the economy of Macroland reports a decline in output. The President of Macroland assembles a group of economic advisors to study this decline in output and to advise the government about appropriate policies to use to address this decline in output.

    a. The first advisor is a Keynesian macroeconomist. How would this advisor explain the decline in output, and what policy(ies) would this advisor suggest to return the economy to its potential output level? Graph an aggregate demand and aggregate supply diagram to illustrate your answer.

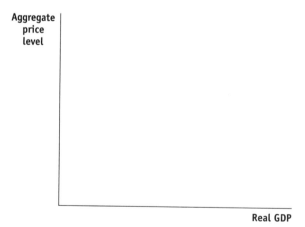

    b. The second advisor is a monetarist. How would this advisor explain the decline in output, and what policy(ies) would this advisor suggest to return the economy to its potential output level? Use an aggregate demand and aggregate supply diagram to illustrate your answer.

   c. The third advisor is an economist who accepts the viewpoints expressed by macroeconomists, in what the text terms, the modern consensus. How would this advisor explain the decline in output, and what policy(ies) would this advisor suggest to return the economy to its potential output level? Use an aggregate demand and aggregate supply diagram to illustrate your answer.

8. Consider the classical macro model and answer "yes" or "no" to the following questions.

   a. Is the economy competitive?

   b. Can there be a prolonged recession?

   c. Is the labour market competitive?

   d. Is labour supply a function of real wage?

   e. If price doubles, does the wage rate double?

   f. If price decreases by 10%, does the wage rate decrease by 10%?

   g. If M doubles, does V change?

   h. If M doubles, does P double?

   i. Is the policy multiplier zero?

   j. Do changes in nominal variables affect real variables?

9. Consider the Keynesian macro model and answer "yes" or "no" to the following questions.

   a. Is the economy competitive?

   b. Can there be a prolonged recession?

   c. Is the labour market competitive?

   d. Is the labour supply a function of real wage?

   e. If price doubles, does the wage rate double?

   f. If price decreases by 10%, does the wage rate decrease by 10%?

   g. If M doubles, does V change?

   h. If M doubles, does P double?

   i. Is the policy multiplier zero?

   j. Do changes in nominal variables affect real variables?

10. Assume an economy in a recession with liquidity trap. Circle which of the following statements is correct.

a. Expansionary monetary policy can increase/decrease/have no effect on the interest rate. Expansionary monetary policy can increase/decrease/have no effect on real GDP.

b. Expansionary fiscal policy can increase/decrease/have no effect on the interest rate. Expansionary fiscal policy has a positive/zero crowding-out effect. Expansionary fiscal policy can increase/decrease/have no effect on real GDP.

Answers to How Well Do You Understand the Chapter

1. flexible, increase, unchanged, long-run, short-run, short-run, macroeconomic policies

2. Industrial, industrial society

3. short-run, business confidence, macroeconomic policy activism, smooth out

4. recovery, inadequate, slump, World War II

5. ineffective, zero, contraction, key, cutting, what, technical, political

6. steadily, constant, more, higher, limit, lower, monetary policy, stable, ratio, erratically, M1, counterproductive

7. natural rate of unemployment, activist, increasing, high

8. political business cycle, instability

9. aggregate demand, vertical, rational expectation

10. expectation, information, monetary policy

11. business cycle, result

12. broad, natural rate of unemployment, fiscal policy

13. broad, independent, inflation target, inflation target, flexibility, asset prices

Answers to Multiple-Choice Questions

1. All of these statements are false. There is general consensus among macroeconomists that expansionary monetary policy is effective in reducing recessions. Herbert Hoover, during his presidency, held firmly to the belief that active intervention into the economy would only worsen the depression: this view reflected the viewpoint that aggressive monetary policy was dangerous and ineffective. In the classical model of the price level, prices are flexible and, hence, the aggregate supply curve is vertical and not horizontal. **Answer: E.**

2. The Great Depression illustrated for economists that short-run economic fluctuations were important and that a theory to understand these fluctuations was needed. The Great Depression threatened economic stability due to the economic pain of extremely high levels of unemployment and the political instability that led to the rise of Hitler in Germany. Although some economists thought that a market-oriented economy was unstable, there were other economists that did not support this view. **Answer: B.**

3. Keynes demonstrated that fluctuations in aggregate demand could cause short-run fluctuations in aggregate output. These fluctuations in short-run aggregate demand were primarily due to changes in "animal spirits," the term Keynes used to describe business confidence. Keynes focused on the short run and the effects of shifts in aggregate demand on a short-run upward sloping aggregate supply curve. **Answer: B.**

4. Macroeconomic policy activism is the use of monetary and fiscal policy to smooth out business cycle fluctuations. Expansionary monetary policy can be used effectively to reduce economic recessions. Large government deficits can be used to effectively fight economic recessions, but may worsen economic expansions. **Answer: B.**

5. In a liquidity trap, expansionary monetary policy is ineffective, since interest rates can fall no further once they are equal to zero. Expansionary monetary policy, if effective, reduces interest rates. Friedman and Schwartz provided proof of the effectiveness of monetary policy as a way of managing the economy. Their work helped to shift macroeconomics from a reliance on fiscal policy to a reliance on monetary policy as a means of managing the economy. This shift meant that macroeconomics became a more technical issue instead of a political issue. Keynes proved there was a role for macroeconomic policy activism. **Answer: C.**

6. Monetarism states that GDP will grow steadily if the money supply grows steadily. Monetarists, like Keynesians, believe that the short run is important and that short-run changes in aggregate demand can affect aggregate output as well as aggregate prices. Monetarism does not believe in the effectiveness of discretionary fiscal policy due to the fact that government perceptions about the economy often lag behind reality. Monetarists believe that steady growth of the money supply will result in less economic instability and will prove better for smoothing out economic fluctuations than the pursuit of discretionary monetary or fiscal policy. **Answer: D.**

7. A monetary policy rule describes the use of a formula by the central bank to determine its actions. **Answer: B.**

8. The NAIRU is the same as the natural rate of unemployment, and the NAIRU hypothesis says that once inflation is built into expectations any attempt to keep the unemployment rate below the natural rate will lead to accelerating inflation. Thus, once inflation is embedded in the public's expectations, then that inflation will continue even if the unemployment rate is high. **Answer: F.**

9. Activist macroeconomic policy does lend itself to political manipulation, since there is an obvious temptation for politicians to pump up the economy in an election year. One of the appeals of a monetary policy rule for a central bank is that it takes policy discretion away from politicians. Political business cycles increase economic instability in an economy. After 1980, velocity was highly unstable and therefore not predictable in the Canadian economy. **Answer A.**

10. New classical macroeconomics returns to the classical model's vertical aggregate supply curve: a shift in aggregate demand, given this vertical aggregate supply curve, will cause the aggregate price level to change, but will have no effect on the level of aggregate output. Answer (b) is a straightforward definition of rational expectations, which is one of the underlying concepts in the new classical macroeconomics. If rational expectations is true (as is assumed in new classical macroeconomics), then individuals and firms will fully anticipate any planned monetary policy: thus, monetary policy is effective only when it is a surprise, and this implies that monetary policy no longer can be used to stabilize the economy. **Answer: G.**

11. Real business cycle theory focuses on the rate of growth of factor productivity and how variations in this growth rate can cause business cycle fluctuations. Subsequent analysis suggests that there is a correlation between the rate of growth of factor productivity and business cycles, but the direction of causation between the two variables is difficult to fully determine. Today, this theory is felt to be limited in its explanatory value, despite its important contributions to our understanding of macroeconomics. **Answer: B.**

12. Classical macroeconomics did not believe that expansionary monetary policy was effective in fighting recessions, while Keynesian macroeconomics believed it was of limited value. Monetarists do believe that expansionary monetary policy can be helpful in fighting recessions. The modern consensus is that expansionary monetary policy is useful, except when the economy finds itself in a liquidity trap where nominal interest rates equal zero and cannot fall any further. **Answer: F.**

13. Table 17-1 in your text provides a summary of the issues addressed in this question. Keynesians upheld the efficacy of fiscal policy as a method for fighting recessions, while monetarists believed that fiscal policy was not effective in fighting recessions. The modern consensus believes that discretionary fiscal policy is useful only under restrictive circumstances. The classical macroeconomists did not believe in discretionary monetary policy. **Answer: B.**

14. Classical macroeconomics emphasized the role of wage-price flexibility to bring about full-employment. The aggregate demand determines price; macroeconomic policies are not needed to fight recession. **Answer: B.**

15. Aggregate demand determines price only, and it cannot be manipulated by policies to change output and employment. **Answer: C.**

16. The Great Depression provided the rationale for Keynesian macroeconomics with a strong emphasis on fiscal policy to fight the Great Depression. **Answer: B.**

17. Keynes did not advocate expansionary monetary policy, because expansionary monetary policy is ineffective in the face of the liquidity trap. **Answer: A.**

18. Keynes was a neither a socialist nor a leftist. **Answer: C.**

19. Velocity of money was not constant. **Answer: C.**

20. If NAIRU is true, the long-run Phillips curve is a vertical line; as a result, there is no trade-off between inflation and unemployment. **Answer: C.**

21. Anticipated monetary policy cannot reduce unemployment. **Answer: A.**

22. According to real business cycle theory, fluctuations in aggregate demand do not cause business-cycle fluctuations. **Answer: B.**

23. According to most economists, discretionary monetary policy cannot be used to fight recession. **Answer: B.**

Answers to Problems and Exercises

1. This classical model of the price level held that the economy, if it was in a recession, would self-correct and return to the natural rate of unemployment and the potential output level on its own. Keynes agreed with this assessment, but recognized that it might take time for the economy to return to this point: during the time that the economy failed to produce at the potential level of aggregate output, some people would be without jobs. Keynes felt that waiting for the long run to arrive in a situation of recession was not the only option: active government intervention in the form of fiscal and monetary policy could help smooth out business cycles. Keynes, by his emphasis on the short run and his use of an upward-sloping aggregate supply curve, was able to provide a model of the economy that illustrated the importance of the short run as well as the potential efficacy of fiscal and monetary policy in addressing business cycle fluctuations.

2. Prior to the Great Depression, the prevailing economic wisdom was that economies tended to full employment of their resources and that any change in the money supply would only result in changes to the aggregate price level, and not changes to the aggregate output level. The classical model of the price level based its analysis on a vertical-aggregate supply curve for both the short run and the long run. With the onset of the Great Depression, economists found their conventional view of the macroeconomy tested: economists were forced to reconsider their model and to question the wisdom of using a model that emphasized only price level fluctuations, without regard to the possibility of aggregate output fluctuations. Thus, Keynes developed a model that considered the impact on the macroeconomy of a upward-sloping aggregate supply curve in the short run: such a model could model economic recessions and could also offer policy prescriptions for a depressed economy in the form of activist fiscal and monetary policy.

After Keynes's work, other economists entered the discussion to question the limits of macroeconomic policy activism. In particular, Friedman revived interest in monetary policy, and his work led to a recognition that management of the economy could be shifted away from fiscal policy and toward monetary policy. This work meant that macroeconomics could be a more technical, less political, issue.

The modern consensus reflects debate and study of macroeconomic issues. The modern consensus agrees that fiscal policy and monetary policy can each be effective in fighting recessions, but are unable to reduce unemployment in the long run. This consensus represents a melding of elements from both the classical model of the price level and Keynesian macroeconomics.

3. Keynes emphasized 1) the short-run effects of shifts in aggregate demand on aggregate output, rather than the long-run determination of the aggregate price level; and 2) that shifts in the aggregate demand curve could be caused by factors other than a change in the money supply. These other factors were lumped together as "animal spirits," or business confidence: Keynes emphasized that changes in business confidence were the primary causes of business cycles in the economy. Therefore, Keynes modeled the economy as having a upward-sloping short-run aggregate supply curve with a shifting aggregate demand curve. Thus, if the aggregate demand curve shifted to the left, this would lead the economy in the short run to experience, not only falling price levels but also falling aggregate output and higher levels of unemployment. The following graph illustrates this idea.

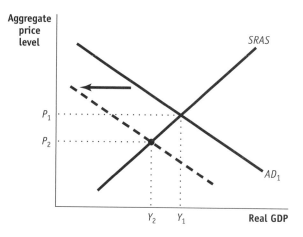

In contrast, the classical view held to a vertical aggregate supply curve (for both the short run and the long run) and thus, a shift in aggregate demand would alter the aggregate price level, but not the aggregate output level. The figure below illustrates this idea.

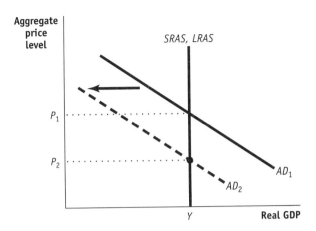

Keynes reasoned that activist fiscal and monetary policy could be used to offset these shifts in the aggregate demand curve, thus keeping the economy at its initial equilibrium. In fact, a failure to engage in activist policy could potentially cause the economy to operate in a recession or depression: Keynes provided a very strong justification for the role of government policy in reducing or eliminating business cycles.

4. The new classical macroeconomic model reverted to the classical view that the short-run aggregate supply curve was vertical: this implies that shifts in aggregate demand alter the aggregate price level, but do not affect the level of aggregate output. The new classical macroeconomic model based its conclusions on two arguments: rational expectations and real business cycle theory.

Rational expectations is the view that individuals and firms make their decisions based upon all available information, and people will therefore take into account not only historical information, but also government intentions with regard to future policy. Thus, any attempt by the government to trade off higher inflation in the short run in order to attain lower levels of unemployment will be noticed by individuals and firms, and this information will be included in the decision-making process. The new classical macroeconomics concludes that government policy to change the level of unemployment can only be effective if it is a surprise: this means that the government no longer can pursue intentionally policies to change the unemployment rate, since people will perceive their intent and act in a manner that eliminates the policy's effectiveness.

Real business cycle theory holds that fluctuations in the rate of growth of total factor productivity cause the business cycle. Rather than looking to shifts in aggregate demand as the cause of business cycle fluctuations (the Keynesian approach), the real business cycle theorists explained economic fluctuations as the result of variation in the rate of growth of total factor productivity. Subsequent research notes a strong correlation between growth rates of factor productivity and the business cycle, but does not identify the direction of causation.

5. Discretionary fiscal policy is rejected as a policy tool by many macroeconomists, because they view it as often counterproductive due to the existence of lags in the implementation and effectiveness of this policy. They argue that by the time the discretionary fiscal policy is implemented and takes effect, the economy is often no longer struggling with the particular economic conditions the fiscal policy was intended to address. In addition, there is concern that the use of discretionary fiscal policy may contribute to greater business cycle fluctuations due to the political business cycle. These economists view the use of discretionary fiscal policy as having a limited role: they advocate its use when monetary policy is ineffective (in the case of the liquidity trap).

6. Central banks, through monetary policy, exert strong influences on the macroeconomy. When a country's central bank is not politically independent, policymakers can adopt inflationary monetary policies that wreck economic havoc. Typically, this havoc is the result of excessive growth of the money supply. When a central bank is politically independent, it can maintain more appropriate money supply growth rates, thereby avoiding high levels of inflation and the resultant economic problems this inflation can cause.

7. a. The Keynesian macroeconomist would explain the recession using an *AD/AS* diagram like the one depicted in the following graph.

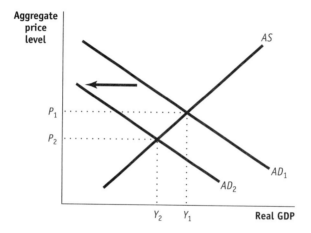

Output, *Y*, has fallen below its potential output level of Y_1 because of a shift in aggregate demand. The current level of production, Y_2, results in a higher level of unemployment. The Keynesian macroeconomist explains the cause of this leftward shift in aggregate demand as a change in "animal spirits," or a decline in business confidence. To remedy the situation, this economist proposes macroeconomic policy activism: the use of monetary and fiscal policy. In this case this policy should be directed at shifting the aggregate demand curve back to the right so that aggregate output can return to its initial level of Y_1.

b. The monetarist advisor would utilize the same diagram as the Keynesian economist to depict the fall in aggregate output. However, the monetarist would caution that expansionary fiscal policy would not restore the economy to Y_1 if the money supply is held constant. The monetarist reasons that the increase in spending (or decrease in taxes) by the government while stimulating aggregate demand will also stimulate money demand. With no change in the money supply this increase in money demand will cause interest rates to rise: the rise in interest rates will crowd out investment spending so that the increase in spending due to the change in fiscal policy will be offset by an equal decrease in investment spending. The monetarist would therefore emphasize the inability of expansionary fiscal policy to address and correct the recession. The monetarist would advise steady growth of the money supply in order to generate steady growth of aggregate output.

c. This third advisor could also use the diagram in part (a) to explain the decline in aggregate output. This economist would assert that expansionary monetary policy could be used to shift the aggregate demand curve back to the right provided the economy was not operating in a liquidity trap. This economist would also advise that expansionary fiscal policy could also be used to shift the aggregate demand curve to the right.

8. Consider the classical macro model and answer "yes" or "no" to the following questions. [Answers in **bold** letters]
   a. Is the economy competitive? **Yes**
   b. Can there be a prolonged recession? **No**
   c. Is the labour market competitive? **Yes**
   d. Is labour supply a function of real wage? **Yes**
   e. If price doubles, does the wage rate double? **Yes**
   f. If price decreases by 10%, does the wage rate decrease by 10%? **Yes**
   g. If M doubles, does V change? **No**
   h. If M doubles, does P double? **Yes**
   i. Is the policy multiplier zero? **Yes**
   j. Do changes in nominal variables affect real variables? **No**

9. Consider the Keynesian macro model and answer "yes" or "no" to the following questions. [Answers in **bold** letters]
   a. Is the economy competitive? **No**
   b. Can there be a prolonged recession? **Yes**
   c. Is the labour market competitive? **No**
   d. Is the labour supply a function of real wage? **No**
   e. If price doubles, does the wage rate double? **No**
   f. If price decreases by 10%, does the wage rate decrease by 10%? **No**
   g. If M doubles, does V change? **Yes**
   h. If M doubles, does P double? **No**
   i. Is the policy multiplier zero? **No**
   j. Do changes in nominal variables affect real variables? **Yes**

10. Assume an economy with recession with liquidity trap. Circle the correct choice of the following. [Answers in **bold** letters]
    a. Expansionary monetary policy **has no effect** on the interest rate. Expansionary monetary policy **has no effect** on real GDP.
    b. Expansionary fiscal policy can **have no effect** on the interest rate. Expansionary fiscal policy has **zero** crowding-out effect. Expansionary fiscal policy can **increase** real GDP.

chapter 18

International Trade

The basis for mutually beneficial international trade is the theory of comparative advantage. A country has comparative advantage in producing a good for which the country has relatively lower opportunity cost. The main sources of comparative advantage are: factor endowments, differences in climate and technology. Why a country has a comparative advantage (lower opportunity costs) in a given good is explained by the Heckscher-Ohlin model, which states that a country has a comparative advantage in a good that uses factors that are relatively more abundant. Gains from trade are explained with the two-country Ricardian constant-cost model. We study trade protection, tariff, and quota, and see the deadweight loss. The arguments for and against trade protection are highlighted in this chapter. We end the chapter with discussions on trade agreements, NAFTA and WTO.

How Well Do You Understand the Chapter?

Fill in the blanks using the terms below to complete the following statements. Terms may be used more than once. If you find yourself having difficulties, please refer back to the appropriate section in the text.

abundant	economic policies	income gap	quota rents
advantage	economies of scale	increase	ratio
agreements	encourage	increasing returns	rise
autark	export	infant industry	scarce
capital	factor endoments	intensive	straight line
capital-intensive	fall	international	tariff
climate	foreign	labour-intensive	technology
comparative	free trade	licenses	temporary
constant	gains	lower	total surplus
deadweight	higher	lowered	trade
decrease	highly educated	new jobs	trade agreements
discourage	import-competing	physical	trade protection
differs	imported	price takers	world
domestic	import quotas	quantity	

1. Most nations engage in _____; their residents produce goods that are sold (exported) to residents of other nations, and they import goods and services that were produced in other nations. Exports and imports have grown tremendously over the last few decades. Nations trade because there are _____ from trade, and these gains arise from _____. A country has a comparative advantage in producing a good if the opportunity cost of producing the good is _____ for that country than for other

427

countries. As long as the opportunity cost of producing goods _____ among countries, there is a basis for trade.

2. The Ricardian model of international trade analyzes international trade under the assumption that the opportunity costs are _____ and the production possibility frontier is a(n) _____. From it, we can see that total consumption in countries will be _____ with trade than in autarky (when a nation does not engage in any trade).

3. There are three main sources of comparative advantage: international differences in climate, international differences in _____, and international differences in technology.

   • Differences in _____ explain why many tropical nations export products such as coffee, sugar, and bananas, while countries in temperate zones export goods such as wheat and corn.

   • The Heckscher-Ohlin model of international trade focuses on differences in _____ to explain trade. According to this model, a nation has comparative advantage in a good whose production is _____ _____ in the factors of production that are _____ in that nation. Factor intensity of production compares the _____ of factors used to produce a good; clothing production is labour-intensive, while oil production is _____ _____ intensive.

   • Japan's success in exporting cars during the 1970s and 1980s seems to be the result of differences in _____. Improvements in technology in Japan _____ the opportunity cost of producing cars, giving the Japanese a comparative advantage in automobile production.

4. Another reason for international trade lies in the role of increasing returns. The production of a good is characterized by _____ if the productivity of labour and other resources rises with the level of production. Increasing returns are known as _____, and they also can give rise to monopolies because they give large firms an advantage over small ones.

5. Leontief found that contrary to the Heckscher-Ohlin model, the United States imported more _____ goods than it exported, something known as the Leontief paradox. The paradox was resolved by understanding that Leontief measured capital as just _____ capital. When human capital was included in the definition of capital, the United States did export capital-intensive goods and imported _____ goods.

6. We can also look at trade using the supply and demand model. In autarky, _____ demand (quantity demanded by domestic consumers) and _____ supply (quantity supplied by domestic producers) determine equilibrium price and output. Once we open the economy to trade, we assume that domestic consumers and domestic producers can buy or sell as much of the good on the world market as they want without affecting the _____ price, the price at which that good can be bought or sold on the world market. Domestic consumers and domestic producers are _____ in the world market.

7. If the world price is lower than the domestic _____ price when the economy opens to trade, the price in the domestic market will _____ to the level of the world price and domestic consumers will begin to purchase foreign-produced goods (imports). Domestic producers will sell _____ and earn smaller _____, while domestic consumers will buy _____ and earn a larger _____. With trade, the _____ in the market increase. The gain of consumer surplus to domestic consumers is _____ than loss of producer surplus to domestic producers.

8. If the world price is higher than the domestic autarky price when the economy opens to trade, the price in the domestic market will _____ to that of the world price and domestic producers will begin to _____ the good. Domestic producers will sell _____ and earn a _____ producer surplus, while domestic consumers will buy _____ and earn a _____ consumer surplus. With trade, the total surplus in the market will increase; the gain of producer surplus to domestic producers is _____ than the loss of consumer surplus to domestic consumers.

9. According to the Heckscher-Ohlin model, a nation has a comparative advantage in producing the good that is _____ in the factor that is abundant in that country. As a nation specializes in the good that is intensive in the factor that is _____, the demand for that factor increases and the price of that factor will _____; as the nation reduces the production of the good that is intensive in the factor that is _____, the demand for that factor will _____ along with the price of the scarce factor. This may explain some of the widening of the _____ between Canada and developing countries. Canada and other developed countries have a comparative advantage in goods and services that require a(n) _____ workforce; those workers already have higher wages than less-educated workers, and the effect of trade tends to increase the disparity of wages.

10. An economy engages in _____ when the government does not attempt either to reduce or to increase the levels of exports and imports that occur as a result of supply and demand. Although most economists advocate free trade, many governments have instituted policies that limit imports, known as _____, Common protectionist measures are tariffs and _____.

11. A(n) _____ is an excise tax levied on imports. Although at one time tariffs were imposed because they were an easy source of government revenue, they are used today to _____ imports and protect import-competing domestic producers. The tariff will increase the market price, domestic producers will produce _____. Imports will fall, producer surplus will _____, consumer surplus will _____, and the government will raise revenue from the tariff. However, the gain to domestic producers and the government is _____ than the loss of consumer surplus. The tariff generates a(n) _____ loss for society.

12. An import quota is a legal limit on the _____ of a good that can be imported and is usually administered through _____ that can give the license holder the right to import a limited quantity each year. We saw in Chapter 4 that the import quota has the same effect as a(n) _____, with the exception of the quota rent. An import quota can limit imports of the good to the same level as a tariff; the difference is that rather than raising revenue for the government, the import quota provides _____ to the holders of the import licenses. The government could charge for the licenses and raise the same revenue as does an import tariff, but in Canada the economic rent goes to the license holder.

13. Three arguments put forth to justify trade protection are national security, job creation, and the _____ argument. The national security argument asserts that we need to protect the industries producing goods that may be vulnerable to disruption in time of _____ conflict. Others argue that by protecting some industries we can create _____ in import-competing industries. The infant-industry argument holds that new industries require a _____ period of trade protection to get established.

14. The primary reason for trade protection seems to be the political power of _____ producers. Tariffs and import quotas _____ producer surplus and _____ consumer surplus. Domestic producers of a good are usually fewer in number, easier to organize, and wield _____ political influence than do the domestic consumers.

15. Nations have attempted to pursue the goal and benefits of free trade through international trade _____. Through them, a nation agrees to engage in

_____ trade protection against the exports of other countries in return for a promise by other countries to do the same for its own exports. Some agreements are between just two or three nations, such as the North American Free Trade Agreement (NAFTA), while others cover most nations of the world. The World Trade Organization (WTO) oversees global trade agreements. It provides the framework for the negotiations involved in major international _____, and it resolves _____ disputes between member nations of WTO.

Learning Tips

TIP #1: In the two-good, two-nation Ricardian model, we can identify which nation has a comparative advantage in a good by comparing the slopes of the production possibility frontiers.

The Ricardian model of international trade assumes that the opportunity costs are constant and not increasing, as we discussed in Chapter 2. The nation whose production possibility frontier has the flatter slope has a comparative advantage in the good measured on the horizontal axis. We see the gains from trade because nations can consume outside their production possibility frontier. Let's look at a hypothetical example of the trade of airplanes and oil between Mexico and Canada. Figures 18.1 and 18.2 show the annual production possibility frontiers for airplanes and oil in Mexico and in Canada.

Figure 18.1

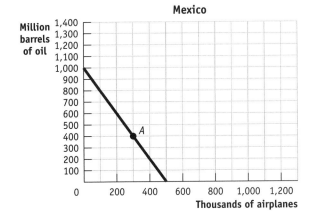

Figure 18.2

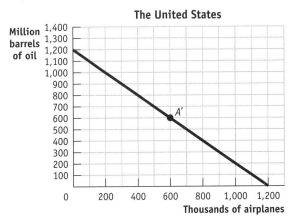

In autarky, Mexico would produce and consume 300 thousand airplanes and 400 million barrels of oil (point _A_ in Figure 18.1) and Canada would produce 600 thousand airplanes and 600 million barrels of oil (point _A'_ in Figure 18.2). The opportunity cost of producing 500 thousand airplanes in Mexico is 1,000 million barrels of oil, or 2 million barrels of oil for each 1 thousand airplanes. In Canada, the opportunity cost of producing 1,200 thousand airplanes is 1,200 million barrels of oil, or 1 million barrels of oil for 1 thousand airplanes. The opportunity cost of producing airplanes in Canada is lower than in Mexico; Canada has a comparative advantage in airplanes and Mexico has a comparative advantage in oil. The opportunity cost of airplanes (how much oil do we have to give up to get 1 thousand airplanes) is the slope of the production possibility frontier. Since the production possibility frontier is flatter for Canada, Canada must have a comparative advantage in airplanes.

If each nation specializes in the good in which it has a comparative advantage, Canada specializes in producing airplanes and Mexico specializes in producing oil; Canada will produce 1,200 thousand airplanes (point B' in Figure 18.4) and Mexico will produce 1,000 million barrels of oil (point B in Figure 18.3). If each nation agreed to trade 600 million barrels of oil for 400 thousand airplanes (a rate of trade of 3 million barrels of oil for 2 thousand airplanes), Mexico could consume at point C and Canada at C' in Figures 18.3 and 18.4. Each nation gains from trade because points C and C' lie outside each nation's production possibility frontier.

Figure 18.3

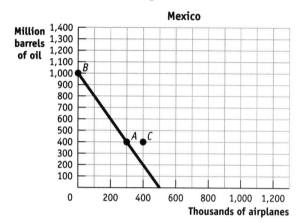

Figure 18.4

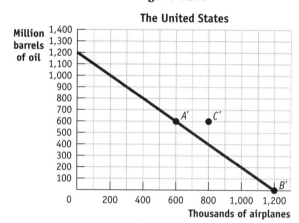

TIP #2: When looking at a domestic market, the increase in total surplus that results when the good is imported (the domestic price in autarky is higher than the world price) or exported (the domestic price in autarky is higher than the world price) represents the gains from trade.

Figure 18.5 shows the domestic demand and domestic supply of peaches. If there were no trade in peaches, the price in the market would be P_A, and Q_A would be exchanged. Consumer surplus would be F and producer surplus would be $G + H$. If the market is opened to trade and the world price of peaches is P_W, the price in the domestic market will fall to P_W. Domestic producers will sell Q_1 units of peaches, domestic consumers will purchase C_1, and the difference between C_1 and Q_1 represents the volume of imported peaches. At P_W, consumers will enjoy a surplus of $F + G + J + K$; domestic producer surplus will fall to just H. Consumers still get their original surplus (F), plus part of producer surplus in autarky is transferred to the consumer (G), and in addition they receive $J + K$. Total surplus has increased by $J + K$. Producers are hurt by the imports, but the gain to consumers more than makes up for the producers' loss. Table 18.1 summarizes the gains and losses of consumer, producer, and total surplus.

Figure 18.5

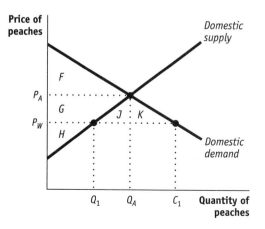

Table 18.1

	At $P = P_A$	At $P = P_W$	Net gain/loss
Consumer surplus	F	$F + G + J + K$	$+ (G + J + K)$
Producer surplus	$G + H$	H	$- G$
Total surplus	$F + G + H$	$F + G + H + J + K$	$+ (J + K)$

Figure 18.6 shows the domestic demand and domestic supply of coffee beans. If there were no trade in coffee beans, the price in the market would be P_A and Q_A would be exchanged. Consumer surplus would be $R + S + T$ and producer surplus would be $U + V$. If the market is opened to trade and the world price of coffee beans is P_W, the price in the domestic market will rise to P_W. Domestic producers will sell Q_1 units of coffee beans, domestic consumers will purchase C_1, and the difference between C_1 and Q_1 will be the volume of exported coffee beans. At P_W, consumers will only have a surplus of R; producer surplus will increase to $S + T + U + V + W$. Producers still get their original surplus ($U + V$), plus part of consumer surplus in autarky is transferred to the producers ($S + T$), and in addition they receive W. Total surplus has increased by W. Consumers are hurt by the exports, but the gain to producers more than makes up for the consumers' loss. Table 18.2 summarizes the gains and losses to consumer, producer, and total surplus.

Figure 18.6

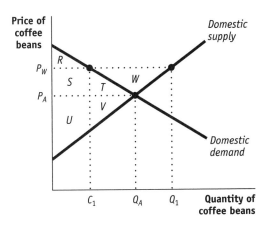

Table 18.2

	At $P = P_A$	At $P = P_W$	Net gain/loss
Consumer surplus	$R + S + T$	R	$- (S + T)$
Producer surplus	$U + V$	$S + T + U + V + W$	$+ (S + T + W)$
Total surplus	$R + S + T + U + V$	$R + S + T + U + V + W$	$+ W$

TIP #3: When the government levies a tariff on an import, there is a deadweight loss.

The tariff, like an excise tax, discourages some mutually beneficial trades, and this creates an excess burden for society. Figure 18.7 shows the market for peaches again. Starting from a position of free trade, we want to analyze the effects of an import tariff. A tariff will increase the price of the good received by the producers and paid by the consumers while decreasing imports. When the government levies the tariff, the price of peaches rises to P_T from P_W; before the tariff, imports equaled $C_1 - Q_1$, and after the tariff imports fell to $C_2 - Q_2$. Table 18.3 shows the gains and losses to consumer surplus, producer surplus, total surplus, and government revenue due to the tariff.

Figure 18.7

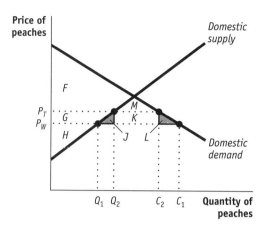

Table 18.3

	At $P = P_W$	At $P = P_T$	Net gain/loss
Consumer surplus	$F + G + J + K + L + M$	$F + M$	$- (G + J + K + L)$
Producer surplus	H	$G + H$	$+ G$
Government		K	$+ K$
Society	$F + G + H + J + K + L + M$	$F + G + H + K + M$	$- (J + L)$

Consumers are worse off because of the tariff; consumer surplus falls by $G + J + K + L$. Producers are better off; producer surplus rises by part of the loss in consumer surplus, G. The government raises K in revenue from the tariff. However, the loss of $J + L$ from consumer surplus is not gained by anyone. This is the deadweight loss associated with the tariff.

TIP #4: An import quota can achieve the same reduction in imports as a tariff but the loss to society may be much larger.

An import quota is a legal limit on the quantity of a good that can be imported. The government usually administers a quota by issuing licenses that give the holders a right to import a particular quantity of a good each year. By limiting the quantity that can be imported, the government creates a quota rent for the license holders. Figure 18.8 shows the effect of a quota in the market for peaches that limits total imports to $Q_2 - C_2$. The price in the domestic market will rise to P_T. Table 18.4 summarizes the gains and losses to consumer, producer, and total surplus due to the quota.

Figure 18.8

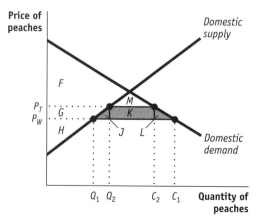

Table 18.4

	At $P = P_W$	At $P = P_T$	Net gain/loss
Consumer surplus	$F + G + J + K + L + M$	$F + M$	$-(G + J + K + L)$
Producer surplus	H	$G + H$	$+G$
Society	$F + G + H + J + K + L + M$	$F + G + H + M$	$-(J + K + L)$

The loss to the domestic economy from the quota is larger than the loss from the import tariff. The government can attempt to minimize the loss by selling the import licenses for a total amount equal to K.

Multiple-Choice Questions

1. The economy of Westlandia can produce 100 units of cotton if it produces no tractors, or 25 tractors and no cotton; the economy of Eastlandia can produce 80 units of cotton if it produces no tractors, or 10 tractors and no cotton. There would be gains from trade if
   a. Westlandia specialized in the production of tractors and Eastlandia specialized in cotton.
   b. Westlandia specialized in the production of cotton and Eastlandia specialized in tractors.
   c. Westlandia specialized in the production of both tractors and cotton.
   d. Eastlandia specialized in the production of both tractors and cotton.

2. In the Ricardian model of international trade, the production possibility frontiers
   a. are convex to the origin.
   b. are straight lines.
   c. show increasing opportunity costs of production.
   d. show decreasing opportunity costs of production.

Use the following figures to answer the next two questions. The figures show the production possibility frontiers for Finland and Germany. Assume that in autarky, Finland produces 500 thousand phones and 175 thousand cars and Germany produces 600 thousand phones and 200 thousand cars.

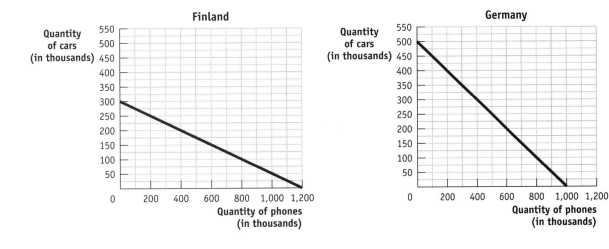

3. Refer to the figures on the proceeding page. The opportunity cost of a phone in Finland is _____ of a car, while the opportunity cost of a phone in Germany is _____.
   a. $1/2$; 2
   b. 4; $1/2$
   c. $1/4$; $1/2$
   d. 4; $1/4$

4. Refer to the figures on on the proceeding page. When the two countries specialize in the production of the good in which they have a comparative advantage, total production of phones will increase by _____ thousand and total production of cars will increase by _____ thousand.
   a. 100; 100
   b. 100; 125
   c. 1,200; 500
   d. 1,200; 1,000

5. The primary source of Saudi Arabia's comparative advantage in oil production is
   a. climate.
   b. factor endowments.
   c. technology.
   d. increasing returns.

6. Trade in manufactured goods between advanced countries probably is based on
   a. differences in climate.
   b. differences in factor endowments.
   c. differences in technology.
   d. increasing returns.

7. According to the Heckscher-Ohlin model of international trade, nations that are abundant in _____ will have a comparative advantage in producing goods that are intensive in the use of _____ in the production process.
   a. capital; labor
   b. labor; capital
   c. capital; capital
   d. None of the above.

8. The Leontief paradox is that in 1951 Canada exported mostly _____ goods and imported _____ goods, in conflict with the Heckscher-Ohlin model. The solution to the paradox was to include _____ in the definition of capital.
   a. labor-intensive; capital-intensive; oil
   b. capital-intensive; labor-intensive; oil
   c. capital-intensive; labor-intensive; human capital
   d. labor-intensive; capital-intensive; human capital

9. As nations specialize in the good in which they have a comparative advantage and trade, we expect the wages of the abundant factor to _____ and of the scarce factor to _____.
   a. increase; increase
   b. decrease; decrease
   c. increase; decrease
   d. decrease; increase

Use the accompanying figure to answer the next two questions. The figure shows the domestic market for soybeans in Westlandia.

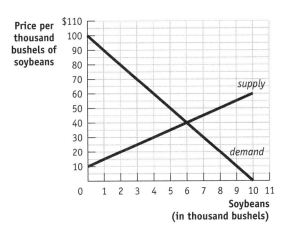

10. If the world price of soybeans is $50 per thousand bushels, domestic producers in Westlandia will produce _____ thousand bushels of soybeans, domestic consumers will buy _____ thousand bushels of them, and the difference between quantity demanded and quantity supplied represents Westlandia's

_____.

a. 6; 3; exports
b. 4; 3; imports
c. 2; 8; imports
d. 8; 5; exports

11. If the world price of soybeans is $20 per thousand bushels, domestic producers in Westlandia will produce _____ thousand bushels of soybeans, domestic consumers will buy _____ thousand bushels of them, and the difference between quantity demanded and quantity supplied represents Westlandia's

_____.

a. 6; 3; exports
b. 4; 3; imports
c. 2; 8; imports
d. 8; 5; exports

Use the following figure to answer the next three questions. The figure shows the domestic market for soybeans in Eastlandia.

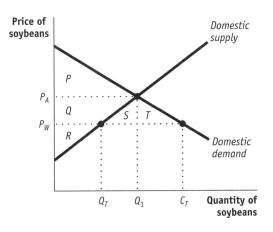

12. In autarky the price of soybeans in Eastlandia is P_A, and the world price is P_W. If Eastlandia opens to trade, consumer surplus will _____ to _____.

a. decrease; P
b. increase; $P + Q$
c. decrease; $P + Q + S$
d. increase; $P + Q + S + T$

13. In autarky the price of soybeans in Eastlandia is P_A, and the world price is P_W. If Eastlandia opens to trade, producer surplus will _____ to _____.

a. decrease; R
b. increase; $R + Q$
c. decrease; $R + Q + S$
d. increase; $R + Q + S + T$

14. When Eastlandia opens its soybean market to trade, the net gain to total surplus is represented by
a. $S + T$.
b. $Q + S + T$.
c. $Q + R + S + T$.
d. $P + Q + R + S + T$.

15. International trade may be a factor in the increased wage inequality in Canada because this nation is abundant in _____ and specializes in goods that are intensive in this factor. In this way, the wages of _____ workers, who have relatively high wages, rise, and the wages of _____ workers fall.
a. land; farm; nonfarm
b. human capital; highly educated; less-educated
c. physical capital; manufacturing; service
d. physical capital; unionized; nonunionized

Answer the next four questions using the accompanying figure. The figure shows the domestic market for soybeans in Eastlandia with a world price of P_W when the government has imposed a tariff that increased the price of soybeans to P_T.

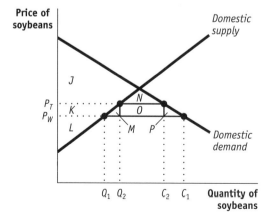

16. When Eastlandia imposes a tariff that raises the price of soybeans to P_T, imports of soybeans will fall from
   a. C_1 to C_2.
   b. Q_2 to Q_1.
   c. $C_1 - Q_1$ to $C_2 - Q_2$.
   d. $C_2 - Q_2$ to $C_1 - Q_1$.

17. When Eastlandia imposes a tariff that raises the price of soybeans to P_T, the net loss to total surplus is
   a. N.
   b. $M + P$.
   c. $M + N + P$.
   d. $M + N + O + P$.

18. Eastlandia could have reduced imports to the same level with an import quota as it did with a tariff. Eastlandia could have issued licenses to import _____ units of imports.
   a. C_2
   b. Q_2
   c. $C_1 - Q_1$
   d. $C_2 - Q_2$

19. Assuming that the quota rents from the tariff go to foreigners, the net loss to total surplus of the quota will be
   a. N.
   b. $M + P$.
   c. $M + O + P$.
   d. $M + N + O + P$.

20. Which of the following arguments to protect an industry from trade do economists find lacking validity?
   a. During wartime, a particular industry is essential for economic stability.
   b. If we limit imports, we can increase the number of jobs in our country.
   c. Industries need some time to establish themselves before competing on world markets.
   d. Both a and b lack validity.

21. Which of the following international organizations rules on disputes concerning global trade agreements?
   a. North American Free Trade Agreement
   b. The European Union
   c. The World Trade Organization
   d. none of the above

22. Importing Bangladeshi cotton shirts will cause all of the following benefits **except**
   a. Canadian consumers will benefit due to lower prices.
   b. the opportunity cost of shirts will be relatively less in Canada.
   c. the average productivity of Canadian workers will increase.
   d. the standard of living in Canada will increase.

Use the accompanying table on the following page to answer questions 23–25.

Assume constant cost.

One hour of labour can produce the following goods in Canada and Mexico.

Country	Wine	Beer
Canada	10 bottles	10 bottles
Mexico	2 bottles	4 bottles

23. Which of the following statements is true?
   a. The opportunity cost of 1 bottle of wine in Canada is 10 bottles of beer.
   b. The opportunity cost of 1 bottle of wine in Mexico is 4 bottles of beer.
   c. The opportunity cost of 1 bottle of beer in Mexico is 0.5 bottles of wine.
   d. The opportunity of 1 bottle of beer in Canada is –1 bottle of wine.

24. Canada has comparative advantage in
   a. both wine and beer.
   b. wine.
   c. beer.
   d. neither good.

25. Mexico has comparative advantage in
   a. both wine and beer.
   b. wine.
   c. beer.
   d. neither good.

26. According to the Heckscher-Ohlin model, Canada
   a. imports more labour-intensive goods.
   b. imports more capital-intensive goods.
   c. exports more labour-intensive goods.
   d. has comparative advantages in all goods that Canada produces.

27. If Ontario imposes a tariff on Chilean wine, the price of Chilean wine in Ontario
   will _____ and the production of wine in the Niagra Region will

   _____.
   a. increase; increase
   b. increase; decrease
   c. decrease; decrease
   d. decrease; increase

28. If Canada is a price-taker in the world-market and if the world price increases,
   a. the total surplus in Canada will increase.
   b. the total surplus in Canada will decrease.
   c. the total surplus in Canada may increase or decrease.
   d. the quantity of output in Canada will not change.

29. One of the arguments for trade protection is that
   a. we need to protect the industries producing goods that may be vulnerable to disruption in time of international conflict.
   b. trade protection increases the economic welfare of a nation.
   c. trade protection increases competition in the domestic market.
   d. trade protection benefits consumers.

30. NAFTA has failed in all the following **except**
   a. it reduced economic welfare and reduced productivity.
   b. it led to some employment losses in Canada.
   c. it failed to exclude Canada's water resources.
   d. it failed to protect publicly-provided Medicare in Canada.

Problems and Exercises

Read each question carefully and then write your answers in the space provided or on a separate sheet of paper.

1. Assume that Canada and China face the production possibility frontiers shown in the following tables for lumber and toys.

Canada

Toys (in millions)	Lumber (in millions of board feet)
0	300
1	250
2	200
3	150
4	100
5	50
6	0

China

Toys (in millions)	Lumber (in millions of board feet)
0	200
2	160
4	120
6	80
8	40
9	20
10	0

a. What is the opportunity cost of producing toys in Canada? What is the opportunity cost of producing toys in China? Which nation has a comparative advantage in producing toys? Which nation has a comparative advantage in producing lumber?

b. Plot the production possibility frontiers for Canada and China in the following figures. What are the slopes of the production possibility frontiers? Which nation has the flatter slope? Does that nation have a comparative advantage in toys (the good measured on the horizontal axis)? How does this answer compare with your answer to part a above?

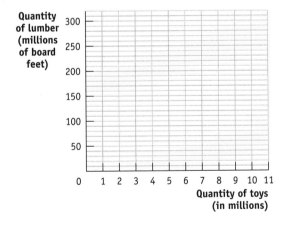

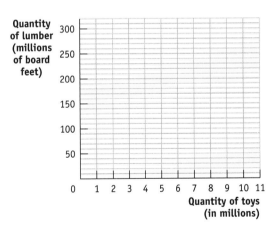

c. Suppose in autarky Canada produces 3 million toys and 150 million board feet of lumber, while China produces 3 million toys and 140 million board feet of lumber. Show how, if each nation specializes in the good of its comparative advantage, total production of toys and lumber for the two nations together can increase.

d. Is it possible with trade for Canada to consume 5 million toys and 120 million board feet of lumber and China to consume 5 million toys and 180 million board feet of lumber? How do we know that both Canada and China gain from trade?

2. The accompanying table shows Canada's domestic demand and Canada's domestic supply schedules for peanuts. Plot the domestic demand and supply curves in the following figure.

Price per ton of peanuts	Quantity of peanuts demanded (in million tons)	Quantity of peanuts supplied (in million tons)
$0	4.5	0.0
100	4.0	1.0
200	3.5	2.0
300	3.0	3.0
400	2.5	4.0
500	2.0	5.0
600	1.5	6.0
700	1.0	7.0
800	0.5	8.0
900	0.0	9.0

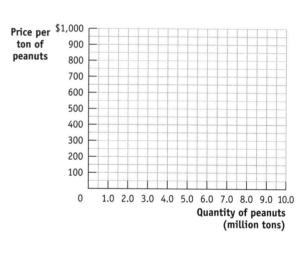

a. What would be the equilibrium price and quantity of peanuts in autarky?

b. If the world price of peanuts is $100 per ton and Canada opens the peanut market to trade, will Canada import or export peanuts? How many peanuts will Canadian producers sell? How many peanuts will Canadian consumers buy? What will be the volume of trade in peanuts? Label the preceding figure and complete the accompanying table to show the gains and losses to consumer, producer, and total surplus.

	In autarky	With trade	Net gain/loss
Consumer surplus	_____	_____	_____
Producer surplus	_____	_____	_____
Total surplus	_____	_____	_____

c. If the world price of peanuts is $600 per ton, will Canada import or export peanuts? How many peanuts will Canadian producers sell? How many peanuts will Canadian consumers buy? What will be the volume of trade in peanuts? Redraw domestic demand and supply curves in the following figure and label your figure to complete the following table to show the gains and losses to consumer, producer, and total surplus.

	In autarky	With trade	Net gain/loss
Consumer surplus	_____	_____	_____
Producer surplus	_____	_____	_____
Total surplus	_____	_____	_____

3. Continuing the peanut example in problem 2, suppose the world price of peanuts is $100 per ton. Fearful that many domestic peanut farmers will go out of business, the government imposes a tariff of an additional $100 per ton on peanuts. Once again draw the domestic demand and supply curves, and show the new price of peanuts in Canada's market.

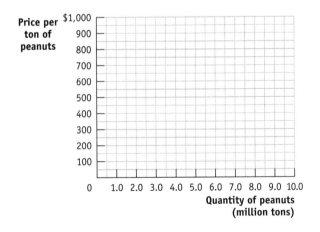

a. How much will domestic producers sell and domestic consumers buy?

b. What will be the volume of trade?

c. How much revenue from the tariff will the government receive?

d. Label your graph to show the deadweight loss from the tariff.

e. Could the government reduce imports to the same level using an import quota? What volume of imports should the government allow? How will consumer, producer, and total surplus with an import quota compare to that of a tariff?

4. The production possibility curves with two goods, *X and Y*, for Canada and Mexico are shown in the accompanying figure.

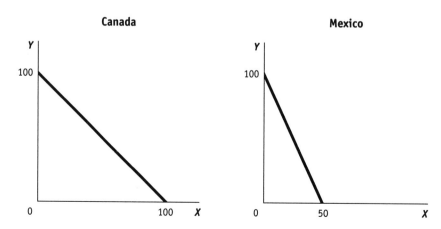

a. What is the opportunity cost of 100 units of good X in Canada? The opportunity cost of 1 unit of X?

b. What is the opportunity cost of 100 units of good Y in Canada? The opportunity cost of 1 unit of Y?

c. What is the opportunity cost of 50 units of good X in Mexico? The opportunity cost of 1 unit of X?

d. What is the opportunity cost of 100 units of good Y in Mexico? The opportunity cost of 1 unit of Y?

e. Which country has comparative advantage in which product? Why?

*5. Consider a price-taking economy with the following demand-supply functions.

$Q^D = 100 - P.$

$Q^S = P.$

a. What is the equilibrium price in autarky?

b. If the world price is $20, what is the amount of import into this economy? What is consumer surplus in this economy?

   c. Suppose the import quota is 30 units. What will be the equilibrium price in this economy? What will be domestic supply?

6. Evaluate the need for trade protection for the textile industry in Canada based on three arguments presented in this chapter.

7. Consider the following demand-supply curves of a small price-taking economy in the world trade market.

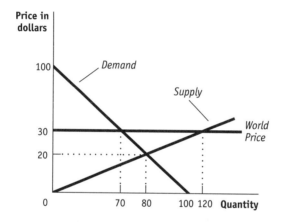

   a. What is the equilibrium price in autarky? Find the value of consumer surplus, producer surplus, and total surplus.

   b. If the world price is $30, what will be total export? Find the value of consumer surplus, producer surplus, and total surplus in this situation.

Answers to How Well Do You Understand the Chapter

1. trade, gains, comparative advantage, lower, differs

2. constant, straight line, higher

3. factor endowments, climate, factor endowments, intensive, abundant, ratio, capital, technology, lowered

4. increasing returns, economies of scale

5. capital-intensive, physical, labour-intensive

6. domestic, domestic, world, price-takers

7. autarky, fall, less, profit, more, consumer surplus, total surplus, larger

8. rise, export, more, greater, less, smaller, greater

9. intensive, abundant, rise, scarce, decrease, income-gap, highly educated

10. free trade, trade protection, import quotas

11. tariff, discourage, more, increase, decrease, less, deadweight

12. quantity, licenses, tariff, quota rent

13. infant industry, international, new jobs, temporary

14. import-competing, increase, decrease, more

15. agreements, less, trade agreements, trade

Answers to Multiple-Choice Questions

1. The opportunity cost of a tractor in Westlandia is 100 units of cotton for 25 tractors, or 4 units of cotton for 1 tractor. The opportunity cost of a tractor in Eastlandia is 80 units of cotton for 10 tractors, or 8 units of cotton for 1 tractor. It is cheaper to produce tractors in Westlandia. Westlandia has a comparative advantage in tractors, and Eastlandia has a comparative advantage in cotton. There will be gains from trade if Westlandia specialized in the production of tractors and Eastlandia specialized in cotton. **Answer: A.**

2. The Ricardian model of international trade assumes that the production possibility frontiers are straight lines. When this is true, the opportunity costs of production are constant. **Answer: B.**

3. Finland can produce 300 thousand cars and no phones, or 1,200 thousand phones and no cars; the opportunity cost of 300 thousand cars is 1,200 thousand phones, or $1/4$ of a car for 1 phone. Germany can produce 500 thousand cars and no phones, or 1,000 thousand phones and no cars; the opportunity cost of 500 thousand cars is 1,000 thousand phones, or $1/2$ of a car for 1 phone. **Answer: C.**

4. In autarky, Finland and Germany produced 1,100 thousand phones and 375 thousand cars combined. With specialization in production, they will produce 1,200 thousand phones and 500 thousand cars. Phone production increases by 100 thousand and car production increases by 125 thousand. **Answer: B.**

5. The primary source of Saudi Arabia's comparative advantage in oil production is its factor endowment. Saudi Arabia has one-fourth of the world's known oil reserves. **Answer: B.**

6. Trade in developed countries can be explained by increasing returns. In the auto industry, both the United States and Canada produce automobiles and their components, but each tends to specialize in one model or component. **Answer: D.**

7. The Heckscher-Ohlin model states that a country has a comparative advantage in a good whose production is intensive in the factors that are abundantly available in that country. If a nation is abundant in capital, it will have a comparative advantage in producing capital-intensive goods. **Answer: C.**

8. The Leontief paradox is that the United States, a capital-abundant nation, appeared to export labor-intensive goods in 1951 while importing capital-intensive goods. Leontief, however, only considered physical capital in his definition of capital. When you include human capital with physical capital, the paradox no longer exists. **Answer: D.**

9. As nations specialize in the good in which they have a comparative advantage, they will demand more of the abundant factor, increasing its price, and less of the scarce factor, decreasing its price. **Answer: C.**

10. The following figure shows that at the world price of soybeans of $50 per thousand bushels, domestic producers will produce 8 thousand bushels of soybeans, domestic consumers will buy 5 thousand bushels, and 3 thousand bushels will be exported. **Answer: D.**

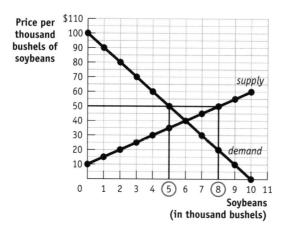

11. The accompanying figure shows that if soybeans are at a world price of $20 per thousand bushels, domestic producers will produce 2 thousand bushels of soybeans, domestic consumers will buy 8 thousand bushels, and 6 thousand bushels will be imported. **Answer: C.**

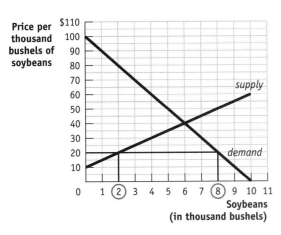

12. The following table summarizes the gains and losses to consumer, producer, and total surplus when the nation begins to trade. Consumer surplus increases to $P + Q + S + T$. **Answer: D.**

	In autarky	With trade	Net gain/loss
Consumer surplus	P	$P + Q + S + T$	$+ (Q + S + T)$
Producer surplus	$Q + R$	R	$- Q$
Total surplus	$P + Q + R$	$P + Q + R + S + T$	$+ (S + T)$

13. Again, the preceding table summarizes the gains and losses to consumer, producer, and total surplus when the nation begins to trade. Producer surplus decreases to R. **Answer: A.**

14. The preceding table shows the net gain to total surplus is $S + T$. **Answer: A.**

15. Increased wage inequality may be the result of Canada having a lot of human capital and specializing in goods that are human-capital-intensive. Wages of highly educated workers (workers with large investments in human capital) rise and wages of less-educated workers fall. **Answer: B.**

16. When Eastlandia imposes a tariff and the price of soybeans rises to P_T, imports will fall from $C_1 - Q_1$ to $C_2 - Q_2$. **Answer: C.**

17. The following table summarizes the gains and losses to consumer surplus, producer surplus, government revenue, and total surplus from the tariff. The net loss to total surplus is $M + P$. **Answer: B.**

	At $P = P_W$	At $P = P_T$	Net gain/loss
Consumer surplus	$J + K + M + N + O + P$	$J + N$	$- (K + M + O + P)$
Producer surplus	L	$K + L$	$+ K$
Government		O	$+ O$
Society	$J + K + L + M + N + O + P$	$J + K + L + N + O$	$- (M + P)$

18. If Eastlandia issued licenses to import $C_2 - Q_2$ units of imports, it would have reduced imports to the same level as did the tariff. **Answer: D.**

19. The accompanying table summarizes the gains and losses to consumer surplus, producer surplus, government revenue, and total surplus from the import quota. **Answer: C.**

	At $P = P_W$	At $P = P_T$	Net gain/loss
Consumer surplus	$J + K + M + N + O + P$	$J + N$	$-(K + M + O + P)$
Producer surplus	L	$K + L$	$+ K$
Government			
Society	$J + K + L + M + N + O + P$	$J + K + L + N + O$	$-(M + O + P)$

20. Economists believe that if job creation is the goal of trade protection, it will not achieve that goal. When a nation imposes a barrier to imports (a tariff or import quota), its trading partners will respond by doing the same. Although we may gain jobs in import-competing industries, we will lose jobs in the export industries. **Answer: B.**

21. The World Trade Organization rules on disputes between countries concerning global trade agreements. **Answer: C.**

22. The opportunity cost of producing shirts in Canada is relatively high and, as a result, Canada imports Bangladeshi shirts, leading to more consumers' benefits, economic welfare, and higher productivity. **Answer: B.**

23. Costs cannot be negative. The opportunity cost of 1 bottle of beer in Mexico is 0.5 bottles of wine. **Answer: C.**

24. The opportunity cost of 1 bottle of wine is 1 beer in Canada, and the opportunity cost of 1 bottle of wine is 2 bottles of beer in Mexico. Therefore, Canada has a comparative advantage in wine. **Answer: B.**

25. The opportunity cost of 1 bottle of beer is 1 bottle of wine in Canada, and the opportunity cost of 1 bottle of beer is 0.5 bottle of wine in Mexico. Therefore, Mexico has a comparative advantage in beer. **Answer: C.**

26. Canada imports labour-intensive goods. **Answer: A.**

27. A tariff will increase the wine price in Ontario, and there will more wine production in Ontario. **Answer: A.**

28. Even though a higher price will reduce consumer surplus, the gain in producer surplus will be greater than the loss of consumer surplus and as a result, the total surplus in Canada will increase. **Answer: A.**

29. Trade protection reduces competition, consumer surplus, and economic welfare. Protecting national security is one of the arguments for trade protection. **Answer: A.**

30. NAFTA has led to some employment losses, and it has failed to protect water resources and Medicare. However, NAFTA has led to more net economic welfare and more productivity. **Answer: A.**

Answers to Problems and Exercises

1. a. Canada can produce either 6 million toys and no lumber, or 300 million board feet of lumber and no toys. The opportunity cost of producing toys in Canada is 300 million board feet of lumber for 6 million toys, or 50 board feet of lumber for 1 toy. China can produce either 10 million toys and no lumber, or 200 million board feet of lumber and no toys. The opportunity cost of producing toys in China is 200 million board feet of lumber for 10 million toys, or 20 board feet of lumber for 1 toy. It is cheaper to produce toys in China; China has a comparative advantage in producing toys. Canada has a comparative advantage in producing lumber.

b. The following figures show the production possibility frontiers for Canada and China.

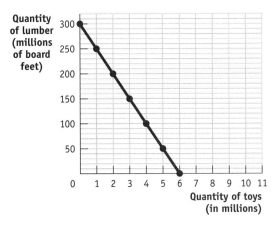
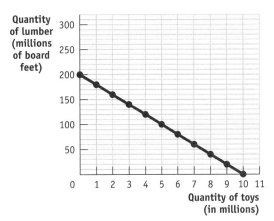

The slope of Canada's production possibility frontier is −50 and the slope of China's production possibility frontier is −20. The slopes are the opportunity costs of producing a toy in each country. China has the flatter slope and has a comparative advantage in toys, which is the good measured on the horizontal axis. Looking at the slopes gives us the same answers about opportunity costs as we found in part a.

c. In autarky, Canada and China jointly produce 6 million toys and 290 million board feet of lumber. If Canada specializes completely in the production of lumber, it can produce 300 million board feet of lumber, while China can produce 10 million toys if it just produces toys. If Canada and China specialize in the good of each's comparative advantage, total production of toys can increase by 4 million and production of lumber will increase by 10 million board feet.

d. If Canada produces 300 million board feet of lumber and trades 180 million to China for 5 million toys (exchanging 36 board feet of lumber for 1 toy), Canada will consume 5 million toys and 120 million board feet of lumber, while China will consume 5 million toys and 180 million board feet of lumber. Since each nation is able to consume outside its production possibility frontier, they both gain from trade.

2. The following figure shows Canada's domestic demand and supply curves for peanuts.

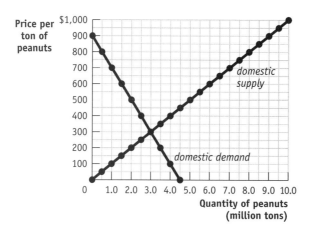

a. In autarky, the equilibrium price is $300 per ton and the equilibrium quantity is 3 million tons of peanuts.

b. If the world price is $100 per ton, Canada will import peanuts (domestic consumers will be attracted by the lower world price and buy peanuts on the world, rather than the domestic, market). Domestic producers will only sell 1 million tons of peanuts, consumers will buy 4 million tons, and 3 million tons will be imported. The following figure and table show the gains and losses to consumer, producer, and total surplus. (Your areas may be labeled differently.)

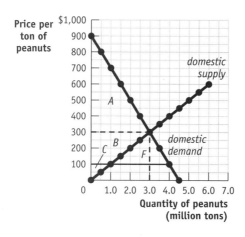

	In autarky	With trade	Net gain/loss
Consumer surplus	A	A + B + F	+ (B + F)
Producer surplus	B + C	C	– B
Total surplus	A + B + C	A + B + C + F	+ F

c. If the world price is $600 per ton, Canada will export peanuts (domestic produc-ers will be attracted by the higher world price and sell peanuts on the world, rather than the domestic, market). Domestic producers will sell 6 million tons of peanuts, consumers will buy 1.5 million tons, and 4.5 million tons will be exported. The following figure and table show the gains and losses to consumer, producer, and total surplus. (Your areas may be labeled differently.)

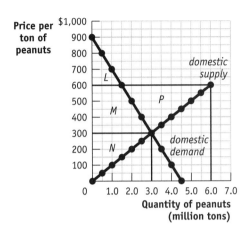

	In autarky	With trade	Net gain/loss
Consumer surplus	L + M	L	– M
Producer surplus	N	M + N + P	+ (M + P)
Total surplus	L + M + N	L + M + N + P	+ P

3. The accompanying figure shows the domestic market for peanuts with a world price of $100 and a tariff price of $100.

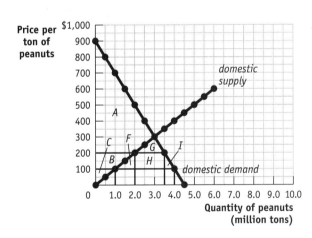

a. With the tariff, domestic producers will sell 2 million tons of peanuts and domestic consumers will buy 3.5 million tons of peanuts.

b. Imports will be 1.5 million tons of peanuts.

c. The government will receive $100 per ton for 1.5 million tons, or $150 million.

d. The deadweight loss from the tariff is F + I.

e. The government could reduce imports of peanuts to 1.5 million tons by only granting licenses to import 1.5 million. Consumer and producer surplus will be the same under a tariff or an import quota. However, the deadweight loss will be larger because there is no revenue to the government. The deadweight loss will be F + H + I.

4. a. The opportunity cost of 100 units of X is 100 units of Y. The opportunity cost of 1 unit of X is 1 unit of Y.

    b. The opportunity cost of 100 units of Y is 100 units of X. The opportunity cost of 1 unit of Y is 1 unit of X.

    c. The opportunity cost of 50 units of X is 100 units of Y. The opportunity cost of 1 unit of X is 2 units of Y.

    d. The opportunity cost of 100 units of Y is 50 units of X. The opportunity cost of 1 unit of Y is 0.5 units of X.

    e. Canada has comparative advantage in X, because the opportunity cost of 1 unit of X is lower. Mexico has comparative advantage in Y, because the opportunity cost of 1 unit of Y is lower.

5. a. Set $Q^D = Q^S$ and solve price in autarky as $50.

    b. At the world price of $20, $Q^D = 80$ and $Q^S = 20$. Therefore, the amount of import is $(80 - 20) = 60$.

    c. With import quota, the available supply in this economy is domestic supply plus 30 units. Therefore, set $100 - P = 30 + P$ and solve P as $35. At $35, the domestic supply is 35 units.

6. The three arguments for trade protection are: national defense, job creation, and the infant-industry argument. The national defense argument is not a valid reason to protect the textile industry in Canada. If we have trade protection for the textile industry, as in the job creation argument, we are supporting inefficient uses of labour in Canada, because the same goods can be produced elsewhere with cheaper costs. Efficient allocation of resources will result in Canada if we don't have trade protection. The infant-industry argument is inapplicable by virtue of the fact that the textile industry is not a new industry.

7. a. The equilibrium price in autarky is $20. The consumer surplus = $3,200 = (80)(80)/2$.

    The producer surplus = $800. Total surplus = $4,000.

    b. At the world price of $30, $Q^S = 120$, $Q^D = 70$ and export = $120 - 70 = 50$. Consumer surplus = $2,450, producer surplus = $1,800, and total surplus = $4,250.

chapter 19

Open-Economy Macroeconomics

This chapter introduces the balance of payments and shows the distinction between balance of payment on current account and balance of payment on financial account. In addition, the chapter considers the determinants of international capital flows and the role of the foreign exchange market and the exchange rate. This chapter revisits the loanable funds model and shows capital inflow (imported funds) or capital outflow (exported funds) at a given world interest rate. We also see how demand and supply of the Canadian dollars in the foreign exchange market determines the exchange rate of the Canadian dollar. The chapter explains the distinction between nominal and real exchange rates and emphasizes the importance of the real exchange rate in the current account; and introduces the concept of purchasing power parity. The chapter also discusses different exchange rate regimes and contrasts fixed-exchange rate regimes with floating-exchange rate regimes. Finally, the chapter considers the effect of open economies on macroeconomic policy when operating under a floating-exchange rate regime.

How Well Do You Understand the Chapter?

Fill in the blanks using the terms below or circle the correct answer to complete the following statements. Terms may be used more than once. If you find yourself having difficulties, please refer to the appropriate section in the text.

aggregate demand	equal(s)	increase
appreciated	euro	large
balance of payments	exchange market intervention	less
Britain		lower
buy(s)	exchange rate	monetary
buying	expensive	monetary policy
capital	exports	nominal
capital flows	factor	positive
capital inflow	fall	purchasing power parity
capital outflow	fallen	real
central	financial account	recession
cheaper	fixed	removing
contractionary	fixed exchange rate	revaluation
current account	floating	rise
demanded	foreign exchange controls	selling
depreciated	foreign exchange market	stimulus
depreciates	higher	supplied
devaluation	imports	trade balance
difference	imposing	zero

1. Many European countries adopted the _____ as their currency, beginning in 1999. However, some countries chose not to adopt the euro, including _____. Britain was unwilling to lose its independent _____ since this would limit its ability to use policy to correct macroeconomic problems. In the context of Canada and NAFTA, similar concerns will be raised if we form a currency union with the United States.

2. The _____ summarizes a country's transactions with other countries. The balance of payments on financial accounts is the _____ between a country's sales of assets to foreigners and the country's purchases of assets from foreigners during a given period. The balance of payment on _____ is the difference between a country's exports and its imports plus net international transfer payments and factor income during a given period.

3. A modified circular-flow diagram can illustrate the flows between a country and the rest of the world. One flow represents the payments that are counted in the _____ (CA): here, the rest of the world sends payments into the country for goods and services (this would be payments for the country's _____), factor income, and transfers, and the rest of the world receives payments from the country for goods and services (this would be payments for the country's _____), factor income, and transfers. A second flow represents payments that are counted in the _____ (FA): here, the rest of the world sends the country payments for assets the world purchases from the country, while the country sends the rest of the world payment for assets it purchases. Since the total flow into the country must be _____ to the total flow out of the country, this implies that the balance of payments on current account plus the balance of payments on financial account must equal _____.

4. The balance of payments on goods and services is the _____ between the sale of goods and services to foreigners (exports) and the purchase of goods and services from foreigners (imports) during a given period. This _____ is the difference between a country's exports and imports of goods. The current account consists of trade balance plus net international transfer payments plus net international _____ income.

5. The financial account shows the _____ between a country's sales of assets to foreigners and its purchases of assets from foreigners during a given time period. This is also referred to as the _____ account. The financial account can be broken into sub-accounts, including the private net purchases of assets by private individuals and the official net purchases of assets, which represent transactions made by _____ banks.

6. The sum of the balance of payments on current account (CA) and the balance of payments on financial account (FA) must equal _____. Thus, if the CA is a positive number, the FA must be a negative number; conversely, if CA is a negative number, then the FA must be a _____ number. Countries can pay for their _____ by selling assets that create liabilities obligating the country to pay for these goods and services at some point in the future.

7. The loanable funds market can be used to illustrate _____ flows between countries. Provided investors think that a foreign asset is as good as a domestic asset and a foreign liability is as good as a domestic one, funds will flow from a country with a _____ interest rate to a country with a _____ interest rate until the difference between the interest rates in the two countries is eliminated. That is, the _____ will equalize the interest rate between the two countries.

8. With a small country assumption, the world interest rate will be the interest rate in the domestic economy. Given the world interest rate, a country can see capital inflow or capital outflow. A country that has _____ must have a matching current account deficit, and a country that has a(n) _____ must have a matching current account surplus. In other words, balance of payment always balances to zero.

9. Movements in the exchange rate ensure that the difference between current account and financial account equals _____. The _____ is the price at which one currency trades for another currency.

10. Currencies can be exchanged for one another in the _____ market. This market determines the exchange rate, or the price for which two currencies exchange. When one currency becomes more valuable in terms of another currency, we say that the first currency has _____. When one currency becomes less valuable in terms of another currency, we say that the first currency has _____.

11. The foreign exchange market brings together demanders and suppliers of Canadian dollars, and it is the interaction of this demand and supply that determines the equilibrium _____. For instance, in the foreign exchange market for our dollars, the demanders in this market are giving up foreign currency in order to acquire Canadian dollars to buy Canadian goods and services and to buy Canadian bonds. Their demand for dollars is influenced by the price they must pay for these dollars: this price is the _____ expressed as the foreign currency per dollar. In the foreign exchange market for Canadian dollars, Canadians supply dollars to buy foreign currency (to buy foreign goods and services and to buy foreign bonds). This supply of Canadian dollars depends on the exchange rate. As the exchange rate increases, holding everything else constant, the quantity

_____ of dollars will decrease, while the quantity of dollars _____ will increase. The equilibrium exchange rate is that exchange rate for which the quantity of dollars demanded _____ the quantity of dollars supplied in the foreign exchange market.

12. When there is an increase in capital inflows into a country, this increases the balance of payments on financial account. This will cause a _____ value of domestic currency, and it will make imports more attractive and exports less attractive for this country: this leads to a _____ in the balance of payments on current account for that country which exactly offsets the (initial) _____ in the balance of payments on financial account for that country. To generalize, a change in the balance of payments on financial account for a country must generate an equal and opposite reaction in that country's balance of payments on current account.

13. The _____ exchange rate is the exchange rate adjusted for international differences in aggregate price levels. The real exchange rate of the Canadian dollar equals the following one:

$eP_{CANADA}/P_{FOREIGN}$

where e is the nominal exchange rate and P is the price.

14. The current account responds only to changes in the _____ exchange rate, and not to changes in the _____ exchange rate. A country's products become _____ to foreigners only when that country's currency depreciates in real terms, and a country's products become _____ to foreigners only when that country's currency appreciates in real terms. _____ refers to the nominal exchange rate between two countries at which a given basket of goods and services would cost the same in each country.

15. The real exchange rate affects exports and imports. When a country's real exchange rate rises, its exports _____ and its imports rise. When a country's real exchange rate falls, its exports _____ and its imports fall.

16. When the government keeps the exchange rate against some other currency at or near a particular target, this is referred to as a _____ exchange rate. A country follows a(n) _____ exchange rate regime when it allows the exchange rate to fluctuate wherever the market takes it.

17. Under a fixed exchange rate regime, the government can affect the exchange rate through three primary activities. The government can affect its country's exchange rate by buying or selling currency in the foreign exchange market: this is called _____, when a government must hold foreign exchange reserves, which are stocks or foreign currency that the government can use to

_____ its own currency when it needs to support its own currency's price. A large part of capital flows represents governmental transactions: these purchases and sales of foreign assets by governments and central banks support their currencies through _____. When the government _____ its own currency, holding everything else constant, this will increase the value of its own currency.

18. The government can also pursue exchange rate intervention through its _____ policy. To support the exchange rate, the government can _____ its interest rate, which will encourage increased capital flow into the economy, causing an increase in demand for that country's currency. Holding everything else constant, an increase in a country's interest rate will _____ the value of its currency.

19. The government can also affect the exchange rate by reducing the supply of its currency in the foreign exchange market. Governments can achieve this reduction by limiting the right of their citizens to buy foreign currency through the imposition of _____. Holding everything else constant, imposition of foreign exchange controls _____ the value of a country's currency.

20. Thus, if the value of a country's currency in the foreign exchange market is _____ than the target exchange rate, the government can prevent depreciation of its currency by _____ the country's currency, by pursuing a(n) _____ interest rate via its monetary policy, or by _____ foreign exchange controls. If the value of a country's currency in the foreign exchange market is _____ than the target exchange rate, the government can prevent appreciation of its currency by _____ the country's currency, by pursuing a(n) _____ interest rate via its monetary policy, or by _____ foreign exchange controls.

21. A fixed exchange rate provides certainty about the value of a currency. A commitment to a(n) _____ by a country is also a commitment to not engage in inflationary policies. Maintaining a fixed exchange rate requires the country to hold _____ quantities of foreign currency, and these holdings typically are a low-return investment. Use of _____ policy to help stabilize an exchange rate may also require a country to forego other goals like the stabilization of output or the inflation rate. In addition, the use of exchange controls, like import quotas and tariffs, distort incentives for importing and exporting, and may lead to _____ transactions costs due to bureaucratic red tape and increased corruption. In short, the pursuit of a _____ exchange rate eliminates uncertainty and volatility of exchange rates but limits monetary policy to pursue domestic income stabilization goals, while the pursuit of a(n) _____ exchange rate leaves monetary policy available for stabilization but creates uncertainty regarding exchange rate values.

22. A reduction in the value of a currency that previously had a fixed exchange rate is called a _____. An increase in the value of a currency that previously had a fixed exchange rate is called a _____. Devaluation makes domestic goods cheaper in terms of foreign currency, leads to _____ exports and _____ imports and, therefore, an increase in a country's balance of payments on current account. Devaluation acts as a(n) _____ to aggregate demand and can, therefore, be used to reduce or eliminate a recessionary gap. Revaluation makes domestic goods more expensive in terms of foreign currency; it leads to _____ exports and _____ imports, and, therefore, a decrease in a country's balance of payments on current account. Devaluation acts as a(n) _____ force on aggregate demand and can, therefore, be used to reduce or eliminate inflationary gap.

23. Under a _____ exchange rate regime, a country retains its ability to pursue independent monetary policy, but the use of monetary policy will affect the exchange rate, which in turn will affect the level of _____ in the economy. Monetary policy in open economies has an effect beyond the effect we have described in closed economies. For example, a decision to use monetary policy to _____ the interest rate will lead to higher investment spending, but it will also provide _____ incentive for foreigners to move funds into the currency and this will reduce the demand for the country's currency. There will also be an increase in the supply of currency as people exchange the domestic currency for foreign currency due to the incentive to move funds abroad, since the rate of return on loans at home has _____ relative to the rate of return on loans in other countries. Together, these two effects cause the domestic currency to depreciate, and this depreciation leads to _____ exports and _____ imports, as well as an overall _____ impact on aggregate demand.

24. Economic events in an economy also impact other economies. Changes in aggregate demand affect the demand for goods and services produced abroad as well as at home: holding everything else constant, a recession in an economy leads to _____ imports and, an expansion in an economy leads to _____ imports. The link between aggregate demand in one country and aggregate demand in another country helps to explain why business cycles are often synchronized between different countries. A recession abroad reduces the demand for Canadian _____, which in turn reduces the demand for Canadian dollars in the foreign exchange market; if Canada has a floating-exchange rate, the Canadian dollar _____. As a result, Canada's exports will increase and imports will _____, and this insulates the domestic economy from a _____ originating abroad. A fixed exchange rate does not provide such insulation.

Learning Tips

TIP #1: This chapter introduces new vocabulary. You will want to learn definitions and be able to apply these definitions.

The chapter introduces an abundance of new terms. You will want to thoroughly understand concepts like the exchange rate, appreciation of a currency, depreciation of a currency, devaluation of a currency, and revaluation of a currency. You will need to think carefully about how changes in the exchange rate affect a country's level of imports and exports. You might find the following table a helpful summary of these relationships.

Appreciation of country X's currency	Country X imports more, exports less
Depreciation of country X's currency	Country X imports less, exports more
Devaluation of country X's currency	Country X imports less, exports more
Revaluation of country X's currency	Country X imports more, exports less

TIP #2: It is important to understand what an exchange rate is and how changes in the exchange rate affect the country's balance of payments.

An exchange rate is the price of one currency in terms of another currency. When a country's exchange rate increases, or appreciates, this makes their domestically produced goods relatively more expensive than goods produced by other economies. This will decrease exports and increase imports for the domestic economy: the balance of payments on current account will increase, while the balance of payments on financial account will decrease.

TIP #3: You will want to be thoroughly familiar with the terminology and the relationships represented in the balance of payments.

The balance of payments (illustrated in Figure 19-1 in the text) shows the flow of money between national economies. It illustrates why the balance of payments on current account must equal the balance of payments on financial account. It illustrates the relationship in a domestic economy between the payments from the rest of the world for goods and services, factor income, and transfers, and payments to the rest of the world for goods and services, factor income, and transfers.

TIP #4: The sum of the balance of payments on current account (CA) and the balance of payments on financial account (FA) must equal zero.

TIP #5: When we consider the loanable funds model with the world interest rate being our interest rate, we can conclude that capital inflow (i.e., positive FA) occurs when demand for loans is greater than the supply of loans and capital outflow (i.e., negative FA) occurs when demand for loans is less than the supply of loans.

TIP #6: A floating-exchange rate system allows the use of monetary policy for the purpose of domestic stabilization, and it also provides some insulation against foreign recession.

Multiple-Choice Questions

1. Which of the following statements is true?
   a. The balance of payments on goods and services is the difference between the value of imports and the value of exports during a given period.
   b. The merchandise trade balance includes the sale of goods as well as financial assets.
   c. A country's international transactions are tracked by the balance of payments accounts.
   d. All of the above statements are true statements.

2. The balance of payments on goods and services plus net international transfer payments and net international factor income
   a. equals the merchandise trade balance.
   b. equals the balance on payments on current account.
   c. equals the balance on payments on financial account.
   d. plus the balance of payments on financial account equals zero.
   e. Both (a) and (c) are true statements.
   f. Both (b) and (c) are true statements.
   g. Both (b) and (d) are true statements.

3. For a hypothetical economy if the balance of payments on financial account equals –$100 million, then the balance of payments on current account must
   a. equal –$100 million.
   b. be greater than –$100 million.
   c. be less than –$100 million.
   d. equal $100 million.

4. The balance of payments tracks the
   a. flow of payments into a country from the rest of the world as well as the flow of payments from the country to the rest of the world.
   b. flow of payments for goods and services, factor income, and transfers in the balance of payments on current account.
   c. flow of payments for assets in the balance of payments on financial account.
   d. All of the above statements are true statements.

5. Suppose that there are two countries with open economies. If the interest rate in the loanable funds market in the first country is higher than the interest rate in the loanable funds market in the second country, we can expect that
   a. this interest rate differential will continue if citizens in both countries view their domestic assets as comparable to foreign assets.
   b. this interest rate differential will be eliminated due to the movement of international capital flows.
   c. the supply of loanable funds in the first country will increase while the supply of loanable funds in the second country will decrease.
   d. the supply of loanable funds in the first country will decrease while the supply of loanable funds in the second country will increase.
   e. Both (b) and (c) are true statements.

6. Which of the following statements is true?
   a. A country that receives capital inflows will have a matching financial account surplus.
   b. The exchange rate is always measured as the price of a dollar in terms of the foreign currency.
   c. The more euros it takes to buy a dollar, the fewer dollars Europeans will supply.
   d. When a country's currency appreciates, exports fall and imports rise.

7. Suppose that the exchange rate (e) of one Canadian dollar is 0.9 euros. Therefore, we can conclude:
   a. If the exchange rate changes to $1 for 0.95 euros, then the Canadian dollar has depreciated.
   b. If the exchange rate changes to $1 for 0.95 euros, then the Canadian dollar has appreciated.
   c. One euro trades for $1.111.
   d. Both a and c are correct.
   e. Both b and c are correct.

8. An increase in capital inflows into a country, holding everything else constant, will
   a. result in an increase in net exports for the country.
   b. result in a decrease in net exports for the country.
   c. result in an increase in the balance on financial account for the country and an equal and opposite reaction in the balance of payments on current account.
   d. Both (a) and (c) are true statements.
   e. Both (b) and (c) are true statements.

Answer the next two questions using the following information. Suppose the aggregate price level for a given market basket of goods in Macroland is 125, while the aggregate price level for the same market basket of goods in Funland is 150. Suppose that currently the exchange rate is 10 Macroland dollars for 1 Funland dollar.

9. Given the previous information, what is the real exchange rate initially?
   a. 10 Macroland dollars for 1 Funland dollars
   b. 1 Macroland dollars for 10 Funland dollars
   c. 1 Macroland dollar for 1 Funland dollar
   d. 10 Macroland dollars for 10 Funland dollars
   e. 12 Macroland dollars for 1 Funland dollar

10. If the aggregate price level of the market basket in Macroland increases to 150, what must the exchange rate be in order for the real exchange rate to be unchanged from its initial level?
   a. 10 Macroland dollars for 1 Funland dollars
   b. 1 Macroland dollars for 10 Funland dollars
   c. 1 Macroland dollar for 1 Funland dollar
   d. 10 Macroland dollars for 10 Funland dollars
   e. 12 Macroland dollars for 1 Funland dollar

11. When the purchasing power parity rate is greater than the nominal exchange rate then,
   a. over time we can expect the purchasing power parity to fall.
   b. over time we can expect the purchasing power parity to rise.
   c. over time we can expect the exchange rate to rise.
   d. over time we can expect the exchange rate to fall.

12. Which of the following statements is true?
   a. When a country's currency undergoes a real depreciation, this causes exports to fall and imports to rise.
   b. Nominal exchange rates almost always equal the purchasing power parity rate.
   c. The current account is affected by changes in the nominal exchange rate as well as the real exchange rate.
   d. None of the above are true statements.

13. If a government wishes to fix the value of a currency above its equilibrium value in the foreign exchange market, it can
   a. engage in monetary policy to reduce interest rates, thereby increasing capital flows into its country.
   b. reduce the supply of its currency by limiting the right of its citizens to buy foreign currencies.
   c. engage in selling its currency through exchange market intervention.
   d. All of the above statements will help the government to reduce the exchange rate to its desired level.

14. Suppose that in the foreign exchange market there is a shortage at the target exchange rate. We know that
   a. the supply of the country's currency is less than the demand for that country's currency.
   b. it is impossible to maintain the target exchange rate unless the government engages in exchange market intervention, changes monetary policy, adjusts foreign exchange controls, or pursues some combination of these three policies.
   c. maintaining a fixed exchange rate will limit the ability of the government to pursue stabilization policy.
   d. All of the above statements are true statements.

15. A fixed rate regime
   a. reduces uncertainty for businesses about the value of a currency.
   b. exposes a country to a potential bias toward inflationary policies.
   c. reduces the amount of foreign currency a country must hold.
   d. creates an incentive to pursue monetary policy to help stabilize the country's economy.

16. A devaluation of a currency, holding everything else constant,
   a. makes foreign produced goods more attractive to purchase in the domestic economy and, therefore, leads to an increase in imports in the domestic economy.
   b. decreases the balance of payments on current account.
   c. may be used as a macroeconomic policy tool since a devaluation stimulates aggregate demand.
   d. Both (a) and (c) are true statements.
   e. Both (b) and (c) are true statements.
   f. All of the above statements are true.

17. Consider a country with a fixed exchange rate currently operating with an inflationary gap. Which of the following statements is true for this country?
   a. A revaluation of this country's currency will reduce its inflationary gap.
   b. A country with a fixed exchange rate regime has no macroeconomic policy tools available to it to combat an inflationary gap.
   c. A revaluation of this country's currency will increase exports and decrease imports, and this will help reduce the country's inflationary gap.
   d. Both (a) and (c) are true statements.

18. When a country pursues expansionary monetary policy, this will
   a. increase the level of investment spending.
   b. decrease the demand for that country's currency in the foreign exchange market.
   c. increase the supply of that country's currency in the foreign exchange market.
   d. All of the above statements are true.

19. Which of the following statements is true?
   a. Demand shocks may originate from outside the domestic economy.
   b. Business cycles in different countries often seem to be synchronized, because changes in aggregate supply affect the demand for goods and services produced abroad as well as at home.
   c. A fixed exchange rate seems to lessen the impact of changes in aggregate demand in one country on the economic performance in other countries.
   d. All of the above statements are true.

20. If the current account (CA) balance is $1.2 billion, then the financial account (FA) balance should be
   a. zero.
   b. $1.2 billion.
   c. – $1.2 billion.
   d. more than $1.2 billion.

21. Suppose the current account (CA) balance and the financial account balance (FA) are zero in Canada. If Canada experiences capital-outflow of $25 billion due to a higher interest rate in the world market, we will see a
   a. lower value of Canadian dollar and a lower current account balance.
   b. higher value of Canadian dollar and a lower current account balance.
   c. lower value of Canadian dollar and a positive current account surplus.
   d. higher value of Canadian dollar and a positive current account surplus.

22. Consider a loanable fund model with demand function for loanable funds in Canada and supply function of loanable funds in Canada. Assume that the interest rate at the intersection of the demand curve and the supply curve is lower than the world interest rate. As a result, Canada will experience
   a. capital inflow and improvement in the current account surplus.
   b. capital outflow and deterioration in the current account surplus.
   c. capital outflow and improvement in the current account surplus.
   d. capital inflow and deterioration in the current account surplus.

23. Consider a loanable fund model with demand function for loanable funds in Canada and supply function of loanable funds in Canada. Assume that the interest rate at the intersection of the demand curve and the supply curve is higher than the world interest rate. As a result, Canada will experience
   a. capital inflow and improvement in the current account surplus.
   b. capital outflow and deterioration in the current account surplus.
   c. capital outflow and improvement in the current account surplus.
   d. capital inflow and deterioration in the current account surplus.

24. Suppose the exchange rate of one Canadian dollar is one US dollar and P_{CANADA} is $1 and P_{USA} is $1. If Canada's price doubles while the U.S. price remains constant, we can expect all of the following, **except**
   a. due to the increase in real exchange rate, Canada's net export will decline initially. Over time, the nominal exchange rate of Canadian dollar will fall.
   b. if P_{CANADA} stays at $2 and P_{USA} stays $1, then over time (other things remaining the same), the exchange rate of one Canadian dollar will be $0.50 US.
   c. inflation in Canada will lead to a depreciated value of the Canadian dollar.
   d. in the long run, the real exchange rate is always more than one.

25. Consider the demand curve and supply curve of the Canadian dollar in the foreign exchange market, where quantity of the Canadian dollar is shown in the horizontal axis and the exchange rate (price) of one Canadian dollar (expressed in U.S. dollars) is shown on the vertical axis. Which of the following statements is false?
a. As we move up along a given supply curve, it implies that we buy more foreign goods due to the appreciated value of the Canadian dollar.
b. As we move down along a given demand curve, it implies that foreigners buy more Canadian goods due to the appreciated value of foreign currency.
c. If there is an excess demand for Canadian dollars at the current exchange rate, this will bring higher value of the Canadian dollar, which will dampen our exports and increase our imports.
d. If there is an excess supply of Canadian dollars at the current exchange rate, this will dampen our exports and increase our imports.

26. Consider an initial equilibrium with a given demand curve and a given supply curve of Canadian dollars in the foreign exchange market, where quantity of Canadian dollar is shown on the horizontal axis and the exchange rate (price) of one Canadian dollar (expressed in U.S. dollars) is shown on the vertical axis. Assume that the world interest rate has increased. As a result,
a. Canada's balance of payment on financial account will deteriorate and Canada's balance of payment on current account will improve.
b. Canada's balance of payment on financial account will not change, but Canada's balance of payment on current account will improve.
c. Canada's balance of payment on financial account will deteriorate, but Canada's balance of payment on current account will not change.
d. The Canadian dollar will appreciate.

27. Consider the fixed exchange rate in a given economy with a large sum of foreign currency with its central bank. As a result,
a. the economy will not observe any volatility (fluctuations) of exchange rate.
b. the central bank can pursue independent monetary policy to fight recession.
c. the economy enjoys complete insulation from foreign recession.
d. The central bank can always keep constant its money supply.

28. In a floating-exchange rate system, all the following are true except
a. the central bank can pursue expansionary monetary policy to fight recession.
b. there is some insulation against foreign recession.
c. expansionary fiscal policy and increased fiscal deficit has positive effect on current account balance in the short run.
d. expansionary monetary policy has positive effect on current account balance in the short run.

29. Consider a recessionary gap in the short run and that policymakers are looking for the correct short-run policy solution. The correct policy is
a. expansionary fiscal policy under a floating-exchange rate.
b. expansionary monetary policy under a floating-exchange rate.
c. expansionary monetary policy under a fixed exchange rate.
d. contractionary fiscal policy under a fixed exchange rate.

30. Consider an open economy with a fixed exchange rate. When this economy suffers from recessionary gap, policymakers should pursue
a. expansionary fiscal policy in the short run.
b. expansionary monetary policy in the short run.
c. expansionary monetary policy mixed with contractionary fiscal policy in the short run.
d. expansionary fiscal policy mixed with contractionary monetary policy in the short run.

Problems and Exercises

1. Use the following table of information to answer this question.

	Payments from foreigners (millions of dollars)	Payments to foreigners (millions of dollars)	Sales of assets to foreigners (millions of dollars)	Purchases of assets from foreigners (millions of dollars)
Goods	200	80	—	—
Services	50	20	—	—
Factor income	70	10	—	—
Transfer payments	10	20	—	—
Official sales and purchases	—	—	100	300
Private sales and purchases	—	—	80	80

   a. Provide a definition or an equation for each of the following items.
     1. Merchandise trade balance

     2. Balance of payments on goods and services

     3. Net international factor income

     4. Net international transfer payments

     5. Balance of payments on current account

     6. Balance of payments on financial account

   b. Given the previous information, compute the value of each of the terms given in part (a).

c. Explain why the sum of the balance of payments on current account and the balance of payments on financial account must equal zero.

2. The following graphs represent the loanable funds market in Macroland and Funland, the only two economies in the world.

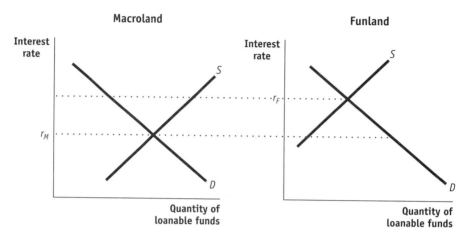

Residents in Macroland and Funland believe that foreign assets and liabilities are as good as domestic assets and liabilities.

a. Given the two graphs, which country is likely to attract capital? Why?

b. Given the Macroland graph, what do you predict will happen to the interest rate in Macroland over time? Explain your answer.

c. Given the Funland graph, what do you predict will happen to the interest rate in Funland over time? Explain your answer.

d. Briefly describe the capital flows between Macroland and Funland.

3. a. Calculate the missing values in the following table.

	Canadian dollar	U.S. dollar	Euro
1 Canadian dollar	1	_____	0.5
1 U.S. dollar	1.10	1	_____
1 Euro	_____	_____	1

b. Calculate the missing values in the following table.

	Canadian dollar	U.S. dollar	Euro
1 Canadian dollar	1	0.98	_____
1 U.S. dollar	_____	1	_____
1 Euro	2.1	_____	1

c. Which currencies appreciated against the Canadian dollar? How it will affect Canada's exports and imports?

d. Which currencies depreciated against the Canadian dollar? How it will affect Canada's exports and imports?

4. Suppose you are shown the information in the following table. Assume net international transfers and factor income equal zero for this problem.

Funland purchases of Macroland dollars in the foreign exchange market to buy Macroland goods and services	3.0 million Macroland dollars
Funland total purchases in the foreign exchange market of Macroland dollars	5.0 million Macroland dollars
Macroland sales of Macroland dollars in the foreign exchange market to buy Funland assets	1.5 million Macroland dollars
Macroland sales of Macroland dollars in the foreign exchange market to buy Funland goods and services	3.5 million Macroland dollars

a. Given the information in this table, compute the values in the following table.

Funland purchases of Macroland dollars in the foreign exchange market to buy Macroland assets	_____
Total sales of Macroland dollars in the foreign exchange market	_____
Macroland balance of payments on current account	_____
Macroland balance of payments on financial account	_____

Suppose capital flows to Macroland from Funland decrease and this causes Macroland's currency to depreciate against Funland's currency, holding everything else constant.

b. How will this affect the demand and supply of Macroland dollars in the foreign exchange market? Use the following graph to illustrate your answer.

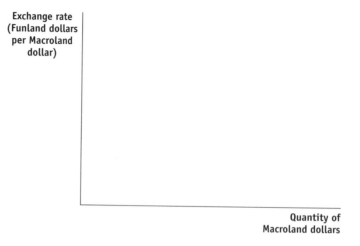

c. How will this depreciation affect Macroland's balance of payments on current account? Explain your answer.

d. How will this depreciation affect Macroland's balance of payments on financial account? Explain your answer.

5. Suppose initially the nominal exchange rate is 20 Macroland dollars per 1 Funland dollar, and the aggregate price index in both countries has a value of 100.
  a. What is the real exchange rate expressed as Macroland dollars per Funland dollar?

  b. Suppose the real exchange rate increases to 25 Macroland dollars per Funland dollar when the aggregate price index in Funland increases to 150. Assuming the nominal exchange rate is unchanged, what is the aggregate price index in Macroland?

  c. Suppose the aggregate price index in Funland is 150 and the aggregate price index in Macroland is 125. If the nominal exchange rate increases to 25 Macroland dollars per Funland dollar, what is the real exchange rate?

d. If the real exchange rate measured as Macroland dollars per Funland dollar increases, holding everything else constant, what happens to the level of exports and imports in Macroland?

6. Suppose that currently the cost of a standardized market basket in Macroland is 300 Macroland dollars, while the same market basket in Funland costs 150 Funland dollars.

   a. If purchasing power parity holds for the two countries, what must the nominal exchange rate expressed as Macroland dollars per Funland dollar equal? Explain your answer.

   b. If the actual nominal exchange rate equals 4 Macroland dollars per 1 Funland dollar, what do you expect will happen to the nominal exchange rate over the long run, holding everything else constant? Explain your answer.

7. Compare and contrast the advantages and disadvantages of a fixed-exchange rate regime and a floating-exchange rate regime.

8. Suppose Macroland has adopted a fixed-exchange rate regime and wishes to target the exchange rate to 2.25 Canadian dollars for each Macroland dollar.

   a. The following figure represents the current situation in Macroland.

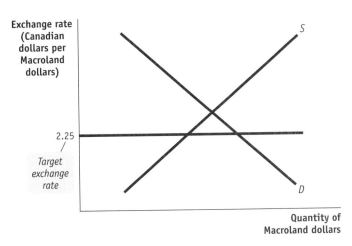

Describe the situation depicted in this figure, given that Macroland would like to maintain a fixed exchange rate of 2.25 Canadian dollars.

b. Given the graph, in part (a), what policies are available to Macroland if it is determined to maintain the exchange rate at 2.25 Canadian dollars? Explain each option.

c. The following figure represents the situation in Macroland six months later.

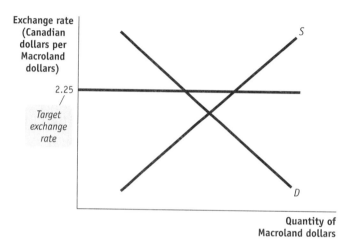

Describe the situation depicted in this graph, given that Macroland would like to maintain a fixed exchange rate of 2.25 Canadian dollars.

d. Given the graph, in part (c), what policies are available to Macroland if it is determined to maintain the exchange rate at 2.25 Canadian dollars? Explain each option.

9. Suppose Canada exports sizeable quantity of crude oil to the United States. If the world price of crude oil doubles, how it will affect the value of Canadian dollar? How it will affect Canada's tourism industry?

10. Consider an economy with a floating exchange rate suffering from a recessionary gap. Trace the effects of expansionary monetary policy and expansionary fiscal policy (with higher G). Which policy is better?

11. Trace the effects of foreign recession under a floating exchange rate and under a fixed exchange rate.

12. The following table shows the demand and supply of the Canadian dollar in the foreign exchange market. In the table, *e* is the exchange rate of one Canadian dollar expressed in U.S. dollars.

e	Quantity of dollars	Supply of Canadian dollars
$0.80 U.S.	$120 million	$ 80 million
0.90 U.S.	110 million	90 million
1.00 U.S.	100 million	100 million
1.10 U.S.	90 million	110 million
1.20 U.S.	80 million	120 million

a. What is the equilibrium exchange rate? What is the balance of payment? If the current balance is +$20 million, what is the financial account value?

b. Suppose the world interest rate increases. As a result, there is a capital outflow and Canada's financial account balance becomes – $50 million. What will the effect on exchange rate, current account balance, and over-all balance of payment?

Answers to How Well Do You Understand the Chapter

1. euro, Britain, monetary policy

2. balance of payments, difference, financial account

3. current account, exports, imports, financial account, equal, zero

4. difference, trade balance, factor

5. difference, capital, central

6. zero, positive, imports

7. capital, lower, higher, capital flows

8. capital inflow, capital outflow

9. zero, exchange rate

10. foreign exchange, appreciated, depreciated

11. exchange rate, exchange rate, demanded, supplied, equals

12. higher, fall, increase

13. real

14. real, nominal, cheaper, expensive, purchasing power parity

15. fall, rise

16. fixed, floating

17. exchange market intervention, buy, exchange market intervention, buys

18. monetary, increase, increase

19. foreign exchange controls, increase

20. lower, buying, higher, imposing, higher, selling, lower, removing

21. fixed exchange rate, large, monetary, higher, fixed, floating

22. devaluation, revaluation, higher, lower, stimulus, lower, higher, contractionary

23. floating, aggregate demand, lower, less, fallen, higher, lower, positive

24. lower, higher, exports, depreciates, fall, recession

Answers to Multiple-Choice Questions

1. The balance of payments on goods and services is the difference between the value of exports and the value of imports during a given period. The merchandise trade balance does not include the sale of financial assets, but does include the sale of goods. The balance of payments accounts provide a set of numbers that describe a country's international transactions. **Answer: C.**

2. By definition, the balance of payments on goods and services plus net international transfer payments and net international factor income equals the balance of payments on current account. In addition, the sum of the balance of payments on current account plus the balance of payments on financial account equals zero. **Answer: G.**

3. The sum of the balance of payments on current account and the balance of payments on financial account must sum to zero: thus, if the balance of payments on financial account equals −$100 million, then the balance of payments on current account must equal $100 million. **Answer: D.**

4. Figure 19-1 in your text reviews this concept: the balance of payments tracks flows of goods and services, factor income, transfers, and assets between a country and the rest of the world. Transactions involving goods and services, factor income, and transfers are measured in the balance of payments on current account, while transactions involving assets are measured in the balance of payments on financial account. **Answer: D.**

5. If two countries are open to trade and allow capital to flow freely between them, then an interest rate differential in their loanable funds market will disappear quickly due to capital flows between the two countries. Capital will tend to flow into the country with the relatively higher interest rate and out of the country with the relatively lower interest rate. Thus, the supply of loanable funds in the market with the higher interest rate will increase, while the supply of loanable funds in the market with the lower interest rate will decrease: this will cause the interest rate to fall in the first country and to rise in the second country until the interest rate differential is eliminated. **Answer: E.**

6. A country that has capital inflows will have a matching current account deficit. The exchange rate may be measured as the price of a dollar in terms of the foreign currency, or it may be measured as the price of the foreign currency in terms of dollars. The more euros it takes to buy a dollar, the fewer dollars Europeans will demand in the foreign exchange market for dollars. When a country's currency appreciates, this means that the exchange rate for that currency in terms of the other currency has risen: this increase in the exchange rate makes goods and services produced in the country whose currency has appreciated more expensive relative to goods and services produced elsewhere. This will lead to a decrease in exports and an increase in imports for the country whose currency has appreciated. **Answer: D.**

7. Since the exchange rate has increased to 0.95 euros from 0.90 euros, one euro trades for $1.053 now. **Answer: B.**

8. When a country has an increase in capital inflows, this causes the exchange rate to increase leading to an appreciation of that country's currency. With this appreciation of its currency, the country will find that its goods and services become relatively more expensive and, therefore, its net exports will decrease. Furthermore, the increase in capital inflows will cause the balance on financial account to increase, and this increase will be met by an equal, but opposite, reaction in the balance of payments on current account. **Answer: E.**

9. To find the real exchange rate, we need to know the nominal exchange rate (in this case, 10 Macroland dollars per 1 Funland dollar) and the aggregate price level in the two countries. We can plug them into formula 19–4 in your text to get the real exchange rate equals (10 Macroland dollars/Funland dollars)(150/125) = 12 Macroland dollars per 1 Funland dollar. **Answer: E.**

10. To find the exchange rate, we need to know the real exchange rate (in this case, 12 Macroland dollars per 1 Funland dollar) and the aggregate price level in the two countries. We can plug them into formula 19–4 in your text to 12 Macroland dollars per 1 Funland dollar equals (the exchange rate)(150/150). Solving for the exchange rate yields an exchange rate of 12 Macroland dollars per 1 Funland dollar. **Answer: E.**

11. Purchasing power parity between two countries' currencies is the nominal exchange rate at which a given basket of goods and services would cost the same amount in each country. When the purchasing power parity rate is greater than the nominal exchange rate, we would anticipate that the nominal exchange rate must increase over time in order for the two countries to have similar costs for a given market basket. **Answer: C.**

12. When a country's currency undergoes a real depreciation this causes exports to rise and imports to fall, since the depreciation reduces the price of the country's goods and services relative to the prices for goods and services produced in other countries. Nominal exchange rates almost always differ from purchasing power parity rates: the nominal rate tends to fluctuate around the purchasing power parity rate. The current account responds only to changes in the real exchange rate, not the nominal exchange rate: it is a change in the real exchange rate that alters the relative cost of domestic goods and services in comparison to foreign produced goods and services. **Answer: D.**

13. When the government wishes to fix the exchange rate to a rate that is above its equilibrium value in the foreign exchange market, it must deal with the fact that there is a surplus of its currency at that desired exchange rate. The government can eliminate this surplus by buying its currency through an exchange market intervention; by pursuing monetary policy that raises its interest rate relative to the interest rates of other economies, thus increasing capital flows into its country (and increasing the demand for its currency); or by reducing the supply of its currency to the foreign exchange market through the imposition of foreign exchange controls. **Answer: B.**

14. When there is a shortage at the target exchange rate, this indicates that the demand for the country's currency is greater than the supply of the country's currency. A government will find that it can maintain the target exchange rate, only if it is willing to give up its use of monetary policy for stabilization purposes and instead use monetary policy, exchange market intervention, and foreign exchange controls to pursue its target exchange rate. **Answer: D.**

15. A fixed rate regime benefits businesses by eliminating uncertainty about the value of a currency while reducing the ability of the government to use monetary policy as a means of stabilizing the economy. A fixed-rate regime reduces, in some cases, a country's bias toward inflationary policies, since it can send a signal to the foreign exchange market about the country's commitment to a stable exchange rate and decision to pursue noninflationary policies in the future. **Answer: A.**

16. A devaluation of a currency is a reduction in the value of a currency that previously had a fixed exchange rate. This devaluation makes domestic goods cheaper in terms of foreign currency and will, therefore, increase the level of exports and decrease the level of imports in the domestic economy. This will stimulate aggregate demand in the domestic economy. The effect of these changes is to increase the balance of payments on current account. **Answer: C.**

17. A revaluation of a country's currency will make domestic goods more expensive in terms of foreign currency and will, therefore, decrease exports while increasing imports. This will cause aggregate demand to decrease and, therefore, help the country reduce its inflationary gap. **Answer: A.**

18. When a country pursues expansionary monetary policy, this causes the interest rate to decrease: this makes investment spending more attractive. In addition, the decrease in the interest rate also affects the foreign exchange market: the demand for the domestic currency will decrease since the domestic economy is now offering a relatively lower rate of return on their loans, and the supply of the domestic currency will increase because there is now a greater incentive to move funds abroad since the rate of return on loans in the domestic economy has fallen. **Answer: D.**

19. Business cycles in different countries often seem to be synchronized, because changes in aggregate demand in one country often have an effect on the level of aggregate demand in other countries. Adherence to a floating-exchange rate regime helps insulate countries from recessions originating from outside their economies, since the movement in the exchange rate limits the level of change in aggregate demand. **Answer: A.**

20. Since the balance of payment is zero under the floating exchange rate, positive current account is negative financial account. Therefore, the financial account balance is minus $1.2 billion. **Answer: C.**

21. With capital outflow, the value of the Canadian dollar will go down and it will increase Canada's current account balance. **Answer: C.**

22. There will be capital outflow and it will lead to the lower value of the Canadian dollar, which will improve Canada's current account surplus. **Answer: C.**

23. There will be capital inflow and it will lead to the higher value of the Canadian dollar, which will decrease Canada's current account surplus. **Answer: D.**

24. All of the statements are true except the last one. In the long run, the real exchange rate is one. **Answer: D.**

25. The last statement is false. If there is an excess supply of Canadian dollars, the value of the Canadian dollar will go down and this will improve Canada's current account. **Answer: D.**

26. A higher world interest rate will cause capital outflow, worsening Canada's financial account; but Canada's current account will improve due to the lower value of the Canadian dollar. **Answer: A.**

27. Under a fixed-exchange rate system, the central bank buys foreign currency or sells foreign currency to maintain a fixed exchange rate. As a result, the exchange rate does not suffer any fluctuation. **Answer: A.**

28. Expansionary fiscal policy brings a higher interest rate and a higher value of domestic currency, which worsens the current account balance. **Answer: C.**

29. Under a floating exchange rate, expansionary monetary policy brings lower interest rate and lower value of dollar, which stimulates net export and improves current account balance as well as GDP. **Answer: B.**

30. Under a fixed exchange rate, monetary policy to fight recession is completely ineffective, but expansionary fiscal policy is more effective in the short run. **Answer: A.**

Answers to Problems and Exercises

1.

    a. 1. Merchandise trade balance = (exports of goods) − (imports of goods) = (payments from foreigners for goods) − (payments to foreigners for goods)

       2. Balance of payments on goods and services = (exports of goods and services) − (imports of goods and services) = (payments from foreigners for goods and services) − (payments to foreigners for goods and services)

       3. Net international factor income = (factor income payments from foreigners) − (factor income payments to foreigners)

       4. Net international transfer payments = (transfer payments from foreigners) − (transfer payments to foreigners)

       5. Balance of payments on current account = (balance of payments on goods and services) + (net international transfer payments) + (net international factor income)

       6. Balance of payments on financial account = (sales of assets to foreigners) − (purchases of assets from foreigners)

    b. 1. Merchandise trade balance = $200 million − $80 million = $120 million

       2. Balance of payments on goods and services = $250 million − $100 million = $150 million

       3. Net international factor income = $70 million − $10 million = $60 million

       4. Net international transfer payments = $10 million − $20 million = − $10 million

       5. Balance of payments on current account = $150 million + (− $10 million) + ($60 million) = $200 million

       6. Balance of payments on financial account = − $200 million

    c. This reflects a basic rule of balance of payments accounting for any country: the flow of money into a country must equal the flow of money out of the country.

2. a. Funland will attract capital, because its equilibrium interest rate is higher than the equilibrium interest rate in Macroland.

    b. Over time the interest rate in Macroland will rise due to capital outflows. Since Macroland initially has a lower equilibrium interest rate than Funland, some Macroland lenders will decide to send their funds to Funland to take advantage of the higher interest rate. Over time this will cause the interest rate in the two countries to equalize.

    c. Over time the interest rate in Funland will fall due to capital inflows from Macroland. As funds from Macroland are attracted to Funland's loanable funds market, due to its initially higher equilibrium interest rate, this will cause the interest rate to fall in Funland. Eventually, the interest rates in the two countries will equalize.

    d. Capital will flow out of Macroland and into Funland. Thus, Macroland will experience capital outflows, while Funland will experience capital inflows.

3. a. Calculate the missing values in the following table.

	Canadian dollars	U.S. dollars	Euros
1 Canadian dollar	1	**0.9090**	0.5
1 U.S. dollar	1.10	1	**0.55**
1 Euro	**2**	**0.1818**	1

b. Calculate the missing values in the following table.

	Canadian dollars	U.S. dollars	Euros
1 Canadian dollar	1	0.98	**0.47619**
1 U.S. dollar	**1.02**	1	**0.4857**
1 Euro	2.1	**2.059**	1

c. Euros appreciated against the Canadian dollar. Depreciated value of Canadian dollar will increase Canada's exports and decrease Canada's imports.

d. The U.S. dollar depreciated against the Canadian dollar. Appreciated value of the Canadian dollar will reduce Canada's exports and increase Canada's imports.

4. a.

Funland purchases of Macroland dollars in the foreign exchange market to buy Macroland assets	2 million Macroland dollars
Total sales of Macroland dollars in the foreign exchange market	5.0 million Macroland dollars
Macroland balance of payments on current account	−.5 million Macroland dollars
Macroland balance of payments on financial account	.5 million Macroland dollars

b. The depreciation of the Macroland currency against Funland's currency will cause the demand for Macroland dollars to decrease at every exchange rate (measured as Funland dollars per Macroland dollars). This will, for a given supply of Macroland dollars, cause the exchange rate to decrease. This is illustrated in the following figure.

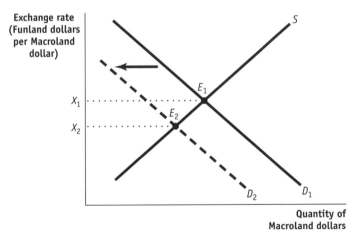

c. This depreciation of Macroland's currency against Funland's currency will cause Macroland's balance of payments on current account to increase, since Funland will now find Macroland goods and services relatively cheaper.

d. This depreciation of Macroland's currency against Funland's currency will cause Macroland's balance of payments on financial account to decrease, since any increase in Macroland's balance of payments on current account must be offset by an equal and opposite reaction in the balance of payments on financial account.

5. a. Real exchange rate in Macroland dollars per Funland dollar = (20 Macroland dollars per Funland dollar)(100/100) = 20 Macroland dollars per Funland dollar

b. To answer this question, we will want to use the equation:

> Real Exchange Rate = (Nominal Exchange Rate)[(Price Index in Funland)/(Price Index in Macroland)]

Thus, 25 Macroland dollars per Funland dollar = (20 Macroland dollars per Funland dollar)[(150)/(Price Index in Macroland)], and solving for the Price Index in Macroland, we find that the Price Index in Macroland equals 120.

c. To answer this question, we will want to use the equation given in part (b):

> Real Exchange Rate = (Nominal Exchange Rate)[(Price Index in Funland)/(Price Index in Macroland)]

Thus, the real exchange rate = (25 Macroland dollars per Funland dollar)[(150)/(125)], and solving this equation for the real exchange rate yields a real exchange rate equal to 30 Macroland dollars per Funland dollar.

d. When the real exchange rate increases this is an appreciation of Macroland's currency, and this appreciation will make Macroland's products more expensive to foreigners: Macroland will export less and import more when the real exchange rate increases, holding everything else constant.

6. a. If purchasing power parity holds in the two countries, then the price of the market basket in the two countries is 300 Macroland dollars equals 150 Funland dollars. This implies that the exchange rate must equal 2 Macroland dollars per Funland dollar or, equivalently, 1 Macroland dollar per ½ Funland dollar.

b. If the actual exchange rate is greater than the purchasing power parity exchange rate, one would anticipate that the exchange rate will fall over time, since nominal exchange rates between countries at similar levels of economic development tend to fluctuate around levels that lead to similar costs for a given market basket.

7. A fixed exchange rate regime provides certainty about the value of a country's currency: this certainty facilitates transactions between countries. In addition, adoption of a fixed exchange regime may help a country commit to not engage in inflationary policies. But, adherence to a fixed exchange rate presents challenges as well as benefits to the country. In order to fix the exchange rate, the country will find that it must hold large amounts of foreign currency: this is typically a low-return investment for the country. In addition, a country with a fixed exchange rate will find that it can no longer use monetary policy to pursue macroeconomic goals like output stabilization and control of the inflation rate. Finally, the adoption of a fixed exchange rate potentially distorts the incentives for importing and exporting goods and services.

A floating-exchange rate regime neither requires the country to hold large amounts of foreign currency, nor constrains the country with regard to monetary policy. It does, however, introduce uncertainty about the value of the country's currency, and that may hinder the level of international trade between the country and other countries. A floating-exchange rate does provide very clear price incentives for the determination of the level of exports and imports at any particular point in time.

8. a. In the graph depicted in part (a), Macroland finds that there is a shortage of Macroland dollars at the target exchange rate of 2.25 Canadian dollars per Macroland dollar. That is, the quantity of Macroland dollars demanded exceeds the quantity of Macroland dollars supplied at the desired exchange rate.

b. When there is a shortage of Macroland dollars, the government of Macroland can intervene in the foreign exchange market and sell Macroland dollars and acquire Canadian dollars to add to its foreign exchange reserves. In addition, the government can act to reduce interest rates in order to increase the supply of Macroland dollars while reducing the demand for Macroland dollars. By reducing the interest rate, the government of Macroland will decrease capital flows into Macroland, thus reducing the demand for Macroland dollars, and increase capital flows out of Macroland, thereby, increasing the supply of Macroland dollars. Finally, the government of Macroland can impose foreign exchange controls that limit the ability of Macroland residents to sell currency to foreigners. Each of these policies will reduce the value of the Macroland dollar.

c. In the graph depicted in part (c), Macroland finds that there is a surplus of Macroland dollars at the target exchange rate of 2.25 Canadian dollars per Macroland dollar. That is, the quantity of Macroland dollars demanded is less than the quantity of Macroland dollars supplied at the desired exchange rate.

d. When there is a surplus of Macroland dollars, the government of Macroland can intervene in the foreign exchange market and buy Macroland dollars and sell Canadian dollars from its foreign exchange reserves. In addition, the government can act to increase interest rates in order to decrease the supply of Macroland dollars while increasing the demand for Macroland dollars. By increasing the interest rate, the government of Macroland will increase capital flows into Macroland, thus increasing the demand for Macroland dollars, and decrease capital flows out of Macroland thereby, decreasing the supply of Macroland dollars. Finally, the government of Macroland can impose foreign exchange controls that limit the ability of Macroland residents to buy foreign currency. Each of these policies will increase the value of the Macroland dollar.

9. If the world price of crude oil increases, it will lead to the higher value of the Canadian dollar. As a result, Canada tourism industry will suffer.

10. With expansionary monetary policy, the interest rate will go down; as a result, the Canadian dollar will depreciate and it will stimulate net export; it will then cause an increase in aggregate expenditure and GDP. With expansionary monetary policy, interest rate will go up; as a result, the Canadian dollar will appreciate and it will dampen net export, which will offset the stimulus of higher government expenditure. Therefore, monetary policy is more effective than fiscal policy.

11. A floating exchange rate provides insulation from recessions originating abroad. With foreign recession and less foreign income, the domestic economy's balance of payment suffers a deficit, which will correct by itself through a lower exchange rate and more current account balance. Trade provides the cushion and insulation under a floating exchange rate. Under a fixed exchange rate, the domestic economy imports foreign recession in the following way. Worsening income abroad reduces the domestic country's trade balance and the exchange rate will decline without intervention from the central bank. To offset the declining exchange rate or keep the exchange rate fixed, the central bank has to reduce money supply in the foreign exchange market by selling foreign currency. This reduction in money supply brings a leftward shift of the *AD* curve and recession.

12. The following table shows the demand and supply of the Canadian dollar in the foreign exchange market. In the table, *e* is the exchange rate of one Canadian dollar expressed in U.S. dollars.

e	Quantity of dollar	Supply of Canadian dollars
$0.80 U.S.	$120 million	$80 million
0.90 U.S.	110 million	90 million
1.00 U.S.	100 million	100 million
1.10 U.S.	90 million	110 million
1.20 U.S.	80 million	120 million

a. The equilibrium exchange rate is US$1 for one Canadian dollar. At the equilibrium, the balance of payment is zero. With the current balance of +$20 million, the financial account balance has to be minus $20 billion.

b. The exchange rate will go down. The current account balance will improve by $50 million. The over-all balance of payment will be zero.